The Arab States and the Palestine Conflict

Contemporary Issues in the Middle East

The Arab States
and the Palestine Conflict

BARRY RUBIN

Syracuse University Press   1981

Library of Congress Cataloging in Publication Data

Rubin, Barry M.
    The Arab states and the Palestine conflict.

    (Contemporary issues in the Middle East)
    Bibliography: p.
    Includes index.
    1. Jewish-Arab relations—1917–   . 2. Arab coun-
tries—Politics and government. I. Title. II. Series.
DS119.7.R75   327.5694017'4927   81-5829
ISBN 0-8156-2253-8   AACR2
ISBN 8-8156-0170-0 (pbk.)

Manufactured in the United States of America

"Interest of State is the main motive of Middle East Governments as of others, and here as elsewhere the idea of interest which determines policy is a blend of two elements: a certain concept of what is good for the State as a whole, and a concept of what is good for the rulers and the group which they immediately represent."

Albert Hourani, *The Middle East and the Crisis of 1956*

"All my friends ...
Have but their stings and teeth newly ta'en out
By whose fell working I was first advanced
And by whose power I well might lodge a fear
To be again displaced; which to avoid ...
Be it thy course to busy giddy minds
With foreign quarrels...."

William Shakespeare, *King Henry IV, Part Two*

BARRY RUBIN is a Fellow at Georgetown University Center for Strategic and International Studies. He is the author of *Paved with Good Intentions: Iran and the American Experience, The Great Powers in the Middle East 1941–1947: The Road to Cold War,* and numerous articles on U.S. foreign policy and on the Middle East.

Contents

Preface

Hundreds of books and thousands of articles have been devoted to the history and contemporary course of the Arab-Israeli conflict. The confrontation within Palestine, the participation of Great Britain, the United States, and the United Nations, and the impact of these events on Jews and Palestinian Arabs have all been endlessly chronicled. Surprisingly little attention, however, has been devoted to the question of how the Arab states entered the battle in the first place.

In addition to tracing the events involved in the growing intervention by Arab states in Palestine, this book attempts to analyze two specific issues. How did internal conditions in the various Arab countries affect their involvement in Palestine? How did the network of alliances and conflict among the Arab governments shape their Palestine policies?

How can one hope to understand the conflict without exploring this essential dimension? If Arab nations have spilled so much passion, spent many lives and so many billions of dollars over this issue—and remain willing to do so—the tale of how they arrived at this position must be a compelling and revealing one. This story should be expected to reveal important principles of international relations and of the connections between domestic politics and foreign policy.

In this sense, the 1948 Arab-Israeli war and Israel's independence represent not only a beginning but also an end. These developments marked the failure of diplomacy and indirect intervention by the Arab states. They seemed to mark as inevitable an evolution of affairs which might often have taken alternative paths.

The remnants of pre-1948 ideas and relationships continued to play an important role until 1956. By then, the collapse of the old order, the rise of a new type of Arab leader and of a new model of Arab politics gained the ascendancy. Yet the importance of the Palestine issue and the distinct roles and attitudes of the different Arab states had been largely set through their earlier experiences.

One other point should be especially stressed here. Analysts and scholars often explain some aspect of an Arab government's foreign policy by presenting it as an attempt to distract public attention from domestic problems. In this light Arab rulers are seen as the masters and manipulators of their political culture. On the contrary, given the powerful and widely accepted premises of Islam and of Arabism, Arab leaders themselves are often seriously constrained. The failure to take certain actions, which may be dangerous and against their personal or national interests, will expose them to the campaigns of domestic and foreign rivals. The ruler may become the subject and even the victim of such necessities. This theme will constantly reappear in the study, and it is an important component in the inner logic of Arab politics.

When the research for this book began I confided my plans to an Arab historian. The idea was, I explained, to write about the efforts of the Arab states over Palestine, particularly in the pre-1948 period. "Oh," he replied with a cynical smile, "they really didn't do very much." I hope this book will convince him otherwise.

Barry Rubin

Introduction

$\mathscr{T}$he origins of Arab state intervention in the Palestine conflict have received surprisingly little attention. Perhaps this happended since, given the variety of powerful factors at work, Arab governments' actions were predictable and inevitable. Yet the course of Middle East history between 1918 and 1956 was not so simple. The pressures which led Egypt, Iraq, Jordan, Lebanon, Saudi Arabia, and Syria to pledge lives, fortunes, and sacred honor for an Arab Palestine should not be lightly dismissed from special study and emphasis. In many ways they provide a key to understanding both contemporary and later events.

Listing these motivations is not difficult. The problem lies in reconstructing the relations between these factors and in showing how some of them gained ascendency at critical points. Arabs outside Palestine opposed Zionism on a religious and nationalist basis, but the expression of this anti-Zionism was largely shaped by the domestic politics and rivalries of these regimes.

The sharply conflicting aims of Zionism and Arab nationalism dictated their clash. The former sought to make Palestine into a Jewish state; the latter wanted Palestine as an Arab state. Dozens of attempts to bridge that gap foundered on mistrust and over specific issues. For the Arabs, their own case was clear and compelling. Palestine and its population had been Arab for centuries in language and culture. By geography and history, Palestine had been an integral part of the Arab world. Religious arguments for Palestine's Islamic character held great appeal among the Arab masses. Alongside this, Pan-Arab and Arab nationalist ideology won the allegiance of the political elite, gradually displacing the traditional concepts. Indeed, Islamic and nationalist sentiments often became impossible to separate.

The battle against Western imperialism — the Anglo-French arrangement which dominated the Middle East after World War I — also became intertwined in the opposition to Zionism. Jewish nationalism became identified as an arm, example, or consequence of the humiliating experience of foreign domination, although this view could never be an unambiguous one. Most Arab leaders spent the years between 1918 and 1948 trying to win the British over to their side in the conflict. In retrospect, this strategy, which almost succeeded, was the most promising route for Arab success.

Nevertheless, the result of these influences was to make Palestine such an emotional and symbolic question as to prompt extraordinary risk and self-sacrifice. An understanding of the development of Arab politics up to 1948 shows the rationality of these decisions, though this made them no less damaging to those who made them. A useful analogy might be made to the East-West Cold War as manifested in American policy toward the Soviet Union. The battle against Zionism became a life-and-death struggle in Arab minds, a fight for self-preservation against a fearful enemy which must be opposed on every level.

Such a description can, however, be most misleading, significantly understating the relative tactical flexibility of some Arab leaders in the years before 1948. One of the most important aspects of the Palestine issue was its dual nature for Arab leaders: it was a political issue (which could be used for partisan advantage), and at the same time it was an issue which transcended all politics. For the underpinning of this latter point it is necessary to take a brief look at the complex of ties between the Arab states and Palestine.

Of course the attempt to classify Arab states as apart from a Palestine entity reveals part of the problem. Such clear-cut boundaries are by no means innate in history. Arab forces conquered Palestine at the same time as the rest of the region in the mid-seventh century. That territory had generally undergone the same series of rulers and had been part of the same cultural and economic developments as had the rest of the area. There is little to distinguish Arab "Palestine" from Arab "Iraq," "Syria," or Arabia beyond the long-term realities of climate and geography.

During periods of decentralization and decay, most notably the thirteenth, fourteenth, fifteenth, and eighteenth centuries, local dynasties had often united Palestine with Syria or Egypt. The main break in this common history had been the trauma of the Christian Crusades, which Arabs saw as analogous to Zionism. Outsiders, their argument ran, had attempted to occupy and de-Islamize Palestine. Their defeat had only been made possible by a united Arab response led by great military-political figures like Saladin. Once again, Arabs concluded, only unity could guarantee victory; failure would endanger the sovereignty of all.

Moreover, the successful Arab response to the Crusades and the periods of Arab unity recalled a golden age of the past. Islam had flourished and Arab culture had been more advanced than that possessed by Europe. These proved attractive memories for the poor and relatively backward states which were emerging into a Europe-dominated twentieth century. A repetition of these triumphs would provide an opportunity for renewed greatness.

For Arab nationalists, to whom the post–World War I borders could only seem artificial, Palestine was as much a part of their patrimony as was any other Arab country. The challenge of Zionism could provide a catalyst for the strengthening of Pan-Arab feelings. Although Palestine was a defensive struggle, it could ignite positive steps toward increased Arab cooperation and eventual political unity.

Those in power in the Arab independent or semi-independent states faced a complex and delicate series of decisions. Their primary concern, of course, was for their own territories and the completion of their independence. In this context, Egypt and Iraq, Transjordan and Saudi Arabia had to operate in regard to different problems and to separate — sometimes conflicting — interests. Such necessities had no legitimacy, however, within the framework of Arab politics and ideology. No ruler could long ignore the powerful currents sweeping the Arab world during these years.

Pan-Arabism, Pan-Islam, and their manifestation in the Palestine question could constitute for such incumbents either a dangerous weapon in the hands of the opposition, a force in public opinion which could not be neglected, and a marvelous tool for furthering their goals. If Palestine was going to be the primary inter-Arab issue and the testing-ground for Arab unity, Egyptian, Iraqi, Syrian, Transjordanian, and Saudi monarchs and politicians were equally determined to place themselves at the head of any such movement.

This does not imply anything beyond the normal measure of political cynicism. The Arabs unanimously believed right and justice to be on their side. If there was any element of double-think among Arab leaders, it was based on tactical necessities. The gap between dealing with the

British and dealing with their publics at home as well as the gap between Arab capabilities and Arab aims required a large amount of political flexibility. On several occasions, most notably in 1948, such contradictions led to major errors, yet Arab leaders never made the mistake of underestimating the appeal of the Palestine issue.

For centuries the primary ideological appeal used by Middle East rulers and the main source of the Arab self-image had been religious in nature. Many things made it imperative for good Muslims to fight to keep Palestine: the Islamic identity as a community of believers (the "umma") obligated to mutual assistance, the importance of solidarity against infidels, the belief that land once controlled by Islam could never be ceded, the confidence in the ultimate superiority of Muslim civilization, and the importance accorded Islamic holy places in Palestine. This view was held by Islamic modernizers as well as by traditionalists and never ceased to have deep roots and broad support among the Arab people.[1]

In contrast to modern Western practice, there was no clear or simple line of demarcation between religion and politics in the Arab world. Despite its particularities, Iran's 1979 revolution, though taking place in a non-Arab country, served as a reminder of that fact. Palestinian Arab leaders did everything possible to reinforce the connection between support for their cause and allegiance to Islamic duty.[2]

Geopolitical and economic influences have often been neglected as important factors in Arab policies. Palestine stood across the traditional invasion and trade routes between Egypt and the Fertile Crescent. The Turks went that way to conquer Egypt in 1516–17. The armies of Napoleon Bonaparte and of the Egyptian ruler Muhammad Ali had marched in the other direction in their campaigns of conquest almost three centuries later. During World War I, General Edmund Allenby's British army had passed through to destroy the Ottoman Empire.

Empires centered in Egypt and Iraq have fought since ancient times to control the resources of the geographic and topographic unit today divided into Syria, Lebanon, Jordan, and Israel. Under the Turks, sections of Lebanon and Syria were even administered in the same province as parts of what would become Palestine. As a market and as an outlet to the sea, Palestine was of vital importance to Transjordan, Syria, and Iraq.[3]

The significant political aspect of Palestine's location certainly did not escape Arab politicians. It sat astride the lines of communication and contact between the eastern and western sections of the Arab world. If Palestine were in alien hands it would be all the more difficult to build and consolidate a contiguous Arab union or federation.

Moreover, Zionism was seen as an inherently expansionist move-ment. Arabs knew that the Zionists wanted Palestine, but many feared a Jewish plan to control all the land between the Nile and the Euphrates rivers. Such an imperium would directly threaten the neighboring Arab states; even a smaller Jewish neighbor could provoke anxiety. Egypt in particular was prompted to take action by this expectation.

Despite all these incentives, there were also significant limits to intervention by the neighboring Arab states. Egypt, Syria, Lebanon, Iraq, and Transjordan each had its own problems in obtaining complete independence from the British and French and in creating viable politi-cal and economic structures. These struggles occupied much of their energies. Further, the importance of maintaining British friendship for Transjordan, Saudi Arabia, Iraq, and Egypt restrained them for many years from making open attacks on the mandatory power's behavior. British aid, logistical support, and protection were required, while Lon-don's leverage in domestic politics (as in Egypt) was also respected.[4]

Nevertheless, as a transcendent political issue on which the position of every Arab leader should be taken for granted, the Palestine question was especially open to manipulation. In countries fighting against foreign control, moderation often becomes equated with treason; and for opposition politicians, free from the yoke of responsibility, dem-agoguery can prove tempting.

In highly stable societies with legitimatized institutions, politics often becomes a race to moderation, in which each candidate attempts to pre-empt the vast center. Where these conditions do not hold and where strong ideological postulates are widely accepted, politics may become a race to militancy. The contradiction between the categorical imperative of Arab unity and the necessity of keeping Palestine Arab and the conflicting interests of real life Arab states and the true balance of forces created many difficulties for Arab politicians.

These leaders were not any less dedicated to the Arab cause in Palestine, but their estimate of proper strategy was quite different from that of the militants, including the Palestinian Arab leadership itself. Diplomatic action and gradualism were deemed to be more likely to yield results than public rhetoric and extravagant promises. Yet each leader and faction also had the need to cope with such pressures, to maintain an aggressive public face. These requirements led to the "double personal-ity" of Arab leaders so often noted by their Western interlocuters.

In fact, there were two separate battles for Palestine. One of them was waged through speeches, resolutions, the daily press, and finally on the battlefields. The second, largely buried until recently in diplomatic archives, was carried out with greater flexibility and pragmatism. Often, what was said in private diverged completely from what was said in public, but ultimately the public image had to prevail. The secret negotiations and initiatives, discredited as the policy which had brought defeat, were only rarely brought to light.

Were these attempts truly at fault, or did the cause of Arab failure lie in the inability of governments to follow through on them? Arnold Toynbee has noted how Egyptian leaders were handicapped for many years by their inability to work out realistic compromises with Britain. The need to maintain domestic popularity was more important than the requirements of a solution. In the short run, such policies were sensible; in the long run they spelled disaster.[5]

Muhammad Mossadegh, the nationalist prime minister of Iran who nationalized the country's oil in 1951, faced a similar choice. After a breakdown in petroleum negotiations with Britain, he told an American diplomat, "Don't you realize that, returning to Iran empty-handed, I return in a much stronger position than if I returned with an agreement which I would have to sell to my fanatics?"[6]

Obviously, this political phenomenon is not restricted to Middle East nations, yet it embodied a particular political logic in the Arab world of that period. A small urban middle class accepting a liberal or totalistic nationalism required mass support. This base could not be built on the basis of their own belief system. Palestine embodied the resentment of foreign domination and the intense desire to eliminate it which struck far deeper chords in the population. Those more traditional politicians, whose ties with the colonizing power might prove an embarrassment, had all the more need to establish their credentials on the issue.[7]

In short, it was precisely because of the sincerity of feeling over Palestine that it proved to be such a potent domestic issue in the Arab states. The simplistic idea that Arab governments used Palestine to distract their constituents from problems closer to home reverses cause and effect. The natural interest in Palestine and the use of it by factional opponents forced the individual regimes to commit themselves.[8]

A complex dialectic was involved. Certainly the use of Palestine in Egyptian or Iraqi politics itself had a deep impact on the future of the Arab-Israeli conflict. As symbol and touchstone of Arabism, Palestine seemed to redefine the national interests of the states involved. To a considerable extent, Arab politicians were as much the victims of this process as they were the manipulators. After 1948, many of them paid dearly for their inability to meet Arab expectations of victory.

At the same time, the Palestine question was interpreted through the ambitions of individual states and leaders. Differing geopolitical positions and perspectives of the various Arab states led them to play different roles in the struggle. The competition among them strongly flavored the direction of Palestine's history at every point.[9]

The underlying contention was over the political disposition of an Arab Palestine: Would it become part of an Iraq-led Fertile Crescent? Part of a Greater Syria under King Abdallah or Syrian nationalists? Part of a united Jordanian kingdom? An independent state under indigenous leaders? Or an Egyptian satellite? Not all of the larger ambitions were directed from the Arab states themselves. Many thought that if the Palestinian Arab leader, Amin al-Husayni, ever came to power he might constitute a danger to his would-be neighbors as well.

These then are the three themes on which this book focuses: the growth of Arab opposition to Zionism and the attempts to find ways to defeat it; the infiltration of the Palestine issue into Arab domestic politics and the need for Arab leaders to blend effective foreign policies which would also satisfy public opinion at home; and third, the conflicts between Arab states (and with the Palestinian Arab nationalist movement) over the proper aims and strategies to pursue.

These factors provide a generally missing dimension toward understanding the evolution of the Palestine question. Even today these historic developments exercise a strong influence on Middle East politics and on the course of the Arab-Israeli conflict.

The Arab States and the Palestine Conflict

1
The Bitter Legacy of Defeat: 1948–81

One could easily argue that the Palestine question has been the key formative experience in shaping the Arab world's political complexion over the last thirty years. Such an approach embodies both analytical virtues and vices. It might be better said that Palestine has been a central element in the rise of Arab nationalism and Pan-Arabism.

Palestine is the unfinished business of this process. As such, it has continually illustrated the contradiction between the here-and-now interests of existing Arab nation-states and the self-conscious interests of the Arab Nation. The day-to-day operations of politicians in power have had to concentrate on the former; opposition politicians and propagandists in both camps have been able to emphasize the latter. Yet the "conventional wisdom" and "ruling ideology" of the Arab world has always been on the side of those who would identify with the idea that the Arabs are one and indivisible and that no price is too high to pay for Palestine's "liberation." This contradiction lies at the heart of modern Arab politics.

"The manifest failure even to approximate unity does not negate the empirical reality of the Arab Nation," writes Professor Walid Khalidi. "The Arab Nation both *is,* and *should be* one."[1] On this level, Palestine plays an intriguing role: providing Pan-Arabism with a cause and a focus, while providing an excuse for its failure to unite the Arabs into one entity.

This seemingly convenient relationship is the root of—or at least the most important illustration of—the vicious circle of Arab politics. If Arab states are merely, in Khalidi's words, "interim caretakers" for the Arab

1

Nation, and if the existing frontiers are "illusory and permeable," there is only so much that incumbent regimes can be expected to accomplish. The Ba'th Party's slogan, "Unity, Freedom, Socialism," places "unity" in first place, since there can be neither freedom nor socialism until the one Arab Nation comes into being.

Here political science categories developed for Western systems are of ..nly limited utility. Palestine cannot be seen as a mere, possibly expendable, foreign policy question for Arab states. Rather, it is a domestic political issue of the highest importance. Most Arabs have accepted that the Palestinian people are by definition an integral part of the Arab Nation. Therefore, by definition, as Khalidi explains, "the injustice suffered by the Palestinian people was suffered by the Nation." Any Arab government must bear this in mind.

Nor does the process stop at the "Arab" level, for this is only one-half of the Palestine issue's substratum. Most Westerners find it difficult to understand how seriously the Muslims take religion and how completely it is intertwined with political thought and practice. The Arab and Islamic factors predetermined that the Arab states would have to keep Palestine from the Jews. But this did not dictate *how* they should do it. That is where the realm of politics in its narrower sense and of diplomacy must begin. On this second level the history of the Palestine conflict becomes a story of politicians, governments, and states, predicated on the interests and rivalries of those entities.

Fundamentally, legitimacy for Arab governments requires a general and overriding faithfulness to the cause. At the least, the formulae over Palestine must be constantly voiced, and even this practice has not been without cost. Iraq and, more recently, Libya and South Yemen can afford rhetorical excesses because their geographic location isolates them from too direct a military and diplomatic involvement. For the states of the Arab heartland, in contrast, a consistent failure to match words to deeds has been a serious destabilizing factor.[2]

To the extent that they were conscious of potential options, Arab governments had to take this, too, into account. From a strictly "national interest" viewpoint, it might seem irrational for an unprepared Egypt to go to war in 1948. Given the contemporary situation, however, a refusal to do so would have created a far more damaging level of domestic conflict and violence. Since each regime's actions and propaganda in response to this situation helped escalate popular emotional involvement in Palestine, the price of failure was equally raised.

All this goes to show that Arab leaders were rarely if ever dominated by blind fanaticism. Under the surface, all of the usual forces of politics were in operation: ambition and localism, competition and calculation, pragmatism and realpolitik. To stay in power, politicians could not stray too far from the mainstream; to gain power they had to be willing to exploit prevailing tides. More often than not, however, statesmen sincerely shared these popular sentiments.

Despite the cultural, ideological, and political necessities on which Arab states' Palestine policies were based, it can still be argued that these positions were disastrous for those who espoused them. This analysis must also be put into perspective. Defeat in Palestine did not so much cause the fall of the old regimes as it did signal their obsolescence, just as Russia's military disasters against Japan and Germany led to the revolutions of 1905 and 1917. The shortcomings of Arab political systems were already clear to the radicals of the 1930s. Parliamentary forms merely varnished the continued rule of socially backward notables and landlords, incapable of achieving progress toward either modernization or the goals of Pan-Arabism.

The new generation of rebels, however, had a firmer grasp on political mobilization techniques than on such matters as economic reform and democratic practices. Since their enemies were England and France, their models became Nazi Germany and Fascist Italy. They had chosen the losing side. The defeat of the Axis doomed their efforts and discredited the survivors. Many were driven out of politics or into exile.

Nevertheless, the revolutionaries of the 1950s were direct lineal descendants of these movements. Many had even served apprenticeships within them. In Egypt, Aziz Ali al-Misri, Young Egypt, the Muslim Brotherhood, and Ali Mahir taught Gamal Abdul Nasser, Anwar al-Sadat, and the Free Officers their political and nationalist principles. Rashid Ali was called back to a position of honor—though not of power—after Iraq's 1958 revolution. The Ba'th, which in its early days rallied to aid Rashid Ali's revolt, took power in Syria in 1963 and in Iraq five years later. Even in Jordan, Sulayman al-Nabulsi, King Husayn's leading domestic rival in the 1950s, came out of the movements led by Muhammad Subhi Abu-Ghanima, a former collaborator of the Germans and the Mufti.

Without underrating the Palestine issue's extreme importance, then, it should be pointed out that Western friends of the old regimes as well as those who overthrew them have often been tempted to overrate it. One would almost think that except for Palestine, Nuri al-Said and Mustafa al-Nahhas, Jamil Mardam and Muhammad Jamali or their political heirs would all still be in power. Arab radicalism and the turn toward the Soviet Union are seen as almost exclusive products of Arab disillusion with the West over Palestine. This line of reasoning ignores the long series of problems and domestic Arab conflicts of which the defeat in Palestine was perhaps merely the proverbial last straw.[3]

In Egypt's case, concentrated land ownership, corruption, domination of politics by a tiny group, continuing inequities of wealth, and struggles with Great Britain over the Sudan and the Suez Canal, provided more than enough motivation for the 1952 coup. Moreover, even after 1948 the traditional elites maintained their friendly ties with the West. The Palestine issue is not required to explain the hatred of England on the part of the Muslim Brotherhood or the Iraqi Istiqlalists. Nasser, on the other hand, seemed quite willing to explore a close relationship with the United States. The break between the new Arab regimes and the United States beginning in the late 1950s had more to do with the Aswan Dam and the Baghdad Pact than it did with American Palestine policy in 1948.

The Palestine war did provide, however, a lesson in the dead end which the incumbent regimes had reached. Military men in Egypt, Syria, Iraq, and Transjordan became convinced that they could do a better job governing than the civilian politicians whom they maintained with their swords. Shame was heaped on the soldiers because of the poor planning and coordination of their rulers. Egyptian officers, often led by politically appointed incompetents and denied proper equipment, came face-to-face with the irreversible degradation of the monarchy. Their real battle was at home, as one dying friend told Nasser.

The Arab debate over Palestine started well before the fighting ended. Opposition leaders understandably saw the chance to make political capital out of the rulers' discomfiture. In Lebanon, the least Pan-Arab of states, Camille Chamoun, the least Pan-Arab of politicians, was already heckling the Beirut government by the end of June 1948. Why, he asked, was a truce signed after only a few weeks of fighting? If the Arabs had been as successful as press reports claimed, then why were their armies unable to penetrate Jewish parts of Palestine? Were the people lied to when they were promised an Arab victory in a few days? Had the government taken effective steps to block establishment of Israel?[4]

Due to Syria's poor showing, Defense Minister Ahmad Sharabati and military commander General Atfe were forced to resign on May 23. Rumors explained the defeat by branding Sharabati a traitor, and in some quarters he was even referred to as "that Jew." General Husni al-Zaim, a political rival whom Sharabati had exiled to Dar al-Zair, was appointed the new chief of staff. A year later, al-Zaim would overthrow the civilian government to become chief of state.[5]

To others, the real crime was the way Palestine had been an Arab political football; the issue was one more proof of the shambles created by Arab disunity. "Every step in planning the war was mixed with the desire to safeguard a special interest," wrote Musa al-Alami. "Special considerations relating to private aims took priority." The Arab armies had been incapable of coordinating their strategies. Egypt and Transjordan had practically sabotaged each others' efforts.[6]

Transjordan had established its own local administration in competition with the Mufti when the Arab Legion marched into Palestine. There was no love lost between Transjordan's king and the Palestinian Arab leader, whom King Abdallah called "a devil straight from hell." When the Egyptians backed the Mufti's ineffective government-in-exile in the autumn of 1948, Abdallah accelerated his plans to annex that part of Palestine occupied by his Arab Legion. He carried out secret negotiations with the Israelis to reach a bilateral peace treaty. The Mufti, with aid from the Syrian government and the Muslim Brotherhood, retaliated by trying to kill the king in March 1949. Two years later, they succeeded.

The murder of Abdallah was intended as an object lesson for any Arab leader who might contemplate reaching a settlement with Israel. Yet after this point, the Palestinian Arabs disappeared for years as an independent political factor. Jordan held the West Bank with little difficulty until the Arab military disaster in the June 1967 war. Meanwhile, the Mufti faded into obscurity in his Lebanon exile. King Ibn Saud died about two years after Abdallah. The whole generation of premodern leaders was giving way to a new order.

King Abdallah, whose political courage was matched only by his inability to face the profound changes taking place in his later years, was not afraid to deny even lip-service to the new verities of Arab ideology. After a Legion retreat in the 1948 war, three thousand Palestinian refugees demonstrated outside Abdallah's Amman palace. The king appeared at the door, pushed through his guards, and gave one of the more prominent slogan shouters a tremendous slap across the face. When the crowd gaped in astonishment, the king shouted, "What nonsense is this? You want to fight the Jews? Very well, there is a recruiting office for the Arab Legion just over there. Those who wish to fight Jews can enlist at once. The rest of you, get away down the hill and make less noise." The crowd dispersed. Such behavior might well serve a tribal chief, but the successful leaders of the 1950s would be those who could place themselves at the head of the demonstrators.[7]

This does not mean that after 1948 the Arab states stood as solidly in private as they did in public against recognition of the war's results. Lebanon and Egypt watched with interest the results of Jordan's peace feelers. Even Syria frequently hinted in 1949 and 1950 that an imposed settlement might be acceptable—as long as Arab leaders would not have to take responsibility for recognizing Israel. Even the Egyptian revolutionaries of 1952 — Nasser and General Muhammad Naguib — wasted little time in assuring Israel that they had no desire to renew the war and would be willing to open secret contacts in the future.[8]

Such talk, of course, was not designed to reach the general public's ears, and little progress toward peace was possible. The point remains, though, that maintenance of the status quo was an acceptable medium-run option. The Arab states would have to build up their military might and settle their internal conflicts before they could seriously consider any second round.

One factor which maintained an impressive continuity was the part played by the Palestine question in the contest between Arab regimes. A government's attitude toward the Mufti had been largely determined by the wider Arab context of alliances and rivalries. The Hashemite alignment between Iraq and Transjordan lasted until the extermination of the family's Baghdad branch in the 1958 Iraqi revolution. The Egyptian-Saudi counteralignment survived vast ideological chasms until its dissolution during the Yemen civil war. At any rate, with the scattering of the Palestinians and the collapse of the Mufti's faction, the receivership of the World War II period returned in intensified form. The Arab leaders became the trustees of the Palestinian Arab cause.

Yet how far could they be trusted? At UN consultations in October 1949, Lebanon claimed western Galilee, Syria wanted eastern Galilee, Jordan asked for central Palestine and a corridor to the Mediterranean, while Egypt sought Gaza and the Negev. At times it seemed that King Abdallah's revolver shot at the Allenby bridge on May 15, 1948, the date of Britain's withdrawal of forces and abdication of the mandate over Palestine, had served to signal the start of a great Arab land rush.[9]

In some ways, the situation after 1948 seemed reminiscent of the order of things after World War I. Palestine was certainly thought of as a rightfully Arab land, but the existence of a particular Palestinian Arab nationalism was considered to be of little importance. Even Palestinian activists accepted this view throughout the 1950s and the first half of the 1960s. They pursued their cause under the banners of different states, parties, and ideologies: Nasserism, Iraqi- or Syrian-oriented Ba'thism, the Arab Nationalist Movement, or loyalty to Jordan. The early Palestine Liberation Organization (PLO) was largely an Egyptian creation, while Al-Fatah enjoyed Syrian patronage. Their gradual establishment of independence was often difficult. To this day, most of the smaller guerrilla groups are dependent on a single Arab state.

Still, they could never completely forgive or forget the contrast between various regimes' promises and performances. Public opinion in the neighboring countries would often be reminded of these contradictions. Why could the Arabs not win? Why could they not unite? Imperialist machinations behind Israel could be used as a partial answer, but self-doubt also flourished. Could there be a basic flaw in the culture, ideology, politics, and military organization of the Arabs? Already the Arabs had been shaken from their feelings of superiority in their nineteenth-century contacts with the West. Colonialism came on the heels of the painful knowledge that the Arab world had fallen far behind Western Europe's scientific and material achievements.

The golden eras of Islamic civilization had always been associated with military superiority over nonbelievers; defeat on the battlefield had foretold periods of decline. The defeat in Palestine challenged the whole notion that an Arab revival was underway. That such an experience could take place indicated that the progress made so far was clearly insufficient. Perhaps the Arab states were headed in the wrong direction altogether; perhaps the whole region might be slipping back under foreign domination again. The destruction of such central Arab premises threatened to undermine all the accepted wisdom built up over the previous thirty years.

Constantine Zurayk, the vice-president of the American University of Beirut, expressed the breadth of Arab humiliation in his devastating appraisal, *The Meaning of the Disaster:*

> Seven Arab states declare war on Zionism in Palestine, stop impotent before it and turn on their heels. The representatives of the Arabs deliver fiery speeches in the highest international forums, warning what the Arab states and peoples will do if this or that decision be enacted. Declarations fall like bombs from the mouths of officials at the meetings of the Arab League, but when action becomes necessary, the fire is still and quiet, and steel and iron are rusted and twisted, quick to bend and disintegrate.[10]

Without credibility there could be no legitimacy. The Arab states had been revealed as paper tigers. They had years to prepare for the day of judgment but failed the test. The immediate reaction was to seek scapegoats, to punish those who had held power. As American Democrats were pilloried for the "loss" of China and as German liberals were punished for the loss of World War I, Arab leaders were overthrown and sometimes murdered for losing Palestine. Of course, as in the two other examples cited, the political and social causes behind these upheavals were much more complex than indicated by these single issues.

The broader problem was the systems which had failed to perform properly. In Egypt, Mahmud Nuqrashi was murdered, King Farouk was dethroned, and the Wafd was destroyed. But the Muslim Brotherhood and Young Egypt were also part of the old order, and they, too, were banished by the new military rulers.

"Egypt has lived through one of the darkest periods in its history," stated al-Sadat in the Free Officers first radio communique after taking power in July 1952. "The army has been tainted by the agents of dissolution. This was one of the causes of our defeat in Palestine." Yet this was only one of a dozen or more factors cited. Nasser spoke truly when he attributed the revolution neither to the results of the Palestine war nor to the arms scandals that grew out of it. Its roots lay deep in Egyptian history. "We were fighting in Palestine," he explained, "but our dreams were in Egypt." Muhammad Naguib could go so far as to state that he had opposed the invasion, preferring continued guerrilla warfare.[11]

Similar events were to be enacted in Syria, where army commanders like Husni al-Zaim and Adib al-Shishakli returned home to throw out the civilians. The 1958 Iraqi revolution, as well, was led by another veteran of 1948, Abd al-Karim Kassem. These rulers were as unforgiving to the militants over Palestine as they were to the moderates. The Istiqlal and National Bloc disappeared as surely as the other forces of the past. Nuri al-Said was killed in the 1958 coup, but Rashid Ali al-Gailani soon wore out his welcome with the Kassem regime.

Palestine's effect on Arab politics must, therefore, be placed in proper perspective. The war and defeat were emotional and political turning points, but Palestine did not bring Arab unity nor did it provide sufficient cause in itself for the Arabs' break with the West.

Indeed, Lebanon, Saudi Arabia, and Jordan never took this route. The early Nasser-Neguib regime's conflicts with Britain and the United States were in no way inevitable outcomes of the Palestine question. They had far more to do with the understandable Cold War priorities and the less comprehendable self-fulfilling prophecies of Prime Minister Anthony Eden and Secretary of State John Foster Dulles. The Suez Canal and Aswan Dam imbroglios were more the legacies of British colonialism in Egypt. Before the mid-1960s, Palestine was rarely a prime consideration in Egypt's foreign policy.

Iraq's radical turn after 1958 is traceable to political trends already visible in the early 1930s, exacerbated over long-term Western support for what many Iraqis deemed a stagnant and repressive dictatorship (far milder than its successors). The common denominator between Iraq and Egypt was their pervasive bitterness at European imperialism. Ironically, the French left behind far fewer grievances than did the British. Paris tried to hold onto Lebanon and Syria as long as possible, but when they left their control was finished. By contrast, the British discredited postindependence regimes in Iraq and Egypt (and Jordan as well) by maintaining an indirect tutelage and special privileges. These things had a corrosive effect on domestic political systems and provided perfect targets for opposition groups. Issues involving modernization, generational conflicts, and the clash of classes all became entangled with these factors.

On the state-to-state level, common Arab opposition to Israel led to only limited areas of Arab unity. The conflicts between governments of the 1940s continued into the Arab cold war of the 1950s, albeit with new ideological justification. Nasserism's greatest success came at a time when Palestine was pushed far to the background. Before 1967, Nasser's main foreign policy thrusts were directed first against Iraq, Jordan, and Lebanon, and later at Yemen and Saudi Arabia. The West's seeming favor toward these rivals, as manifested in the Baghdad Pact and the Eisenhower Doctrine, enhanced Nasser's anti-Western themes. Despite his differences in style and ideology, Nasser was to a surprising extent heir to Farouk's inter-Arab postures.

Nasser also rediscovered the immense power of radical nationalist rhetoric in Arab state competition, a formula which had been latent since the destruction of the 1930s rebels. The electrifying effect of Nasser's nationalization of the Suez Canal opened the way for his domination of Arab politics to a greater extent than any of the earlier leaders.

Yet Nasser's generation would also learn that rhetorical promises raised expectations. A militant, interventionist foreign policy could be a two-edged sword. The Egyptian disaster in Yemen and the calamitous June 1967 war provided destabilizing echos of 1948. When Israel once again crushed its Arab opponents, governments fell in Iraq and Syria, while Jordan lost the West Bank. Escalation of confrontation as a tactic in inter-Arab rivalry, and the triumph of confidence over realistic assessment functioned in 1967 in very much the same way they had in 1947.

The Arab regimes' 1967 failure led Palestinian Arabs to question the value of their protectors. The Palestinians began to emerge as a separate factor for the first time since the Mufti's downfall. Yet the lessons of the 1930s and 1940s had to be relearned; the PLO's relations with the Arab countries remained as complex as those of the Arab Higher Committee.

Division over strategy and tactics remained as potent a force as did

Arab alliance against Israel. At one time or another, the PLO clashed, sometimes violently, with every Arab government. At times the quarrel between PLO leader Yasir Arafat and King Husayn seemed a reincarnation of the old battle between the Mufti and Abdallah. Their September 1970 war was far bloodier than anything seen before. PLO forces fought the Lebanese and Syrian armies in the following years. President Anwar al-Sadat's trip to Jerusalem was an even greater shock.

Abu Iyad, one of the key PLO leaders, voiced this disillusion in his autobiography: "We thought, for example, that Egypt would be on our side forever, that Syria would never, even for the briefest of intervals, lend a helping hand to the Christian Right against us in Lebanon. We would never have imagined that Iraq, even given the political differences that separate us, would have our most outstanding militant fighters abroad assassinated."[12]

But his solution—that the PLO appeal to the Arab masses over the heads of their governments — was unlikely to solve the problem. This strategy advocated by the Popular Front for the Liberation of Palestine (PFLP) and its off-shoot, the Popular Democratic Front for the Liberation of Palestine (PDFLP), helped produce the September 1970 debacle. Funds from the Arab oil-producing states on which the organization is dependent would dry up. Yasir Arafat has wisely been careful to avoid any unnecessary breaks.

By the close of the 1970s, the PLO had succeeded in winning the Arab states' recognition as the sole legitimate representative of the Palestinian people. Yet the fact that no Arab leader seemed able to produce a plan leading toward either peace or victory, with the exception of an isolated Egypt, still limited the value of this designation.

Arab failures in the post-1948 period make possible a greater appreciation of the problems faced by the Arab states in the years up to 1948. Was there historically no escape from a tragic determinism of events in that era? Were there alternatives to the ways in which the Palestine conflict developed? There are three potential areas for investigation here: the program adopted by the Zionists, the opportunities offered by various compromise proposals presented along the way, and the distinctive attitudes of different Arab states.

The maximum concession generally conceived by Arab regimes was a Palestine settlement in which Jews would accept "minority rights." Palestine would then become part of a larger Arab federation or would gain independence as a unified country. The maximum concession considered by Zionists was a single binational state. Even Chaim Weizmann's most moderate proposal was far different from the Arab view of a political system in which Jews had no national standing.

Agreement to a "minority rights" solution was totally contrary to Zionism's nationalist aims and to the unpleasant experiences produced by such systems in Europe. As Weizmann wrote Wauchope in June 1937: "Jews are not going to Palestine to become in their ancient home 'Arabs of the Mosaic Faith' or to exchange their German or Polish ghetto for an Arab one. Whoever knows what Arab government looks like, what 'minority status' signifies nowadays, and what a Jewish ghetto in an Arab state means—there are quite a number of precedents—will be able to form his own conclusions as to what would be in store for us if we accepted the position allotted to us in these 'solutions.'"[13]

Weizmann employed similar imagery in his testimony before UNSCOP eleven years later: "I will not discuss whether it is a good or a bad fortune to be a minority in an Arab state. I would leave the Jews of Iraq, or Yemen and of Tripoli... to pronounce on that. Here I would say that this was not the purpose for which under international auspices we were encouraged to come to Palestine. Those of us who made our homes there did not do so with the object of becoming Arab citizens of Jewish persuasion."[14]

As far back as the 1919 Weizmann-King Faysal meetings, if not before, Zionist leaders had attempted to make an agreement with the Arab states. This was aimed at securing a position for a Jewish state among its neighbors, perhaps involving mutual aid in independence struggles. The Arab states would provide a means for bypassing the Palestinian Arabs. David Ben-Gurion was always willing to explore such a possibility.

But Palestine's future as designed by the Arab states held little attraction for the Zionists. The worsening situation of the Jews in the Arab world heightened this resistance. Today, Jews emigrating to Israel from Arab countries and their descendants are the majority in Israel's population. The driving out of these people by Arab governments made a tremendous contribution to the success of their enemy; cases of mistreatment destroyed Arab credibility of possible coexistence. With or without the existence of Zionism, rising Arab nationalism would probably have led to the same end.

Arnold Toynbee, a staunch anti-Zionist, explained this process in 1925: "The overthrow of indigenous institutions was accompanied by the wholesale elimination of minorities from the population of the Islamic world; and the two phenomena were logically inseparable," when the Ottoman balance was destroyed. Where "the free play of local forces was not interfered with by the effective intervention of some extraneous Power, the elimination of minorities, by massacre, eviction, flight or expatriation" was likely. Aside from political nationalism, economic competition encouraged the destruction of the minorities' influence in commerce, banking, shopkeeping, artisan enterprises, and the import-export business.[15]

In short, Zionism, the life-and-death necessity of escape from Europe, the pressure on Jews in the Arab world, and the very mistrust engendered by the escalating conflict led the Jews to refuse the Arab states' limited promises. Even King Abdallah never shook this determination. "Your King Abdallah will never sit upon the throne of David," Weizmann told Alec Kirkbride in January 1945, though some binational scheme might be possible involving both sides of the Jordan river.[16]

It is equally easy to explain the Arab states' opposition to the creation of a Jewish state. Islamic belief and Arab nationalism militated against it, as did strategic and partisan political considerations. Fundamentally, the Arabs had nothing to gain from any such arrangement, except for Transjordan and the Lebanese Maronite Christians with their particular interests. The early thoughts of cooperation against Britain or France and of mutually beneficial economic collaboration could not offset the far deeper conflict of interests.

Yet even given this the Arab states had a real margin for compromise before the 1948 war, not because they might have been expected to make greater concessions, but because the suggested solutions were relatively favorable. The 1937 Peel Commission proposal, the London conference and the British White Paper of 1939, Britain's 1946–47 offers, the November 1947 partition proposal, and the April–May 1948 U.S. truce plan, all gave the Arabs far more than did the results of the 1948 war. If they had played the diplomatic game better and if they had adopted a more integrated strategic approach, the Arab states could very possibly have prevented the creation of a Jewish state. Yet each proposal was ultimately treated as a trap rather than as an opportunity.

While opposition to any Jewish state can explain the Arab position toward the Peel Commission and UNSCOP plans, it does not account for the rejection of the other four possibilities, or of the UNSCOP minority report until it was too late. The Arabs, of course, believed in the total justice of their cause, but incorrect evaluations of the political balance of forces and the race toward militancy resulted in that cause's defeat.

At the same time, Arab governments did propose many plans; some leaders wanted to adopt a more flexible attitude toward the above-mentioned proposals. Nuri al-Said and Abdallah, in particular, made various offers to the Jews, while Egypt and Saudi Arabia tried to compromise over the heads of the Zionists with Great Britain and the United

States. Such efforts were blocked by radical forces, particularly by the Palestinian Arabs' own leadership. Thus one might well question John Glubb's analysis: "the Arab governments were largely responsible for the ruin of the Palestine Arabs. By raising the hopes of the latter, they made them intransigent. Had they, on the contrary, restrained the Palestinians and used their considerable influence in (the UN) to secure a modification of the partition plan, the result for the Palestinian Arabs would have been far better."[17]

Perhaps the opposite was more accurate: Palestinian leadership repeatedly forced Arab states into intransigent positions and the rejection of several proposals which offered a transitional plan for the independence of an Arab Palestine. The Mufti limited the diplomatic options of Arab regimes by appealing over the heads of incumbents and by forming alliances with opposition groups. These measures tended to neutralize the bargaining leverage of these governments in relation to Britain and the United States.

The Arab states were thus forced to grant veto power on their most essential policies to a "foreign" movement over which they exercised little control. Consequently, they sought to take advantage of the Mufti's removal from the scene during and immediately after World War II to eliminate this problem. The Arab League's intervention into Palestine Arab politics and its refusal to allow a Palestinian Arab government to be formed, however, only stepped up the interstate conflict.

Of course, the Arab Higher Committee justified its strategy as one of self-defense. They were trying to hold in line a series of unreliable allies. Arab regimes might make more concessions to the British or the Zionists than would the Arab Higher Committee. Some of them clearly wanted Palestine for themselves. Yet their tactical approach was also more likely to achieve success than was the Mufti's abstentionism. This was the paradox which the Palestine issue faced in Arab politics.

Once these factors were set in motion the ambitions of different Arab states and leaders did the rest. The U.S.-proposed retreat from partition in 1948 was sunk by Iraq's and Transjordan's determination to intervene. The Husaynis opposed the Hashemites' aims but not their militant means. The real victims of this outcome were Egypt and the Palestinian Arabs themselves. But the Palestinian Arab leadership held a larger share of responsibility than did most of the Arab states.

Since 1948 the Arab "moderates" have been discredited for a variety of reasons and over a variety of issues, both domestic and foreign. Arab hindsight condemns them as having been too conciliatory, too willing to cooperate with Britain and America. Israel is often portrayed today as a creation of the United States and Britain. A study which shows the missed opportunities for the Arab cause and the British governments willingness to go a long way toward Arab demands throws doubt on this view. The race to militancy in the framework of Arab state rivalry seems a more likely villain than was the vacillation of moderation.

If Jews have sometimes overstated the anti-Zionist aspects of British diplomacy, Arab intellectuals and writers tend to understate this factor. This is a tempting interpretation: How could the Arabs hope to win against such an overwhelming force? Just as Nasser could only explain the crushing June 1967 defeat with the myth that Western air forces helped Israel, Arab leaders could explain away 1948 by attributing Zionist victory to British machinations. This is far removed from the fearless exposure of Arab shortcomings favored by Zurayk and others. Moreover, in protecting their political standing, the older generation of Arab leaders sacrificed their historical reputations. If British (or American) policy was deterministically pro-Zionist then, it is argued, Muhammad Mahmud and Ali Mahir, al-Said and Jamali, King Ibn Saud and King Abdallah could only have been traitors and Western agents for having pretended otherwise.

Ironically, the Zionist version of the story reaches similar conclusions. For them, too, the Arab leaders only reflected London's policies. Foreign Office Arabists created and encouraged Pan-Arabism with one concession after another, this school argues, and eventually begat the Arab League which made a solution to Palestine impossible by "the extravagant rhetoric and inflated ambitions conjured up." As long as Britain asked for Arab state cooperation on Palestine, "They would naturally refuse it, but once they knew that Mr. Churchill and Mr. Roosevelt supported a Jewish National Home, they would acquiesce. The moment they sensed a flaw in this support they would become negative, arrogant, and destructive." Ben-Gurion said in 1939 that "only by use of British arms can the (Jewish) immigration be stopped, just as only by British arms would it be possible to establish an Arab state in Palestine."[18] This ignores the force of Arab pressure on England. No British match was required to light the Arab world's fuse.

Could there be a more visceral issue for the Arab states than the question of Zionism? It combined in the sharpest form a presumed challenge to Arab nationalism and religion. This is well known. Less appreciated is the depth of interstate rivalry that lies beyond this common ground. The interests of each Arab state differed with its size, domestic politics, ambitions, geopolitical needs, and proximity to Palestine. What is most telling, however, is the ways in which these interests often remained surprisingly consistent, transcending coups, revolutions, ideologies, and vastly different personalities. A brief survey of Arab countries' individual strategies both before and after 1948 confirms this view.

Lebanon was and is relatively small and weak, a status which necessarily limits its ambitions. Involved in its own independence struggle against France, Lebanon did not become heavily engaged with Palestine until after World War II. Palestine provided Lebanon a way of proving its dedication to Arabism and in so doing to stabilize and insulate its ethnic heterogeneity. A few Maronite Christians might want to make common cause with Israel, but they would remain a minority as long as the National Pact protected the Muslim-Christian balance within the country. Arab nationalist preoccupation with Palestine distracted attention from the continued Christian predominance in Lebanon. Only after the Lebanese civil war of the mid-1970s, when under Syrian-Palestinian-Muslim attack and with their favored position already being dismantled, would some Maronite nationalists truly break Arab ranks.

There were also many Lebanese Muslims whose Pan-Arab sentiments were equal to any in the Arab world, but they tended to concur that Lebanon's interest was in keeping the Palestine crisis at arms length. Lebanon's prosperous mercantile character as well as its internal ambiguity presupposed a preference for a stable environment. The problem was resolved in 1948 and afterward by coupling strong rhetoric with inaction. Ironically, Lebanon was the sole Arab country to benefit from the disaster. Beirut took over Haifa's harbor business, winning the transfer trade for Jordan, Syria, and the Arabian peninsula.

After 1948, Lebanon was the only one of Israel's neighbors never again to go to war. Yet its protective weakness became its undoing. As PLO headquarters and as the base for guerrilla raids into Israel, the country became the target for Israeli retaliatory raids. The more than two hundred thousand nonassimilated Palestinian refugees helped upset the domestic communal balance. These became contributing factors toward Lebanon's civil war, and the resulting political and economic collapse, amply illustrating the reasons for Lebanon's historical caution over Palestine.

Syria, which had no such hesitations, was generally restrained by its own independence struggle until 1945. As a fragment of the Ottoman empire with little internal cohesion, Syria was an especially ardent advocate of Pan-Arabism. But the National Bloc strenuously resisted absorption by Transjordan or Iraq. Palestine, still seen as "southern

Syria," symbolized Syria's potentially leading role in the Arab world. This led to a dualist relationship with the Palestinian nationalist movement. Syria kept close ties with the Arab Higher Committee and with the PLO, yet always maintained its own candidates for Palestinian leadership. In 1947–48 they backed Fawzi al-Qawukji's army; in the 1960s and 1970s, they supported the second largest PLO group, Al-Saiqa.

It was therefore never quite clear where fraternal support ended and where Syrian ambitions began. While domestic opinion constricted the precarious Ba'th regimes as it had the pre-1948 civilian rulers, Palestinian interests would not be allowed to interfere too far with Syrian aims. PLO activities were tightly controlled within Syria, and the Syrian military opposed any intervention on the PLO's side during its September 1970 war against Jordan. The Syrian army even briefly fought against the PLO when Damascus invaded Lebanon to dampen the civil war there. Yet any open break was always prevented by the intertwining of the Palestine issue and internal politics.

Saudi Arabia was a unique case. The profoundly Islamic nature of Ibn Saud's kingdom made its emotional ties to Palestine particularly deep and its opposition to a Jewish state especially strong. Western analysts often found this difficult to understand in relation to the country's moderation on so many other issues. Before 1948, Saudi Arabia's poverty, backwardness, and distance from Palestine limited its involvement. The Saudis' unique role was as mediators with the British and later the Americans. Their dependence on Western aid and defense enhanced their diplomatic moderation.

Many of these characteristics continued in later years. They supported the PLO as they had helped the Mufti, but never agreed with the politics of either. So suspicious were they of radicalism that Ibn Saud and his successor King Faysal were convinced that Zionism was a front for Soviet communism. Yet while remaining inwardly conservative, the Saudis funded the most radical Arab forces.

The Saudis increasing petroleum wealth raised their importance in the Arab world, but control of the purse strings bought them more insurance than influence. The suspicion of the Hashemite states, Iraq and Jordan, continued even after the Iraqi monarchy had disappeared. Unlike the Mufti and his Syrian and Iraqi allies or their political descendants thirty years later, the Saudis fought Israel to maintain Arab stability, not to set off regional revolution. Nevertheless, their passion over the Palestine cause led them to initiate the 1973 oil embargo and to break with Egypt after al-Sadat's adherence to the Camp David agreements with Israel.

Iraq's stand in relation to Palestine remained remarkably consistent over fifty years. Baghdad never allowed itself to be outflanked by any-one in taking a hard-line stand. This stridency was often aimed against other Arab states for domestic purposes or as a tool in inter-Arab rivalries. To a remarkable extent, though, this militant rhetoric was almost never matched by concrete action. The country was far enough from Palestine to reap the greatest propaganda value at the least cost, while Egypt, Syria, and Jordan did almost all of the fighting.

The most radical wing of the Ba'th and the most conservative of Nuri's cabinets under the Hashemites had much in common in this respect. After preaching the most violent interventionist line in 1947–48, the Iraqis almost completely avoided battle. They removed their troops from Palestine to avoid having to sign a truce with Israel—a luxury not open to the neighboring states. They would hurl fire in speeches while cheating on the 1973 oil boycott. Iraqi rulers from Hikmat Sulayman to Kassem would wave Palestine to answer suspicions about their Pan-Arab zeal.

Nonetheless, Iraq had squandered its head start in independence. Its candidacy as the Arab Prussia would fade with these failures to match words with deeds. The continued suspicions of Syria, Jordan, and Saudi Arabia would screen Iraq from becoming a power center. On the other hand, when al-Sadat's decision to make peace with Israel provided a classic opportunity, Baghdad could once again take some limelight.

And what could be more impressive than the consistency of Jordan? If Syria wanted Palestine the most on an abstract plane, Jordan needed it the most and was willing to do what was necessary to pay the price. The West Bank was annexed and was ruled from Amman for almost twenty years. Jordan implicitly modelled itself as the representatives of the Palestinians. Consequently, the rivalry between Arafat and King Husayn replaced the rivalry between the Mufti and Abdallah. They would embrace at one point and shoot salvos at each other a few months later. The PLO's attempt to conquer Jordan in 1970, followed by the "Black September" offensive of the Jordanian army, recalled the clashes of the late 1930s.

The loss of the West Bank in the 1967 war posed a difficult question for King Husayn. How high a priority would he place on winning back that territory? His confidence could not match that of his grandfather. Where once the Arab Legion was unsurpassed and Transjordan could boldly act independently in Arab affairs, Jordan was now a minor power wedged between relatively mighty states. The British subsidy had been replaced by payments from the Arab oil-producing states. Thus its neighbors could impose far greater limitations on Amman's policies.

Moreover, King Husayn had to cope with the problem which had brought his grandfather's death: Would Jordan finally swallow the Palestinian Arabs or would that more educated and numerous group come to dominate Jordan? So while Jordan remained moderate and sought to maintain a calm border with Israel—after all, a potential common enemy still existed—Husayn's strategy had to be far more restrained than that of King Abdallah.

Perhaps most intriguing of all were the parallels in Egypt's behavior during the first and second thirty-year cycles of the conflict. Egypt's involvement with Palestine had always demonstrated more emotional and political distance than the other Arab states. Cairo could be the relatively moderate purveyor of peace proposals—the London conference and White Paper of 1939 and the American truce plan in 1948. It was the last to make the decision for war in 1948 and the first to agree to a truce with Israel several months later.

When Egypt threw itself into the Palestine conflict, King Farouk had already spent several years moving toward a more activist role in Arab world politics. Egypt made its first efforts toward Arab leadership at the start of the Arab League. Nasser followed in Farouk's footsteps in this regard. Both men began their rule with a preoccupation toward eliminating British influence; Cairo's irredentia were the Sudan and the Suez Canal. Gradually, they looked for foreign successes in part as a measure in domestic political base building. Yet both also miscalculated badly in trusting an unprepared army—twice, in 1948 and in 1967, resulting in shattering defeats.

Anwar al-Sadat witnessed these failures, observing a severely weakened Egypt after the 1967 war. The new president laid more emphasis on Egyptian nationalism that on Pan-Arabism and developed a different strategy aimed at regaining Sinai. He courted the United States, fought a limited war in October 1973, and visited Israel. At Camp David he reached a segmented peace agreement with the Jewish state: bilateral in the immediate sense, but with a timetable aimed at a comprehensive settlement.

Certainly, Egypt had paid a higher price in the battle over Palestine than did any other Arab country, including the suffering of 75 percent of all Arab military casualties. Despite this, Egypt had shown itself to be tempermentally the Arab country which could most easily take such a step. Other Arab leaders tried to bring political and economic pressure against Cairo, but this rejection front was hampered by continual Arab conflict.

The conflict's unbearably heavy financial and human costs plus domestic pressure to regain the Sinai were the key objective factors prompting Egypt's action. As development efforts came to a halt and as social problems steadily worsened, only a dramatic policy shift could avoid instability or even political collapse. In short, the domestic political factor—which usually militated against concessions—became a force for peace. Cairo's acceptance of Israel's existence was also made easier by the cumulative failure of military means to destroy the Jewish state and by the fact that the political influences of Islam and Arabism, though far from negligible, were relatively weaker in Egypt than elsewhere.

Whether other Arab states could follow this course may depend on the specific details of what they are offered (return of occupied territories and a settlement of Palestinian grievances) and on what they need offer Israel in exchange. Beyond this, however, the traditional quartet — Islam and Arabism, domestic politics, inter-Arab rivalries — will determine their policies. A conjunction of such factors favoring peace is least likely in Iraq or Libya, where marginal costs will never outweigh the internal and external benefits of a hard line. Jordan and Syria face more serious burdens, while both require foreign Arab subsidies and fear subversion from neighbors and opposition elements. Concessions might foment crises rather than alleviate current problems.

This does not mean that Arab positions always follow the line of least resistance. The Palestine issue has often overpowered empirical national interests. To reverse this process, the rationale for giving up such strongly based traditional stands must be compelling indeed. Establishment of an independent Palestinian Arab state in the West Bank and Gaza might provide a way out for Arab governments who have tired of the long struggle.

Up until now, though, rejectionism and even defeat have been made to serve definite purposes in the Arab world. The unresolved Palestine question has kept Pan-Arabism more fully alive, providing a rationale for its failures. As William Cleveland argues in the case of Pan-Arab philosopher Sati al-Husri: "In order to sustain the argument that the Arab nation is a natural entity, he must show that intrusive rather than inherent factors have denied that nation its rightful unity."[19] While the Palestine issue often prompted Arab unity, its history is also the record of the greatest failures in cooperation among the Arab states.

Hisham Sharabi has explained modern Arab political history as lacking any deep-going social reform movement or any leadership capable of promoting rapid modernization. He writes that "the Arab Awakening at its crucial point was haunted by a sense of impotence and fear. Its leaders took to scape-goating."[20] The Arab governments of the region's "liberal age" failed not because of individual treasons, but because of the weakness of their state systems and due to the very real conflicts between the interests and objectives of particular states. By hiding these conflicts, the dominant ideology interfered with Arab efforts.

The other side of the ledger shows a great deal of faithfulness to a fraternal cause. Palestinian bitterness over the long receivership and its many disappointments should not erase the fact that the Arab states kept alive an issue which might otherwise have faded. Regardless of the justice or merit of its complaint, the PLO would have been only an historical footnote without the financing, sanctuary, and political support provided by Arab governments. The fate of the Kurds, South Moluccans, Ukrainians, and Biafrans is instructive on this point. In contrast, the PLO's international diplomatic success has been in inverse proportion to its unremitting military failures and organizational weaknesses.[21]

The PLO itself has enjoyed much leverage in this relationship. One might well argue that the PLO has had more success in shaping the public statements and policies of the Arab states than the reverse. Western hopes that a given Arab state or states could "deliver" PLO acquiescence to some settlement or that Arab regimes might be convinced to abandon its goals has generally been in vain. Within the PLO, the guarantor for this strategy has been Al-Fatah, which has opposed the demands of the smaller groups seeking to undermine their benefactors.

Thus the Palestine issue continues to stand at the center of Arab politics. As long as Arab states can punish those who would deviate from opposition to the outcome of 1948, progress might be blocked. As long as internal opposition groups could successfully appeal to public opinion on this score, the regional situation was frozen into a cycle of war and hostility. Such mechanisms transcended principle and ideology. Kassem, the most inward-oriented of Iraqi rulers, chided his fellows by advocating a Palestinian government in exile; King Husayn taunted Nasser into the 1967 war.

On a general level, Arab experience clarifies two often-neglected aspects of foreign policy-making. First, national interest cannot be defined merely by geographic, economic, or strategic factors alone. The nation's political culture also plays an important role. One can argue whether or not a Jewish state in Palestine would comprise a "real" threat to Iraq or Egypt. The Arab belief that the Zionists sought territorial expansion "from the Nile to the Euphrates" clearly has little basis in the thought and politics of the Zionist movement. Yet regardless of such considerations, the Islamic and Arabist foundations to the thinking and practice of these leaders predisposed them to adopt such views.

Second, historians and political scientists often over-simplify the relation between domestic politics and foreign policy. The explanation of last resort is that actions abroad seek to distract attention from problems at home. Obviously, multiparty democracies require the forming of coalitions, the winning of elections, the shaping of public opinion, and the response to mass media necessary to gain and remain in power. But "domestic politics" should not be viewed too narrowly. The term can also cover the competition between political factions, individual politicians, and underground oppositions. It might be necessary to respond to potential internal subversion or the discontent of military officers. Since Arab politics rested on a clear set of definitions over what was "right" and "wrong," deviations from these norms could be expected to bring retribution. In other words, foregn policy could not be insulated in such societies to the extent that it was in nineteenth-century European polities or in contemporary communist totalitarian states.

To Western observers, Arab foreign policies did not always seem "rational" because they were not formulated solely within the realm of "objective national interests." They were, however, by no means arbitrary. They followed a rationality of their own built on the basis of domestic political culture and domestic politics which, in turn, defined the national interest. Indeed, large elements of these latter categories were transnational—Pan-Arabism, Islam, the Istiqlal or Ba'th parties, and even the migrations of many of the politicians themselves. In retrospect, Arab Palestine policies do not seem to have maximized benefits either for the Arab states, the Palestine Arabs or (in the long run) for specific Arab regimes. Nevertheless, an alternative point should not be ignored. Failure to follow such lines of policy might have intensified and accelerated the onset of internal chaos, disunity, and instability. Certain policies, Arab leaders concluded, might lead to disaster, but refusal to adopt a militant stand, they reasoned, would definitely lead to disaster.

To detach either the Islamic/Arab base or the nation-state/factional superstructure from each other in considering Arab states' decisions over Palestine would lead to a serious misunderstanding of this vital issue and the central role it has played in the modern Middle East.

There can be no doubt on this point. "When I was in Iraq in 1924," wrote John Glubb, "I took an Iraqi with me to Jerusalem. He looked upon the place as if he had been in China and said he wanted to go home.... But anybody who has been in the Middle East lately will know that every step, every incident of the Palestine situation is followed in Baghdad and in Damascus."[22]

Ancient tradition, historic religion, and common language might have knit together the Arab world regardless, but Palestine did this in a special manner whose repercussions are still being felt today. As Sharabi remarks, "It is in confronting an external threat or in embarking upon a course of collective action that a social group has its greatest need for ideology."[23] From 1918 to 1948, and from 1948 to the present, the Palestine conflict decisively shaped the political and intellectual structures of all the Arab countries.

2
Zionists, Hashemites, and Pan-Syrians: 1897–1930

*T*here was a time, "the British Peel Commission said in its 1936 report, "when Arab statesmen were willing to concede little Palestine to the Jews, provided that the rest of Arab Asia was free."[1] Whether or not this was ever true, the statement reveals important principles of British and Zionist thinking during and after World War I. On this basis, London sought to reconcile its promises to Jews and Arabs, while Zionists hoped for a bloodless fulfillment of the Balfour Declaration in creating a Jewish national home.

Arab nationalists also held high expectations for a smooth transition from the Islamic legitimacy of the Ottoman Empire, which the war had destroyed, to a new Arab state, uniting millions of their brethren under a common government. The Anglo-French partition of the region dashed this possibility for the immediate future. New entities emerged—Lebanon, Syria, Iraq, Transjordan, and Palestine—to establish quickly their own structures and political interests.

These states were preoccupied with expanding their own scope of independence and establishing their own identities. Although this coexisted with the growth of Arab nationalism toward establishing itself as the dominant ideology, the realities of the period limited the interstate interaction of these newborn regimes.

Perhaps the Arab group with the greatest interest in fostering such contacts was the Palestinian Arabs themselves. For them, the neighboring states were obvious allies in their struggle against Zionism. After the immediate postwar period, however, this effort developed only very slowly. During the 1920s, the Zionists were often more active in this contest and, although their eclipse seemed inevitable, they even scored some successes. Yet the idea of an Arab-Zionist alliance along the lines recalled by the Peel Commission proved impossible.

Equally disappointing were the efforts of two other forces who hoped to unite the Arabs under their banner: the Hashemite dynasty and the Pan-Syrian movement. Both factors would continue to have importance in the 1930s and 1940s.

In short, this period, which composes the prehistory of the Arab-Israeli conflict and of the modern Middle East, set in motion the key elements of what was to follow: the doctrine of Arab unity at odds with the conflict among the Arab states, the beginnings of Arab anti-Zionism at odds with Britain's expressed support for Zionist aspirations, and the difficulty in defining Palestine's fate. The human element must also be considered, for all those who would rule the Arab world until 1948 had their formative experiences in this period, and many of them were active participants in these events.

It is common today to say that early Zionism ignored the existence of the Arabs, but this is somewhat misleading. More accurately, it ignored any Arab problem, believing that the two nationalist movements might be easily reconciled. The political maneuvers before the onset of World War I might have fed this hope at the time, but a careful reconstruction of these events shows the already deep-seated nature of Arab opposition.

In 1897, at the time he was founding the Zionist movement, Theodor Herzl met Mustafa Kamil, the founder of modern Egyptian nationalism. Herzl was impressed by the young leader and expressed support for Kamil's efforts to end British colonial rule of Egypt. Five years later, when he visited Cairo, Herzl became convinced in the eventual victory of the nationalists' cause and was surprised that the British did not understand this.[2]

The idea of Arab-Jewish collaboration, which appealed to Herzl though he did little to further it, was often to recur in the following years. While Zionism was at best a very secondary factor in Middle East politics before World War I, however, some of the small number of Arab nationalist intellectuals and newspapers already saw Zionism as a future rival. Yet they faced many more immediate problems as semiunderground Arab factions, competing Ottoman parties, and European great powers took part in a rapidly changing series of alliances.[3]

Still, the Syrian Arab reformer Rashid Rida wrote of his suspicions of Zionism as early as 1897, though he thought it had some features which Arabs might copy. Negib Azouri, a Syrian Christian Arab living in Paris, predicted in 1905 that Arab nationalism and Zionism would battle until one triumphed. On this struggle, he noted dramatically, would depend the future of the entire world. The Young Turk revolution of 1908 gave immediate relevance to these obscure debates.[4]

For four centuries the Fertile Crescent had been ruled by the Ottoman Empire. Relatively isolated from the industrial revolution and intellectual ferment of the West, it had fallen further and further behind Europe. The overthrow of this structure by a group of military officers— the Young Turks — marked a turning point in the history of the Arab world. Having brought down the Sultan-Caliph, though, their problem was what to put in place of the Islamic solidarity that had cemented together a multinational empire. Their turn toward an intolerant ethnic Turkish nationalism undermined Arab loyalty while offering nothing better than the prospect of forced assimilation.

Since much of this long-range program remained only on paper, most Arabs continued to accept the Ottoman government out of habit, vested interest or lack of alternatives until its collapse in World War I. At the same time, it is not surprising that growing numbers of intellectuals, notables, and army officers embraced Arab nationalism. The earliest and most consistent advocates of this ideology had been Christian Arabs, who lacked any Islamic loyalty to Ottoman rule. The Young Turks, by themselves challenging Islamic legitimacy in the name of nationalism, fostered demands for an Arab state stretching from Morocco to Iraq which would be built on the linguistic, cultural, and historical identity of the Arabs.

A third group rejected both support for the Young Turk regime and profession of such a Western concept as ostensibly secular nationalism. They championed the empire's traditional Islamic identity, as embodied in the person of the Sultan-Caliph.

Each of these factions had their own reasons for opposing Zionism. To loyalists, it was still another nationalist, secessionist movement threatening the empire's unity. To Arab nationalists, Zionism threatened to steal away an important portion of their projected nation. To traditionalists, Zionism was a subversive, anti-Islamic force whose tentacles lay even behind the Young Turks.[5]

Often these ideas were combined in various ways. The first Arabic anti-Zionist book, published in 1911, claimed the Zionists had enough money to dominate the entire Ottoman empire and that their ultimate aim was a state stretching from the Nile to the Euphrates. This belief was later widely accepted by Arabs outside as well as inside Palestine. The effect on Arab regimes was clear: a movement seeking to conquer their land as well as Palestine itself was a direct as well as an indirect threat.[6]

For a brief period in 1912–13, as the Turkish-Arab conflict loomed large, both sides temporarily courted the Zionists. The Young Turks had always been cautious in this regard lest their enemies charge them with pro-Zionism, but the regime's financial weakness and military losses in the Balkans prompted some effort at rapprochement. The Jews, the Young Turks hoped, would help shore up the empire with loans and pro-Turkish lobbying in European capitals.

In response, the opposition Decentralization party, representing moderate Arab forces, made a counteroffer. Zionist support for the Arab movement, it was suggested, could be exchanged for Jewish immigration into Palestine. Rafiq Bey al-Azm, the party's Syrian president, commented on the value of "Jewish capital, manpower and intelligence" for the rapid development of the Arab provinces.

These offers were limited in both scope and seriousness. Neither Young Turks nor Arab politicians could accept Zionist political aims. Both used these feelers as bargaining chips in their own bilateral negotiations. When they reached momentary agreement they lost interest in continuing talks with the Jews.[7]

Only one Arab group, the Maronite Christian nationalists of Lebanon, still had thoughts of common interests with Zionism. A Jewish Palestine, some of them told Zionist emissary Sami Hochberg, would be the best guarantee for achieving their dream of an autonomous Christian Lebanon. This potential friendship often seemed promising, but always remained unrealized, in the following decades.[8]

Many of these issues would be profoundly reshaped by World War I. The Young Turks made a fatal decision to join Germany and Austria-Hungary against Russia, Britain, and France. While the Ottoman regime suppressed Zionism and Arab nationalism within its borders, both groups were courted by London. After ensuring British support, Sharif Husayn of Mecca, founder of the Hashemite dynasties, launched an Arab nationalist revolt against the Turks. Dozens of Ottoman army officers, often members of secret Arab nationalist societies, joined him in the struggle for Arab independence.

Although a direct British assault on the Turkish heartland failed in 1915, Allied forces gradually wore away stubborn Turkish defenses. One column drove into Iraq, while the Hashemites, accompanied by British advisors, cleared the enemy from Arabia's Red Sea coast. Powerful British armies from Egypt finally broke through into Palestine and Syria in 1917, driving the shattered remnants of the Turkish army before them. The Ottoman Empire was finished.

On the diplomatic front, much attention had been devoted toward redrawing the map of the Middle East. To secure their support, London made territorial pledges to the French, Arabs, and Jews, creating one of the most controversial issues in Middle East history.

To the Jews, the Balfour Declaration offered a national home in Palestine, with the reservation that indigenous people's rights not be affected. To the French, the Sykes-Picot accords conceded dominion over Lebanon and Syria. Iraq would be British while Palestine would be jointly controlled. For the Hashemite allies, the Husayn-MacMahon correspondence spoke of a large independent Arab kingdom, excluding certain areas along the Mediterranean.[9]

In the short run, these were all intended as wartime measures, to strengthen the British position while undermining the Turks. Immediately after the war, they would be manipulated to whittle away at France's interests. Whether or not Palestine was included in the area earmarked for the Hashemite kingdom has been under much dispute. What is generally neglected, however, was the British belief that conflict could be avoided through construction of an Arab-Jewish alliance. Not only would this provide stability in Palestine, but it would also guarantee the dependence on Britain of both movements.

While the Balfour Declaration was not well received by the Arabs in Palestine, Hashemite reaction was different. Zionist aid might well prove helpful in achieving their kingdom. For them, Palestinian Arab leadership was too distant and too disorganized to count. Thus Sharif Husayn's own newspaper in Mecca welcomed the Jews as "original sons of the country" whose return would benefit their "Arab brethren" materially and spiritually.[10]

British diplomat Sir Mark Sykes was a key architect in this policy of support for Arab, Jewish, and Armenian aspirations. As the war ended, he told both Sharif Husayn and Zionist leader Chaim Weizmann that Arab-Jewish entente would be the best way for their causes to gain universal recognition. If Jews supported Arab sovereignty outside Palestine, Sykes believed, the Arab leaders would accept Jewish aims.[11]

This would not include Zionist desires for a Jewish state, which were generally not voiced at the time. When D. G. Hogarth, a leading British Arabist in government service, visited Sharif Husayn to explain the Balfour Declaration, he assured the Hashemites that Jewish settlement would be allowed only insofar as would be "consistent with the political and economic freedom of the Arab population." On this basis, Sharif Husayn declared readiness to promote such an objective and he so informed his Cairo representatives and military leaders.[12]

T. E. Lawrence, General Edmund Allenby, and other British Middle East officials shared Sykes's analysis. The Zionists would help the Arabs in Syria while the Arabs would make way for the Jews in Palestine, thus allowing abrogation of the Sykes-Picot agreement and keeping France out of both areas. Allenby himself promoted a successful meeting between Weizmann and Prince Faysal, the ablest of the Sharif's sons and commander of the Hashemite army. All sides expressed enthusiasm.[13]

This led to a second conference in January 1919, concluding with an agreement for use at the forthcoming Versailles peace conference. The accord called for mutual collaboration in the development of the Arab state and Palestine. The boundaries between these two would later be determined by a joint commission. Jewish immigration, freedom of religion, and the safety of holy places in Palestine would be guaranteed. To this, Faysal added his famous reservation: implementation would depend on the success of Arab demands in Syria.[14]

Weizmann saw this strategy as one of bypassing the Palestine Arabs, who could be expected to be hostile, through an agreement made with external Arab leaders. The former, in whom Weizmann wrote "the Sharif is little interested," could be politically ignored. Faysal's presentation at Versailles in February 1919 might have reinforced this view. The Arab world, Faysal said, was a single unit with common language and natural frontiers demanding full independence, but Palestine would be left for the "mutual consideration of the interested parties." Yet Weizmann and the above-mentioned British officials had miscalculated both on Faysal's power and on London's willingness to back him against the French.[15]

An alternative Arab leadership was already forming, led by veteran nationalists like Jamil Mardam. This group, which had the support of Palestinian Arab notables, saw Palestine as part of Syria. True, this tendency — represented by its own delegation at Versailles — did not explicitly oppose Jewish immigration, but its insistence on Palestine forming a part of a Syrian federation could not fail to affect the fate of the Balfour Declaration.[16]

In 1918 and for a number of years thereafter, Palestine remained a relative backwater in the Arab world, as it had been in the Ottoman Empire. The idea that its future would be decided by events elsewhere — and by Arabs from Syria or the Hijaz — did not then seem surprising or inequitable. Nevertheless, the Balfour Declaration and Jewish settlement, perceived by Arabs as the Zionist challenge, was already beginning to give Palestine a new importance.

By the end of 1919, it was already becoming clear that, as one British intelligence officer warned, the Weizmann-Faysal agreement was "not worth the paper it is written on." Faysal could not be regarded as a representative of the Palestine Arabs. While the Arab historian George

Antonius exaggerated when he argued that the great majority of political-minded Arabs including the Hashemites regarded Palestine as "an integral part of Syria ... bound to remain in the area of Arab independence" in early 1919, he was only advancing this conclusion by a few months at most.[17]

The popularity of Pan-Arabism, in both its Hashemite and Syrian-centered varieties, could be easily explained through historical and contemporary factors. The postwar Middle East settlement was to leave both Palestine and all the neighboring Arab lands under European control. Lebanon and Syria were claimed as League of Nations mandates by France while Transjordan and Iraq were under a British mandate. Although these countries were supposed to be guided toward independence, the French treated the areas under their control as colonies. Egypt faced heavy British influence and intervention. Only remote Arabia and backward Yemen were fully independent.

Arab anger at what were perceived as broken European promises spurred nationalist reaction, but its roots went far deeper. The dream of a united Arab state was no mere abstraction. Arab nationalists in the Fertile Crescent did not need to strain their memories to recall the area's centuries-long unity under the Ottomans. Many of them served in the empire's army or bureaucracy. With this cosmopolitan background, they had little stake in any particular portion of the domain; possessing the common language, culture and world-view of the Arab world, all boundaries within it seemed artificial to them. They thought the governing elite for the entire Arab nation already existed in themselves. This relatively compact educated group formed Arab public opinion. By 1919, their ideas were beginning to gain hegemony over the masses.

Tactically they were more aggressive than Faysal; strategically, they put little store in an alliance with Zionists or with the British. When Faysal established a Syrian government to contest French claims, it soon evolved beyond his control. The Syrian Congress, elected in July 1919, rejected a plan for a future Palestine government submitted by Chaim Kalvarisky, a Zionist expert in Arab affairs who had been invited to Damascus by Faysal.

Quickly, the congress called for an independent Syria, including Palestine, with Faysal as king—a demand which the U.S investigating delegation, the King-Crane Commission, believed to reflect popular sentiment. Within Palestine, such resolutions were supported by petitions and demonstrations. Faysal himself realized that any indication of acquiescence toward the partition of Syria would threaten his entire political position. Faysal's power depended on his fulfilling Arab nationalist demands. Any commitment to a Zionist alliance might destroy the Hashemites' political base.[18]

Even without such problems, Faysal had difficulty in controlling Damascus. While he was away negotiating in Paris, politicians led by Yasin al-Hashimi came out against the separation of Lebanon from Syria, a step already agreed to by Sharif Husayn. In March 1920, the Syrian Congress repudiated Faysal's agreement with the French government and demanded full and undivided independence. The congress also called for Iraq's independence under the rule of Faysal's brother, Abdallah. The projected kingdoms' boundaries were left vague.[19]

Arab notables in Palestine carefully followed these moves, while hoping their own April 1920 anti-Jewish riots might discourage London's pro-Zionist policy. A young nationalist named Amin al-Husayni, soon to emerge as leader of the Palestinian Arab movement, was responsible for liaison with Faysal. Both Faysal and some high-ranking British officials —who were not averse to a Syria-Palestine federation—encouraged the oppositionists.[20]

The French quickly put an end to all these hopes. Their army marched into Syria, easily routing the Arab forces and capturing Damascus. Overnight, Faysal was transformed from king to refugee. The British, however, had not completely forgotten him. When he travelled through Palestine into exile in August 1920, British High Commissioner Herbert Samuel received him with official honors, and there the deposed leader made a final attempt to obtain Jewish assistance in regaining Syria.

Samuel, though Jewish and pro-Zionist, had leaned over backward to prove his fairness to the Arabs in administering Palestine. He favored a loose confederation of Arab states, each with its own government. In Samuel's scheme, Faysal would be king of Syria and honorary head of a primarily economic union of which Palestine would be a member. Like Weizmann, he thought such an agreement would provide a place for a Jewish Palestine. This idea, which Samuel advocated for many years, made little headway.[21]

With Faysal and Syria removed from consideration by the French, the British were forced to redefine the Hashemites' role in the new Middle East order. Eventually the problem would be neatly solved: London put Faysal on the throne of Iraq and helped make Abdallah the emir of Transjordan. As for their father, Sharif Husayn, both Britain and the Palestine Arabs sought his support in defining Palestine's status.

Toward the end of 1920, Britain offered Sharif Husayn a treaty guaranteeing the borders of the Hijaz, his home domain in western

Arabia. Although the British dangled continuation of their subsidy before him, Sharif Husayn refused to sign an agreement recognizing Zionist claims in Palestine and French claims in Syria. Faysal, more sadly familiar with European might, advised acceptance of the new borders as a tactical measure, citing the Arab saying, "A locust in the hand is better than ten in the air."[22]

Husayn's opposition was stiffened by the Palestinian Arab appeals he began to receive in 1921. Clinging to his demand to be recognized as leader of the Arab world, he claimed the right to appoint major religious officials in Arabia, Iraq, and Palestine as well as recognition of his supremacy over all Arab rulers. These conditions prefigured his widely ignored March 1924 claim to the Islamic caliphate. Their failure also marked the last Hashemite effort to establish immediate Arab unity under their auspices.[23]

With France's crushing of independent Syria and with the eclipse of Hashemite ambitions, Arab nationalists began to adapt to European-imposed realities. The process of regrouping would take almost a decade. Palestine, where the British promised to restrict Jewish immigration to the country's "absorptive capacity," remained relatively quiet. Meanwhile, a new personality came on the scene to compete for influence there.

This was Abdallah, Sharif Husayn's younger son. He had marched northward with a small army in 1921, nominally to retake Syria from the French. The British, needing to distract this embarrassing march against their allies and having to dispose of the sparsely inhabited strip of territory east of the Jordan River, created Transjordan as Abdallah's kingdom. To obtain this realm, Abdallah had to sign a treaty accepting the British mandate over Palestine and the Balfour Declaration, a step his father had refused to take. Thus began the long, tangled relationship between Abdallah and Palestine.[24]

Transjordan's political status was not entirely clear, partly due to the earlier unimportance attributed to the territory. It had nominally been part of Faysal's Syria, but this had little effect on local life. After France's conquest of Syria, Transjordan fell into Britain's hands by default. London quickly realized that the centralized administration and special commitment to Zionism which prevailed in Palestine held little attraction for Arabs east of the Jordan. On the other hand, anarchy in that land might result in Bedouin raids, a breakdown in food exports to Palestine, and transformation of the territory into a center of anti-Zionist and anit-French propaganda. A separate and stable government in Transjordan was required.[25]

Such a regime, Abdallah and the British agreed, should maintain close links with Palestine. Abdallah tried to convince British Colonial Secretary Winston Churchill to make him king of Palestine as well as Transjordan, and his choice of Palestinian Arab nationalists, like Awni Abd al-Hadi, as advisors indicated the extent of his ambitions.[26]

For their own reasons, Zionists also objected to any separation of Transjordan from Palestine. Such a state, they argued, would be neither viable nor sensible. Despite these complaints, the League of Nations approved the British plan. Anglo-Transjordan treaties of 1922 and of 1928 recognized Abdallah's government and provided for internal autonomy under British guidance.[27]

These events did not dampen the belief of Abdallah and the Zionists that there might be some basis for a bilateral accord. The Jews saw in Abdallah what they had seen in his brother Faysal—a foreign Arab leader who might help secure their role in Palestine. On a more modest level, there was the possibility of economic cooperation and Jewish settlement in Transjordan. To Abdallah, who had inherited Hashemite ambitions, Jewish acquiescence could pave the way to his own control of Palestine.[28]

Yet Abdallah's goals sprang from more than desire for added territory. The political and economic connections between Palestine and Transjordan were very close, with active trade and constant communication. For Abdallah, joining Transjordan to Palestine was no mere whim—it was a necessity. By itself, Transjordan lacked capital, markets, and an outlet to the sea. Its administration was largely staffed by Palestinian Arab expatriates and by Pan-Arabist refugees from Faysal's Syrian regime. As a traditional politician, Abdallah had little use for ideologies and parties. Rather, through personal diplomacy he sought to build alliances with the Jews, the British, and the Palestine Arabs to strengthen his position.

While seeking Abdallah's friendship, the Zionists could never really accept his patronage or become his subjects. The whole point of the Zionist movement, after all, was the creation of a Jewish state. Still, in the 1920s many Zionist leaders adhered to Weizmann's belief that neighboring Arab states could be brought to accept a Jewish Palestine as an ally and as a partner in development. Even knowing this, Abdallah could understandably consider the prospects for a Jewish state to be quite dim. Sooner or later, he reasoned, the Jews would be happy to accept his protection, finding him the most acceptable Arab ruler.[29]

Although Palestinian Arab leaders might already speak of mobilizing the Arab world against Zionism — and against the British if they continued to support it—fulfillment of such threats still lay well in the future. In March 1921, a Palestinian Arab delegation met with Churchill, and its leader, Musa Kazim al-Husayni, gave a warning that many British officials would echo a decade later: "The Arabs are the key to the East and they possess its doors and passes, Arabia, on the Red Sea and the Persian Gulf, is the way to India." To preserve imperial communications, England must keep the Arabs' friendship, and this meant concessions over Palestine. If Britain did not take up the Arab cause, he concluded, Germany or Russia might do so.[30]

This was prophecy of a high order. Many Arabs did look to Nazi Germany in the early 1940s and toward Russia beginning in the mid-1950s, but all this lay far in the future. Within Palestine, Amin al-Husayni, the former Faysal supporter, was still trying to consolidate control over the Arab nationalist movement. Outside Palestine, the issue had not yet become a focus for nationalist activity. British power remained unchallenged. Many Pan-Arab activists even took up the talks with Zionists earlier pursued by Faysal.[31]

In 1921 Weizmann began a long series of talks with Riyad al-Sulh, then a young nationalist in exile from Faysal's defeat (and years later prime minister of Lebanon). Frederick Kisch, Jewish Agency representative in Palestine, met many Arab political figures during 1923 and 1924 visits to Egypt.

Among his interlocuters was Aziz Ali al-Misri, a prestigious nationalist leader during World War I who was in eclipse at the time. "He wants the Orient for the Oriental and regards the Jews as such," Kisch optimistically concluded. "I think he is a man with whom we can cooperate." Attempts were also made to encourage the attendance of Egyptians at the ceremonies marking the inauguration of Hebrew University.[32]

The most important set of meetings also took place in Cairo. On the Arab side they involved Rashid Rida, then president of the central committee of the Syrian Unity party, Riyad al-Sulh, and Emile al-Ghuri, then foreign editor of the Egyptian newspaper Al Ahram. The Jewish side was led by David Eder, head of the Political Department of the Zionist Executive in Palestine, Egyptian Jewish leaders, and Weizmann's personal representative. At the outset these talks were cordial and promising. Some source of outside assistance for development was needed, the Arab delegates stated, and the Jews—whose "settlement does not constitute a political danger"—would be preferable to a European nation which might threaten Arab independence.

Their proposals were a modification of the 1919 Faysal-Weizmann agreement, and there were indications that Faysal himself, now king of Iraq, promoted the approach. The Jews would help the Arabs expel France from Syria and would repudiate the Balfour Declaration to deal with the Arabs "nation to nation." The Arab countries would be fully independent within a single federation, while the Zionist movement would have full opportunities in Palestine.

These exchanges continued for several months. In the fall of 1922, an Arab delegate went to Palestine to convince Arabs there to avoid disturbances during the negotiations. In Geneva, two Zionist emissaries met Shakib Arslan and Ihsan al-Jabiri of the Syro-Palestine Congress, the Arab nationalist lobbying group in Europe whose membership included Rashid Rida and Musa Kazim al-Husayni.

At this point, efforts stalled. Both Britain and France were hostile to an Arab-Jewish alliance potentially aimed against their Middle East positions. Pressure was brought to bear on both sides, and London even persuaded Egyptian nationalist leader Sa'd Zaghlul to cancel a planned meeting with Weizmann. French authorities in Syria suppressed Zionist activities there. Ironically, Kisch considered these officials to be more anti-Zionist than their Arab counterparts, because Paris considered Zionism to be a British tool.[33]

Thus ended the second serious effort for an Arab-Zionist alliance. To blame this failure on British and French opposition, however, would be simplistic. These contacts had been of an exploratory nature, and their survival was largely due to the vagueness of their aims. Would the Zionists have risked an open break with the British or abandoned their nationalist ends? Could the Arabs have braved their own public opinion or delivered concessions over Palestine's future?

New, conflicting forces were already stirring. Palestinian Arab nationalists were finally exercising more autonomy. By 1923, Pan-Syrianism was fading. The demand for Palestine's self-determination within a broader Pan-Arab perspective tended to take its place.[34]

Zionists had already decided to focus on what Zionist activist Arthur Ruppin called "the real centers of Arab politics," Baghdad, Cairo, and Damascus. Now the Palestinian Arabs began to compete on these fronts. Their Supreme Muslim Council sent out its first delegation to rally Arab support in 1923, ostensibly soliciting funds for restoring two great Jerusalem mosques. Amin al-Husayni, finally emerging as leader of the movement, participated in the 1926 Caliphate Conference in Egypt, strove to mediate between rival Syrian exile factions in 1926–27, and convened a World Islamic Congress in Jerusalem in 1931.[35]

When Arthur Balfour, who as wartime British foreign minister had authored the Balfour Declaration, visited Syria in March 1925, Palestinian students called for local demonstrations against him. Non-Palestinian Arabs also served as mediators in the sharp conflicts between Amin al-Husayni, by then the Mufti of Jerusalem and head of the Supreme Muslim Council of Palestine, and his factional opponents.[36]

Syria maintained its special interest in Palestine throughout the 1920s and as late as June 1928 the Syrian Constituent Assembly, in its draft constitution for the republic, included Lebanon and Palestine as part of Syria. This position was accepted by senior National Bloc leaders, many of whom had been Faysal supporters, and by younger militants like Shuqri al-Quwatli. Yet remaining under tight French control — the French high commissioner controlled foreign relations — and partitioned by the French creation of ethnic enclaves for Druze and Alawites, Syria had little scope for foreign involvement.[37]

Transjordan and Iraq, ruled by the Hashemite heirs Abdallah and Faysal, played the predominant role in trying to affect Palestine developments until well into the 1930s. Transjordan's ties were especially close. This was symbolized by the country's use of Palestine currency, which carried Hebrew as well as English and Arabic inscriptions. When Abdallah's relations with the Jews were good, those with the Mufti, Amin al-Husayni, prefigured a clash. Abdallah began to support the Mufti's main opponents, the Nashashibi and Tuqan families, and in retaliation the Mufti backed the tiny opposition in Transjordan.[38]

In his discussions with Kisch, Abdallah stressed how important it was to find a solution to the Palestine issue before the Arabs lost patience. Kisch proposed in 1924 a joint Jewish-Palestinian Arab committee to discuss common interests. Abdallah would be the chairman, the Zionist official suggested, but Abdallah's father opposed the idea and it went no further.[39]

From time to time, Abdallah would make proposals of his own. In August 1928, for example, he suggested an Arab-Jewish settlement could be found only in the context of a wider Arab federation. Zionists would have difficulty in reaching an understanding with the Palestine Arabs, so they should rather seek an alliance with those of Iraq, Transjordan, and Arabia. This, of course, had been Weizmann's original idea. As a first step, Abdallah encouraged Jews to work and invest in Transjordan: "I guarantee your safety. Together we will work for the benefit of the country."[40]

Good personal relations were maintained during this period between members of the Palestine Jewish community, the Yishuv, and some Egyptian intellectuals. During the mid-1920s, some Egyptian newspapers, particularly *Al-Ahram* and *Al-Muqattam,* advised Arabs to take more moderate positions toward the Palestine mandate. Liberal Egyptians were suspicious of what they saw as reactionary Pan-Islamic movements which threatened to undercut Egypt's independence. Such thinking was found only among a small minority. One case was Dr. Mahmud Azmi, editor of the Liberal Constitutional party's organ, *Al-Siasa.* In 1925 he visited Palestine for the inauguration of Hebrew University and met with Weizmann, Labor party leader Chaim Arlosoroff, Arabist Chaim Kalvarisky, and others.[41]

There were also occasional contacts with those met in earlier years, like veteran nationalist Ihsan al-Jabiri. He visited Jerusalem in 1928 and tried to serve as a mediator, bringing Jews together with several leaders of the Palestine Istiqlal Party, a Pan-Arab group with ties to Faysal's Iraq.[42]

The Palestinian Arabs, particularly the Husaynis and their supporters, carefully watched such relations between Zionists and neighboring Arab countries. There was anger and protest in the local Arab press over official Egyptian-Zionist exchanges, but satisfaction was expressed over the demonstrations against Balfour's 1925 visit to Damascus and the pro-Zionist Alfred Mond's trip to Baghdad in 1928.[43]

Within Palestine, the Arabic-language press evidenced this new Arab internationalism. Extensive coverage was given to the Riff revolt in Morocco and the Druze-led uprising in Syria. Most foreign Arab leaders received favorable attention, though some publications linked to the Mufti were already beginning to attack Abdallah. Political groups organized demonstrations and raised funds for nationalist battles in neighboring countries—for example, protests against the visit to Palestine in 1927 of the new French high commissioner for Syria.[44]

The Mufti also began his own diplomatic campaign keyed to religious appeals through the Committee for the Defense of the Wall, established in October 1928. Claiming a Jewish threat to major Jerusalem holy sites—the Temple Mount area which included the Dome of the Rock and Al-Aqsa Mosque as well as the Western ("Wailing") Wall of the Jewish Temple—the Mufti asked the Islamic world to help defend them. In early 1929, he visited Egypt to raise funds for mosque repairs and to rally supporters. His opponents accused him of exaggerating a minor issue for political advantage and appealed to Egypt's King Fuad to ignore these requests.[45]

It was a mistake to think that disputes over the holy places were a passing conflict. In August 1929, Arab rioting broke out after a small right-wing Zionist demonstration at the wall. Jews were massacred in several cities, particularly Hebron. By the time the British regained control, more than 250 people had been killed on both sides, and several hundred more were wounded. The British investigation conducted by the Shaw Commission saw growing Arab anti-Zionism as the underlying cause of the disturbances.[46]

Events in Palestine now for the first time gained the attention of the Arab world, particularly in religious-oriented circles. Syrian government officials helped smuggle arms to Arab insurgents, while anti-Jewish riots broke out in Damascus. During one demonstration, crowds stopped by the offices of the Saudi Arabian mission to acclaim King Ibn Saud, who had driven Sharif Husayn out of Arabia and was building a fundamentalist Islamic state there. They were disappointed by a Saudi government statement that the British would undoubtedly be fair in Palestine.

Iraq remained relatively quiet during the conflict, although in the southern city of Basra demonstrators forced their entrance into the British consulate to protest. Beirut saw a one-day strike of shopkeepers and a large, orderly march led by a broad alliance of religious dignitaries. One of the organizers was Riyad al-Sulh, who had earlier sought negotiated solutions.[47]

Even in Egypt the news was closely followed and public opinion sympathized with the Palestine Arabs. Egyptian Jews fearfully avoided expressing their feelings and requested special police protection. Shaykh Mustafa al-Maraghi of the prestigious Al-Azhar mosque-university warned the British that no Muslim could accept foreign influence on the Al-Aqsa Mosque, which he called the second holiest site of Islam. "The enmity of the Jews to Muslims is mentioned in the Koran," he wrote, and Muslims always see a religious basis for quarrels with Jews. Moreover, he added, they believe that the prophet Muhammad promised that victory would always go to the Muslims. Such situations were inherently inflammatory.[48]

In Transjordan, Abdallah maintained calm by urging restraint on his people. Earlier, a number of influential religious and tribal leaders had openly discussed the possibility of a military march across the river and of raising money for arms.

Many of the stories spread in neighboring countries were wildly inaccurate. Some Egyptian newspapers proclaimed that Islam's most essential rights were under attack in Jerusalem. Visitors to Palestine from Egypt and Syria came expecting to find the Jews claiming possession—and even in actual occupation—of Muslim holy sites. They were surprised to find nothing of the kind. Up to two years later, reports were still circulating in Baghdad attributing the original riots to Jewish bomb attacks on Jerusalem mosques. Nor were such ideas excluded from the political elites. King Ibn Saud, despite his moderation toward the British, firmly believed that the Zionists had thrown hand grenades into the Al-Aqsa shrine.[49]

The 1929 riots had provided a dramatic end to the quiet and apathy which had marked Arab attitudes toward Palestine throughout much of the 1920s. The period of readjustment and realignment following the quick downfall of postwar expectations was nearing an end. Sporadic Arab-Jewish negotiations had failed to produce anything approaching the hoped-for bilateral alliance; the political differences between the two camps and the growing activity of the Palestinian Arabs made such a solution seem increasingly remote.

Both Arab nationalism and Zionism had come a long way from those pre–World War I days when both were embodied by a scattered group of intellectuals. Securing British patronage, each held greatly improved positions when the dust of battle had cleared. Yet European support, as the Arabs in particular had learned, had its price.

The downfall of the Ottoman Empire had created a Middle East political vacuum which many ideas and forces sought to fill. The traditional order, based on membership in a religious community, could not be reconstructed. Arab nationalism was the new ideological glue of the postwar polities, and Arab unity was its goal.

Still, the apocalyptic expectations of the Hashemites had not materialized. They had lost prosperous Syria to the French and their home base in the Hijaz to Ibn Saud's expanding empire. On the positive side, Faysal and Abdallah were respectively king of Iraq and emir of Transjordan. Both of them harbored hopes of reviving Hashemite leadership on a wider scale and both, for this and other reasons, saw Palestine as an element in the political equation.

While ideas leaped boundaries, politicians had to deal with such obstructions. How could Arab states gain coherence and how could local Arab regimes gain legitimacy if they were only shards of a larger, as yet unrealized nation? How could Arab policies be coordinated when each entity possessed a different relationship toward Britain or France? How could a philosophy of seamless unity deal with very real differences of interests between these states? These problems remained embryonic in the 1920s. European control was most tightly exercised on the realm of international relations, and Arab leaders were clearly circumscribed there.

Although all sides involved drew lessons from the 1929 upheavals, these conclusions came more profoundly from the preceding decade of experience. The British government, noting the Shaw report, began to count up the costs of supporting Zionism and began to edge away from their commitments to the Jews. The tactical rationale of their wartime promises had proven erroneous, but the far more real tangible strategic benefits were in their hands. Partial fulfillment of pledges still seemed to hold future advantages. Individual Arab states would be moved toward independence though their special ties to Britain would be maintained. Jewish immigration and institutions in Palestine would be fostered, but with limitations and careful regulation of entry permits.

The Zionists had only become more convinced that the road to Jerusalem lay through Cairo and Baghdad or, in Kisch's words, that understanding with the Palestine Arabs "will be achieved only by our developing relations with the ... real leaders who enjoy unquestioned authority in the neighboring Arab countries."[50]

As for the Palestinian Arab nationalists, they had understood that support from neighboring Arab states was not only desirable but logistically and politically necessary. Demonstrations and armed attacks could be quickly organized in all parts of the country, while religious appeals were another useful channel for mobilizing foreign Arab sympathy. From the Mufti's point of view, the prospects for material and diplomatic aid seemed gratifying and full of promise for the future.

3
Entrance of the Arab Kings: 1931—36

The August 1929 riots had produced an apparent sense of solidarity between the Palestinian Arabs and the neighboring countries. Yet it was a number of years before such sentiments would have an impact on the political scene. Between 1931 and 1936, the Mufti attempted to foster this relationship in every possible way. Religious appeals, whose effectiveness had been demonstrated in 1929, continued to play a central role in his campaign.[1]

Such a choice was a natural one. Amin al-Husayni's leadership among the Palestine Arabs was institutionally based on his religious position as Mufti of Jerusalem and on his control of the Supreme Muslim Council. Given European domination over the diplomatic options of the Arab regimes, ostensibly religious cooperation could be one of the few sanctioned inter-Arab channels. The presence of the holy places in Palestine made it a focus of Islamic interest.

Moreover, the Arab masses had still absorbed relatively little of modern politics and nationalist ideology by the early 1930s. Religion remained the single most important component of their world-view. Even nationalist appeals succeeded to a great extent not because of their denunciation of foreign rule *per se* (the Turks had, of course, not been Arabs), but because that foreign rule was at the same time Christian rule. Finally, the Mufti's religious approach was necessary to overcome the reluctance of Arab rulers to become involved in the conflict and to eliminate their suspicion that al-Husayni's ambitions might pose a political threat to them.[2]

King Faysal of Iraq and Emir Abdallah of Transjordan maintained a special interest in Palestine as part of their broader plans to fulfill the hitherto thwarted Hashemite ambitions. Faysal supported the Istiqlal party within Palestine while Abdallah backed the Nashashibi clan. The Transjordanian leader also continued to court the Zionists, hoping to get them securely on his bandwagon. Egypt and Saudi Arabia, in contrast, stayed relatively aloof from events in Palestine during the first half of the 1930s. Ultimately, the crisis of 1936 brought in all of these forces on an official basis.

While the Young Turks had deprived the Caliph of real power, their secular-oriented successors after the war completely abolished the office. For centuries, Muslims had accepted the Caliph as the legitimate political as well as religious leader of the Islamic lands. Although the institution had degenerated over the centuries, fallen into non-Arab hands, and lost control over many Islamic domains, many Arabs thought its revival to be essential for political unity and for a renaissance of Arab power and culture.

Sharif Husayn had aspired to this role and often had pressed the British to recognize him as Caliph. By the time he proclaimed his candidacy for the post in 1924, such a claim could not be taken seriously: he could not even protect the traditional seat of the Hashemite dynasty from the advancing armies of Ibn Saud. Ironically, one of the few groups recognizing his bid was the Supreme Muslim Council of Palestine, while the Nashashibi group opposed him.[3]

With the disappearance of the caliphate and the failure of Sharif Husayn, no political or religious figure could claim allegiance from anyone outside his own country's boundaries. To win such status — which also carried enhanced domestic prestige — Arab leaders became avid participants in the search for a new source of authority. King Fuad of Egypt organized a conference on the caliphate for Cairo in May 1926; King Ibn Saud, whose control over the holy cities of Mecca and Medina gave him special appeal, held his own meeting the following month. This latter conclave gave the Mufti the idea for a similar gathering five years later.[4]

The Mufti was able to stir much Arab interest over the state of the holy places in Palestine, and these contacts had borne fruit when religious representatives from throughout the Arab world testified before the Shaw Commission. This marked Britain's first acceptance of intervention by outside Arabs.

Shortly after his well-received 1931 pilgrimage to Mecca, Amin al-Husayni and his lieutenants decided to call an Islamic conference in Jerusalem. This promised benefits on the international level but, they quickly realized, it might have negative repercussions at home. Cooperation between Muslim and Christian Arabs had always been an important part of their movement. A specifically Islamic conference might provoke antagonisms, particularly at a time of agitation against Christian missionaries and of Muslim exultation at Turkey's military victory over Christian Greece. Jealousy among Muslims resulted from the high government offices and business successes achieved by the more urbanized and educated Christian Arabs. By treading carefully in this sensitive area, the Supreme Muslim Council managed to avoid serious problems.[5]

More problematic were the inevitable attempts of the Nashashibi and other anti-Husayni forces to portray the Mufti's "foreign policy" as a selfish ploy to gain factional advantages. They had already tried to influence the Egyptian government and were developing contacts with Abdallah. If he invited foreign Arab involvement in Palestine, the Mufti might also be fostering his neighbors' interference in internal Arab politics. He had no assurances that such actions would always help his side. This became a serious problem at several times in the future.

Finally, the British must be somehow persuaded that foreign Arab involvement would not harm their interests. Generally, there was no restriction placed on nonviolent activities, but the British — like the Mufti's internal Arab opponents — would try to use the participation of neighboring Arab states to their own advantage.

In the case of the December 1931 Islamic Conference, this last difficulty was easily solved. The Mufti promised the British high commissioner that the meeting would only deal with religious and educational questions. Good will would be furthered between England and the Muslims. No discussion would touch on political questions. With permission quickly granted, the Mufti helped draw up a program focused on the strengthening and guarding of Muslim traditions, principles, and holy places.[6]

If British concern was soothed, the Arab states themselves were not so easily persuaded. None of them was enthusiastic. Ibn Saud interpreted the Mufti's call as a direct challenge to his own religious efforts. Egypt's reaction was the most hostile. Even after the Mufti personally went to Cairo to give written assurances that Egypt's domestic affairs would not be discussed, the government still decided not to send an official delegation.

Like Ibn Saud, Egypt's King Fuad feared that others might be named Caliph. Egyptian religious notables worried that the conference might establish an Islamic university in Jerusalem to threaten the primacy of their own Al-Azhar. Modernist intellectuals thought the meeting reactionary, as threatening to reverse the evolution toward separate, secular states which they supported. There was some concern that the extension of Arab-Jewish conflict to Egypt would cause intercommunal strife.[7]

Almost immediately the Jerusalem meeting did become an issue in Egypt's internal politics. The domestic line-up on the question illustrates the curious role reversals into which Palestine often led Arab parties and politicians: while the "conservative" palace and religious factions opposed participation in the meeting, the "liberal" and "secular-oriented" Wafd party supported it. The reason was simple: the king's strongman, Prime Minister Ismail Sidqi, had suspended democracy and engineered a repressive campaign against the Wafd. Participation in Jerusalem not only allowed the Wafd a platform for denouncing these actions, it also let the party portray itself as the true Arab patriots in Egypt.

Personalities also played a role. At that time, the Wafd still contained a number of men who would soon leave the party to follow a more consistently Pan-Arab policy. Typical of these was the Wafd's delegate to Jerusalem, Abd al-Rahman Azzam, the future first secretary-general of the Arab League. During his speech at the Jerusalem meeting, Azzam launched an intense verbal attack on King Fuad. When he went on to blast Italian colonial policy in Libya, where his family had originated, the British authorities expelled him from Palestine.[8]

Given the apathy and misgivings of Arab governments, the December 1931 Jerusalem meeting fell short of the Mufti's expectations. None of the heads of state and few of the political parties invited sent delegates and few of the 150 people present represented any real forces. On several occasions, official delegations withdrew from sessions to avoid embarrassment to their governments.

To make matters worse, the Mufti's opponents held their own one-day alternative congress attended by about fifteen hundred people, including a number of Palestinian Arab mayors. They also made attempts, though with little success, to convince delegates to withdraw from the Mufti's meeting.[9]

Despite these obstacles, the Jerusalem conference brought to light a number of positions and ideas which would characterize Arab policies in later years. Among these were resolutions calling for a boycott of Jewish goods, the formation of an agricultural association to purchase and farm Arab lands to keep them out of Zionist hands, and the proposal to systematize anti-Zionist propaganda throughout the Arab world.

Iraqi delegate Said Thabit invoked an ominous new tactic. If Jews continued their activities in Palestine, he warned, Jewish communities elsewhere in the Arab world would be punished. Within eighteen months, bloody anti-Jewish riots in Aden and Algeria, while probably spontaneous, seemed to echo his words.[10]

The Mufti worked hard to build a permanent organization out of the conference. To gain contributions, al-Husayni and his close Egyptian collaborator, Muhammad Ali Alluba, toured Iraq and India. In 1934 the executive committee they had established sent a peace delegation to mediate the Saudi-Yemen border war. But in the end, the Mufti's group seemed destined for demise. Despite these efforts, the inter-Arab scene between 1932 and 1936 continued to be dominated by the Pan-Arab proposals of the Hashemite heirs, Faysal and Abdallah. The Zionists maintained diplomatic contacts with both groups, while trying to build relations with Egypt and Lebanon.[11]

King Faysal was particularly active. Along with Syrian nationalist Faris al-Khuri and Palestinian activist Awni Abd al-Hadi, the king tried to organize his own Pan-Arab conference. After a 1933 visit to Palestine, where he promised local Arab delegations that he would intervene for them in London, he began a campaign to change English policy.

During talks with British Foreign Secretary Sir John Simon, Faysal laid out his Pan-Arab plans unaware that, due to British commitments toward the Jews and French, Simon had already decided to discourage him. Faysal's plan for Palestine was similar to his ideas in 1919. An agreement with the Jews would be worked out to guarantee their right to settle in Palestine in exchange for their acceptance of an Arab confederation. Next, the accord would provide a basis for negotiating an Anglo-Palestine treaty similar to the Anglo-Iraq treaty which provided Faysal's new realm independence. Since British strategic interests in Palestine would be safeguarded, the mandate could be terminated and independence granted.

Seeing himself as the natural leader of the federal Arab state, Faysal dispatched Yasin al-Hashimi to Palestine and neighboring countries to test public opinion. In press interviews al-Hashimi urged the Jews to give up aspirations for an autonomous state and to immigrate to Palestine under Arab protection.

Faysal particularly stressed two points in his discussions with British officials. Iraq needed a line of communication to the Mediterranean Sea through Syria or Palestine. He preferred the latter since his ties were to Britain; the French were Faysal's enemies. Also, unless his plan were adopted, there would be more Arab-Jewish fighting in Palestine. Continued Jewish immigration was raising tensions and must be limited. Failure to solve the problem coupled with renewed conflict, Faysal added, would make it difficult for Iraq to maintain friendly relations with Britain. His ideas were all rejected.[12]

Iraqi intervention in Palestine was by no means limited to diplomatic efforts. The Palestine Istiqlal party was the local branch of a Pan-Arab political group linked with Iraq. Led by Abd al-Hadi, it was never able to challenge Husayni leadership (institutionalized after 1935 in the Mufti's own Palestine Arab party), but the Istiqlal did succeed in gathering together a number of Palestinian Arab intellectuals. Abd al-Hadi himself had been associated with Faysal since 1918. He had worked for Abdallah after Faysal's expulsion from Syria but was himself expelled from Trans-jordan in 1924 because of his criticisms of Abdallah's pro-British policy.[13]

As implied by Faysal in his London proposals, his supporters were interested in trying to work out a solution with the Zionists. For his part, David Ben-Gurion, whose Labor party was gaining hegemony in the Zionist movement, thought it would be easier to deal with the modernist, Pan-Arab Istiqlal than with the patriarchal, Palestine nationalist Husayni group. Ben-Gurion and Abd al-Hadi met several times in 1934 to search for common ground, but they essentially talked past each other. Ben-Gurion saw two separate nationalist movements which would eventually build separate states, whereas the Palestine Istiqlal could only think of Palestine as part of a unified Arab nation.[14]

On an ideological level, Zionists had more in common with Maronite Christians who in the 1930s were developing a non-Arab Lebanese nationalism. The Society of Young Phoenicians, formed by poet Charles Corm and politician Albert Naqqash to redefine Lebanese Christian identity, often cited the Zionist revival of Hebrew culture as an example to be followed. Victor Jacobson, a Jewish Agency emissary, visited Beirut in 1932 to discuss the possibility of a Lebanese-Zionist social-cultural association or even a joint company for using southern Leba-non's Litani River for electricity and irrigation. These plans were blocked by the French and by the growing tension in the area.[15]

Exchanges with Egypt, which had been started in the 1920s, also continued. Makram Ubeid, Wafd general secretary, visited Jerusalem to speak on the importance of Arab-Jewish conciliation. While a Jewish state would meet with strong opposition from the entire Arab world, he said, a Jewish spiritual homeland would be welcome.

In general, Egyptian policy in these years maintained a distinct aloofness and remoteness from Palestine. Contacts remained on a largely sporadic and individual level. Abd al-Hamid Said, president of the influential Egyptian Young Men's Muslim Association, tried to mediate among the feuding Palestine Arab factions; King Fuad received Nahum Sokolow, head of the World Zionist Organization; and Fuad's throne-seeking relative, Abbas Hilmi, even suggested himself as king of a decentralized Palestine. All this was marginal.[16]

The same cannot be said for the continued efforts of Abdallah, who constantly generated new ideas and proposals. One of these would lead to a major public controversy. In February 1931, Jewish Agency representative Fred Kisch went to Amman. There he met with Prime Minister Hassan Khalid, the aged Sharif Husayn, and Emir Abdallah himself. All spoke of their desire to establish friendly relations between Jews and Arabs. Some of the talk was along traditional lines: neither side would benefit from a clash in Palestine, Abdallah said, and while he appreciated the Jewish connection with Palestine (which was even mentioned in the Koran) a solution must be found consistent with Pan-Arab aspirations.

Alongside this there was a new and significant proposal. Jewish help might be welcome, Khalid hinted, in the development of Transjordan. Kisch convinced a Jewish specialist on Transjordan to set up a survey office in Amman and urged Weizmann to go to Transjordan's capital in person. This last proposal was blocked by British pressure. If the Zionists did reach an agreement with Abdallah, they feared, violence might be instigated by Palestinian Arabs who opposed it. Moreover, although Abdallah's energy for making plans seemed unending, he had no authority to carry out such negotiations.[17]

Abdallah remained undeterred, and he quickly moved forward on his idea. In 1930 Mithqal al-Fa'iz, head of the most important Bedouin tribal confederation in Transjordan, the Banu Sakhr, and a close friend of Abdallah, suggested selling thirty thousand dunams of land in Transjordan to the Zionist Executive for economic reasons. Other tribal leaders seemed amenable. About a year after Kisch's visit, Abdallah offered a promising tract of seventy thousand dunams.

The Jewish Agency quickly agreed and on January 7, 1933, they signed a contract for a ninety-nine-year lease on a six-month option. Not surprisingly, publication of this accord enraged Abdallah's Palestine Arab opponents and worried the British. The mandatory government abrogated the agreement.[18]

Abdallah was by no means finished. In response, he launched another political offensive. He made a four-point proposal to the Jewish Agency. Palestine and Transjordan would unite under Abdallah; the Arabs would recognize the mandate, including its guarantee of Jewish rights; each state would keep its own legislative council and prime minister subject to Abdallah's direction; and a joint agreement would be concluded over future immigration and land purchases. Moshe Shertok, head of the Jewish Agency Political Department, and Arabs representing both the Nashashibi and Husayni factions were invited to discuss this. Both sides rejected the offer.[19]

From this point on, the strain between the Husayni camp and Abdallah reached a peak of bitterness. The emir was openly denounced by the Mufti's supporters as "the Jews' friend." In contrast, the Nashashibis stepped up their support of Abdallah and called for Palestine's merger with Transjordan. Once again, the Nashashibi National Defense party sought to counter the Mufti's foreign policy, sending missions to Egypt and Saudi Arabia to present their side of the story. The Transjordan People's party, composed of Abdallah's followers, denounced the Mufti and his press while tightening links with the Nashashibis.[20]

This conflict also opened a rift between the two branches of the pro-Hashemite forces. Abd al-Hadi, head of the pro-Iraq Istiqlal, attacked Abdallah in letters to Syrian, Iraqi, and Saudi officials. To his patron, King Faysal, he pleaded for drastic action, since Abdallah "had failed in his duty by opening the gateway of the Arabian peninsula to the Jews." Abd al-Hadi had, of course, carried out his own negotiations with the Zionists about the same time.[21]

During minor 1933 disturbances in Palestine, sympathy strikes took place in Transjordan. Abdallah wrote to the high commissioner protesting Jewish immigration in a revealing letter. There were two sides to the accelerating influx of Jews, spurred by Hitler's rise to power in Germany. On the one hand, it was a "calamity" for the Arabs to receive such people "with first-class European educations in science, the professions, and in the mechanical and military fields." They would certainly not fit in with traditional Arab societies, while their presence would provide the Zionists with economic and political advantages over the Arabs.

On the other hand, Abdallah realized that the harnessing of these abilities for the development and prosperity of his own backward kingdom — or in a Palestine joined to his kingdom — was a tremendous opportunity, and one worth some risk to gain. Not only did Abdallah court the Zionists, he also never underestimated their power. His analysis of the conflict and its probable outcome was quite different from that of other Arab leaders, who maintained confidence in an easy victory over the Jews right down to those fatal days of 1948.[22]

This strategy made the Mufti equally determined to destabilize Abdallah's position. If Abdallah would support the Nashashibis, al-

Husayni would support the much weaker opposition party in Transjordan. He also tried to bring other Arab leaders into a coalition against Abdallah. Ibn Saud was the obvious candidate for this purpose. He had driven the Hashemites out of Arabia and his Wahabi tribesman continued to launch fierce raids on Transjordan. His eldest son, Prince Saud, received a spirited reception during a September 1935 visit to Palestine. The courtly Musa al-Alami, a moderate Arab intellectual, explained Palestinian respect for the Saudi kingdom's independence with an Arab proverb, "When we have not beautiful eyes we admire the beautiful eyes of our neighbor."

When the crown prince visited Amman, the different atmosphere there was unmistakable. After Abdallah presented Prince Saud with a magnificent gold-and-silver inlaid sword, he approached a British officer who had attended the ceremony. "I saw you smile and I know why you did it," Abdallah confided. "I was thinking the same thing but I did not smile. You thought that Saud would return one day with his beautiful sword and cut off my head."

Such fears were premature. When a group of Syrian and Palestinian Arabs appealed to King Ibn Saud for intervention into their problems, the Saudi king knew he was still too weak to offer much effective aid. Political events were being set in motion to make such involvement a reality. Yet when the Arab states became intertwined in Palestine the following year it was a coordinated effort.[23]

To understand these developments, it is necessary to retrace the political evolution of the major Arab states up to 1936. The differences between their political structures and geopolitical positions goes far toward explaining their various roles in the Palestine conflict.

Saudi Arabia and Transjordan can be termed "monocentric" states. King Ibn Saud and Emir Abdallah held full power within their respective countries. There was no meaningful political party system or opposition. Both were highly traditional societies where rulers based their power on tribal pastoralists. Although public opinion sometimes had to be taken into consideration, it was a limited and unorganized force. In short, domestic considerations played a relatively small role in the making of their foreign policy.

More important were the personalities and objectives of the individual rules. These were shaped, of course, by their backgrounds and by the position of their country. Ibn Saud's conflict with the Hashemites was in many ways a personal duel, a continuation of the war for control of Arabia which Abdallah's father had lost. Palestine was Transjordan's doorstep and its future was central for Abdallah's realm. Saudi Arabia was remote in those days of slow travel, and Palestine was a more marginal concern. Abdallah saw himself as the rightful heir to Hashemite ambitions on the inter-Arab stage, while Ibn Saud, as protector of the holy cities of Mecca and Medina, saw himself as a guardian of Islamic rights.

An additional factor was the importance for both of the British connection. While Ibn Saud was independent and Abdallah was under British mandate, both were to a large measure dependent on British subsidies. These were poor countries even in relation to their neighbors. Money was needed to pay for the upkeep of royal courts and for the loyalty of tribes. They could have no illusions about their ability to pull the British lion's tail and survive.

There is a probably apocryphal story designed to demonstrate the average Saudi tribesman's attitude toward Palestine in the early 1930s. "To what tribes do the Arabs in Palestine belong?" he asked. On being told that most were agriculturalists with no such affiliation, he lost interest. Clan loyalties or enmities were not aroused.[24]

This was beside the point. If the Palestine Arab was not likely to belong to a tribe, he was still likely to belong to the community of Islam. For members of the Wahabi sect, which dominated Saudi Arabia, the idea of non-Muslim rule over the holy places and over part of the Islamic heartland was painful enough. For a king who reigned over the holiest places of Islam it was inadmissible.

The significance of this last point in elevating Ibn Saud's status should not be underestimated. Only a few years earlier, Sharif Husayn tried to use his rule over that territory as a springboard for Hashemite rule of the Arab world. When Britain made Sharif Husayn's continued subsidy conditional on his recognition of the new territorial status quo, he refused in the belief that London could not afford to do without his cooperation. Ibn Saud was well aware that this miscalculation had helped cost Sharif Husayn his kingdom, but he also knew the exalted status which had made him so stake it.

Yet after his conquests Ibn Saud turned inward. The bywords of his policy were internal consolidation and the maintenance of good relations with Great Britain. In his Arab strategy, he sought to prevent formation of a strong hostile Hashemite bloc. When his Syrian advisers or his English friend H. St. John Philby suggested involvement in Palestine beginning in 1930, he would demur. His policy was never to intervene in the internal affairs of the mandates, he replied. The king was confident that the British would one day invite him to use his prestige to solve matters there. He would wait.[25]

Meanwhile, Saudi Arabia played an important role in a period of growing Arab cooperation. Ibn Saud negotiated a peace treaty with Yemen and boundary agreements with other neighbors. He initiated the April 1936 Treaty of Arab Brotherhood and Alliance and an accord with Egypt the following month. The king's popularity throughout the Arab world rose to new heights.[26]

The Hashemite regimes in Iraq and Transjordan obviously did not share in this admiration. They knew that the Saudi policy of concord was designed to eliminate any chance for their leadership of the Arab world. This rivalry also extended to Palestine. When faced with Abdallah's attempt to gain part of that territory in 1937, Ibn Saud threatened to invade Transjordan. After 1945, Saudi Arabia paired with Egypt to form an alternative bloc to that of the Hashemites. Three years later, this conflict played a central role in the Arab decision to go to war.

Just as Saudi Arabia was the creation — and in some ways the personification—of Ibn Saud, Transjordan was built around the personality and ambitions of Emir Abdallah. Born in Mecca in 1882, Abdallah was Sharif Husayn's second son. After education in Istanbul and in the Hijaz, Abdallah became a member of the Ottoman parliament and developed an interest in Arab nationalism. He returned home to become his father's foreign minister and later the commander of the Hashemite forces. After being badly defeated by Ibn Saud's army, Abdallah marched north against Syria. In March 1921, he abandoned this operation in exchange for the throne of Transjordan.

To gain control of Palestine, Abdallah believed it necessary to cope with three factors: the British, the Palestine Arabs, and the Jews. He developed concurrent strategies for all three fronts.

Toward the British, he attempted to prove his unswerving loyalty. He would gain London's support by showing himself to be their most dependable ally in the Arab world. The Anglo-Transjordan treaty of 1928 institutionalized British influences, bases, and advisers there. Given his country's weak economy, Abdallah was dependent on British subsidies, but London's money and officers also provided him with the most impressive army in the Arab world.

Moreover, the ever-buoyant Abdallah always seemed confident that in the long run Britain would back his claims. "Great Britain will finally fulfill her promise to the Arabs," he said in 1935. "Arab independence and the interest of England are bound together by mutual interest." His attitude toward the 1936 Palestine general strike, the 1937 partition proposal, and the Allied cause in World War II, would all be in line with this conception.[27]

Among the Arabs, he encouraged confidence in British intentions. More important, his policy differed in two ways from that of Ibn Saud. The Saudi ruler, despite Hashemite suspicions, was generally satisfied with the territorial status quo. Abdallah, by contrast, made no secret of his revisionism. His designs on Syria and Palestine made him many enemies in those countries and elsewhere. Further, he courted and subsidized opposition movements in various states which he hoped would remain loyal to himself and his vision.

He did not choose his friends well. Abdallah's support for the Shahbandar group in Syria earned him the enmity of the triumphant National Bloc majority. In Palestine, he fared equally poorly with his assistance to the Nashashibis against the Mufti's leadership. This latter collision was probably inevitable. The conflict between the Mufti's desire for an independent Arab state under his leadership and Abdallah's goal was as great as the gap between the Mufti and the Zionists.

In addition to his links with Raghib al-Nashashibi's National Defense party, Abdallah employed many Palestinian Arabs in the highest positions of his own government. They included Ibrahim Hashim (from Nablus), Samir al-Rifai (from Safad), and Tawfiq Abu al-Huda (from Acre), who served as prime minister between 1939 and 1944. Both Hashim and Abu al-Huda were veterans of Faysal's Syrian regime. These officials and others provided skills which native Transjordanians could not supply, but they also augmented Abdallah's claim that his government could represent Palestinian aspirations.[28]

While Abdallah sought to avoid a Jewish state if possible, he wished to stay on good terms with the Zionists. To gain all of Palestine, Abdallah wanted the Jews to prefer some degree of autonomy under his rule rather than any other arrangement. If partition seemed inevitable, Abdallah was willing to gain every possible square inch of territory for Transjordan. Like almost every other Arab leader, Abdallah had no personal difficulties in dealing with Jews. In sharp contrast, Ibn Saud's anti-Semitism approached the pathological.

Abdallah's Jewish policy began in 1922 when he offered Weizmann a Jewish national home and implementation of the Balfour Declaration in exchange for Jewish acceptance of him as sovereign of Palestine. Contacts continued throughout the 1920s. As time went on, Abdallah's determination intensified. Not only was the economic situation in Palestine increasingly attractive, but also merger with Palestine was seen as the first step toward Abdallah's long-range goal of a "Greater Syria" under his auspices.[29]

The Zionists were also interested in maintaining good relations with

Abdallah, though they had no desire to become his subjects. With confidence in their ability to eventually win statehood, they did not feel the need for Abdallah's preferred protection. Some did have great hopes for settling in Transjordan while others, particularly but not exclusively the Revisionists, wanted to add it to Palestine on their own terms.[30]

While the policies of Abdallah angered both the Mufti's forces and Istiqlal, their leverage against the emir was limited. Jamil al-Husayni, the Mufti's cousin and chief adviser, admitted the strength of Abdallah's domestic support. The Transjordan tribes supported the Palestine Arabs' cause but resented their interference. Not that Abdallah underestimated the danger: "God alone knows the trouble it is costing me to preserve peace in Transjordan with cries from Palestine daily rending the ears of my people ... and zealots seek to stir them up through religious and racial agitation," he wrote in June 1936. Such echoes within his domain must have further convinced Abdallah that a solution to the Palestine problem was necessary for his own survival.[31]

Palestine's economic importance to Transjordan also cannot be neglected. Transjordan was far less developed than its neighbor, and in some years Palestine purchased its whole agricultural surplus. During the years 1936–39, bilateral trade doubled, with the balance heavily in Transjordan's favor. Palestine's ports were its best route to the outside world. These facts were recognized by the 1928 Anglo-Transjordan treaty which confirmed Transjordan's right to equal harbor facilities and eliminated customs' barriers.[33]

Thus both Transjordan and Saudi Arabia had their own particular reasons for special interest in Palestine. The growing involvement of Egypt and Iraq even further expanded the scope of foreign Arab participation. Further, while for Abdallah and Ibn Saud Palestine was primarily a foreign policy issue, for the more advanced and complex societies of Iraq and Egypt, the issue had profound domestic implications as well.

4
ᗞomestic ᑭolitics and ᑭalestine: Iraq and Egypt

I raq and Egypt, in contrast to Saudi Arabia and Transjordan, were "polycentric" societies. Power was widely dispersed among the royal palace and a number of political parties. They were riven by personal and factional rivalries and ideological debates. There were elections, legislatures, a relatively free press, voluntary associations and, in short, the full panoply of institutions which apparently provide for democracy and the expression of public opinion.

In practice, all of these forms were adapted to contemporary Arab political and cultural organization; they never really took root in divided and rigidly stratified states only a few years away from Ottoman autocracy. Their youth, along with the Pan-Arab doctrine which denied the validity of such separate states, deprived them of legitimacy. Internal conflict often paralyzed them while British influence humiliated them. Beginning in 1949 these structures collapsed, to be replaced in Syria, Egypt, and Iraq by one-party military dictatorships.

The weaknesses of this intervening period of liberal experiment were manifold. For example, political parties were, in Albert Hourani's words, "alliances of independent leaders, held together by precarious agreement." Their emphasis was on gaining independence, but they had no clear idea of what should be done once independence had been won. Generally, they had no systematic program for modernization and development. With the exception of the Egyptian Wafd, their political base was generally limited to small circles of urban notables and intellectuals, to the great families and the large landlords.[1]

The Palestine issue's impact on Iraq and Egypt was filtered through

53

these realities. Islamic and Arab sentiments dictated the direction of their sympathies and geographic proximity its measure of urgency. Events in Palestine and elsewhere determined the timing of interventions. The interplay of domestic politics, however, played a major part in helping to set the strategy and tactics employed.

In the early period, the Palestine conflict was far more central for Iraq than for Egypt. Sayyid Talib of Basra, one of the first Arab opponents of the Young Turks, accused them of being "pro-Zionist, anti-Muslim and anti-Arab." They had, he added, proposed to sell Palestine to the Jews in their own interest. These wild charges provided the first example of the Zionism issue's usefulness in attacking political rivals.[2]

Existence of a Zionist enemy was an important factor encouraging Arabs to band together. This was clearly demonstrated in Iraq's nation-building process. Population diversity and a traditional localism made it difficult for the central government to win allegiance and obedience from its subjects. A strong ideological Arabism evolved as an answer to this problem.[3]

Those who ruled Iraq during the years up to 1958 tended to have two things in common. They had been born outside the country or at least had spent much of their early lives abroad in the service of the Ottoman Empire and the Hashemites. Although themselves Sunni Muslims, they had been imposed by Britain on the Shi'ite and Kurdish minorities, as well as on local nationalists. Any group would have had difficulties in establishing a legitimate state in Iraq, but this elite had special problems in that regard.[4]

Second, their backgrounds, experiences, and ambitions made them determined Pan-Arabists. Iraq had a special mission to build a united Arab nation, they believed, and educators like Sami Shawkat passed on such sentiments to the 1930s' generation. "Sixty years ago," he said in his 1933 speech, "The Profession of Death," Prussia had dreamed of uniting the German people, now Germany was a powerful nation. "What is there to prevent Iraq ... from dreaming to unite all the Arab countries?" Shawkat asked.[5]

King Faysal agreed. Iraq's early independence and its 1932 membership in the League of Nations implied a special obligation of leadership. Faysal's service to the Arab and Hashemite causes had brought him recognition and popularity throughout the Arab world. Many thought the wartime Hashemite military commander and monarch of the ill-fated Syrian kingdom the most likely ruler for a Pan-Arab state. Ibn Saud once confided to the Mufti, "I was never scared of any man but Faysal."[6]

Faysal's death in 1933 ended this personal appeal, but these doc-
trines continued to be widely spread among Iraqi students and soldiers.
As directors-general of Iraqi education, the Pan-Arab theorist Sati al-
Husri and his successor Shawkat imported many Syrian and Palestinian
teachers. Their purpose was, in al-Husri's words, to "spread faith in the
unity of the Arab nation and to disseminate its past glories." The
primary school syllabus ended its world history section with an extensive study of Italian and German national unification.[7]

Iraq's political style quickly developed the dangerous practice of
running with the British fox while hunting with the militant nationalist
hounds. From the 1920 on, Iraqi politicians repeatedly created or
utilized domestic crises for partisan advantage. Civilian leaders' willingness to employ the army and violent means to gain power created a
lasting tradition, giving rise to permanent military rule after 1958.

There are many examples of this spiralling race to militancy. For
instance, Faysal, Nuri al-Said, and Yasin al-Hashimi organized an anti-
British campaign to win the right to enlarge their armed forces through
conscription in 1928. Once this succeeded, they tried to tamp down the
agitation to enable maintenance of the vital British alliance. Obviously, it
was easier to foster such movements than it was to control them. The
counterrevolutions had a way of devouring their own children.[8]

Such controlled demagoguery was also involved in gaining Iraq's
independence. During the preparatory period, the Ikha and Watani
parties threatened Faysal and his negotiators, as well as each other, for
lack of nationalist zeal. Yet they all knew that concessions were necessary. When Rashid Ali al-Gailani came to power in 1933 and made a *pro
forma* remark friendly to London, his Watani rivals denounced him as a
reactionary traitor to national interests. Such rhetorical over-kill toyed
with thunder.[9]

Between 1933 and 1936, Iraqi politics generated a crescendo of bitter
conflict which owed much to individual competition. In the former year,
the Ikha party used the army's defeat of the Assyrian Christian minority
to play on majority chauvinism. When Ali Jawdat and Jamil al-Midfai
came to power in 1935, the displaced Ikha politicians incited the tribes of
the middle Euphrates River to revolt. The uprising was not easily controlled and once again the army was called out. By making military
commander Bakr Sidqi into a national hero, the civilians created their
own nemesis.[10]

By 1936, Iraq was little closer to stability. Having used the tribes to
come into power, Ikha leaders Taha al-Hashimi and Rashid Ali al-Gailani
sought to entrench themselves by tightening control and repressing the

tribes. A propaganda campaign at home and abroad sought to win confidence by advocating a strong Pan-Arab policy. Syrian and Egyptian nationalists were invited for visits, and the carefully courted Syrian press began to refer to Taha al-Hashimi as "Bismark of the Arabs." King Ghazi, Faysal's son, supported these efforts.[11]

For the new left-of-center reform party, the Ahali, al-Hashimi and al-Gailani had sold out to the British, while other groups criticized the government for insufficient nationalism.[12] As for Palestine, Iraq had not been particularly active. British Foreign Secretary Sir John Simon could comment with some accuracy that the regime and its predecessors had not "taken any action to prejudice the position of the British Government in Palestine."[13]

In addition to the Islamic, Arab, and Hashemite links, Iraq had two unique ties to Palestine before 1936—the economic connection and the minority question within Iraq.

From the "third millennium B.C. down to the thirteenth century of the Christian era," wrote Arnold Toynbee in 1935, "Palestine had lain on the line of communication between one great center of population and productivity in Egypt and a comparable center in Iraq." With the commercial development of aviation and transdesert motor traffic, the shifting routes from sea to land, the reemergence of Iraq from its 700-year-long eclipse, and the economic rehabilitation of Palestine through an inflow of Jewish enterprise, Toynbee concluded, Palestine could again play this role for both Iraq and Egypt.[14]

Up to 1918, of course, the entire Fertile Crescent had been part of the Ottoman Empire, and goods moved freely throughout the region. These trade routes were not disrupted by the postwar settlement. In the 1920s and 1930s, Palestine remained Syria's chief customer in the region, buying cement, butter, cheese, eggs, vegetables, fruit, cereals, and other products. Through Palestine, Syria reexported wool, cotton, silk, textiles, and other commodities.[15]

Palestine was also a major market for other Arab neighbors. In 1937, for instance, it took 150 percent more Arab exports than all the Arab states together, purchasing five times more goods than did Egypt or Syria and seven times more than Iraq. Palestine ranked fourth among importers of Iraqi goods, and bilateral trade increased dramatically in the 1930s. In 1935–36, Palestine took over one-quarter of Iraq's exports, far more than Syria, Saudi Arabia or Egypt. As with Transjordan, the balance of trade was very much in Iraq's favor.[16]

The development of infrastructure favored such commerce. In 1933, a direct Haifa-Baghdad road opened as well as a telegraph line. In

Haifa's new port, third largest in the eastern Mediterranean, a free zone was opened for Iraqi goods. These arrangements began to shift Iraq's trade from the long sea passage around the Arabian peninsula and through the Suez Canal to the shorter Haifa Mediterranean route.[17]

Iraq's oil pipeline through Haifa opened in January 1935. The company was given special railroad rates and tax reductions for shipments across Palestine. Toynbee wrote at the time that Palestine seemed "destined to become the *entrepot* for the vast new oil-extracting industry" which was promising—or threatening—to transform life in the region.[18]

So impressed was Weizmann with these economic factors that he attributed Iraq's later hard line to them. Without doubt, this was an exaggeration, but Palestine's status as Iraq's Mediterranean outlet made its disposition a matter of prime national interest in Baghdad.[19]

Iraq's handling of minority problems was closely watched by Jews in Palestine as an indication of what Arab rule mighr bring them. The rapid disintegration of British promises to the Assyrians increased Zionist skepticism over the prospects for minority guarantees within an enlarged Arab state. Threats against the large Jewish community in Iraq, expressed as early as the 1931 Jerusalem conference, had a similar effect. League of Nations demands that Iraq safeguard minority rights proved ineffectual. Iraqi leaders offered such provisions to Jews in exchange for their abandonment of demands for a state. After the first major outbreak of anti-Jewish violence in Baghdad, the proposal was rejected.[20]

Nuri al-Said was the Iraqi politician who played the greatest role over Palestine. As architect of the Anglo-Iraq treaty, al-Said had been attacked for being pro-British, but he was as aware as any of his compatriots of the nationalist and Pan-Arab grounds for concern. Further, the tremendous prestige which would accrue to any statesman who could win Arab gains on the issue was always attractive.

Indeed, it was precisely because of their worry over maintaining good Anglo-Iraq relations that moderate politicians became preoccupied by Palestine. "The Palestinian question is the root of all evils which disturb and weaken Anglo-Iraqi relations," al-Said later told al-Gailani. He later recalled, no element in all Iraqi-British relations of the period 1937 to 1941 was more detrimental than the "tragically mishandled" Palestine issue.[21]

As a consummate politician in the Iraqi tradition, al-Said understood the need to diffuse the appeal of radical Pan-Arab groups like the Muthanna Club of Baghdad (core of the Palestine Defense Committee), the Jawwal Society, and Shawkat's Futuwwah group.[22] "God, being the personification of virtue, does not have to be propitiated," he once explained. "But the devil, always on the alert to do mischief, needs to be." Activism on the Palestine issue was a necessity for successive Iraqi regimes.[23]

The contrasts between Egypt and Iraq were broad and deep. To a great degree, these differences help to explain why in the period between 1936 and 1948, as after 1970, the Egyptian attitude was generally moderate while the Iraqi attitude was generally radical.

While Iraq's boundaries were artificial, and its topography and population diversity made it difficult to rule, Egypt was heir to a civilization thousands of years old with a strong tradition of centralized control. While Iraq had been part of the Ottoman Empire and sought to reassemble its Arab provinces, Egypt had been in practice independent for centuries. Iraqi rulers and ideologues had far fewer roots in the country than did their Egyptian counterparts. The history of Egyptian nationalism was by no means identical with that of Pan-Arabism.

The Palestine question only gradually attracted Egyptian attention in the 1920s and 1930s. Emotionally and politically important as it was, Palestine never seemed to touch Egypt quite as deeply as it did the Fertile Crescent Arab states. At times the distinction might seem a small and relative one, but it is nevertheless quite important.

During the interwar period, Egypt was preoccupied with its own problems: the battle for full independence against the British, power struggles between the Wafd party and the king, and intellectual debates over Egypt's future course. Concepts of European-oriented modernism and Egyptian nationalism competed with Pan-Arabism and a traditional Islamic self-definition.

While the view of the Palestine issue in Iraq remained fairly static, in Egypt the question was perceived in an Islamic context in the 1920s, as a central principle of Arabism by the mid-1930s, as an important point in domestic political conflicts in the late 1930s and, finally, as a vital challenge to Egyptian state interests in the post-1945 period.

Although a particular group of Pan-Arabists, who might be called the "Palestine lobby," were primarily responsible for promoting Egyptian concern, they often disagreed as to the nature of an Egyptian response. Political, religious, and economic realities also played a role. Among these should be numbered the failures of the liberal parties, the Islamic culture of most Egyptians, the model offered by the new ideology of Arabism elsewhere, Egypt's geopolitical position, the growing conflict within Palestine itself, and the vision of Egypt as the Arab world's leader.

Egypt had often ruled Palestine in the past or, more correctly, both had been ruled by the same outsiders. Ayyubids and Mamluk dynasties united them against Mongol and Crusader invasions. Muhammad Ali, founder of the modern royal house, conquered Palestine in the 1930s. Thousands of Egyptian laborers participated in Britain's World War I victory in Palestine.

Of all Egyptian frontiers, wrote historian Bernard Lewis, "that in the north-east has always been the most challenging — and the most vulnerable." In response, Egyptian rulers tried to maintain a bridgehead to the east of Sinai or in southern Palestine.[24]

Religious interest in Palestine and its Muslim holy places was also strong. Al-Azhar was an important center of Islamic thought while the Young Men's Muslim Association and the Muslim Brotherhood — both active over Palestine — were predominantly Egyptian organizations. It was Egypt's grand mufti Muhammad Abdu who spoke of all Muslims' duty "to aid in maintaining the authority of Islam and Islamic rule over all lands that had once been Muslim."[25]

Pan-Arab thinkers sought to win Egypt for their movement, in which Palestine was a most potent issue. Many of the writers, journalists, and demonstrators who advocated this cause in Egypt were themselves of Palestinian or Syrian origin, but they were willing to appeal on the basis of Egyptian interests. One of them, political theorist Sati al-Husri, assured Egypt of its natural right to assume the leadership of Arab nationalism.[26]

But it was an uphill fight. While Egyptians undoubtedly wished well for the eastern Arabs after World War I, there was little interest in joining them in a single state. Perhaps typical of Egyptian nationalists was Wafd leader Sa'd Zaghlul's derisive attitude toward Pan-Arabism. "If you add one zero to another zero to another zero," he told Azzam, "then you add another zero what will be the sum?" "Our problem is an Egyptian problem and not an Arab problem," he said at the 1918 Versailles conference.[27]

These sentiments represented a majority, though not the universal, view in the Wafd and Liberal Constitutional parties. To extend Zaghlul's mathematical analogy, these Egyptians saw the attempt to combine Arab states as an artificial and ill-fated process. For Pan-Arabs, on the contrary, European intervention had illogically balkanized a viable Arab union. Concern over Palestine never led to the extended Arab state of Pan-Arab dreams, but it did help break down the exclusive Egyptian nationalism of Kamil and Zaghlul.

Anglo-Egyptian relations also had an important effect on Egypt's

Palestine policy. London's reserved rights in Egypt seriously limited the powers of that country's foreign affairs ministry. For example, Cairo could conclude treaties only after consultation with London. Removal of such British tutelage in 1936 was a precondition for an active Egyptian diplomacy.[28]

Egyptian policy-makers were not always sure how the Palestine question would affect their attempts to cajole concessions from Britain. At first, they tended to stifle protests, fearing they would damage more immediate interests. As World War II approached, they saw London's need for Egypt's strategic cooperation and understood how such Arab leverage might foster a more advantageous Palestine settlement. The British Foreign Office was aware of and responded to this factor.[29]

The style of Egyptian politics differed greatly from that of Iraq. Instead of conflicts between rapidly shifting coalitions of politicians, in Egypt there was a fairly continuous contest between the Wafd party and the palace. Those whose ambitions or inability to accept Zaghlul's (and his successor's) one-man rule drove them from the party eventually ended in the king's camp. The Wafd's popular base was not affected by these defections, and its legitimacy as leader of the nationalist movement pushed its rivals into the shadows. The king often used his constitutional prerogatives and rigged or suspended elections to keep the Wafd out of power. Meanwhile, his advisors avidly sought an ideology, issue, or alternate organization to smash the Wafd's hold on the people.

The Wafd did, however, have two weaknesses. Focusing on the anti-British struggle, it made little effort to deal with Egypt's profound social inequities and maldistribution of land. The power of the palace and its supporters was not challenged at its root. As time went on, the Wafd itself became more and more subject to factionalism and corruption.

In addition, the Wafd's seeming modernist, secular, and Egyptian nationalist learnings made it vulnerable to opposition on traditional, Islamic, and Pan-Arab grounds. This was the direction taken by the palace politicians and the Muslim Brotherhood, which sincerely advocated these answers to Egypt's problems. It was certainly no secret that, as even Emir Abdallah noted, Wafd leaders knew little of other Arab countries and were preoccupied with Egyptian issues.[30]

For some time, Zionists failed to grasp this new atmosphere, continuing well into the 1930s to believe that Zaghlul's "isolationism" still held. "The recent hostility toward our movement," Kisch wrote in 1931, "seems to have left Egyptian circles quite untouched."[31]

Attempts by Kisch and Weizmann to use Egypt as, in the words of one Egyptian Jew, "a center of conciliation" could not compete with the appeal of Arab and Islamic fraternal ties. Reactions to the 1929 riots had shown Egypt's inevitable support for the Palestinian Arabs, though ambiguity over the 1931 Jerusalem conference demonstrated the relatively cautious nature of Cairo's commitment. Between 1931 and 1936, Palestine remained relatively calm and Egypt remained relatively detached. The events of 1936 brought this situation to a rapid end.

First was the Wafd's election victory, ending an internal crisis and setting the stage for the long-awaited Anglo-Egyptian treaty. Pan-Arabs had long suggested that Egypt's isolation had made it harder to force British concessions, but developments happened in reverse: only the treaty's completion made possible a more active Egyptian international role.[32]

King Farouk's accession to the throne in April 1936 was also of fundamental importance. His first years in power were marked by a major anti-Wafd offensive in which the Palestine issue was to play some part. The young king's advisers, like the politician Ali Mahir and Al-Azhar rector Shaykh Mustafa al-Maraghi, spearheaded this effort. Farouk's youth and screen-star good looks made him seem a stirring symbol around whom Egypt could unite.[33]

In the second half of the 1930s, the intensification of the conflict within Palestine coincided with the presence around the king of Egypt's leading advocates of greater Arab consciousness and responsibility. Unlike their counterparts in Iraq, though, they assigned the Palestine issue a relatively low priority. As men of the establishment they did not advocate violent actions or mass popular mobilizations. As incumbents, they endorsed quiet diplomatic measures. The best way to achieve Arab demands was to reach an accommodation with Britain. In contrast to Iraq, the palace politicians did not have to escalate rhetoric to match extremist opponents since they themselves were on the offensive against the Wafd.

Since attainment of Arab leadership was a vaguer, less passionate ambition in Cairo than in Baghdad, only marginal elements were willing to openly attack their own government on its Palestine policy. The Muslim Brotherhood's rise after 1945 changed this situation, but in the 1930s the focus on Anglo-Egypt bilateral relations and the Wafd-palace conflict made Palestine only one question among many. All these factors combined to produce a more moderate, if no less determined, Egyptian stand on that specific dispute.

The careers of three of the palace's chief strategists illustrate some of these points. Abd al-Rahman Azzam, whose fiery performance at the

1931 Jerusalem conference brought him much attention, was the most consistent Pan-Arab activist in Egypt. Born of a Libyan family in 1893, he had grown up in Egypt and had briefly studied medicine in England. Although frail, sallow, and diabetic, Azzam possessed a remarkable amount of energy.[34]

Azzam was an early Wafdist and friend of Zaghlul. He wrote for Pan-Arab publications, authored a book advocating Arab unity, and organized an abortive Islamic organization. Later, Azzam served in Parliament and, between 1936 and 1939, in the Egyptian diplomatic corps. While more of a political technician than a politician, he came to symbolize inter-Arab cooperation as the Arab League's first secretary-general. Emir Abdallah accused him of always working for Egypt's national interest rather than for the benefit of all Arabs. Certainly, his experiences deeply stamped him with a distinctively Egyptian point of view.[35]

Ali Mahir, ten years older than Azzam, was a lawyer, wealthy landowner, and a close adviser of the king. Although a founder of the Wafd, he soon became a conservative royalist. Between 1924 and 1935, Ali Mahir was several times elected to Parliament and served at various times as ministers of education, finance, and justice. He was prime minister and foreign minister in 1936 and again in 1939–40, until forced from office by British pressure over his pro-German sympathies. For this reason he became a hero in nationalist circles and briefly served as the first prime minister after the 1952 revolution.[36]

Muhammad Mahmud, born in 1878, was also a charter member of the Wafd. He later joined the Liberal Constitutionalists and briefly served as prime minister until pushed out by his old Wafd comrades. Mahmud again occupied that post from December 1937 to 1939, when he was replaced by Mahir. An accomplished speaker, Mahmud was considered ambitious even by his compatriots.[37]

All three of these men had been members of the Wafd but had broken from it, turning toward the palace as a route to power. All were advocates of an Arab orientation, though Mahmud and Mahir were far less loyal to this conception than were their Iraqi colleagues. Perhaps they overestimated the ease of finding a solution to the Palestine problem, certainly they did so in the 1939 negotiations. Most of their efforts went into combatting the Wafd and British at home. Support for the Palestine Arabs could be taken for granted, but what should be done on their behalf was not so easily resolved.

Students, journalists, and extremist political groups were those who most strongly accentuated the Palestine issue in Egypt. Gamal Abdul Nasser would later recall his participation in secondary school strikes on the anniversary of the Balfour Declaration. To this he attributed his "first elements of Arab consciousness," but he was far more concerned at the time about British power in Egypt and could not understand except on sentimental grounds his anger "for this land which I never saw." Many of the student activities were promoted by Syrian and Palestinian students who were transmitting Arabism to their counterparts.[38]

This also held true among the journalists. The two newspapers most supportive of the Palestine Arab cause, *Al-Ahram* and *Al-Muqattam*, were strongly influenced by Gabriel Takla and Faris Nimr respectively, both Syrian Catholic immigrants. Ironically, these two newspapers had been relatively lenient toward the Zionists in the 1920s, and perhaps for the same reason. Many Christian Arab intellectuals had sought an alternative to Pan-Islam in secular, Western-style nationalism. In the mid-1920s it was still possible to find some kinship between this movement and Zionism, which represented similar things to the Jews. With the consolidation of an Arab nationalism apart from religion—and in conflict with Zionism — any such mutual understanding was foreclosed. Arab Christians thus strongly supported the Arab cause in Palestine, though they always sought to cast the issue in secular terms. Christian journalists therefore insisted on calling Palestine Arabs "our Arab brothers" and "fellow nationalists," criticizing references to them as "our Muslim brothers."[39]

Some Egyptian groups and politicians became particularly identified with the Palestine issue. Foremost among them was Muhammad Ali Alluba, one of the Mufti's first foreign allies and an organizer of the 1931 Jerusalem conference. A founder of the Wafd, Alluba broke with Zaghlul in 1920. He joined the Liberal Constitutional party and broke with it in 1936. As Egyptian Bar Association president, he organized the anti-Zionist Cairo Parliamentary Congress in 1938. A political maverick, Alluba always remained an outsider. His fate contrasts sharply with those political figures who rode to power with a Pan-Arab ideology in the far more congenial atmosphere of Iraq.[40]

The two major Egyptian radical parties also made Palestine one of their key areas of activity. The fundamentalist Muslim Brotherhood, which had direct links to the Mufti, demonstrated, agitated, collected funds, and distributed pamphlets over Palestine beginning in 1936. Their greatest impact came after the postwar polarization of Egyptian politics. Before then, despite their heavy criticisms of Egyptian society, they were sometimes courted by the palace's top advisers as a possible counterforce to the Wafd.[41]

Another militant party, Young Egypt, began work on Palestine in

1938. As opposed to the Islamic orientation of the Brotherhood. Young Egypt leader Ahmad Husayn was a Fascist-style Egyptian nationalist who envisaged his country as the center of a great Middle East empire, a parallel to the Iraq-as-Prussia view so prevalent in Baghdad. Yet such ideas could muster nowhere near as much support in Egypt.

More representative of Egyptian thinking was its emphasis on pragmatic, Egypt-centered reasons for greater involvement in Palestine. These included the danger of Jewish industry stifling nascent Egyptian factories and "closing Eastern markets to us," the inspiration Zionism might offer European communities in Egypt seeking to maintain their privileges, and the political threat of European intervention in Palestine. Most telling was the fear of a powerful Zionist state of Egypt's eastern border, a sure security problem in the future.[42]

Young Egypt, like the Brotherhood, found friends in the king's camp, most notably Ali Mahir. When these two parties began to harass Egyptian Jews in the late 1930s, however, the government stood against them. They had little real effect on policy-making until the war crisis of 1947–48.[43]

In both Iraq and Egypt, the Palestine issue became entwined with domestic politics, but it did so in very different ways. For Egypt, Palestine was only one of a number of issues up to 1946 or 1947. Its importance, both directly and as part of the complex of Pan-Arab questions it represented, was far less than in Iraq or Transjordan. The Palestine issue in Egypt was not a point on which governments would rise or fall nor one on which heavy criticisms of incumbents could be based. There could be no doubt of Egyptian support for the Palestine Arabs but the level of support was lower than in Iraq, more concerned with a negotiated settlement with Britain (and later the United States) than for maximalist positions.

What was marginal in Egypt was central in Iraq. The level of violence and the use of the army in domestic political struggles made such options seem more acceptable means of settling foreign disputes. Moderate politicians were on the defensive, constantly being forced to prove their Arabism and challenged over their militancy. Since the concept of an Iraqi state had far less legitimacy than that of an Egyptian nation, Baghdad's political debates looked outward to a far greater extent than did Egypt's. Even in its central foreign policy dispute, Egyptians were mostly concerned with British powers and interference within their own country.

These are often fine distinctions, but they are all important in shaping those two countries' political cultures and histories. Part of the difference is one of timing. Iraq produced a large radical generation in the 1930s whose political fortunes were destroyed after their collaboration with the Axis. In Egypt, these forces, favoring a far different social and political order from that endorsed by the old-style politicians, survived the war and did not come to full blossom until the late 1940s. After the 1952 revolution, their aims were both fulfilled and tamed by the Nasser regime.

For both states 1936 marked a significant turning point. Sporadic intervention became continuous involvement. The Palestine Arab general strike and request for help to the Arab kings, followed by British acceptance of Arab state participation, made Palestine occupy for the first time the place it would ever after hold in Arab politics.

5
The General Strike and the British Invitation: 1936

*T*he April 1936 Palestine Arab general strike marked a turning point for Arab state intervention. Both the British, who had previously sought to avoid this, and the Palestine Arabs now strenuously sought the Arab kings' participation in finding some solution. In the long run, neither was satisfied. The British discovered themselves facing a more complex strategic position and a reinforced Arab opposition to their policies; Palestine Arab nationalists, who had once been annoyed by their neighbors negotiations with the Zionists, were later often disconcerted by direct Arab state talks with Britain.

Within Palestine itself, much had changed since initiation of the British mandate. Zionist objectives must have still seemed fantastic in the early and middle 1920s. Jewish settlements were few and far between, and the average Palestine Arab had little contact with them. The Arab population seemed to possess a secure majority. The prevailing social peace of the 1920s was closely related to the low rate of Jewish immigration, prompted by Palestine's early economic depression. Moreover, the British Churchill White Paper of 1921 and London's reactions to the 1929 riots seemed to promise future limitations.

The early 1930s brought major changes to this picture. Adolf Hitler's rise to power and increased discrimination against Jews in Eastern Europe made a sharp upward swing in the immigration figures. The founding and expansion of Jewish agricultural settlements and urban neighborhoods were quite noticeable, and commercial competition became a factor. Jewish land purchases and the Zionist policy of hiring only Jewish workers were also seen as threatening.

Psychological pressure was as important as material conflict. Nothing appeared likely to halt the gradually changing balance of power in the country. No perceptible progress toward Palestine's independence had been made. The hour of decision was arriving, Palestine Arab leaders believed. Only disaster could result from further passivity.

Growing great power tensions, the first signs of the coming world war, and the advancement of Arab nationalism elsewhere contributed to this atmosphere. British domination of the Mediterranean, the imperial lifeline's most important link, had been unchallenged since 1918. Italian dictator Benito Mussolini made no secret of his determination to change this. With a foothold in its Libyan colony and with more than half of its oil and some other strategic materials coming from the Middle East, Italy soon launched a challenge. The 1935 conquest of Ethiopia was a foot in the region's back door. Could Hitler's Germany be far behind?[1]

Such activism offered opportunities for Arab political leverage. Egyptian politicians like Mahmud, Mahmud Nuqrashi, and Azzam spoke openly of using these conflicts to pry concessions from the British. English diplomats and Foreign Office officials were quick to appreciate the importance of keeping the Arab world pacified, even at some cost to past assessments and commitments.[2]

The Arab states' continuing march toward complete independence gave them more ability and appetite to act abroad. At the same time, their progress could only add to the frustrations of Palestine Arabs, whose situation appeared increasingly anomalous. In April 1936, negotiations were concluding for the Anglo-Egypt treaty (signed August 21) and the Anglo-Iraq treaty (ratified June 30, 1936). Although later disavowed by French leaders, concurrent accords with Syria (signed September 9) and Lebanon (signed November 13) seemed to be bringing those mandates to an end. Only Palestine would be left behind, to stagnate or be wrested from Arab hands.

Direct contacts with these struggles could only add to the Palestine Arab determination to act. When Syrian nationalists called a general strike and massive demonstrations in February, solidarity meetings, fund-raising, and demonstrations were held in Palestine. Local political organizations and newspapers called on the Palestine Arabs to follow Syria's example.[3]

A similar appeal was issued by a visiting Iraqi parliamentary delegation in March. "Oh Arab brethren," said the group's leader Said Thabit in a speech to a Jaffa rally, "launch a Holy War and the Arab nation will stand behind you." A few days later he explained, "Don't expect us to send an expeditionary force. You have to begin and the remainder is upon us."[4]

Such statements coincided with the decision of the Husayni-led nationalist forces to begin a general strike aimed at ending Jewish immigration and attaining independence. The mobilization of Arab and Islamic opinion on behalf of these demands was expected to have as powerful an effect as the strike itself.[5] Palestine Arab leaders hoped a relatively brief protest showing their strength coupled with Arab state intervention would quickly bring British concessions.

Shortly after the strike's start, the Mufti convinced King Ibn Saud to carry this message to the British. Through his deputy foreign minister, Yusuf Yasin, himself born in Palestine, the Saudi king warned of the building pressure in the Arab world. Unless Palestine was soon solved there would be serious damage to Anglo-Saudi relations and danger for the security of British imperial trade and communications routes. In light of Italian advances, Yasin concluded, London should carefully mend fences with the Arabs.[6]

This early initiative revealed the Mufti's understanding that his own forces would not actually be able to defeat Britain's power without outside aid. He would, however, be able to demonstrate his movement's unity and broad support. By bringing in Ibn Saud and other Arab monarchs, the Husaynis could offset Abdallah's continuing call for a Palestine-Transjordan merger.

Between April and July 1936, the Palestine strike produced a strong echo in the nearby Arab countries and particularly in Iraq. There were special prayers for Arab victory in mosques, extensive press coverage, and petitions from the Young Men's Muslim Association and law students. Senator Naji al-Suwaydi led a parliamentary deputation to the British embassy, while schoolboys collected funds in the streets.[7] Prime Minister Yasin al-Hashimi and Foreign Minister Nuri al-Said warned, in terms similar to Ibn Saud's, of growing popular feeling over Palestine and of the danger to Anglo-Iraq relations unless action was taken to meet Arab demands.[8]

While visas were denied an Iraqi delegation to Palestine, a group of Palestine Arabs, including the Supreme Muslim Council's secretary, travelled to Baghdad to seek support. There they found firm allies, including the new Palestine Defense Committee led by Thabit, which collected relief money and tried to exact contributions from the Baghdad Jewish community. So violent was Thabit's propaganda—with accusations of British torture and "horrible human butchery" against Arabs— that the Iraqi government told him to moderate the language or face censorship. Reminiscent of the 1929 charges were the committee's claims that Jews were taking over Muslim holy sites.[9]

The restraint imposed by Nuri al-Said was due in part to his desire to personally mediate the Palestine dispute. Opposition politicians took up the slack, embarassing a government whose treaty with Britain was predicated on its ability to maintain order.

In Egypt, too, negotiations with Britain made the government momentarily circumspect. The Mufti had concentrated on winning sympathy from the Egyptian press and during the strike dispatched many letters to them, some with falsely inflammatory information. Stories of British brutality toward Arab women and children and about the desecration of mosques were widely distributed. In mid-May, emissaries were sent to Egypt to organize public opinion and to gain support from religious circles.[10]

By June, the Egyptian newspapers were confirming the statements of Saudi and Iraqi leaders: Palestine was being carefully watched in the Muslim world, and Britain should beware of raising Arab public opinion against herself. As in Iraq, British complaints about some of the wilder tales circulating brought some government action. Prime Minister Mustafa al-Nahhas called in the proprietors of *Al-Jihad, Kawkab al-Sharq,* and *Al-Balagh,* which had carried dispatches about atrocities and mutinies within the British army, and asked them to moderate their reporting.[11]

There were several short student strikes at Al-Azhar, the Islamic university, and at other schools, often led by Palestinian Arab students there. Fund-raising efforts, however, were not particularly successful, and Alluba's attempts to organize a delegation to Palestine was blocked by the British. Though Nahhas and Muhammad Mahmud contributed £50 to the Palestine aid effort, political, and public involvement fell somewhat short of Iraqi standards.[12]

Nahhas was by no means inactive but publicly laid more stress on his confidence in Britain and, like Nuri al-Said, his hopes for quiet diplomacy. In private, he pressed for British concessions. Only a miracle was preventing demonstrations in Egypt, he said, and lack of progress would push local opinion over the brink. Besides, Nahhas warned, if the British made martyrs of Palestine Arab leaders they would face an uprising in Palestine equivalent to Egypt's 1919 revolt over the exile of Wafd leaders. The problem should be settled peacefully.[13]

There was no question of the widespread support for the Palestine Arabs in Egypt, but there was an element of hesitation as well. To large elements in the liberal parties, ratification of the Anglo-Egypt treaty might be endangered. On the other end of the political spectrum, the conservative magazine *Rose al-Yusuf* labelled some of the leading Palestine agitators in Egypt "agents provocateurs" supported by the Italians. Overreaction, it argued, would only cause the shedding of more innocent blood and might irretrievably lose Palestine. While the Chamber of Deputies and Senate passed resolutions, both declarations were mild and vague, toned down from stronger originals.[14]

Indeed, both the Wafd party regime and the British had a common interest in keeping King Farouk out of the Arab monarchs' appeal which would end the strike in October. The British sought to keep the country containing the Suez Canal out of the contentious Palestine issue; the Wafd feared an increase in the king's prestige. Although Nahhas showed a greater interest in playing a mediating role after the Anglo-Egypt treaty was safely sealed, Cairo remained a secondary factor in the crisis.[15]

The same could be said of Syria and Lebanon, which were still under tight French control. There were public meetings in Damascus, though the National Bloc, the main Arab party, preferred printed protests over strikes. They feared, as did their incumbent compatriots in Iraq and Egypt, that too much unrest might damage pending treaty negotiations. There were a few small demonstrations, mostly by students, who tried to organize a boycott of Jewish shops. Merchants in both Lebanon and Syria were hurt by declining trade due to the general strike and sometimes, according to some sources, ignored the embargo by profitably selling food to Jewish customers in Palestine.[16]

Transjordan seemed least affected by the strike though all was not necessarily calm under the surface. On July 2, 200 tribal sheiks representing 100,000 Bedouins met. Some urged a march into Palestine and the launching of a holy war. "Freedom for Transjordan is useless without freedom for Palestine," one said. But as in 1929, Abdallah avoided an explosion, a particularly difficult task since many of his government officials were themselves Palestine Arabs. Later, in 1937 and 1938, Palestine Arab guerrilla groups would cross the Jordan River in an attempt to eliminate the emir and bring Transjordan into their revolt.[17]

Thus the Supreme Muslim Council's turn to Abdallah, after London ignored Ibn Saud's initiative, was a sign of their desperation. As usual, Abdallah followed a triple strategy. He told the Palestinian Arabs to send their own delegation to London and urged moderation. The disturbances should end so that a British royal commission might investigate the problem. England should accede to immediate Arab demands, he explained to the British resident in Amman, so that talks could begin on Palestine's future.[18]

This is what most interested him. By positioning himself between the Palestine Arabs and British, he could promote a Transjordan-Palestine merger as an equitable compromise. However, the emir was asking too much of London. Rather than suspend immigration, British authorities arrested several strike leaders. Strong measures, they believed, would command respect. The first round of discussions broke down.[19]

Meanwhile, Abdallah had not neglected the third factor in his plan by approving negotiations with a Jewish delegation. The Arab conferees, George Antonius and Musa al-Alami, were by no means Abdallah's agents, but their proposals were somewhat parallel to his line of thought. Antonius put forward a "Greater Syria" concept, which he had advocated for several years. An Arab state would extend "from the Taurus mountains to the Sinai Peninsula." Within it there would be plenty of room for the Jews.[20]

This came up against the same clash of interpretations which had plagued such "broader" solutions from the beginning. The Zionist representative Pinhas Rutenberg, managing director of the Palestine Electric Company, agreed that—as Weizmann had said—they "should aim not at a temporary accord with Arab leaders in Palestine but at a permanent settlement with the Arab world as a whole." He even agreed that Palestine and Transjordan should be considered a single unit and that the latter must be brought into any agreement. But he envisaged a separate and independent Jewish Palestine within this framework, precisely what the Arabs were seeking to avoid. The talks ended there; a similar initiative put forward by Nuri al-Said to Weizmann failed in the same way.[21]

The historian Michael Cohen has concluded these negotiations were "more the result of tactical approaches made under pressure than genuine efforts at compromise." Both sides were dealing with the immediate problem of ending the strike on the best possible terms for themselves. There is much truth in this, but as so often happens in the writing of Palestine's history, the inter-Arab dimension is neglected. Abdallah genuinely seemed to believe that developments were moving toward his favored program of Palestine-Transjordan unity. In addition, for him as for Nuri al-Said, these talks were useful ways to bypass the Mufti, who was already rejecting compromise suggestions, and to gain advantages for Transjordan or Iraq respectively. Finally, both men were genuinely interested in fostering regional stability and in preventing Anglo-Arab rifts.[22]

The British were equally interested in solving these problems, and though they did not accept the Mufti's terms as offered through the Arab rulers, the idea of using neighboring governments as conduits for negotiations seemed to have merit. On June 4, the British high commissioner in

Palestine proposed to Abdallah that he intervene. By early July, after Ibn Saud had reiterated his willingness to help restore peace, London added Saudi Arabia, Iraq, and Yemen to their list of mediators. Egypt was nominally left out because of King Farouk's youth and as a reserve in case the other four states failed, but the pending Anglo-Egypt treaty and the determination to avoid imperiling the Suez Canal also were considerations.[23]

Ibn Saud's effort failed. As the strike continued with solid Palestine Arab support, the Mufti was not yet ready to step down. The terms offered by him, with the support of Yemen and Iraq, were still too high for London: an end to Jewish immigration and the beginning of talks toward the establishment of a Palestine national government.

Next, it was once more Abdallah's turn. On July 26, he met with a Palestine Arab delegation in Amman. The strike had been a success, the emir said, but it caused hardships for the Arabs. If the violence now ended, a British royal commission could proceed and the Arabs would have a strong case. The Mufti made a counteroffer. Unilateral action would seem to be a surrender but if Abdallah would appeal for the strike's end, the Arab Higher Committee, the nationalist movement's directorate, would accept.

Nothing came immediately from this proposal, though it would shortly become the basis for a settlement. The British were too determined that concessions were possible only after peace was restored. They believed that a show of weakness would not lead to the moderation of Arab demands. On the other hand, expansion of the conflict must be avoided. Thus they hinted that if the strike ended, a partial amnesty and temporary suspension of Jewish immigration would be granted.[24]

Given these mutual peace feelers, the situation seemed auspicious for Nuri al-Said's August 17 offer of his services as mediator. Pledging to work "as an Arab and not as the Iraqi minister for foreign affairs," he promised rapid results. Yet this was a difficult if not impossible distinction for him to make. In his talks with Weizmann, for example, al-Said had suggested incorporating a Jewish national home into an Iraq-dominated Arab federation.

Palestine High Commissioner Arthur Wauchope was willing to let al-Said try, but Colonial Secretary W. Ormsby-Gore questioned how disinterested he would prove. Lacking an alternative, they compromised. Nuri might undertake talks to develop recommendations for the coming royal commission. Nuri's dislike for such a limited mandate and the leaking of the secret talks in the *Palestine Post* torpedoed this attempt.[25]

Thus, two rounds of initiatives by Arab leaders had failed to find some solution. The mutual distrust of Iraq, Saudi Arabia, and Transjordan had not helped matters, nor had British proposals. London now decided to crush the strike, announcing military reinforcements and martial law on September 7. While admitting the failure of Arab state intervention, the Foreign Office had kind words for all three Arab leaders.

Yet this strategem had shown a way out for all concerned. With the British refusal to back down, the approach of the profitable citrus season, and the gradual internal collapse of the months-long strike, as well as British military success against armed Arab bands, the Mufti and Arab Higher Committee looked for a quick settlement. Such a solution must leave unimpaired their unity and prestige. Hence, they returned to the idea of having the Arab kings issue a peace appeal.[26]

The way in which this proposal was actually handled held important repercussions for the future of Arab state involvement in Palestine. First, the Arab Higher Committee only wanted to request action from Ibn Saud, King Ghazi of Iraq, and the Imam of Yemen. Transjordan's exclusion was deliberate—the emir had his own designs on Palestine in conflict with the Husaynis. This conflict was amply demonstrated when Raghib al-Nashashibi, the Mufti's main internal rival, called for Abdallah's inclusion in the appeal.[27]

Second, the Foreign Office had also accepted the idea of Arab state intervention, even after the disorders ended, through diplomatic channels. The Zionists recognized the extent to which this shifted the balance of forces against them. "If the Arab kings had a right to intervene to stop the strike," said Professor Lewis Namier of the Jewish Agency in a meeting with Ormsby-Gore, "next time they could intervene to start one."

Third, by using the Arab states as an excuse for making concessions, the Palestine Arab leadership was able to maintain its image of unbending militancy. Hence, they did not absorb the lesson of political compromise to obtain an important objective, a strategy well understood by many of the politicians in neighboring countries. Over the next decade, the Mufti would over and over again adopt an abstentionist or maximalist stance when a softer line would have achieved far greater results. Moreover, his ability to exercise a veto on moral and ideological grounds over Arab state actions toward Palestine forced them to adopt his position even though his material forces were far smaller than theirs.

The Arab side could well argue their right to Palestine on ethical, historical, and political grounds. They could justify a refusal to dilute the principle of self-determination or the pace of independence. But the shortest distance between two points in a political conflict is not necessarily a straight line. The Zionist movement's history clearly illustrates the value of strategic flexibility and tactical virtuosity. Victory is the goal in political engagements, and freedom of maneuver is a necessary technique for success.

In the short run, however, the Arab kings' appeal worked smoothly. Saudi and Transjordanian representatives hammered out the exact wording in meetings with the Arab Higher Committee. These two countries along with Yemen and Iraq released the call on October 8 "To our sons the Arabs of Palestine." They should faithfully return to peace and quiet in order to avoid further bloodshed, "relying on the good will of our friend the British government and her declared intention to fulfill justice." The Arab states would oversee the process, continuing their efforts on the Palestine Arabs' behalf. Less loftily, Ibn Saud sent an accompanying note, pragmatically citing the heavy Arab losses suffered as a reason for changing tactics.[28]

Everyone understood the significance of the appeal and its acceptance by the Arab Higher Committee. The Peel Commission, which investigated the strike, called the Arab world's concern and involvement its "most striking and far-reaching" result. The Palestine newspaper *Al-Difah* applauded, "The Palestine Arabs are recognized as part of the Arab federation and therefore they are no longer alone."[29] So, at least for the moment, it seemed.

Others were not so pleased. Zionist leaders criticized this "dangerous precedent." The London *Times* approved the ingenious way in which the conflict had been resolved but argued the British government should not recognize "any right of formal intervention" by the Arab kingdoms in Palestine affairs, for this "would be an obvious breach of the terms of the Mandate."[30]

From Iraq came the strongest Arab reaction to the strike's end from both government and citizenry. Nuri al-Said had been actively involved in the earlier negotiations, but his diplomatic efforts had fallen far short compared to Abdallah or Ibn Saud. Indeed, he had so misrepresented Arab and Jewish positions in talks with the Foreign Office that one pro-Arab Englishman accused him of sabotaging a settlement.[31]

Thus his attempts to claim credit for the king's appeal in press interviews angered Ibn Saud. The Saudi king, after all, had received plenty of proof that he was the Mufti's favored mediator. Now, he complained, London was paying more attention to al-Said than it was to Ibn Saud. Despite surface appearances, British diplomats were equally annoyed with al-Said's attempts to interject Iraq between Britain and the Palestine Arabs.[32]

As the strike ended, al-Said quickly suggested establishment of an Iraq bureau in Jerusalem to coordinate Arab demands on Palestine, to be directed by him and two close political allies, Jaafar al-Askari and Rustum Haydar. High Commissioner Wauchope refused but set another precedent by allowing al-Said to testify before the Peel Commission. The Iraqi proposal was not entirely repugnant to Wauchope since at that very moment he was supporting creation of an "Arab Agency" to parallel the Jewish Agency in Palestine. Just as the Zionist movement representing Jews from other countries possessed official standing under the mandate, he believed, the scales might be balanced by participation of Arabs from other countries. This might allow Britain to by-pass the Mufti and find more flexible negotiating partners. London disagreed.[33]

Nuri al-Said also hoped to bypass the Mufti—by establishing his own direct contacts with the Zionists. His direct talks with Herbert Samuel and Shertok, however, did no better than those of Abdallah, deadlocking over Arab demands for limiting immigration. Since al-Said seemed genuinely confident of a pro-Arab report from the Peel Commission he was not overeager to reach a settlement with them.

Nor was such an eventuality likely given Iraq's political atmosphere. The Mufti was popular and had his own links with opposition elements. Even Prime Minister Yasin al-Hashimi contributed to the armed volunteers organized to infiltrate Palestine, supplying government arms and autos. Thabit and the Palestine Defense Committee assembled a unit of 100 Iraqis and 100 Syrians. At the last minute, al-Hashimi had second thoughts and moved to stop them from crossing the border.[34]

In Baghdad, violence began against both Jews and British installations. Zionist organizers in Iraq had been harassed as early as 1935. Emissaries had been deported, Jewish and Palestine newspapers had been banned, and Jewish civil servants had been dismissed. (In Egypt, by way of contrast, the Zionist movement operated with relative freedom into 1948.) Now a half-dozen murders of Jews in October 1936 alone illustrated the tension. Though not all were directly traceable to politics —one Muslim killed a Jewish competitor who outbid him on a government contract—anxious Jews requested and received police protection. Police plainclothes observers attended Thabit's Palestine rallies as his campaign took on an increasingly inflammatory and anti-Semitic tone.[35]

Jewish concern over the strained situation was exemplified by the

Baghdad chief rabbi's public denial of any connection with Zionism. When a small meeting was held by Jews in the city's Exchange Square to complain of discrimination, a Muslim slapped the speaker and Muslim-Jewish street fights broke out.

Thabit's rallies were more successful. "The enthusiastic audience had its racial feelings gratified," and five thousand Palestine pounds were raised, reported *Al-Liwa* after one August meeting. Political poems were read, and an Egyptian troupe put on a play. In September, a Palestine Arab leader from Tulkarm travelled to Baghdad to participate in "Palestine day" activities. Jaafar al-Askari, the minister of defense, called on soldiers to contribute to the Palestine Relief Fund.[36]

Religious institutions were also important. Many special sermons were delivered in mosques and a *fetwa* (decree) from a leading Iraqi religious scholar ordered Muslims to protest "the Zionization of Palestine." The Mufti himself sought petitions from senior officials and Muslim judges in Iraq and Egypt demanding the British end Jewish immigration or face the "revenge of God Almighty."[37]

Yet all this was only a part of the Iraqi political scene in the autumn of 1936. The regime of al-Hashimi and al-Said was falling out with the king and was rumored to be aspiring to dictatorship. At a speech inaugurating new government offices, al-Hashimi expressed the wish that he live another ten years to devote himself to Iraq's welfare. Hikmat Sulayman, his archrival even then planning a coup, remarked that the prime minister's motto was not "Vive le Roi!" but "Vive le moi!" Six weeks later, moving from witticism to armed criticism, Sulayman rode to power on the crest of a military coup.[38]

The cooperation of four Arab monarchs graphically illustrated the potency of united Arab action. Politically active Arabs greeted it as a model of interstate coordination. The success of the kings' appeal made a particularly strong impression in Egypt, which was still skeptical over the value of Pan-Arabism. Would victory really come so easily? Only if the Arab governments maintained their own stability and their united front with the Palestine Arabs could progress continue.[39]

Challenges quickly emerged on both of these fronts. The breaking of ranks by the Arab Higher Committee seemed simply resolved but warned of problems to come. The kings' appeal, by providing a graceful excuse to end the strike, blinded the Mufti to his own weakness. The Palestinians would boycott the British investigating commission, he declared. This did not help the Arab states convince London of his reasonable state of mind, at a time they were trying to arrange an amnesty for strike leaders. Saudi Arabia, Iraq, and Transjordan forced the Arab Higher Committee to abandon this abstentionism.[40] This did not reconcile the Mufti to Abdallah, whose Nashashibi allies had been the first to denounce the boycott.[41]

The coup in Iraq was a far more serious shock for the Arab world. Not only was it the first military takeover in one of the new states, it was also the first real crack in the legitimacy of the post-1918 political systems. Lack of militancy over Palestine was one of several issues employed against the Yasin al-Hashimi/Nuri al-Said regime. Even the fact that the government had concurred with ending the strike—though at the Mufti's request—was used against them. Thus this upheaval marks a significant escalation of Palestine's use in Iraqi domestic politics.

Yet the coup had little to do with either Pan-Arabism or Palestine. Army officers led by Bakr Sidqi, civilian politicians led by Hikmat Sulayman, and reform-minded intellectuals in the Ahali party led by Kamil al-Chadirchi among others, had come together in a strange coalition. Sidqi, a Kurd and a colonel in the Ottoman army during World War I, only joined Iraq's army in 1921. Sulayman, too, had limited Arab nationalist credentials. As a member of the Young Turks party, the Committee for Union and Progress, and as director of education in Baghdad for the Ottoman regime, he had fought against the Hashemite Arab revolt. A long visit to Turkey in 1935 led Sulayman to praise the Attaturk regime when Arab-Turkish relations were at a low point. Even the Ahali group had clashed with the Arab nationalists because of its domestic and leftist orientations.[42]

All these handicaps made it imperative for the new government to stress its Arabism over the Palestine question. Moreover, many of the middle-level army officers who assured the coup's success were strong Arab nationalists, concerned about Palestine's salvation and convinced of Iraq's destiny to unite the Arab world. Thus while the Palestine Arabs initially reacted to the coup with concern about the new regime's future policy, Sulayman, Bakr, and other Iraqi leaders were soon making speech after speech pledging a firm stand for Palestine.[43]

Taking up Nuri al-Said's earlier call for official Iraqi mediation in Palestine—a view Ibn Saud continued to reject—the new regime also spoke of adding both Palestine and Transjordan to their state. Even this, and their intensified efforts over Palestine, did not save them from attack by the Pan-Arabs in the Muthanna Club and the Palestine Defense Committee. Sulayman was forced to make even more lavish promises to them, abandoning the socioeconomic program of his Ahali allies. Even the coup's exiled opponents—Rashid Ali al-Gailani, Nuri al-Said, and Yasin al-Hashimi—tried to play on this theme to arouse Arab governments and the foreign Arab press against the "anti-national" regime in Baghdad. All sides were stoking fires which eventually would consume them.[44]

Predictably, Britain refused to accept Iraq as intermediary between London and the Palestine Arabs. Egyptian Prime Minister Nahhas' similar offer was also rejected.[45] No Arab leader or individual country had succeeded in gaining a special status in Palestine, but by the end of 1936 the Arab states had collectively won the right to participate in the negotiating process.

The 1936 general strike demonstrated the Palestine Arab national movement's coming of age. Its organizational structure was sufficient for a protracted struggle; its popular appeal was capable of mass mobilization. Yet the strike's end, in which that leadership abrogated its own responsibility onto the backs of neighboring Arab governments, gave rise to a mistaken evaluation on the rewards of tactical inflexibility. Furthermore, while advancing the Palestine Arabs political cause the strike did not advance their material position. The British were not afraid to make a show of strength while the Jewish economy within Palestine, thrown on its own resources, was actually strengthened.

In this sense, the importation of outside Arab influence was the most significant effect of the strike. Truly, the upheaval brought the Palestine problem as such onto the international political agenda. No longer could day-to-day administration continue, passively leaving a settlement to some distant future. The search for solutions to the Palestine problem began in the aftermath of those events, and it has scarcely ever halted since then. Yet at this very dawn the whole issue was tightly locked into much broader questions of relations between Britain and the Arab states, between the Arab states and the Palestine Arabs, and among the Arab states themselves.

Two particular dialectics were set up in this process, ripening in the events of 1936. First, if the Arab states were to be involved in Palestine, the Palestine issue was to intervene in Arab state politics. Arab governments could pressure the Palestine Arab leadership, take sides in its factional disputes, and presume to pass judgment on the country's fate. Iraq or Egypt could propose themselves to the British as mediators, while Transjordan might campaign over the Mufti's head for possession of Palestine. The Arab regimes, seeking a settlement in Arab interests, would see fit to pressure both the British and the Arab Higher Committee. Eventually they would move toward completely supplanting any indigenous leadership.

This was no mere one-way relationship. Palestine might also be an apple of discord among and within the Arab states. While superficially promoting unity, as in the case of the Arab monarchs' appeal, Palestine also nurtured jealousies. In 1936 the mistrust between Saudi Arabia and Iraq, Saudi Arabia and Transjordan, and Iraq and Transjordan were already becoming visible.

The upheaval in Iraq showed this as a double-edged scimitar. If Arab regimes would pledge their reputations on saving Palestine, they would be taken at their word. If they promised victory, no less than victory must be delivered. Hikmat Sulayman could ridicule Yasin al-Hashimi for his weakness and the latter might become an accuser in his own right. Greater activism only raised demands for still more action. Faster and faster the wheel might turn with the speed of many revolutions.

And if Amin al-Husayni had his weaknesses in the face of the full-blown states, he also had his own moral — and hence material — leverage. As the symbol of the Palestine Arab nationalist movement, his regiments could be counted in Arab public opinion. He could stand unbending, invoking sacred principle; it was for the Arab states—as with the monarchs' appeal—to counsel compromise. For them, perhaps, such advice might be the essence of political realism, but this could have the public appearance of cowardice. Incumbents might tremble or fall on such distinctions.

Second was the dialectic between Britain and the Arab states. In the short run, London had approved Arab state intervention as a way of moderating the Arab Higher Committee's demands. By the autumn of 1936 this seemed to work. Nonetheless, an alternate possibility was still to come: The Arab Higher Committee and the Palestine question might reverse the process by radicalizing the Arab states. Such a development was by no means entirely in Britain's hands. With or without London's permission, Palestine would be a very important factor affecting regional politics.

Underneath this lay the strategic situation's evolution. Italy's Mediterranean build-up and Hitler's growing challenge in Europe were starting an overture for British appeasement and an atonement in world war. In light of such problems, London must avoid alienating the Arab states. A Palestine solution satisfactory to them seemed indispensible. Sanctioning their involvement in the diplomacy of Palestine was a calculated risk. Either they would help weave a solution or they might be dragged into direct collision with Britain. Once begun, such involvement could be neither calibrated nor regulated. Each step of the way Arab governments would have to take a position on the British proposals put forward.

In 1936 every Arab regime confidently accepted this test. The following year the trial began in earnest. Britain's partition proposal would be met by a full-scale Arab revolt in Palestine. It was soon apparent that there would be no easy answers.

6
Opposition to Partition, Support for Revolt: 1937–38

*P*alestine's demographic changes in the years up to 1936 had been truly dramatic. In the brief period since Adolf Hitler took power in Germany, the Jewish community in Palestine grew by 83 percent, to total 400,000. Jewish Tel Aviv became the largest city in the country, and new Jewish settlements sprang up with astonishing speed. Though Jews still owned a relatively small proportion of the land, their purchases and reclamation projects steadily added to this amount.

The Palestine Arab population also expanded at a remarkable though slower rate. From the end of World War I to the end of 1936, it grew by 67 percent, to a total of nearly a million people. During the same time span, however, the Arab proportion of the population fell from 90 percent to 70 percent. Although many peasants had migrated into the developing cities, some two-thirds of the Palestinian Arabs still lived in villages concentrated in the hill districts of central and northern Palestine.

Jewish immigration was regulated by the British in accord with their estimates of the land's "absorptive capacity." These are now known to have been underestimates, but at the time many Arabs and British experts feared Palestine would soon be filled up. Even worse from the Arab viewpoint was the political implication of the changing balance of population wrought by immigration. The day was in sight when Arabs would become the minority in what had been their own country. For them, such an eventuality was too horrible to contemplate.

So the 1936 strike was launched to cope with the essential factors behind this fatal trend. The Arab Higher Committee demanded an end to

Jewish immigration, a ban on land sales from Arabs to Jews, and establishment of a national government leading to an independent Arab Palestine. Until then, Arabs would neither buy from nor sell to Jews. The country would be economically paralyzed.

These activities were supplemented by sporadic acts of violence and sabotage. Arab guerrillas, particularly active in the hill regions, barricaded and mined roads, derailed trains, attacked Jewish villages, and burned crops and forests. The British responded to this repertoire of protest with curfews, searches, and arrests.

The Arab governments successfully served as intermediaries between the British and the Palestinian Arabs. London hinted at future concessions in exchange for restoration of peace. Only after order was established would a royal commission be appointed to look into Arab (and Jewish) grievances. Policy changes could only be considered after the commission presented its report. Given the strike's failure to force immediate change and the difficulties in keeping it going, the Arab Higher Committee elected to request the Arab monarchs' appeal. London duly appointed the Peel Commission to find some solution.

If the Arab governments took their first step toward extended involvement in Palestine through the negotiations over the strike, the Peel Commission report forced a decisive second step. While the nature of the commission's recommendations created a rift between Transjordan and the other Arab states, its rejection by them led to a wave of violence in Palestine far greater than that seen in 1936. Support of this revolt by groups or even governments in the neighboring Arab states opened the Anglo-Arab conflict to a dangerous extent. Debates within the Arab states over how much effort to devote to Palestine and over how to settle the problem increasingly thrust the issue into the realm of domestic politics. The temptation offered by Germany and Italy as alternative allies to Britain also helped to deepen and define the split in the Arab world.

The Arab Higher Committee, controlled by the Mufti's supporters, had already shown its adeptness during the strike at taking a militant public posture while forcing the Arab governments to accept the onus of urging restraint. British fear of an Arab-Axis alliance provided the Arabs an opportunity to secure an advantageous settlement. The Arab regimes, however, were unable to convince the Husayni leadership to accept a process through which Arab demands might be won. The Mufti's all-or-nothing attitude took him into a disastrous adhesion to the German camp.

Politicians of the older generation, including those in and out of power in Egypt and a more limited circle in Iraq, were concerned over maintaining good relations with Britain. Many of them had seen first-hand the dangers of direct confrontation with a major European power in their post-1918 defeat by France. Their experience also told them that the best way to gain concessions from Britain was through a step by step series of diplomatic advances. Analyzing the international balance of forces and London's need for their cooperation, they concluded that the same techniques might work in Palestine. Strikes, violence, and guerrilla activities would provide valuable added pressure but could not substitute for state-to-state dealings. Britain need only open the door to Arab power in Palestine; the Arabs could use this opportunity to build a governing apparatus, even if it took five or ten years.

The new wave—one is tempted to say the new political generation— approached these matters from a different perspective. The British could not be trusted. Only direct action leading to immediate results would be satisfactory. Both London and the establishment politicians were the enemy, and flexibility would be equated with treason. The Husayni leadership of the Palestine Arabs would play a leading role in promoting these theses in the Arab world, but the Muslim Brotherhood in Egypt and the radical Pan-Arab forces in Iraq (which absorbed many establishment politicians) also accepted them.

This conflict, which would become entangled in the clash of national interests among the Arab states, was not yet visible in early 1937. Yet the maneuvers which preceded the Peel Commission's report gave some clues of the events to come.

Neither the Mufti nor Abdallah had any intention of leaving things to chance. From March 1937 on, Amin al-Husayni led delegations to Saudi Arabia and other Arab countries, deliberately avoiding any contact with Transjordan. Arab border and customs patrols looked the other way in Syria and Transjordan as arms were smuggled into Palestine for any future showdown. Guerrilla forces which had retreated into Iraq and Syria after the strike's end stayed in readiness.[1]

For his part, Transjordan's emir tried to block shipment of weapons across his territory and his subjects' participation in support activities for the Mufti's forces. Travelling to London in April for King George's coronation, he attempted to convince the British to give him all or part of Palestine. There were already rumors that the Peel Commission would recommend partition and that Abdallah and the Nashashibis favored this solution.[2]

The rumors daily grew in intensity. Jewish leaders were not enthusiastic about Abdallah but commented that they could work with him. When the emir returned from Britain on June 13, he met a spirited welcome from Palestine Arabs and Transjordan officials. His party proceeded by special train to Jerusalem where they spent the night as the high commissioner's guests. The next day Abdallah spoke of his highly satisfactory London trip. Denying any knowledge of a partition plan, he claimed to have laid the foundations for future cooperation with the British government.[3]

Since Abdallah was acting like the victor, local Arabs concluded that he was about to be proclaimed king of Palestine as well as of Transjordan. In explaining British strategy to an American counterpart, one British officer explained the ideal scenario. Abdallah would be king and Raghib al-Nashashibi would be his prime minister. The Mufti, still president of the Supreme Muslim Council, would be reduced to an exclusively religious position.[4]

Nazi Germany, beginning to explore its possible intervention into the Middle East, drew similar conclusions over British intentions. Obviously, Berlin's Foreign Ministry noted, German interests were opposed to any Jewish political structure in Palestine. Germany should clearly express understanding for Arab national aspirations, "but without making any definite promises." When the Mufti and Iraqi representatives visited German diplomats to seek advice and support against partition, they received a warm welcome but little concrete assistance. The Nazis did not seek a clash with Britain in the region and were still skeptical about Arab strength and determination.[5]

Just before the commission's report was released, veteran Zionist leader Chaim Weizmann was in Paris meeting with Lebanese Christian nationalists. Maronite Patriarch Antoine Arida expressed support for a Jewish state, which he hoped would have a common border with Lebanon. Emile Eddé, one of the most influential Lebanese Christian politicians, held a similar view. He and Weizmann had a long and rambling conversation on the day the commision's report was to be officially signed. After a half hour, Eddé glanced at his watch, stood up, and declared, "Now that the Peel Commission's report is an official document, it is my privilege to salute the first president of the coming Jewish state." One of Weizmann's first acts, Eddé suggested, should be to sign a friendship treaty with Lebanon.[6]

This would be about the last kind word for the Peel report heard from any Arab leader. The commission, whose conclusions were released July 7, concluded that previous British policies and attempts at conciliation had failed. The promises to the Jews embodied in the Balfour Declaration could only be fulfilled through repression against an unwilling Arab population. Already, Britain had been unable to maintain public security and conflict would only increase in the future.

The report did call for limitations on immigration and land sales but, most importantly, this was in the framework of a partitioned Palestine. A small Jewish state, taking about 20 percent of the land, would be established in the Galilee, Jezreel Valley, and the coastal plain. The rest, including Jaffa, would be tied to Transjordan, except for a small enclave around Jerusalem which remained under British control. The Jewish state would pay an annual subsidy to its Arab neighbor.

While the report provoked heated debates among the Zionists, partition was accepted as the basis for further negotiations. Weizmann and David Ben-Gurion argued that increasing persecution in Germany made it essential to obtain some territory where refugees could find asylum.

Weizmann worried, however, about British willingness to implement the plan. Even before the report's release he had written Ormsby-Gore of the "very grave dangers" involved in Arab state intervention. The British government was too impressed by the "bogey" of Pan-Islam and Arab nationalism, he argued.[7]

The views of the German Foreign Office and U. S. State Department did not entirely agree with Weizmann, but they were little kinder to British policy. The report, said the American analysis, sought "permanent appeasement" of the Arabs to protect Britain's strategic position in the eastern Mediterranean and the Red Sea. Once the bulk of Palestine was freed from the mandate, London could organize an Arab entente, bound by treaties of mutual assistance against Italian encroachments. This approach was all very well, but it was based on the questionable assumptions that the Arabs would accept partition and that Britain would implement it. Washington doubted both ideas.[8]

At the same moment, Otto von Hentig, head of the Middle East division of the German Foreign Ministry, urged caution in estimating the Arab reaction. Doubtless they were opposed to a Jewish state, but would they quarrel with England over it? Only Iraq and the Mufti, he continued, would really commit themselves against partition. Ibn Saud and Egypt would be lukewarm, while Transjordan might follow the British lead. Given this, it was "out of the question" to support the Arabs with arms or money over Palestine.[9]

Both of these perspectives had something to recommend them, but the American one was more accurate. Since the British had sought a solution which would patch up their strategic relations with the Arabs they were hardly likely to enforce a settlement against the wishes of the

Arab states. While von Hentig was right in making distinctions between the intensity of the Arab states' response, he misunderstood that they would oppose it strongly enough to block partition. His idea that "England considers the question important enough to impose her point of view by force of arms, without restrictions," was quite wrong.

The concept of partition itself might easily have been enough to guarantee Arab opposition. The Palestine Arabs opposed the surrender of a rich portion of the country even as the price for saving the rest. Most Arab politicians feared a Jewish state as such, regardless of size. What made matters worse was the nature of the suggested partition. If Arab Palestine was subsumed by Transjordan the Mufti and his supporters would be completely shut out of power. Thus the Husayni-controlled Arab Higher Committee had every incentive to oppose the Peel Commission report. By giving the prize to Abdallah, the plan also made inevitable strong opposition from Iraq and Saudi Arabia.

Abdallah and the Nashashibis were predictably pleased by a plan which would give them most of Palestine, a $10 million grant from Britain, and a subsidy from the Jewish state. In Transjordan itself, the people were at first delighted, convinced that the Palestine problem was solved. The British flag was hauled down in Nablus, a Nashashibi stronghold, and replaced by Transjordan's flag.[10]

Some British leaders were also enthusiastic. Ormsby-Gore told the League of Nations that the Transjordan Arabs were positive about the plan. Their emir contacted the Jewish Agency, promising autonomy for any Jews living in his new state. Newspapers in Syria under his influence also reacted favorably. Abdallah told *Filastin* that the report should be accepted.[11]

He was more careful in replying to an Arab Higher Committee inquiry, but added that "there is a lesson for men who want to learn" in the Arabs' 1936 confrontation with Britain. Within Palestine, the Nashashibis were more outspoken, walking out of an Arab Higher Committee meeting which opposed the report. Under pressure, to Abdallah's disgust, they would soon recant.[12]

Transjordan's triumph was short lived. After the majority of the Arab Higher Committee declared complete opposition to the Peel proposals, a tidal wave of hostility engulfed Abdallah. Five days before the report was issued, Ormsby-Gore had warned against Abdallah counting his chickens before they hatched. Yet London had done little to incubate its own plan. The commission's suggestions had undoubtedly seemed a reasonable compromise to its members. The promise to the Jews would be kept by providing them a national home, but the Arabs would receive the bulk of Palestine. Despite its even-handed intentions, British policy seriously misestimated Arab politics.[13]

One by one each Arab state declared opposition. In Syria, still under the French mandate's heavy hand, Prime Minister Jamil Mardam protested to the French high commissioner and the League of Nations. His National Bloc organized strikes and marches.[14]

Egypt's Wafd regime was cautious in public and politely negative in private. Prime Minister Nahhas told British High Commissioner Miles Lampson at a July 24 dinner that he was sure the Arabs would never accept the proposal. He could not allow a Jewish state on Egypt's borders — it might even one day claim Sinai. Why, he asked, didn't Britain establish an allied Arab state? This ran counter to the mandate, Lampson replied. Then, Nahhas countered, the mandate should be scrapped. Still, the prime minister did not reject Lampson's request to wait while the British government and Parliament considered the report. Saudi Arabia had already asked him to join a united front of Arab rulers, excluding Transjordan, explained Nahhas, but he would stand aloof to keep open his options.[15]

While *Al-Misri,* a Wafd newspaper close to the government, published a long editorial finding some positive aspects to the proposals, the palace opposition strongly attacked them. Mahmud called on Egypt to exert fullest efforts against this "sacrifice of fellow Muslims in Palestine." Against such embarrassing criticisms, Nahhas maintained silence for several weeks. The prime minister staved off calls for parliamentary debates by invoking Egypt's national interest in avoiding a public commitment. He assured the senate of his efforts to safeguard Arab rights and interests, working through discussions with the friendly British government. The request for open debate was withdrawn.[16]

Nahhas held off attacking the commission's report as long as possible and when necessary moved to mild opposition. Such moderation reflected his own views: Palestine was only one of many issues, he said, and it was necessary to "keep a sense of proportion." He condemned the "irresponsibility" of Iraq in taking an extreme rejectionist stance.[17]

Ibn Saud also valued highly his British connection, but the strengthening of Transjordan and establishment of a Jewish state were anathema to him. Saudi Foreign Minister Hafiz Wahbah told the Foreign Office that his king regarded Abdallah as untrustworthy and unfriendly. If London turned most of Palestine over to Transjordan, the Saudis would retaliate by demanding large parts of Abdallah's kingdom—including the strategic towns of Aqaba and Maan — and a common border with Syria.

The Saudis were sorry, Wahbah added, such a comprehensive plan had been presented. The investigation might have better been limited to ways of stopping Jewish immigration. Could the report be changed to make it acceptable to the Arabs? Perhaps, Wahbah hinted, but he seemed terrified of becoming identified with even a modified Peel plan.[18]

After all, Wahbah and Nahhas were criticizing Iraq's hardline because they knew their countries would be pressured into matching its rhetorical militancy. As long as London did not strike against Sulayman, Wahbah complained, Britain could hardly expect restraint from other Arabs. When pro-British Iraqi politicians were deposed, murdered, or exiled, England had done nothing to interfere. This implied that England would neither reward its friends nor punish its enemies, the Saudi diplomat heatedly concluded.[19]

No Arab leader could afford to appear less nationalistic than his counterparts at home or abroad. If Iraq could attack the Peel report and British policy yet remain unscathed, Egypt and Saudi Arabia must follow suit. Both resented Baghdad for dragging them into such a dangerous escalation.

They never doubted that failing to fall into line would pose the most dire risks. By late July 1936, Saudi officials were suggesting that the king's position at home would be severely shaken if he accepted the Peel proposals. This might be dismissed as a mere pretext to side-step British urgings, but there are reasons to accept it as sincere. The kingdom was facing severe financial difficulties which were causing some discontent. Religious figures in the puritanical Wahhabi sect, on which Ibn Saud's legitimacy largely rested, raised strong religious objections to the creation of any Jewish state.

Muslims outside Saudi Arabia, among whom Ibn Saud retained some special status, sent a stream of telegrams begging him to reject the plan. So great was the pressure, the king told Wahbah, that he had not slept properly for five nights. "Every Muslim and every Arab," wrote Wahbah to the Foreign Office, "looks on the establishment of this new Jewish state as the first step in a policy which aims at the destruction of Islam and the Arabs."[20]

Despite all this, the Saudis managed to maintain a low profile throughout the summer of 1937, making occasional protests and a first attempt to reach the American government through the California-Arabian Oil Company. Yet beneath the surface important doubts had been raised in Ibn Saud's mind. On one hand, British weakness toward Iraq made him wonder if he need seek other protectors or even switch sides entirely. On the other, he perceived the voice of Arab public opinion calling for a break with the English. Still, he saw Italy, Germany, and even Turkey as wolves which would devour a Saudi Arabia deprived of British protection. These contradictory forces would cause him to seek German aid and arms at the end of 1937 while hesitating to throw in his lot with the Axis. In the end, he correctly judged Britain's superior strength.[21]

Psychologically and religiously, Palestine posed special difficulties for Ibn Saud. The traditional tenets of Islam were for him what Pan-Syrianism was for the Syrians, what Pan-Arabism was for the Iraqis, what territorial expansion was to Abdallah, and what the desire to secure their borders was for the Egyptians. His anti-Semitic views were not in outright conflict with Islamic ideology, but they stretched it to an extreme. "Praise be to God," he later said, "for 1400 years there had been no Jews in my territory."

His feelings on this score went so far as to warrant a misrepresentation of the Koran. While Christians were "People of the Book," fellow monotheists who should be protected by Muslims, he told a visiting American delegation, Jews "have no right to that consideration." If any Jew ever entered Saudi Arabia, he swore, the man would be murdered on the spot. To him, Jews, like a misanthropic snake, were greedy, perfidious, and false. A Jewish state, even a small one, might be a foothold from which might spread "the disease of Judaism."[22]

As politically potent as his sentiments were, they remained a personal idiosyncrasy nevertheless, which might be reined in to preserve his British alliance. Iraq's far more active position over Peel sprang from more orthodox political motives on the part of men who flourished at home in direct proportion to the intensity of their attacks on British policy.

Within days of the Peel report's release, Iraqi public opinion was already enflamed. Sulayman was genuinely horrified by the proposals and would hear no argument in their favor. He was aware that he was generally, and not unfairly, thought to be relatively indifferent to Palestine. Motivated by his desire to hold onto power, as well as by his hatred for Abdallah and fear of internal chaos sparked by anti-Jewish pogroms, he had to place himself at the head of the opposition to the Peel plan.[23]

While Egypt and Saudi Arabia hesitated and Transjordan barely suppressed its glee over the report, Iraq was urging the Arab Higher Committee to reject the commission's conclusions. Prime Minister Sulayman even directly threatened Abdallah. Any person venturing to act as head of a partitioned state, he warned, "would be regarded as an outcast throughout the Arab world, and would incur the wrath of

Muslims all over the East.'' Such an act would "stab the Arab race to the heart" for the sake of personal ambition. The newspaper of the pro-Iraq Istiqlal party in Palestine proclaimed, "Should the British find some creature willing to stoop so low he would have a serious account to settle with the Arabs."[24]

Sulayman went so far as to turn toward Nazi Germany for aid in a July 15 meeting with Fritz Grobba, Berlin's Baghdad representative. If Iraq could obtain a German loan and thus escape British financial pressure, Sulayman said, a successful struggle could be waged against creation of a Jewish state. Although the Germans were noncommittal, from that time on Iraq-German ties tightened. Berlin offered long-term commercial credits, sent more agents into the country, and stepped up radio coverage of Palestine.[25]

Iraq's press was packed with Palestine news and with reports of the hundreds of telegrams protesting the commission's report sent to the king and prime minister. Army Chief of Staff General Bakr Sidqi, the regime's strongman, pledged the military's willingness to fight in Palestine. Fawzi al-Qawukji, an honored exile in Iraq and a guerrilla leader in the 1936 fighting, expressed readiness to renew the struggle. Religious notables discussed a possible decree forbidding any Muslim from accepting the throne of a partitioned Palestine.[26]

On July 16, thousands marched under Istiqlal party leadership to oppose the Peel plan. Their placards attacked these proposals and the Jews but carefully refrained from any direct criticism of Great Britain. Demonstrators beat up thirty Jews and pillaged a number of shops. Nor was Abdallah forgotten. Newspapers received government permission to take the offensive against him.[27]

Iraq countered the partition idea with a call for an independent Arab state in Palestine, with a constitution like Iraq's and a treaty alliance with London. Jewish population would be limited at 30 percent, though this was negotiable. Both Sulayman and his exiled opponent al-Said put forward separate feelers along these lines.[28]

Ironically, violence came first to Iraq. Bakr Sidqi's assassination by a soldier removed the military underpinning for the government. Although Sulayman's stand on Palestine had strengthened his regime, he could hardly continue without Sidqi. On August 17, he resigned to be succeeded by Jamil al-Midfai, who immediately recalled Nuri al-Said as Iraq's chief negotiator over Palestine. While anti-Transjordan articles in the press and protests continued, the upcoming League of Nations session and the inter-Arab conference planned for Syria seemed to offer opportunities for more positive action.[29]

Since joining the league, Iraq had often used it as a forum for debates on Palestine. The very first speech ever made by an Iraqi delegate called for Palestine's independence; such appeals were often repeated. In a September 1937 session, Iraqi Foreign Minister Tawfiq al-Suwaydi again challenged the legitimacy of the mandate and the Balfour Declaration. Taking a different tack, he argued that the declaration had already been fulfilled. The Jews could now enjoy its fruits in an undivided, independent Palestine that would "take its place among the other Arab nations." Otherwise, there would be disorders in Palestine which would have repercussions in Iraq.[30]

Nonetheless, al-Said and al-Suwaydi were relatively conciliatory toward London's position. Speaking confientially, al-Suwaydi said he would be prepared to cooperate with some kind of partition plan if all other solutions proved impossible. Division might be based, for example, on current land ownership or, when British delegates said this was impractical, on giving the arid south to the Jews. He particularly noted Iraq's special interest in Haifa's port, claiming "the Arabs" did not have a single harbor. Obviously, this argument did not apply for Egypt or Lebanon. In reply, British representatives explained that London was committed to partition but not to the details of any particular scheme.[31]

Egypt's delegation was even more careful to placate Britain, as in Foreign Minister Wassif Butrus Ghali's September 18 speech. He supported the Arab Higher Committee's argument that partition was contrary to both Britain's wartime promises to the Arabs and to the League of Nations Covenant. It would also, he added, complicate Arab-Jewish relations in the Middle East without helping Jews in Europe.

British diplomats and Zionist observers considered the Egyptian position as moderate despite their disagreements. Ghali's expression of sympathy for Jewish suffering, his appeal for calm, his opposition to violence, and his call for Arab-Jewish cooperation in Palestine, were considered evidence of goodwill. Yet they were distressed to find that even Egypt could no longer stand apart from the tide of opposition sweeping the Arab world.[32]

The Cairo correspondent of the Zionist magazine *Palestine* took a cynical view, seeing Egyptian politicians as snatching slogans to strike at opponents.[33] True as this might have been, it in no way negated the seriousness of the situation. The Wafd's reaction was largely defensive. The palace's appeal to Arab nationalism was dangerous for them. Throughout the Arab world, the ante was being raised: it was becoming impossible for any Arab leader to avoid taking a militant stand, at least for public consumption.

As real as the problems facing the Peel plan were, the available evidence indicates possible tactics which might have saved it. By combining the formation of a Jewish state with the Palestine-Transjordan merger, London had produced too big a pill for the Arabs to swallow. Opposition to such a windfall for Transjordan guaranteed the opposition of the Arab states and of the Arab Higher Committee. Might a partition plan based on an independent Palestinian Arab state have provoked the same degree of animosity? Some of the statements of Wahbah, al-Suwaydi, and Nahhas provide grounds for wondering on this point.

Further, the failure of Britain to press harder for implementation of the Peel plan doomed it from the start. London's policy seems to have been poorly conceived, badly coordinated, and unimaginative. It was true, of course, that England could not afford to antagonize the Arabs for strategic reasons. But given the importance of their British alliance to most of the Arab rulers, London seemed to have had more room for maneuver than its policy-makers realized.

The Zionists had moved toward a large concession in order to maintain peace and to save the refugees from Europe. They would never again be willing to settle for so little. Indeed, in retrospect the Arabs would never again have such a clear opportunity to take 80 percent of Palestine. While seeming an inevitable failure, then, the Peel plan was a missed opportunity for Britain and the Arabs.

The September 1937 Arab conference at Bludan, Syria, moved the Arab states further down the road toward confrontation. The meeting, hosted by the Palestine Assistance Committee of Syria, brought activists together to oppose partition and to plan further action. Most of the delegates came from Islamic groups, Palestine support committees, and parties in Palestine, Syria, and Lebanon. There were hardly any from Egypt or Saudi Arabia and no official government representatives.[34]

Although the National Bloc supported the meeting, much of the money and impetus came from the Mufti during his June 1937 visit to Damascus. While the bloc would have liked to have openly participated, British protests encouraged the French authorities to deter them. Saudi Arabia's abstention, the uninfluential Egyptian delegation (led by Al-luba), the absence of the Nashashibi, and the fact that most of the Transjordanians present were exiled opponents of Abdallah, made the conference seem a feeble effort to some observers.[35]

Such a conclusion would have been in error, for the tone set there would dominate Arab politics for several years to come. Certainly it was a well-organized effort. The meeting hall was decorated with Arab national and Islamic flags. A thirty-one-page pamphlet prepared by the

Palestine Defense Committee was distributed to all present. Entitled "The Jews and Islam," it quoted anti-Jewish statements from the Koran and added some new inventions, including a Jewish attempt to assassinate the prophet Muhammad. This focus was due not only to the Islamic flavor of the meeting—only one Christian attended—but also to a tactical decision to stress attacks on the Jews while avoiding criticisms of Great Britian.[36]

The strong Iraqi contingent included members of the influential Muthanna Club, the Palestine Defense Committee, the Young Men's Muslim Association, and the Islamic Guidance Association. Naji al-Suwaydi, a former Iraqi prime minister and brother of the current foreign minister, was elected the conference's president. Alluba and veteran Pan-Arabist Shakib Arslan were vice-presidents, while Nuri al-Said chaired the political committee.[37]

Yet al-Suwaydi represented a radical position which differed fundamentally from that of his brother and al-Said. They, like the established leaders in Egypt and Saudi Arabia, preferred to protect their links with London and to operate using diplomatic methods. Naji al-Suwaydi argued that all European powers were equally untrustworthy, but that alliance with Britain's enemies was preferable. Violence, too, would be a worthwhile tactic, since Europe only respected power. "We must make Britain understand that it must choose between our friendship and the Jews," he argued. Britain must change its policy in Palestine or the Arabs would side with the Germans and Italians.[38]

Obviously, this was an option which Palestine Arabs by themselves could not have exercised. As al-Suwaydi himself pointed out, close coordination between the Arab states would be necessary to make such a threat credible. Certainly, the British would have to take seriously such a possibility. The same day al-Suwaydi was speaking, Nazi propaganda chief Joseph Goebbels called on nations throughout the world to join the German crusade against decadent democracy.

Even Naji al-Suwaydi was somewhat moderate compared to many of the conference's participants, and he had to work hard to tone down its resolutions. The final conference declaration called for abolition of the Balfour Declaration and the mandate, an end to Jewish immigration, Palestine's recognition as an integral part of the Arab world, and an independent Palestine which would sign a treaty with Britain. Further actions would involve an anti-Jewish and—if possible—an anti-British boycott, prevention of Arab land sales to Jews in Palestine, encouragement of inter-Arab trade, and establishment of a central Arab propaganda office. Although only the Iraqis spoke with any real authority, those present pledged their respective countries to support this program.

As many as half of the participants were dissatisfied with such insipidly general resolutions. On September 12, about 100 Palestinian and Syrian delegates held a secret meeting in Damascus to discuss the organization of armed resistance. A letter from al-Qawukji was read and the decision made to smuggle arms, ammunition, and volunteers into Palestine under the Mufti's supervision.

Perhaps in response to these decisions, violence soon broke out in Palestine, beginning with the assassination of a high British official. The British moved quickly to outlaw the Arab Higher Committee and to remove the Mufti from the presidency of the Supreme Muslim Council. Warrants were issued for Jamil al-Husayni and others. Many Palestine Arab leaders, including these two men, escaped across the border to Lebanon or Syria.

Now all-out war had come to Palestine. Small rebel bands attacked Jews and the Arab opponents of the Mufti, especially the Nashashibis. See-saw battles resulted in the guerrillas alternately occupying and being driven out of various areas of the country. Extensive assistance including 200–300 volunteers a month came from the Arab states, particularly Iraq and Syria. Palestine Defense Committees grew rapidly. Some aid also came in from Italy and perhaps from the Germans.[39]

Here the involvement of the Arab states had entered a new stage. Without their help it would have been far more difficult for the Palestinian Arabs to have maintained the revolt for eighteen months. For the radical oppositionists, the struggle in Palestine was only the most advanced of a whole series of actions to be carried out against the British and their Arab allies. The established politicians also contributed to the cause, but for them it demonstrated the urgency of pressing a negotiated solution with London. The Peel Commission's plan had for all practical purposes been sunk. The field was open for new ideas.

As might be expected, Iraq was most closely involved in both aspects of these new developments. Naji al-Suwaydi became leader of the Palestine Defense Committee which, along with the Muthanna Club, was the center of agitation. Relief funds collected from government officials, members of parliament, and the general public were used to buy arms. The government was reluctant to supply military hardware directly but chose to ignore smuggling. Consequently, much of the military supplies came from army officers with radical Pan-Arab sympathies. Religious leaders and the press were in the forefront of the money-raising effort.[40]

Although out of office, Nuri al-Said continued his diplomatic activities, generating one idea after another for solving the Palestine conflict. He negotiated with Judah Magnes and other Jews favoring a binational state, but misled London in claiming they would accept an Arab king and a ban on immigration in exchange for a small semi-autonomous Jewish region. Given their experience with his 1936 intervention, neither the British nor the Zionists would accept his mediation. Neither would the Mufti, who confidently told him that the "terror of 1936 buried the mandate" while "the terror of 1937" would soon do the same to the partition plan. Undaunted, Nuri proposed in March 1938, an Iraq-Palestine-Transjordan confederation to dilute the Jewish presence — an idea which Ibn Saud saw as a front for Hashemite ambitions. All in all, al-Said's personal activities had little success.[41]

The National Bloc of Syria also threw itself into the Palestine struggle. Their partisan control of the issue, however, alienated the rival Shahbander faction which moved closer to Transjordan and Abdallah's "Greater Syria" plan. Some of Shahbander's supporters, like the Nashashibi in Palestine, refused involvement in the fighting.[42]

Abdallah aimself maintained a low profile, stressing the virtue of patience: "We are only sorry for all that has happened," he told Transjordan's assembly in November 1937, though wishing the Palestine Arabs "peace, blessings and success." Transjordan was doing everything possible "without expecting any reward," he said on another occasion, and "the dear sons of Holy Palestine know it."[43]

The Mufti's supporters did not agree. Throughout 1938 and early 1939, they tried to extend their rebellion into Transjordan and to undermine its emir. Armed bands attacked rural police posts, cut telegraph lines, and damaged the Kirkuk-Haifa pipeline three times. Bombs were placed in Irbid and one, which failed to explode, was planted in Abdallah's palace. When British military pressure increased in Palestine in 1938, guerrillas crossed into Transjordan to spread the insurrection. They failed, as did a second such wave in April 1939. The well-disciplined Arab Legion wiped them out in one month.[44]

Egyptian involvement was less direct but steadily increasing. When several of the Mufti's aides travelled to Egypt in October 1937, their appeals were well received. At the same time, there was less enthusiasm for their proposal to organize a major logistical base in Egypt, since that country lacked an extradition treaty with Palestine. Cairo would not go so far in jeopardizing relations with London. The Wafd regime's fall in December 1937, shifted power to the palace politicians, however, and opened the door for Egypt's more activist role beginning late in 1938.[45]

Saudi Arabia was the scene of the greatest changes at the end of 1937. Ibn Saud had been reluctant to supply arms to the Palestine Arab rebels although he offered them help against Abdallah. He was also considering a change of alliances. On October 25, he told a British friend that "for a Muslim to kill a Jew or for him to be killed by a Jew ensures him an immediate entry into Heaven and into the august presence of God Almighty." The Jews not only wanted Palestine, he warned, but the land to the south as far as Medina and eastward toward the Persian Gulf. In short, he feared a direct threat to Saudi Arabia.[46]

The following month, Ibn Saud's representative Yusuf Yasin met with Grobba in Baghdad. The Arabs were uniformly opposed to the Peel plan, he told the German diplomat, and asked for a German mission in Jidda to balance British influence. Ibn Saud also wanted German arms and a loan. Unwisely, the German economic ministry turned down the proposal because of foreign exchange shortages. The Italian dictator Benito Mussolini was less reticent, but he too was scarcely willing to challenge Britain's sphere of interest there.

Ibn Saud was playing a complex game, and it was never clear how serious was his approach to the Germans. They were convinced that the king or some of his advisers were acting as British agents. Though he again sought their support in the early days of 1939, he was later quickly convinced that Britain would defeat Germany in the war. Thus his motive in these flirtations might have been to accumulate some leverage with London on forcing a change in its Palestine policy.[47]

The sincerity of his concern over Palestine was beyond question. After listening to a BBC report on the hanging of one Palestinian Arab guerrilla, his eyes filled with tears. The British had the right to maintain order in Palestine, he acknowledged, and the man had broken the law: "Nevertheless," the king concluded, "if it had not been for the Zionist policy of the British Government that Arab would be alive today."[48]

Growing Arab antagonism toward Britain's position on Palestine, the mounting Italian-German threat, and the possible combination of these two forces could not be ignored by London. The debates within the British government from the latter half of 1937 focused on the importance of maintaining friendship with Egypt, Iraq, Saudi Arabia, and Yemen. Strategic planners knew that a European war would leave England only limited forces to hold the Middle East and keep open the Suez Canal. Peace in Palestine was essential for this purpose.[49]

The Jews, British policy-makers knew, would not pose much of a threat since they could scarcely oppose England in any conflict with Nazi Germany. Zionist strategy was based on the inevitably losing argument that they would be a more reliable ally than the Arabs. It was precisely the unreliable nature of Arab support that forced British concessions. Otherwise, they might imperil not only the canal, but other sea and air routes to the east as well. Within Palestine, help from the Jewish defense forces proved useful in putting down the Arab revolt, but this posed a potential political embarrassment. Few in the Foreign Office doubted the need to shelve partition and the priority of ending the fighting in Palestine.[50]

A Foreign Office memorandum of November 11, 1937, for example saw the small Jewish state proposed by the Peel Commission as "a kind of time-bomb" with "insecure foundations" and a "perilous future." Partition could only earn Britain "the undying hostility of the Arabs and Muslim world," driving them into an alliance with Britain's enemies.[51]

While the Colonial Office was skeptical over the extent of Arab opposition, the Foreign Office believed that Palestine could not be isolated from wider considerations of Arab nationalism's formidable force. For example, Egyptian nationalism and religious sentiment, "always readily inflammable, may be roused to new excitement by sympathy with their Arab co-religionists." British Palestine policy might involve large, unaffordable military commitments. Saudi Arabia and Yemen were turning toward Italy, while anti-British feeling was increasing in Egypt and Iraq.

Palestine must be dealt with in this regional context, the Foreign Office concluded, "All our evidence goes to show that it is now dominating every other question throughout the Middle East, and that our whole future relations with Middle East states depend almost exclusively on our handling of it."[52]

Such talk was perhaps exaggerated but these were not imaginary concerns. Using the 1936 monarchs' appeal as an opening wedge, the Arab states gained a major chance to affect British policy. Their opposition defeated the partition proposal and convinced London of the need for a more pro-Arab approach. This was an impressive result after a little more than twelve months' labor.

At the same time, the importance of Palestine in the domestic politics of the Arab states was also greatly increased during that period. Those who staked prestige on saving Palestine for the Arabs risked being discredited if they could not provide results. Yet the very factors which pushed them toward diplomatic activism inhibited them from successfully using Britain's weakness to obtain one.

Passionate anti-British feelings on the Palestine issue brought pressure for a break with Britain and alliance with its enemies. Impatience with negotiations led the militants to support outright rebellion. A deep-seated conviction in the rightness of the Arab cause made compromise unpalatable and ultimate victory unquestionable. Such attitudes, reflected in Arab public opinion, hardly made the task of Arab foreign ministers easy.

The strong reaction to the Peel Commission's proposals seemed to energize a hurricane of rejection. One might well argue that this was inevitable, but London's greatest mistake was not necessarily the idea of partition itself as it was the role envisioned for Transjordan. By offering Arab Palestine to Abdallah, the commission guaranteed the opposition of the Arab Higher Committee and of all the other Arab states. Further, the hesitancy of Egypt and Saudi Arabia in attacking the plan indicated a possible basis for further negotiations over modifications.

Although the Arab states had not moderated Palestinian Arab demands as Britain had hoped, their new level of involvement could not be reversed. Parallel with the deteriorating situation in Europe, London's attempts to reach an accord with the Arab states over Palestine had to continue.

7
Partition Abandoned, Compromise Denied: 1938–39

*H*aving committed themselves to find a solution to the Palestine question, the Arab states used the period between the beginning of 1938 and the start of World War II to work out some settlement with Britain. Aid to the Arab rebellion in Palestine was continued as were the constant round of meetings and demonstrations in neighboring countries.

London was equally eager to reach an agreement. A confrontation with Germany could clearly be seen on the horizon, and Great Britain could hardly afford a new front in the Middle East. The 1939 London Conference and the subsequent White Paper represented British attempts to work out a compromise accord with the Arabs which would satisfy their main demands.

Yet a growing hard-line faction of Arab nationalists, particularly in Palestine and Iraq, saw no need to conclude a pact with Britain. They were convinced of British perfidy toward Arab interests. Imported parliamentary institutions, modelled after Western European constitutions, held no attraction for them. More appropriate for Arab countries, they believed, was a decisive dictatorship backed by mass mobilization and legitimatized by romantic nationalism. Nor was British protection necessary. An alternative existed in the very powers which embodied these characteristics: Germany and Italy. Compromise or patience over Palestine was not only treasonous—it was unnecessary.

At odds with this view stood Nuri al-Said and Abdallah. Indeed, they realized that the surest way to make peace was to discover a formula which might win Jewish approval. The Iraqi government suggested a complex scheme to divide Palestine into fourteen Arab and seven Jewish cantons which would have local autonomy within a federal state. Nuri's vision went even further: a Palestine settlement might provide the first step toward Arab federation.[1]

Yet long-range plans could not stand entirely apart from short-range aims. Arabs sought the clear and final elimination of the Peel proposals; Zionists wanted to calm disturbances in Palestine and to guarantee immigration from Europe. Prevailing opinion in Iraq was not moving in Nuri's direction, however, as shown by an exchange before the parliamentary budget committee. When al-Said's ally Rustum Haydar attributed British policy to a fear of the Jews international financial power, one nationalist member replied that it made no difference. Whether it was a matter of gold or guns it was clear that might made right. Force rather than more talk was the answer.[2]

Transjordan's plans actually fed such sentiments by heightening the suspicions of other Arab leaders. While al-Said proposed limiting Jewish population in Palestine to 35 percent while allowing immigration into other Arab states, Abdallah was willing to forego any limits. His rule over a united Palestine and Transjordan, rather than any demographic statistics, would guarantee Arab rights. Even the Nashashibi would not endorse such an idea, which *Palestine & Transjordan* called a "miniature theme of partition." Of equal importance, Abdallah was willing to allow the mandate to continue for ten years before independence.[3] Perhaps their identification with Transjordan's ambitions further discredited the ideas of partition and a transitional period in Arab eyes.

In a letter to the Young Men's Muslim Association, he defended his unity prosposal. It was his religious and racial duty, Abdallah explained, to foster such a union. This would not suppress the rights of Palestine's inhabitants, he concluded, since they outnumbered those of Transjordan and would "ably take over the leadership of the administration of such a state."[4] Something like this would happen after the 1948 war when Transjordan annexed the West Bank. At the moment, though, Transjordan's policy was too discredited among the Arab states to have much influence.

The end of 1937 was a turning point in Saudi Arabia's involvement in Palestine; it was a moment when that issue started to affect wider policy decisions. For Egypt, the summer of 1938 marked a similar transition. In January 1938, eighty legislators had issued a petition supporting the Arab Higher Committee. Alluba helped arrange a May 28 parliamentary declaration calling for a permanent end to Jewish immigration and establishment of an independent Arab regime. The following month, he organized a call for a "World Interparliamentary Congress of Arab and

Muslim Countries for the Defense of Palestine." The British, for whom Egypt was the most significant Arab domino, tried unsuccessfully to block the meeting.[5]

Palestine was becoming a partisan issue in Egypt more slowly than in Iraq. Anti-British speeches distinguished a new radical camp which included the Muslim Brothers, the Young Men's Muslim Association, and student activists. The palace politicians in power even had to worry about the Wafd's use of the Palestine issue against them. Unless the British soothed Muslim discontent, Prime Minister Mahmud warned, he would have to escalate official protests. Otherwise, Nahhas might seize on the Palestine question for an antigovernment campaign. This prophecy seemed fulfilled in July as the Wafd busily issued its own statements over Palestine and launched a fund-raising campaign.[6]

The Wafd faced its own dilemmas. How could they support a conference organized by Alluba, a known partisan of the king? When the Wafd decided to boycott the meeting, Mahmud leaped in to give the conference semiofficial recognition. He appointed Chamber of Deputies President Baha al-Din Barakat to preside. But Mahmud was not motivated merely by the desire to gain advantages over the Wafd. In contrast to Bludan, Iraq's King Ghazi, Ibn Saud, Syrian President Hashim al-Atassi, and Emir Abdallah, all endorsed the Cairo meeting. Their support signalled the Arab world's increasing radicalization over Palestine and the rulers' attempt to moderate its tone. The Foreign Office actually commended the Egyptian and Iraqi governments in this regard.[7]

As always, Abdallah went farther than his colleagues. In his June 1938 letter to the Young Men's Muslim Association he boldly attacked the radical analysis. Rather than trying to find a workable solution, they "are content with weeping and wailing and calling for help to those who cannot aid them." He argued this was leading to the Arab loss of Palestine, and the only way to save it was by gaining a foothold in governing the country. Under a transitional compromise arrangement, "There would be a parliament to represent the people and an army to defend them. Finances would be unified and the shores of the state would be well patrolled and its gates shut to prevent clandestine immigration."

Palestine "would have a breathing spell in which to recuperate, while at the same time its neighboring sister ... countries would be enabled to make not a little progress toward strengthening the bonds and ties between them." Such arguments, to be made by the Egyptians only six months later after the London roundtable conference, ran against the prevailing mood in the Arab world.[8]

The capacity of the Palestine issue to both unite and divide the Arabs was amply demonstrated by the October 1938 parliamentary congress and by Egyptian reaction to it. The Wafd had belittled the meeting, accusing it of being a tool of the Mahmud regime. Still, they could not allow the palace to monopolize the limelight over Palestine nor could they ignore a gathering which drew twenty-five hundred participants. The party was forced to relent, and members attended the concluding sessions in considerable numbers. Nahhas himself gave a tea for delegates, apologized for the earlier criticisms, and pledged support for the "most worthy cause in recent Arab and Muslim history."[9]

This did not mean the Wafd had been wrong. King Farouk's government would certainly not forego such an opportunity to build up his prestige. Delegates cheered Farouk as "Commander of the Faithful," and some spoke of him as a possible caliph. Mahmud and Farouk held receptions for those attending, praising the gathering and presenting their own credentials as fighters for Palestine.[10]

Arab harmony coupled with Arab state competition permeated the conference. Faris al-Khuri led the Syrian delegation in introducing a resolution advocating the absorption of Palestine and Transjordan by Syria. Both the Iraqis and Palestinians strongly opposed this idea. The Syrians also attacked their Lebanese Maronite neighbors as being as much a "bone in the Arabs' throat" as were the Jews. King Ibn Saud, who decided at British request not to send an official delegation, also came under attack. Alluba complained of the king's broken promise. Jamil al-Husayni said he was not surprised: Ibn Saud was not reliable. Perhaps the pilgrimage to Mecca should be suspended until he cooperated. Ibn Saud had sold out to England and sought to strengthen his own country" on the backs of the Palestinians." The resolutions of al-Khuri and al-Husayni were voted down.

A third contentious issue was over whether the Arabs should conduct any more negotiations with the Jews. A Syrian delegate pointed out that Arab leaders had met Weizmann in the past, but Alluba, al-Husayni, and Awni Abd al-Hadi opposed any more such talks. Nevertheless, the political committee decided to impose no limitations on future Arab diplomacy.[11]

Like Bludan, the Cairo conclave called for independence for an undivided Palestine under an Arab government and a ban on Jewish immigration. The new feature at Cairo, however, was not only a higher level of official participation but also a greater awareness of the leverage provided the Arabs by the European crisis. Alluba once again pointed out that support for Zionism would hurt British interests, though it was hardly reassuring when he said that Arabs were only asking for what

London had given the Sudeten Germans at the Munich meeting some weeks before.[12]

There was also a greater willingness to attack Britain. The main resolution declared that the British attitude was hostile toward the Arabs and forced them to respond with a similar hostile policy. Farouk had also become more outspoken. The British carefully noted every such omen. It was obvious to them that conflict could be avoided only if Egypt and the other Arab states were coaxed into a diplomatic soulution.[13]

Aware of the danger to them posed by Arab-British rapprochement over Palestine, Zionists sought to discount these trends. The British were being deceived by "the mirage of a united Arab world," they argued, in spite of the more important conflicts between Arab states. Yet this blithely ignored the fact that much of the Arab division was due to competition over Palestine.

Further, despite the Cairo meeting's indecision on the subject, even the idea of direct Arab-Zionist negotiations was becoming unacceptable to Arab public opinion. Arab representatives were now afraid to talk to Jews, Saudi diplomat Hafiz Wahbah told Ben-Gurion. A few years before, calling for peace in Jerusalem, Wahbah had mentioned that Jerusalem was a holy city for Jews and Christians as well as for Muslims. The response was a stack of cables protesting this. "How many thousands of pounds did you get from the Jews?" one asked. Compromise could not take place, he concluded, in an atmosphere where everyone was afraid he might be accused of treason.[14]

The anger and impatience of the Arabs had a profound effect on the Palestine situation in the late 1930s, but this was only half the story. King Ibn Saud, for example, hated and feared the Jews, was disappointed at the lack of British support for his territorial claims against Oman and the Trucial states, and was pressed by outside Arabs and Muslims as well as his own religious views over lack of progress on Palestine. All of this might have been insufficient to prompt action against British policy without an additional factor: the alternative offered by the expanding power of Italy and Germany.[15]

The British knew that German and Italian radio and press propaganda aimed at the Arab world made heavy use of the fighting in Palestine. One provision of the April 1938 Anglo-Italian treaty was Rome's pledge to abandon Arabic-language broadcasts and its assurances not to create friction over Palestine. The Foreign Office, which deemed this intervention as having been most effective, was greatly relieved. British Foreign Minister Lord Halifax even thanked the Italians for playing down the Palestine conflict.[16]

The Germans cautiously advanced step by step to take their place. To the Arabs, Palestine could be used to present the picture of "perfidious Albion" as a treacherous enemy; for the German public, Hitler's regime used London's difficulties in quelling the revolt as proof of weakness. British intelligence thought Ibn Saud was serving as a German conduit to supply the Mufti with arms. Iraqi Prime Minister al-Midfai even told Grobba that Iraq would remain neutral in any Anglo-German war out of sympathy for Berlin.[17]

Given such concerns, the British government moved steadily away from any partition solution. The Foreign Office area specialists, who had always been skeptical, won over Prime Minister Neville Chamberlain because of the wavering Saudi attitude. Miles Lampson's repeated warnings about the gathering storm in the Arab world were also influential. Even the Colonial Office, under its new secretary Malcolm MacDonald, moved to join them. The Palestine Arabs themselves, MacDonald concluded, were "intractable" and "intransigent." Ibn Saud, seen as the most prestigious regional leader, might even raise the Arabs in revolt against Britain as Sharif Husayn had done against the Turks. The best prospect would be to work through Iraq and Egypt which MacDonald thought were ultimately dependent on Great Britain. The Arab states might still produce a moderate solution.[18]

From Egypt, Lampson tirelessly hammered away at the need for a more pro-Arab British policy. "Unless the Arabs get satisfaction over immigration," he wrote, "we must face the fact that, if war comes, we shall have to take on the Arabs as well as the Italians and Germans. What would our position then be in the Near East? I shudder to think." Even aside from Palestine, he told Chamberlain, Cairo was moving toward "re-insurance with Italy" because it feared "that we are not strong enough to protect Egypt adequately in the event of an Italian attack." His aide, Oriental Secretary Walter Smart, was equally blunt. Unless the Palestine question was resolved "in a manner favorable to the Arabs," he said, it might lead to the destruction of the entire British Empire.[19]

When the Woodhead Commission (organized to reinvestigate the ground cover by Peel) made another partition proposal, its report was quickly buried. In October 1938, the British government decided its new policy: Arab goodwill must be safeguarded at all costs, Jewish immigration must be drastically curtailed, Jews would remain a minority, and Palestine would become part of an Arab federation. The Arab states would be invited to a conference over Palestine which would set up an interim agreement along these lines, for the time being maintaining British rule over Palestine.[20]

This decision was taken at the height of the Czechoslovakia crisis, a war scare resolved by the Munich agreement. At this moment of high drama, MacDonald and Halifax contacted Iraq's Foreign Minister al-Suwaydi, Nuri al-Said, and Egyptian Prime Minister Mahmud. Perhaps, it was reasoned, these men could moderate the Mufti's hard line. Arab leaders were told that an independent, united Palestine might be possible within the framework of a new agreement. In exchange, the Arab states were expected to smooth the way to conciliation, as London openly stated in announcing the meeting.[21]

The Jewish Agency executive knew that such a plan could bring them no benefits, and they objected to the invitations for Arab governments. Iraq and Egypt, they said, had no more rights in the matter than any other League of Nations member or the United States. Zionists bitterly concluded that the London conference's outcome had been determined in advance—a reasonable analysis as events would show.[22]

The Mufti was equally unhappy with the British plan, for he feared that Britain was correct in hoping that the Arab states would be willing to compromise. He and his cousin Jamil were often sarcastic in private over the aims of their Arab neighbors, whose designs might curtail Palestine's independence or displace his leadership. A deal between the British and the Arab states might exclude him as well as the Zionists.

There was some material evidence for this fear provided by British suggestions that Palestine's integration into a broader Arab federation might avoid giving power to the Mufti. The Peel Commission had offered Arab Palestine to Transjordan; Syria and Iraq had staked claims of their own. Jamil al-Husayni's attacks on Ibn Saud at the Cairo conference showed that even Saudi Arabia was not considered to be above reproach.

Far from viewing Palestine as the passive object for other Arabs' ambitions, the Mufti began to have plans of his own. As leader of the Palestine revolt, he was in the forefront of the radical Arab faction. He had gone further than his compatriots in breaking with England to join with Germany. An Anglo-German war could only bring more opportunities. Why should he defer to Egyptian and Iraqi politicians? Perhaps his future would be brighter than their's.[23]

The Mufti therefore demanded stiff preconditions for his participation in the London meeting: guarantees for Palestine's independence and the exclusion of the Nashashibi faction from participation. Britain's refusal must have heightened his anxiety. On the other hand, contemporary developments in Iraq seemed to confirm the correctness of his analysis.[24]

The Palestine Defense Committee in Iraq was openly critical of its government's acceptance of the British invitation. The balance of power in Baghdad continued to shift toward the Mufti's allies. Inflammatory reports of alleged British atrocities in Palestine filled the newspaper columns. Violence against Jewish institutions and Jewish-owned stores in Baghdad was on the upswing. It would be difficult for the Iraqi government to give any ground over Palestine.[25]

In fact, al-Midfai's government did not stay in office long enough to see the London conference. On December 25, 1938, the army forcibly replaced him with Nuri al-Said. One of seven reasons given for the coup was the government's failure to sufficiently support the Palestine revolt. Behind al-Said's presence as a moderate figurehead, a junta of militant army officers controlled the new regime. The hard-line opposition groups intermingled with the political establishment. Minister of Defense Taha al-Hashimi became president of the Palestine Defense Committee, whose fund-raising campaigns attained a semiofficial status. Anti-Jewish violence continued to escalate. In such circumstances, al-Said's mission to the London conference assumed the air of a last, desperate attempt to settle the Palestine dispute peacefully.[26]

All the Arab states would be represented by top-level delegations. King Ibn Saud chose his son and foreign minister, the Emir Faysal, and Deputy Foreign Minister Fuad Hamza, himself of Palestinian origin. Transjordan was represented by Prime Minister Tawfiq Abu al-Huda (also born in Palestine). Egypt sent Ali Mahir with Azzam as one of his advisers, while Yemen dispatched Prince Sayf al-Islam al-Husayn.[27]

The conference's timing coincided with the height of Jewish desperation over persecutions in Europe. No country was willing to take many of the existing refugees at a moment when new areas of oppression threatened to open in Italy and the Balkans. Palestine's immigration quotas cut off that escape route. While some British policy-makers might have been personally sympathetic, such problems were not seriously considered alongside London's strategic interests—and those lay clearly on the Arab side.[28]

Warning signals of the coming war multiplied daily. The conference's opening day, February 7, 1939, was marked by Italian newspaper threats of violence if Egypt tried to deny Mussolini's aspirations in North Africa. To drive this point home, a German general toured Italian fortifications in Libya. Such reminders were never far off. The London conference itself had been planned under the pressure of the Munich crisis; Hitler occupied the rest of Czechoslovakia during its sessions.[29]

In this context the immense strategic significance of the Arab Middle

East could never be far from the thoughts of British policy-makers, with obvious consequences for the urgency of solving the Palestine problem. No matter how strong British forces were in the area, they would be insufficient if the local population turned against England in a crisis. Arab friendship was deemed an absolute necessity. Once Palestine was amicably dealt with, they reasoned, there need be no fear of an Arab fifth column.[30]

Yet despite the strong temptations this posed for contemporary Foreign Office specialists, it would be most misleading to attribute Britain's Middle East problems exclusively to the Palestine problem. London's heavy-handed tutelage over Egypt and Iraq was equally at the root of Arab nationalists' antagonism. British diplomats constantly interfered in the domestic politics of these countries, favoring particular parties and individuals. Those whose ambitions were blocked, those who demanded faster social and economic development, and those who felt such influence a humiliation, all had powerful grievances.

Even moderate leaders tried to turn away from London during the dark days of 1939–41. If German or Italian might was bound to replace Britain in the region, Arab rulers like Ibn Saud did not plan to be on the losing side. Few failed to seek some accommodation with the self-proclaimed new order. Further, Arabs, like the Germans and Italians, wanted revision of the boundaries set by the World War I peace settlements. Iraq, Syria, Transjordan, and even Egypt became animated with ambitions to redraw borders and to establish their own spheres of influence. The Axis might bring change; Britain and France stood for imperialism and the unpleasant status quo.

Axis ideologies also contained much that appealed to the new generation of Arab nationalists. They were responsive to pan-ethnic nationalism, irredentism, unity and social mobilization behind a single party and a charismatic leader, romantic nationalism, contempt for Western parliamentary structures, and hatred of the Jews. They sought a totalistic world view to parallel (or supplant) Islam. They yearned to dedicate life and loyalty to their nation's sacred mission. Many of these themes would later appear in the Arab adaptation of Marxism in the 1950s and 1960s.

Such features could be most clearly seen in Iraq. Officers there had already aided one armed uprising against the British. Close contacts with radical politicians reinforced their desire for Iraq to unify the eastern Arab world. Their December 1938 coup was a first step. By February 1939, the Palestine Defense Committee's new weekly called on Iraqis "to be prepared for that dreadful hour chosen by Allah when you

will be called upon to serve the Arabs and lift them out of their misery."
The tone was xenophobic, attacking Armenians and Assyrian Christians
as well as Jews, and expansionist, adding Kuwait to the territories which
Iraq should annex.[31]

Abdallah, most friendly to Britain of the Arab leaders, was isolated,
as he had been since rejection of the Peel proposals. While nominally
optimistic, he well realized that the tide was running in the Mufti's favor.
Dr. Khalil Totah, the well-informed educator, explained that "Emir
Abdallah hasn't an honest friend among the Arabs of Palestine." Transjordan did not even bother to send its delegates to the preconference
Arab consultations in Cairo.[32]

The other delegations gathered on January 17, to decide on common strategy. They would not negotiate with the Jews. They would
demand a total ban on Jewish immigration and land purchases and
creation of an independent Palestine with an Arab majority. The per-
centage of Jews in the population would be frozen, but those already in
the country would have civil and political rights guaranteed. Mahmud
suggested offering autonomy to towns, giving Jews some self-rule in
Tel-Aviv and elsewhere. Perhaps most important, it was agreed that the
Palestine Arabs would have the decisive voice in the negotiations. The
other Arab states would support them. Although the Iraqis and Egyptians stressed their own country's interest in Palestine, these conditions
had given the Mufti veto power over any settlement. This doomed the
Anglo-Arab talks from the beginning.[33]

Chamberlain, Halifax, and MacDonald represented the British side
in London, shuttling between the Zionist and Arab delegations, which
met separately except on three occasions. Chamberlain told the Arabs
that the presence of the neighboring states implied recognition of a
"commonality of interest and sentiment which characterizes the Arab
world." He assured them of Britain's desire to maintain and strengthen
friendship with the Arabs. Both sides kept British strategic considerations to the fore. MacDonald noted that trouble in Palestine would have
repercussions throughout the region, and the Arab delegations understandably played on this theme. With such a trump card in their hands,
the Arab newspapers at first waxed enthusiastic over the progress
being made.

In meetings with the Jewish side, MacDonald frankly presented the
reasons for the change in British policy. If ten years of peace could be
assured in Europe, he explained, the British could afford a different
stand, but unhappily this was not the case. Halifax was even more blunt:
"Gentlemen, there are times when the most ethical consideration must
give way to administrative necessity."

A week later, MacDonald gave the Zionists a more detailed picture. Egypt commanded the routes to Asia and Africa, while also containing the Suez Canal and its defenses and Alexandria, the only naval base suitable for defending the eastern Mediterranean. Iraq commanded the air and land passage to Asia and was an important oil center. A hostile Saudi Arabia could threaten lines of communication to Iraq and Aden. In the event of war, all of these must be available to the British side.[34]

Moshe Sharett attempted to counter these arguments. If the Palestine question was settled, he said, Arab governments would only raise other issues. Jewish support would be more reliable than Arab pledges in the event of war. Ben-Gurion agreed. Regardless of British policy on Palestine, the Arab governments would follow their own interests. Such arguments fell on deaf ears. There was equally little agreement at the first informal Arab-Jewish meeting. When Ali Mahir called for an independent Palestine in which cooperation with the Arabs, rather than treaties, would guarantee the Jewish community's security, Weizmann and Ben-Gurion demurred. The Arab states, they replied, could not even guarantee the safety of their own Jews, nor could Zionist demands for immigration be abandoned.[35]

With both sides standing firm after these preliminaries, the British began their series of concessions to the Arabs. MacDonald, who believed that war might break out in the spring, was in a hurry. A Palestine constitutional conference would be held in autumn, he proposed, to establish a Palestine executive council. Although he had earlier spoken of equal Jewish-Arab representation, he now offered a 3 to 2 ratio in the Arabs' favor. In addition, the period before which Jewish immigration would be subject to Arab veto would be cut from ten to five years. While the Zionists considered walking out of the conference, the Arab press celebrated this news. In Baghdad, *Al-Iraq* and even *Al-Istiqlal* spoke of their optimism at the prospect of a favorable solution.[36]

These high spirits did not last long. The Palestinian Arab delegation quickly rejected this plan. Instead they demanded an immediate provisional government, a transition period of only three years, and a ban on immigration and land sales. The Arab states favored the British proposals and even some of the Mufti's followers wanted to accept, but the majority of their delegation refused to budge. Trapped by their agreement in Cairo, the government delegations were forced to fall into line behind them.

The triumph of the hard-line faction was indicated by Nuri al-Said's deteriorating position. As the militants in Iraq consolidated their position and forged a special alliance with the Mufti, Ibn Saud interpreted this in traditional terms. The king accused al-Said of trying to maneuver

Palestine into Iraq's orbit, thus disturbing the balance of power among the Arab states. Actually, al-Said was under continuing attack from home. Soon, to ensure the uncompromising purity of Iraq's stand, Tawfiq al-Suwaydi was sent to replace him.[37]

The second Arab-Jewish meeting, on March 7, centered on the immigration issue. Weizmann and Ben-Gurion spoke of its importance in light of the worsening situation in Europe. "Romania Plans to Force Out 50,000 Jews a Year; Germany 100 a Day," read one contemporary headline. This desperation was augmented by the Zionist delegates' belief that the Arabs and Britain had joined forces against them. "They have called this meeting... to tell us to give up," Ben-Gurion whispered to Shertok. When Ali Mahir asked the Jews, "for the sake of peace," to stop or limit immigration, Weizmann suggested this could be done in exchange for Arab concessions, but his own delegation vetoed the hinted compromise.[38]

Faced with this impasse, MacDonald embarked on another round of concessions to the Arabs. Not only would Jewish immigration be under Arab veto after five years, but during that time it would be limited to seventy-five thousand people. The ratio on the executive council would not be 3 to 2, but 2 to 1 in the Arabs' favor. Again the Arabs stood firm. On March 15, Hitler occupied the rest of Czechoslovakia, marking another step toward international confrontation. Two days later the London conference ended in failure.[39]

The European crisis "which has arisen since the end of the conference," wrote Lampson on March 23, "makes it all the more essential that [a] rapid end should be put to disturbances in Palestine." The Arab states were also interested in a quick settlement. Despite the breakdown of the London meeting, the Arab delegations once again met in Cairo to propose a new basis for agreement. Their plan was not too far from the latest British proposals, and the changes mainly aimed to ensure the completion of the transition period. A Palestinian state would be established within ten years, and consultations with the Arab states would be held if this schedule could not be met. Immigration would be reduced, and the Jewish population of Palestine would be frozen at 33 percent. Palestinian ministers would be chosen to begin the preparation for independence. The Arab states were still optimistic. If his country backed a settlement, Egypt's ambassador assured the Foreign Office, the Mufti would not be able to interfere.

Again, the British gave in on most of these points. Chamberlain explained, "We are now compelled to consider the Palestine problem mainly from the point of view of its effect on the international situation.

... If we must offend one side, let us offend the Jews rather than the Arabs." Surely such an attitude must put an Anglo-Arab accommodation within Britain's grasp. There was, Lampson wrote, "substantial agreement ... on all the main issues." Nevertheless, the Palestine Arabs were still not likely to accept, he continued, therefore the accord must be reached directly with the Arab states. The Egyptians were confident that this method would work. Mahmud claimed that he would simply invite the Mufti to Cairo and "make him toe the line."[40]

Since 1936, British policy sought to win the Arab states to a solution short of the Mufti's full demands. The worsening series of international crises had given Arab governments their own leverage in forcing British concessions. Yet London acted on the premise that such a settlement would strengthen British security in the coming war. Rapid independence for Palestine under a Husayni-led regime would not meet this requirement. Britain was in no hurry to abandon such a strategic territory to a group with such strong anti-British and pro-German feelings. This explains London's insistence on a longer transitional period and its attempts to prevent the Mufti's exercise of political power in Palestine for the foreseeable future. Otherwise, the whole exercise would only dangerously weaken Britain's position in the region.

With these thoughts in mind, the Foreign Office knew that either it must quickly reach agreement with the Arab states or issue a unilateral White Paper defining their policy. An agreement was certainly preferable and seemed possible. As late as April 28, after talking with Arab negotiators, Lampson reported matters "are going more favorably than expected."[41]

At that moment, things began to go wrong. The Arab states would agree on limiting Jewish immigration to seventy-five thousand over the next five years and to a 33 percent ceiling on Jews in Palestine, but they demanded an acceleration of the independence process. A constituent assembly would be formed to draw up a constitution within the next three years. Ministries composed of Palestinians would be set up to start administering the country. This new provision, the British realized, came from the Arab Higher Committee itself.[42]

"This is just what we expected and feared," wrote C. W. Baxter, head of the Foreign Office's Eastern Department. The Arab states had come to terms "on all the most difficult outstanding points," when Mahmud had miscalculated. Overestimating his own leverage vis-a-vis the Arab Higher Committee, he invited their representatives to Cairo from their place of exile in Beirut. Rather than force them to "toe the line," Mahmud was forced to accede to their position.[43]

Now came the greatest missed opportunity for the Arabs at the peak of their leverage over Britain. The failure of compromise in 1939 would doom the Arab regimes to the disaster of 1948. Never again would they have such a golden chance to create a unified, Arab Palestine. Did the Mufti and Arab Higher Committee really want a settlement in April 1939? Their abandonment of negotiations with Britain because of the proposed timetable could only mean that they believed they could achieve their ends more quickly by fighting against London. Only an Axis military victory combined with a larger Arab uprising than had taken place in World War I would suffice. If this was the Mufti's line of reasoning, it was a gross miscalculation of the balance of political and military forces.

Unwilling to make a further retreat on the schedule for independence, it was London's turn to dig in its heels. They informed the Arab states that unless further progress was made, a White Paper on Palestine would be issued May 17 on the basis of the earlier proposals.[44]

The Egyptians, as main intermediaries with the Arab Higher Committee, now made one more desperate attempt to talk the Palestine Arabs into an agreement. On May 17, Prime Minister Mahmud and Ali Mahir, soon to be his successor, met the Mufti's delegates, Mahir spoke first. London's plan should be accepted, he argued, since the Jews opposed it and were seeking to gain time. True, only limited independence was being granted, but many European states were also circumscribed by the great powers—independence was a relative concept.

Most important, he continued, was the opportunity offered by the White Paper. Not only was it the best deal which the Arabs could obtain at the moment, it also gave them concrete advantages. Cooperation with Britain was better than being "at the mercy" of the Jews. Sympathetic Arab regimes would help open the door to further gains.

Mahir had another and different argument. Independence did not consist only in signing agreements, it also required the training of administrators, preparation for defense, and a moral power which modern political scientists would call "legitimacy." Although Mahir did not say it, this nation-building policy was precisely that of the Zionists in Palestine. It would be the foundation of their victory in 1948.

A transitional period might do the same for the Arabs, Mahir continued. Further, the battle could more efficiently be carried by a step-by-step advance. "The position," Mahir summed up, "is the same as two armies fighting against each other. One army is vacating some of its front trenches. Would you refrain from jumping into them and occupying them?"

Like a Greek chorus, the Palestinian representatives retorted, "If we accept, the revolution will end."

Undaunted, Mahir began again. "Do you believe that Great Britain is unable to crush your revolution, with all its modern satanic war implements and inventions? Is it not better for you to come nearer to the British authorities and get them to forsake the Jews?" Then they would not have to ask London to stop immigration. They could directly regulate it! The Arabs would not have to demand independence rhetorically, they would control key positions in the government and after a few years in a parliament as well.

Mahmud did not attempt to gloss over the political situation. The Palestine Arabs could decide for themselves, but war was on the way and would not strengthen their hand. Britain would lose patience and turn Palestine over to military rule. The other Arab countries would be too involved with their own problems to help. In fact, Mahmud and Mahir could not have been unaware that the Palestine revolt was already being stamped out by a British offensive.

Again their interlocuters demurred: "When the revolution started, we had aims in view to attain. We cannot now tell our people, 'Stop the revolution because we got some high posts.'"

"You can tell your people," Mahir answered, "that you shall be able to control your country's administration; to stop persecution, exiles and harsh measures." They could set Palestine's budget, limit the Jewish population to one-third, and point to the Arab governments' advice for their acceptance. The Palestine Arabs would not even have to sign anything, but would merely have to agree to cooperate with the White Paper. None of his arguments made any headway.[45]

There can be no doubt that the 1939 White Paper did go a very long way toward satisfying Arab demands. A unitary Palestine state (the British had conceded to Arab opposition over the word "federal") would be established in ten years. In large areas of Palestine, land sales to Jews would be prohibited. Relatively few Jews would be allowed to immigrate for five years after which the Arabs themselves would decide how many—if any—more would be admitted.[46]

The Jewish Agency had no illusions about this plan. They strongly protested the White Paper as contrary to the mandate's provisions. Other observers also noted the vast advantages being presented to the Arab side. Even the Soviet ambassador accused Great Britain of selling out the Jews for its own benefit.[47]

The Arab governments were not blind to this chance, but they had painted themselves into a political corner. As much as they wanted a favorable settlement, they feared the explosive potential of the issue in domestic politics. With war rapidly marching over the horizon, no one could predict who would end as victor or vanquished. Immediate or future revenge might be taken against anyone deemed to have faltered over a prime Arab cause. Already, virtually every Arab leader had hedged his bet by trying to establish contacts with the Germans or Italians. Thus while they would seek compromise in private, none would openly clash with the Mufti. Even if they did, they could scarcely force implementation against the will of the Arab Higher Committee. With the Palestine rebellion already in eclipse—the kings of Saudi Arabia and Iraq were urging Arabs there to "down arms"—there were few alternatives.[48]

Only Transjordan, along with the Nashashibi party in Palestine and the allied press in Syria, said anything publicly favorable about the White Paper. Despite its shortcomings, they explained, it might initiate "a new era of cooperation" between the British and the Palestine Arabs. This was but a straw in the wind.[49]

Although the most ardent advocates of accepting the White Paper in private, the Egyptians were the first to denounce it. Mahmud declared the negotiations at an end, though he continued secret efforts well into July. For its part, the Wafd attacked his rejection as being too soft. The White Paper, they said, showed only that Britain sought to hold onto Palestine "forever."[50]

The growing tension within Egypt had some detrimental effect on the local Jewish community. Among the Egyptian elite, Palestine seemed to evoke less passion than elsewhere in the Arab world. Mahmud could still warmly welcome Weizmann to Cairo, express admiration for Zionist accomplishments, and suggest bridging the Arab-Jewish gap through technical cooperation. Nevertheless, the militant and growing fringe groups made increasingly credible threats.

Alluba had asked Egyptian Jewish leaders about their stand on Zionism but refused to accept their response that the community would support the government's policy. "Anything less than a complete condemnation of Zionism," he warned, "would brand them as foreigners." The Egyptian people, he hinted, might not be so restrained in taking action as were the officials. Young Egypt called for a boycott of Egyptian Jews, and several members were arrested after bomb attacks on Jewish stores. This offensive only ended with the outbreak of the war and the imposition of martial law.[51]

Following the Arab Higher Committee's lead, Iraq and Saudi Arabia also rejected the White Paper. Iraqi Foreign Minister Ali Jawdat indicated the ambiguity of the Arab governments. He objected to the length of the transition period and to allowing any further immigration. On the other hand, he called the policy a great Arab victory and confided that he and Nuri al-Said had tried to convince Jamil al-Husayni to accept it. The regime also sought to calm the Palestine Defense Committee's more outspoken agitation against the plan. Instructions were issued to newspapers not to publish anything which might damage Anglo-Iraq relations. Still, Baghdad would not cooperate in the request of Awni Abd al-Hadi to support a moderate pro-White Paper group of Palestine Arabs. The moment for a straightforward settlement with Britain had passed.[52]

In retrospect, the 1939 negotiations appear as the high water mark for Arab diplomacy over Palestine. The British need for regional stability and for the support of the Arab states led London to make a number of important concessions. The arguments made by Arab leaders since 1936 seemed justified: cooperation with the British could lead to a satisfactory settlement. The three main provisions of the 1936 Peel Commission proposals—partition, an independent Jewish state, and a direct role for Transjordan—had all been withdrawn. These achievements had been due more to the geopolitical weight of the Arab states than to the Palestine rebellion.

Yet although the role of the Arab governments had been so essential and although the outcome of the Palestine conflict so directly affected their own interests, they were to have little ultimate control over any agreement. Only the leadership of the Palestine Arabs would be able to give the signal for accommodation with Britain.

In principle it was quite reasonable that only the Arab Higher Committee could take such a step. Their's was the fate to be settled; their's was the future to be forged. On smaller tactical points Arab pressure had carried the day; the Mufti and his supporters held a veto on this most essential issue. If necessary, they could call on Arab public opinion and their political allies in Iraq and elsewhere.

But the Arab Higher Committee did not see things the same way as did the Arab rulers. Blinded by bitterness toward the British and by overestimates of German power, the Mufti fundamentally misunderstood political and military realities. He stuck to his maximal demands. Diplomatically experienced Arab politicians abroad grasped how the British offers could be widened into an incremental road to independence. Using such methods, the Zionists had driven inch by inch, day by day, and hectare by hectare toward their goal. Such a program was not in the Mufti's traditionalist strategic inventory. Both the Arab states and the Palestine Arabs would pay dearly for this shortcoming.

Just as strategic requirements defined Britain's new orientation, they also determined its limits. The Arabs might be given the keys to Palestine, but they would have to wait. On the eve of international conflagration, Palestine would not be turned over to those who had waged war for almost three years against Britain. Anti-German stability would not be built by strengthening those who had thrown in their lot with Berlin.

The White Paper stood to propitiate the Arabs even if they did not formally accept it, but it could not be fully implemented. With the defeat of the radical Arabs in Iraq and of the Germans in Russia and North Africa, Arab leverage would dissipate. Although the Palestine issue was seemingly in suspended animation, profound changes were taking place in the balance of forces there.

8
Fortunes and Misfortunes of War: 1939–42

Despite the refusal of any Arab state to approve it, the 1939 British White Paper was the governing document for Palestine during the next six years. The Arabs were aided by its restrictions on Jewish immigration and land purchases, but their rejection blocked steps aimed at leading Palestine toward independence. As Egyptian leaders had warned the Arab Higher Committee, the war froze the situation in a way that damaged Arab interests in Palestine.

Each Arab leader was forced to choose between the Anglo-French alliance and the German-Italian axis. The radical faction—particularly the Mufti's followers and the Iraqi militants—had already decided that Berlin had more to offer. Their alliance of convenience with the doomed Nazi cause would severely damage their position in later years. In contrast, Abdallah's strong commitment to the British would bring him rewards in the postwar era. London's preference for him over the Mufti, demonstrated in the 1936 Peel proposals, was confirmed by this experience.

Within Egypt, a similar division ran between the Wafd and the palace. When Nazi forces triumphed all over Europe in 1940–41 and the Afrika Corps stood at Egypt's gates, King Farouk and Ali Mahir prepared to welcome General Rommel. The British nipped in the bud any such plan by applying the most intensive pressure. The king's surrender and the Wafd's support of the Allied cause damaged them in the eyes of the young nationalist generation, while Mahir's ouster made him their hero.

Nuri al-Said and King Ibn Saud adopted a relatively more successful middle course. They were willing to work with the Germans but were ironically refused. Both their enemies in the radical camp and the German government itself distrusted them as British agents. Ibn Saud out of shrewdness and al-Said out of necessity soon realized the likelihood of British victory. They smoothly moved to benefit from their appearance of loyalty.

British strategy was based on the importance of Arab support in time of war. Concessions on Palestine would help preserve and reinforce this alliance. Since Jewish backing was already ensured in any battle against Hitler, it was not necessary to placate the Zionists. These premises motivated the replacement of partition by the London conference and the White Paper.

The very success of British arms on Middle East battlefields makes difficult an evaluation of this thesis. The Arabs gave little active or material aid to the war effort. Only Transjordan's Arab Legion participated in the fighting. Arab declarations of war on the Axis, a precondition for joining the United Nations, came late and had little effect.

Of course, the central British concern had been to keep the Arabs passive and neutral, to avoid an anti-British uprising. The critical factor here, however, was the course of the war rather than the efforts of diplomacy. If Rommel had broken through into the Nile Valley or if German armies had turned into the Middle East from southern Russia, it is hard to believe that Arab leaders would have stayed so acquiescent to British power. The Palestine element in British policy might be judged relatively secondary in affecting these events either way.

Nevertheless, the British course was set on the side of maximum strategic safety—a view which did not end with Hitler's defeat. Maintaining good relations with the Arab states remained a high priority for British governments in the post-war era. While wartime support for Pan-Arabism was often exaggerated in later times, at least rhetorical gestures had been made in that direction. Economic and political competition with the United States and the Soviet Union continued to make such actions necessary to maintain British influence in the region.

All this seemed far ahead in 1939, with German power on the rise and the future still so invisible to mortal eyes. In January 1939, when Germany opened formal diplomatic relations with Saudi Arabia, Ibn Saud told Grobba his hope that Berlin would help him curb British strength in Arabia. Since he had helped finance the Palestine rebellion, the king continued, he had earned the right to more German aid and arms. In exchange he promised Saudi Arabia's benevolent neutrality when war began.[1]

The Germans were in no hurry to make such commitments, though an arms agreement was signed on July 18. Perhaps they were all too aware of the king's caution. He supported the Palestine Arab rebels, but only in secret. Although often moderate in practice, he had taken a harder line than Iraq or Egypt over the White Paper. He sought German assistance but never followed through on these initiatives. When World War II began, he quickly made clear his support for Britain.

The reason for these seemingly contradictory policies lies in Ibn Saud's special position at home and among Arabs abroad. Saudi Arabia was poor, backward, and remote, even relative to other Arab countries. These factors strictly limited any real Saudi interventions in international affairs. Ibn Saud's high personal prestige as a politico-religious figure meant, however, that he was expected to uphold the Islamic cause against the Zionists. Since the king's own mind was attuned to the views of the Arab masses, he was moved to strong public pronouncements and private lobbying: letters to President Franklin Roosevelt, diplomatic protests, and newspaper interviews, but Saudi Arabia's material weakness made any substantive break with Britain out of the question.

At best, the king—a realist when it came to power politics—might seek support from another Western state to balance off his dependence on Britain. Italy, already established across the Red Sea in Eritrea and Somaliland, was too close for comfort. Germany seemed a better bet. Yet the king never neglected portraying himself to London as the most trustworthy of allies. He could thus maintain good relations with both sides. Ibn Saud's skill at this strategy allowed him to stay in the victorious camp while the Mufti, Rashid Ali al-Gailani, Ali Mahir, and others made the mistake of an irrevocable alignment with the Axis. Instead, Ibn Saud could seek backing from an Allied power. He found his alternative source of subsidies and protection in the United States. There, the increasing importance of Saudi oil gave him new leverage over Palestine.[2]

While Saudi Arabia coolly dallied, Iraq plunged into the treacherous currents. As early as January 1939, Rashid Ali al-Gailani had moved to place himself at the head of the radical forces. He demanded the government strengthen the army and press harder over Palestine, doing everything necessary to "save that Arab land from destruction." Baghdad's hesitation over the White Paper brought more criticisms from the Chamber of Deputies, though Palestine was only one of several issues reflecting the nationalists' hatred of Great Britain. Such indications only accelerated al-Said's attempts to find some settlement, a quest which in August took him to Amman, Beirut, and Cairo.[3]

When the Mufti escaped—or was allowed to leave—French-ruled Lebanon in October, he supplied a catalyst for those dissatisfied with al-Said's approach. Four army colonels, the "Golden Square," drew on all the varieties of militant Iraqi Pan-Arabism which had emerged over the last decade. These were augmented by a large Palestine Arab exile community. So many Palestine Arab activists had fled to Iraq, Glubb recounted, that by the beginning of the war there was "less anti-British feeling in Palestine than there was in Damascus and Baghdad." The Mufti furnished Iraq's government with educated Palestinians (and some Syrians) to fill bureaucratic and educational posts while stiffening the radicals' resolve.[4]

From the time of the Mufti's arrival, they acclaimed him a national hero. Every leading personality in Baghdad from the prime minister down, as well as all manner of political clubs, threw parties in his honor. Iraqi politicians and Syrian and Palestinian exiles turned these events into Pan-Arab demonstrations with anti-British and Iraqi expansionist overtones. Nor was support expressed only by verbal means. The Iraqi parliament granted the Mufti a special fund of £18,000 a month, plus £1000 a month from secret service funds and a 2 percent tax on government officials' salaries. Additional contributions came from Egypt and Saudi Arabia. Although he had promised al-Said not to engage in political activity within Iraq, the Mufti played political king-maker, assisting Nuri's replacement by Taha al-Hashimi and later helping Rashid Ali al-Gailani into power.[5]

Painfully aware of this explosive situation, al-Said pressed for a settlement over the White Paper. During a trip to Cairo in November, he proposed an Iraq-Egypt alliance which would try to persuade the Mufti to accept the White Paper as a basis for negotiation. At least they might suggest an amnesty to allow the Mufti to return to Palestine. Neither Ali Mahir nor the British were enthusiastic. The Egyptians were losing interest in Palestine for the moment as they focused on the far more immediate friction in Anglo-Egypt relations under wartime conditions.[6]

The opposite was true of Iraq. With the Mufti's presence and the intensity of Pan-Arabism, feelings over Palestine and the domestic power struggle were mutually reinforcing. The critical barrage against British policy mixed together with attacks on the Baghdad government itself. The Palestine Defense Committee organized protests on both targets in February 1940. *Al-Istiqlal* warned that Palestine, not Nazism, was responsible for Arab-British conflicts. "Promises are no longer enough," it warned. "There is beneath the surface growing unrest among the Arabs."[7]

Nuri al-Said's attempts to defend his efforts over Palestine met a wall of opposition in the Chamber of Deputies. The militants had rejected the White Paper, but complained over alleged British violations on the smallest points. The extremists openly sympathized with the Axis, but attacked Britain as ungrateful for their supposed contributions. For example, after al-Said spoke to the legislators, one deputy replied that British authorities in Palestine "are intent on exterminating the Arabs in Palestine or reducing them to a minority." The Arabs had dutifully "declared themselves" for the Allies in the war and "called off the rebel movement" in Palestine lest it be exploited by the Axis. Thus the Arabs "gave proof of their good will" and "faithfulness" to Britain, hoping London would reciprocate and give "a fair and just settlement to the Palestine problem." The British, however, had responded with ruthless repression.[8]

When al-Said called for moderation, another deputy complained, "I do not suggest that the Arab countries should dispatch armies for the deliverance of Palestine but I do say that England and ... France ... should improve their policy toward the Arabs of Palestine and Syria. The question of Palestine is one of life or death for the Arabs." A colleague continued, Iraqi interests required "that Palestine should form an outlet for Iraq on the Mediterranean; but how can this hope be realized so long as British policy seeks to establish the Zionists in that country?"

"Iraq will remain Iraq," Nuri responded, "Palestine Palestine and Syria Syria. Do not let us imagine a large Iraq or a small one," he warned, such ambitions might lead to disaster. For the moment, al-Said's line held. The Chamber of Deputies applauded the minister of finance's proposed appropriation for Palestine relief and then adjourned.

Working against time, Arab leaders continued approaches to Britain on amnesty for Palestine Arabs sentenced during the revolt. Saudi Arabia suggested further steps. London might appoint Palestine Arabs to head local government departments in order to demonstrate continued progress toward independence. Or, more modestly, they could simply announce that the White Paper policy was still in force. On this basis, Arab governments might make one more attempt to win Palestine Arab cooperation.

An amnesty was seriously considered in the Foreign Office, but British policy-makers were embittered by their experiences during and after the London conference. They sought to avoid any show of weakness and to forego strengthening potential enemies. "Whatever we say or do will be deliberately turned against us," lamented one official. They were well aware of the double game played by many. For example, Azzam told British diplomats of his efforts to win Arab declarations of war against Germany, while confiding to others that Egyptian interests had more in common with Berlin than with London.[9]

Nor did the Mufti's activities seem to merit concessions. He clearly augmented Iraq's animosity toward the war and plotted against the government with anti-British elements. Everything possible was done to block his planned visit to Ibn Saud. The Mufti had broken his word to Iraq to abstain from political activity, reported the British ambassador in Baghdad; by allowing him to do so, Iraq had broken its word to England. In light of al-Husayni's pro-Axis intrigues, the Foreign Office even considered a propaganda campaign to discredit him.[10]

The more modest proposal to simply restate the White Paper principles, on the other hand, seemed feasible. German successes had already begun to sway the Arabs, L. Bagallay of the Foreign Office Eastern Department pointed out in June 1940. Further concessions would not satisfy Arab aspirations, but, on the contrary, might merely confirm the Arabs in believing that they had unlimited leverage over England. The Allies could truly strengthen their position only by persuading the Arabs that they would win the war. This could only be done by military successes or propaganda about coming military successes.

Still, he wrote after a War Cabinet meeting, there was no question of abrogating the White Paper. If this were to be done even the Arabs who wanted Britain to win ("though believing that we shall lose") would begin to prefer a German-Italian victory. Anything, they would argue, would be better than the specter of Zionism. This analysis carried the day: no new promises would be made, but the Arabs would be assured that Britain would act in their interests. The Zionists would not like this policy, the Foreign Office noted, but "It will be kindest... in the long run to tell them the truth finally and plainly now."[11]

Such was the cold calculation. No matter how infuriated the Zionists were, they could not make common cause with their Nazi persecutors, whereas Arab hostility presented a formidable threat to vital British positions. By preventing tens of thousands of European Jews from reaching a safe haven, British policy decreed their deaths. Appeals were ignored. English policy-makers were unshakeably convinced, as historian George Kirk later wrote, "that this cruel ban was essential for the political stability of the Middle East theater of war."

Whether or not it was essential, it was certainly not sufficient. Bagallay's assertion that only victories—not promises or policies over Palestine—would hold the Arabs in line was quickly borne out. If the radical faction shared ideological beliefs with the fascists, for most Arab nationalists they simply provided a potential means for winning greater independence from Britain or France. They waited to see if this would be an effective option. In September 1939, the Allies had a substantial superiority in the Middle East, but after the fall of France, the Nazis seemed likely victors. Farouk and al-Misri in Egypt as well as al-Gailani and the Golden Square in Iraq reacted accordingly. If the Germans penetrated further, any British concessions over Palestine would have been far too late to save the day.[12]

Perhaps the best indication for this can be found in an unpublished manuscript by George Antonius, a leading Arab nationalist intellectual and activist. Born in Syria, he worked for the British in Egypt during World War I and later entered the Palestine government's Department of Education. In 1939, Antonius was secretary-general of the Arab delegations at the London conference, where his research became the basis for an influential book, *The Arab Awakening*.

By 1940, Antonius was at work in Beirut on a second book, a study of Arab public opinion and the war. He travelled to Palestine and Egypt, interviewing many leading fixtures in Arab politics. When he visited his estranged wife in Jerusalem in October, he gave a summary to George Wadsworth, the U.S. consul. Antonius died a few weeks later, and his work was never completed. Nevertheless, the available fragment remains a valuable contemporary record.[13]

Arab political circles were full of "uneasy forebodings" over their countries' future, Antonius wrote. Britain was considered "a satisfied Power" and as such was "less harsh than the others in her exploitation of weaker nations and less intolerant of their national aspirations." The "blackest mark" against her was Palestine, although her pro-Turkish policy was also resented. The new government of Prime Minister Winston Churchill, who had replaced Chamberlain after the military debacle on the continent, was thought more pro-Zionist than its predecessor.

Most Arabs, Antonius continued, had no love for either Germany or Italy—they thought all European powers imperialistic—but there were distinctions to be made. Italy was "needy, over-populated and, in her colonial methods, ruthless," as her behavior in Libya and Ethiopia had shown. On the other hand, "Nazi Germany is also ruthless; but, being less in need of mass colonization and better equipped in technique, she might content herself with oil concessions and other economic privileges (which it would pay us to grant) and leave us free to govern ourselves."

Germany might even curb Italian excesses, he commented, a view shared by Ibn Saud, though Antonius probably did not know that. Equally, it was certain that "both Germany and Italy would give very short shrift to the Jewish national home and rid us at any rate of *that* incubus." Yet who could know what would happen? Was the unknown devil really preferable to the known one? The only guarantees were the verbal and somewhat specious assurances emanating from the daily Berlin and Rome radio broadcasts.

In some quarters, particularly in Egypt and Iraq, "a certain degree of undisguised admiration of Nazi achievements and power is expressed." In others, Britain was considered "the natural ally of the Arabs": British victory would result in the elimination of France from Syria and the achievement of Arab unity through a "chain of separate states bound to each other and to Great Britain by treaties of alliance."

Few Arabs thought their best hope lay in a stalemate. Some chose sides on the basis of ideological predilection; most sought the best possible deal for their own and Arab national aspirations. When things looked bleakest, even such practiced Anglophile moderates as Ibn Saud, Nuri al-Said, and Musa al-Alami had considered jumping ship. For many of the Syrian and Palestinian Arab emigres and Iraqi politicians and officers, already inclined in that direction, the fall of France signalled their clear decision. In June 1940, the Mufti wrote Franz von Papen, German ambassador to Turkey, to offer his services.

To the moderate Iraqi politicians, few of whom believed that Britain would triumph, the Anglo-Iraq alliance now seemed a personal and national liability. A dramatic step was necessary. London, equally aware of the danger of more defections, dispatched Col. S. F. Newcombe to Baghdad in July 1940, to investigate. Newcombe, whose work with the Hashemite forces in World War I left him with many good Arab contacts, explored new ways of satisfying Arab demands. He met with al-Said, the Mufti, Jamil al-Husayni, and al-Alami. Judging from German documents, the Mufti had already made his own decision and opposed Newcombe's efforts to patch Anglo-Arab differences. His vision was to obtain from the Axis in World War II what the Hashemites had failed to gain from the Entente in World War I: creation of a Pan-Arab state under his leadership.

This was a far cry from al-Said's plan. If Britain implemented the White Paper, gave independence to Palestine after ten years, arranged for Syria's independence, and supplied arms to Iraq, al-Said suggested, Iraq would enter the war on England's side. Churchill refused additional guarantees. Nuri could hardly deliver his side of the bargain, while the Mufti was already an outright enemy.[14]

Nothing if not tenacious, al-Said did not give up. In August, he went directly to Cairo to lobby for his own case. Even implementation of the White Paper would not be enough, he told Richard Casey, British minister of state in the Middle East. There must be Palestinian Arab ministers as well in the mandate's government. Even though there were none qualified to actually run governmental departments, he argued, such appointments would have great symbolic value.

Again frustrated by British rejection, al-Said sought the best terms from the Axis camp. Yet Iraq's Palestine Arab guests had already taken up jobs as Berlin's gate-keepers. The Mufti rejected al-Said's offer, made through Jamil al-Husayni and Musa al-Alami, to work with them if Iraq's independence was guaranteed. The Mufti and his ally, Minister of Justice Naji Shawkat, also undermined al-Said's approach to the Italians. As late as December 1940, Nuri was still unsuccessfully trying to find some place for himself in the new order.[15]

As Antonius had shrewdly noted, the Germans made few promises. In March 1940, however, recognizing how Iraq had been kept out of the Allied side, they began a subsidy to the Mufti. On a political level, Berlin acknowledged the complete independence of all the Arab states. Britain was determined to stop any German-Iraq rapprochement. They complained that Baghdad had not fulfilled its treaty obligations and demanded that relations with Germany remain suspended. London had no confidence in Prime Minister Rashid Ali al-Gailani, the British ambassador warned, and Iraq would have to choose between him and her friendship with Britain.

The situation in Baghdad was extremely tense. British pressure collided with the aims of the Mufti and the Golden Square. The ever-energetic al-Said made one more attempt to bridge the gap. Some progress over Palestine, he told al-Gailani in a December 15 memorandum, might provide an excuse for reconciliation with London while satisfying the militant pro-Axis elements. Ignoring the broader issues at stake, al-Said tried to attribute the conflict exclusively to differences over Palestine and to an Anglo-Iraq "misunderstanding."

His was an understandable strategy: he was trying to provide al-Gailani with a way out of the impasse. But did al-Gailani and his allies want a way out? The people and government of Iraq, wrote Nuri, "are unanimous in seeking the safety of their country before anything else and in following the road which leads to that safety." That was hardly an accurate description of the political atmosphere in the country, nor was his conclusion that, wanting to "enforce the letter and spirit" of the Anglo-Iraq treaty, the regime would avoid any action which seemed to violate it.[16]

Nuri was correct that conflict with Britain would bring disaster for

Iraq, but wrong in thinking that the radicals could be deterred from an open break. The king did force Rashid Ali to resign on January 31, 1941, due to British pressure; Taha al-Hashimi's new government did try to transfer the officers involved in planning subversion. But the result was the Golden Square's military coup of April 3, bringing Rashid Ali al-Gailani back to power. Given the contemporary military situation, they had ample reason to believe that they were right while Nuri al-Said was wrong. German armies smashed deep into the USSR; other columns converged on the Middle East through Greece, Crete, and the Sahara. In Lebanon and Syria, the Vichy French rulers actively collaborated with the Axis.

Egyptians were reaching similar conclusions. They saw the Italians advance eighty-five miles into their own territory. While Prime Minister Ali Mahir was pressured by Britain to sever relations with Italy, he drew the line at declaring war against her. The British forced him out of power, while also obtaining the resignation of General Aziz Ali al-Misri as Egyptian army chief of staff. Indeed, Cairo's armed forces were virtually disarmed and demobilized since their loyalty to the Allies was highly suspect.

Such perceptions were not inaccurate. Many officers saw the war as "a foreign conflict in which we had no interest," as one of them, Anwar al-Sadat, later recalled. Even though the Italians were decisively defeated, Rommel's German troops again drove to the gates of Egypt in January 1942. "Great Britain stood alone," al-Sadat wrote. "Her weakness in the Middle East was apparent to everyone" and her military position in the Mediterranean "had become untenable." When German agents approached al-Misri and the officers' group in which al-Sadat participated, both agreed to supply copies of Egyptian defense plans and maps of fortifications.

Determined to guarantee Egypt's political loyalty before the showdown with Rommel, British authorities threatened to unseat Farouk unless he replaced the palace regime with Nahhas' more reliable rule. Farouk backed down to Britain's overwhelming military force, a humiliation Egyptian nationalists would long remember. Demonstrators in Cairo's streets shouted for a German victory, but the political and military tide had turned. The Wafd entered office, German agents were rounded up, and al-Misri was thrown into prison.[17]

Other British responses offered more positive incentives for Arab cooperation. On May 29, 1941, Foreign Secretary Anthony Eden spoke to endorse a greater degree of cultural, economic, and political ties between the Arab countries. Practically every contemporary observer saw this Mansion House speech as the start of a comprehensive plan to stimulate Arab unity under pro-British leaders. When the Arab League was formed after the war, its enemies and many of its friends, saw a British hand behind it. In fact, the British pledge to support such efforts was intended strictly as a short-term war propaganda measure. Many Foreign Office officials actually thought any such scheme would be impractical. Besides, they argued, greater Arab unity might well be detrimental to British interests.[18]

Arabs already inclined toward England greeted the Mansion House speech as a major step toward realizing the Pan-Arab dream; those placing their hopes on the Axis looked rather to the Iraqi revolt. Egyptian dissidents, al-Sadat explained, "wanted to attack the British and make Egypt a second Iraq. Rashid Ali had given the signal for the war of liberation, it was our duty to rush to his aid." Leaders of the nascent Ba'th Party in Syria felt the same way. General al-Misri was more knowledgeably skeptical. "You don't know Iraqi politicians as well as I do," he told al-Sadat; they would not be able to remain united.[19]

He was right. Their own bickering, Iraq's isolation among the Arabs, and German errors doomed the uprising. Berlin's inadequate intelligence and the vacillation of the German high command delayed their intervention. Rashid Ali and his military supporters also did not plan well. Although some nine thousand Iraqi troops surrounded and beseiged the Royal Air Force base at Habbaniya, they did not make any decisive attack. In early May, British planes ended the one-month "sitting war" by driving off the Arab force. Only then, on May 5, did the junta ask for German military supplies and air support.

The Wehrmacht was favorable, dispatching an He-111 fighter-bomber squadron, 750 tons of arms and ammunition, and a military advisory team. This airlift reached Damascus on May 12, but was ordered to await further instructions from Baghdad. Since the Iraqi army mistakenly shot down the German liaison officer, Major von Blumberg, when he tried to land, the necessary data never arrived. Reconnaissance flights and bombing raids against Habbaniya failed due to poor coordination with Iraqi ground forces.

Meanwhile, a British column, supported by the Arab Legion and the Transjordanian Frontier Force, crossed the desert from Amman to Baghdad and defeated the insurgents. On May 30, as they reached the outskirts of Iraq's capital, Rashid Ali and the Mufti ingloriously fled to Germany.[20]

Other offensives further consolidated the Allied position. British troops invaded Syria and Lebanon on June 8, capturing Damascus three weeks later. The Vichy French collaborators were expelled. In North Africa, Rommel's defeat at El Alamein October 19, coupled with American landings in Morocco and Algeria marked the beginning of an Axis debacle in North Africa. The Russian victory at Stalingrad ended the threat from the north. By the close of 1942, the Middle East was securely held by the Allies. The Axis alternative had been smashed, and the radical faction had clearly misplaced their bets, but they would not disappear without some revenge. Before occupation forces entered Baghdad on June 3, Rashid Ali's supporters massacred at least 180 Jews, injured a thousand more, and looted thousands of homes and businesses.[21]

Abdallah, as the only Arab leader to provide positive support, and Nuri al-Said, who had been forced into exile by the Rashid Ali coup, now voiced their claims for reward. England should consolidate Arab support by furthering some Pan-Arab plan. Many Englishmen agreed, and even some Zionists were not opposed. In a *New York Times* article, Weizmann revived his old proposal for an Arab federation to live peacefully alongside a Jewish state.[22]

As early as July 1940, Abdallah wrote London requesting the unification of Syria and Transjordan. A year later, after the Free French promised Syria independence, the Transjordan Legislative Council repeated the proposal. British Minister of State in the Middle East Oliver Lyttleton asked them to postpone the claim until after the war. The emir was not deterred. In March 1942, during a Jerusalem speech, he asked for unification of all geographic Syria — a designation which included Palestine—into a single state. The demand was based on his status as last surviving leader of the World War I revolt and on the 1920 resolutions of the Syrian Congress.

When a Zionist conference passed the "Biltmore program," openly demanding a Jewish state for the first time, Abdallah offered an alternative. Palestine would be absorbed into a federation with Transjordan, Syria, and Lebanon. Local government would be organized by proportional representation and limited Jewish immigration would be permitted. The Mufti, he argued, had forfeited his position by collaborating with the Axis; Transjordan was entitled to determine the area's future. Yet these grandiose visions were beyond Transjordan's means. It remained a small, poor, and weak state with few outside Arab allies. Egypt, Saudi Arabia, and Iraq all opposed its ambitions, seeing themselves as more qualified for Arab leadership.[23]

Such was the essence of Nuri al-Said's plan. Though similar in form to Transjordan's Scheme, his Fertile Crescent unity would place an Iraqi monarch on the Arab throne. Like Abdallah, he was willing to offer some degree of autonomy for Jews in Palestine. If a greater Arab state could be established, he promised, the Arabs would "deal generously with all the Jews living in their midst whether in Palestine or elsewhere."[24]

The renewed ability of Arab states to propose Palestine's disposition was made possible, of course, by the virtual disintegration of the historic Palestine Arab leadership. The Mufti and his lieutenants were either exiled in neighboring Arab states or in Germany. This began a brief period in which non-Husayni politicians attempted to rebuild the movement on a new basis and a longer era during which Palestine would be placed in virtual Arab state receivership. Awni Abd al-Hadi returned from Egypt to organize, particularly in his native city of Nablus. He also started a national fund to keep land in Arab hands. Musa al-Alami, specializing in propaganda, also tried to build an independent base.[25]

Too late, in the aftermath of their military defeat, the Germans stepped up propaganda to the Arab world. The Mufti and Rashid Ali cooperated in Berlin, helping to raise Arab units for the German army, but this had no impact on the course of the war. Several dozen Arab exiles were directly on the payroll of German military intelligence or of the information ministry. More lived on subsidies funnelled through the Mufti or Rashid Ali, who bitterly quarrelled over precedence.

The Germans planned to install the two men as heads of puppet governments in their respective countries. Currency was printed and uniforms manufactured for the projected Iraqi regime, though this would have been better done in 1941 than in 1942. Germany's challenge in the Middle East had ended in anticlimax.[26]

As London had correctly predicted, the Jews threw themselves behind the Allied cause. The Zionists were at the same time able to carry out their own aims: lobbying for a Jewish brigade in the British army, using military training to strengthen the Haganah, continuing "illegal immigration" beyond the quotas permitted by the White Paper, and independently gathering intelligence.[27]

The Baghdad pogrom encouraged formation of a Jewish underground in Iraq, printing Zionist books, distributing arms, teaching Hebrew, and smuggling emigrants across the border. Increasing government pressure through restrictions on Jewish economic activity disillusioned many in the community. Local Jewish leaders, nevertheless, remained optimistic about their future in Iraq; al-Said's regime won good will by paying compensation for the riot damage.[28]

Dovish Zionists also worked to keep open lines of communication with moderate Arabs. Aharon Cohen and Chaim Kalvarisky of the League for Rapprochement and Cooperation visited Syria and Lebanon in September 1942. They met members of the Naqqash family, with whom good relations had been established in the 1930s, Riyad and Sami al-Sulh, Lebanese Muslims who would later become prime ministers, and Jamil Mardam and Hashim al-Atassi, leaders of the Syrian National Bloc. They found no interest in discussing a Jewish state, but there was a willingness to maintain contacts. Other Zionists went to Transjordan, Egypt, and Iraq while influential Arabs from those countries also came to Palestine.[29]

But the most important new factor in the aftermath of the German collapse was the entrance of the United States into the Palestine controversy. True, the Zionists had long lobbied in Washington and Ibn Saud had tried to work through the American oil companies. Nevertheless, only during World War II did U.S. interests clearly extend to the Middle East. As an ally of Great Britain, America's first objective was to keep the Arabs as friendly as possible toward the Allies. King Ibn Saud became something of a special American responsibility. In May 1942, Secretary of State Cordell Hull, writing for President Roosevelt, promised him that U.S. policy would make no decision on Palestine without full consultation with both sides.[30]

Like Britain, the United States saw the Palestine problem in a military-strategic context, and this meant concern over its effect on the Arab states. "There are only 16,000,000 Jews throughout the world. But there are 320,000,000 Moslems," noted General George Strong, chief of staff for army intelligence. To antagonize them would endanger Allied supply routes to Russia, Middle East rear areas, and oil reserves. Conduct of the war required avoiding any outbreak of violence among the Arabs. This in turn meant soft-peddling any appearance of U.S. sympathy for Zionism. Already, congressional resolutions had fostered anit-American feeling in Egypt, Lebanon, Syria and Iraq. For Washington's policy-makers and military commanders, Palestine was defined at this early date as a potential barrier to improved relations with the Arab states. This view would profoundly shape their postwar recommendations for a stand on the issue.[31]

Given such pressures, there was strong temptation to seek some quick fix to resolve all contradictions. Churchill and Roosevelt were open to such suggestions. As always, there was no shortage on panaceas being offered by various official, semiofficial, and free-lance figures. One bizarre adventure centered around H. St. John Philby, English convert to Islam, close friend and sometime-adviser to King Ibn Saud. If the king was paid £20 million, Philby told his many contacts, he could become leader of the Arab world. In exchange, he would cede Palestine to the Jews.

Philby never quite said whether or not the king himself knew anything about this scheme, but Churchill judged it a capital idea. As Weizmann prepared to leave for America in March 1942, the British prime minister startled him with his plan to make Ibn Saud "Lord of the Middle East — the boss of bosses — provided he settles with you." Weizmann could only assume that Churchill knew something; President Roosevelt chose to do the same. Several months later, British and American representatives actually broached the matter to the king, who was outraged at what he called an attempted bribe. As with so many earlier mediation attempts, the whole affair ended in confusion and contradiction.[32]

Such debacles should not, however, prove misleading about the impact of the early war period on Palestine's future. Never had so little happened within the country itself, yet a whole new era had begun in the relations between the Arab states and that tangled issue. First, the defeat of the radical faction in Iraq and Palestine as well as its allies elsewhere set back the overthrow of the post–World War I regimes by a decade or more. The revolutions in Iraq and Egypt would come too late to affect the fate of mandatory Palestine. Two important corollaries of these events were the discrediting of the Palestine Arab leadership in the West and the weakening of its hold at home. The Mufti's decision to cast his lot with the Germans had a heavy cost. Transjordan's position revived in inverse proportions to the problems of the Husayni party. Amman's loyalty to the victorious side enhanced Abdallah's standing with Great Britain.

Second, the idea of greater inter-Arab cooperation and unity had also increased its legitimacy at home and abroad. The defeat of the militant Pan-Arab school in Iraq might have made an apocalyptic merger less likely, but it cleared the way for collaboration on a state-to-state level. The implied acceptance that such entities as Syria, Iraq, or Egypt would not disappear in the immediate future removed a barrier to their working together in their present status. The British accepted that such a state of affairs might not be a bad thing, while the *de facto* decline in French influence made possible for the first time real participation by Syria and Lebanon.

This had been achieved by two conflicting phenomena: the ability of the Arab states to pose a threat in the late 1930s and, conversely, the need to reward them for their wartime assistance. These factors, combined with the weakness of the Palestine Arab leadership, meant much greater influence for the Arab states in Palestine. Indeed, they seemed to become custodians or trustees of Palestine Arab interests. In 1939 they had been unable to carry the White Paper against the Mufti's opposition. Two years later, Iraq and Transjordan were once again openly planning to annex Palestine. In a sense, it was a triumph for a trend visible since 1936–37: the response of the Arab states to the Palestine question had now become more important to Britain (or the United States for that matter) than developments in Palestine itself.

By 1943, all Arab leaders who had survived this turbulent era were looking toward the postwar readjustments which were so clearly necessary. The questions of Palestine, Anglo-Egyptian relations, Syria and Lebanese independence, and Arab unity would surely come onto the international political agenda. The masters of Egypt, Iraq and Transjordan could all hope that these issues offered opportunities for exercising leadership, but the stabilization of separate Arab states also entailed the heightening of competition between them.

In the last three years of the war, the Arab states were deeply involved in plans, plots, and counterplots designed to favorably place them in the new alignment of forces. The Arab League would symbolize the positive aspects of this new order, while Palestine would be a prime object and a prime subject in its definition.

9
The Division over Unity: 1943–45

The Arab political crisis of 1941–42 had brought many changes. Nuri al-Said was returned to power by the British; his militant opponents were imprisoned or fled to Germany. The Wafd displaced the palace politicians in Egypt, though its dependence on British bayonets to regain power damaged its popularity. Transjordan's loyalty to the Allies broke Emir Abdallah's post-1937 isolation. The removal of the Mufti and his closest supporters gave more moderate independents a chance to fill the vacuum in Palestine Arab leadership. In short, the radical factions had been destroyed for the time being. With these internal conflicts settled, the focus of Arab politics once again shifted toward interstate competition.

Many Arab leaders were optimistic over the opportunities offered by this reshuffle. For the first time since 1918, Pan-Arab proposals seemed capable of gaining British sponsorship. Iraq and Transjordan considered expansion into Syria or Palestine. To avoid this, Egypt and Saudi Arabia advocated a looser Arab confederation of equals. Nevertheless, any Arab state could spin out plans for Palestine without worrying about the local leadership's response or the Mufti's veto.

Although Palestinian Istiqlalists like Ahmad Hilmi, Awni Abd al-Hadi, and Rashid al-Hajj Ibrahim tried to rebuild the Palestine Arab movement, the task was not an easy one. The July 1943 and February 1944 preparatory conferences leading toward the Arab League met without Palestine Arab representation.[1]

Privately, the British had little enthusiasm for either the Fertile Crescent or Greater Syria merger plans, but it was not useful to publicly

133

state such doubts. Eden's continued speeches encouraged both Nuri al-Said and Emir Abdallah to further press their proposals. They winked at the very real British reservations that such schemes would be acceptable only if approved by all Arabs—a most unlikely prospect.[2]

Still insecure over his reintegration into Arab councils, Abdallah presented his most hard-line program toward the Zionists. Jewish population in Palestine should be set at 33 percent while immigration would be prohibited. In exchange, he did not even offer local autonomy but only promised them an effective administration. Beyond Palestine, however, he wanted control of Lebanon and Syria as well. Indeed, if Palestine posed too much difficulty, he was willing to omit it from the projected federation.

The basis of his claim, said the emir, was his effective assistance to the Allies, his inheritance from the Sharif Husayn, alleged (and rather doubtful) 1921 promises from Churchill to make him head of Syria, and the supposed — equally doubtful — support for him among the local peoples. He was not reticent about placing these arguments before inter-Arab meetings, where they deepened the suspicions of his fellow rulers.[3]

Nuri al-Said, who saw Greater Syria as only a part of a larger state to include Iraq, offered Jews in Palestine a "semi-autonomous administration" in areas where they formed a majority. They might have their own schools, policy, and health institutions as a Jewish national home under supervision of the Fertile Crescent government. Their safety would be ensured by Arab "good will." While al-Said admitted that minority guarantees had not functioned well in Europe—not to mention Iraq—he was sure that problems could be resolved.[4]

Egypt's Prime Minister Nahhas took a third approach which was the most conciliatory toward the Zionists. His Wafd party, by disposition and in line with Egypt's national interests, did not want any such federation. After a successful five-day visit to Palestine in June 1943, he declared an Arab-Jewish understanding necessary for any settlement. The Jews should be invited to a conference of Arab nations to discuss terms, he suggested. Since King Farouk was only awaiting an opportunity to dispose of the British-imposed prime minister, however Nahhas could scarcely carry forward any such plan.[5]

The Saudis had no positive blueprint to compare with those spelled out by Iraq and Transjordan, but King Ibn Saud was as determined as ever to yield nothing to Zionist claims. Any Western support for Zionism, he warned in a May 1943 interview, would cause conflict with the Arabs. Jewish refugees should return to Europe or go to America. At any rate, he concluded, he knew the Jews would never have a state, based on his reading of the Koran.[6]

Such complaints were not taken lightly in London or Washington, as both governments sought to dampen domestic campaigns in support of a Jewish state. They agreed to make a public statement postponing any decision over Palestine until after the war. At the last minute, the United States backed away, a retreat due to American disenchantment over British Middle East policy as well as to Zionist lobbying. With the beginnings of Anglo-American competition in the region, the U.S. government was not eager to tie itself to any British policy there.[7]

Besides, a whole new problem soon arose. In January 1944, a resolution introduced in Congress advocated Palestine's transformation into a national home for the Jewish people. The United States would "take appropriate measures" to support free immigration of Jews so that they "may ultimately reconstitute Palestine as a free and democratic Jewish commonwealth." State Department specialists were horrified by the potential effect on Arab-American relations. Already, Iraqis had read pro-Zionist advertisements in the *New York Times* as implying official U.S. endorsement for evicting all Arabs from the territory. As one intelligence officer put it, the danger was equivalent to a "trainload of dynamite."[8]

American oil executives actively fought the proposed resolution, persuading Secretary of War Henry Stimson to intervene with the two foreign affairs committees. Its passage, he told them, threatened the war effort. Wallace Murray, senior State Department advisor on the region, concurred. The Arabs, he told Secretary of State Edward Stettinius, were "bewildered and disillusioned by U.S. policy" and might therefore turn to Moscow or London for political and commercial succor. President Roosevelt was convinced of the danger posed by the resolutions, and they disappeared in committee, never to be seen again.[9]

This showed the potential Arab leverage over U.S. policy. Zionist lobbying might be effective in relation to election campaigns — pro-Zionist planks appeared in both Democratic and Republican platforms— but what really counted was the execution of policy by the White House and State Department. Here, rather than on public opinion, was where the Arab case met the best response. Iraqi, Egyptian, and Lebanese prime ministers simply explained how their desire for close relations with America could only be realized if Washington kept its distance from Zionism.[10]

Ibn Saud coordinated Arab efforts toward the United States. He organized a letter-writing campaign by Arab heads of government and strongly suggested to Arabian-American Oil Company executives that they ensure representation for the Arab case on Palestine. If Britain and the United States did not support Arab interests in Palestine, he told the American minister in Jidda, they would lose Saudi friendship. The Arabs would fight to the last man against any further Jewish immigration.

When the king met with Roosevelt in February 1945, he tried to make the president understand the seriousness of the conflict. Roosevelt, preoccupied by the recently ended Yalta summit meeting, was naive about Arab sentiments, confident as usual that he could charm opponents into flexibility and compromise. Obviously, Ibn Saud did not succumb. When asked by James Byrnes, powerful advisor and future secretary of state, how the conversation had gone, Roosevelt twice changed the subject. Finally, Byrnes cornered him. "Mr. President," he said, "I fear you were not very successful." "Oh yes," Roosevelt lamented, "I had an exceedingly pleasant meeting with Ibn Saud and we agreed about everything until I mentioned Palestine. That was the end of the pleasant conversation."[11]

Roosevelt's famous aplomb was momentarily shaken by the encounter, and certainly Ibn Saud conveyed the potential tension of the issue. Roosevelt later told Congress that he learned more about the conflict "by talking with Ibn Saud for five minutes than I could have learned in exchange of two or three dozen letters." But this did not imply, as some contemporaries thought, that the king had convinced the president of anything. Ibn Saud was only able to extract a renewed American promise of consultations before any action was taken. This was cold comfort when coupled with Roosevelt's declaration of support for unrestricted Jewish immigration and for creation of a Jewish state.[12]

The Arabs had gained a hearing in Washington without obtaining any meaningful commitments. Roosevelt was more than happy to leave the prickly problem to his successor. The Arabs had, however, persuaded State Department Middle East experts and some War Department strategists that support for Zionism spelled trouble with the Arab states. Such opinions had their value for the Arabs in the decisive days of 1947 and 1948, but they would not be enough to carry the day.

Arab unity over Palestine seemed the most effective way of impressing the West, and this was much easier to achieve than was cooperation on broader questions. At the October 1944 Arab conference in Alexandria, Egypt, Saudi Arabia strongly attacked the merger plans proposed by Iraq and Transjordan. They literally shouted down the Fertile Crescent proposal and, though this hardly dampened Baghdad's enthusiasm, placed on record the infeasibility of any political union.[13]

Discussions over Palestine went far smoother. True, at first the Arab states were hesitant about Palestine Arab participation—this was, after all, a meeting of independent states — but Abdallah unexpectedly emerged as their champion. This was a sound political move. With the Husayni group momentarily out of the picture, Transjordan had a priceless opportunity to help consolidate a more moderate faction. Musa al-Alami had talked five Palestine Arab parties into designating him their joint delegate. Moreover, al-Alami was willing to accept the White Paper. Though Nahhas' call for a more conciliatory line toward the Jews was rejected, the chance seemed bright for producing a new and more successful Arab position.[14]

Alami's acceptance as an observer and participant was emotional and dramatic. During earlier sessions, he sat at a small side table. When it came time to discuss Palestine it seemed incongruous that he remain in the corner like a "bad boy." He was welcomed to the main table with kisses and embraces; his calm and quiet speech, which stayed on generalities, moved some delegates to tears. Ibn Saud brought the session back to earth by warning against too strong a resolution during the U. S. election campaign. He and al-Alami suggested such practical measures as establishing an Arab land development fund and a string of Arab information bureaus in the West.

Palestine and Syrian independence were the only major issues on which the conferees agreed, but they did lay the basis for the Arab League. Egypt, Iraq, Saudi Arabia, Syria, Lebanon, Transjordan, and Yemen all joined in declaring Palestine an important part of the Arab world. Infringement of Arab rights there, they added, might threaten regional peace and stability. On a tactical level, they had aided a more moderate Palestine leadership whose views were in line with those of the Arab governments. Their expressed confidence in the White Paper was a second step toward a diplomatic solution.[15]

Transjordan's emir worked hard to build ties to the new Palestinian Arab activists. Only he, among all the Arab leaders, accurately gauged the Zionists' power and organization. He pulled no punches over the Arabs "backward state of development" in Palestine, while the Jews "are constantly increasing their hold on the country." While the Zionists were "cultivating the sandy areas, boring wells, recovering dead lands and converting them into gardens of paradise," he wrote, "Arab parties are still fighting over the claims to leadership of those men who were responsible for the ruin of their country." Since the Mufti's strategy had clearly failed, Abdallah argued, someone else should be given a chance.[16]

The British were already conscious, however, that the heat of war had only provided them a brief respite from dealing with the Palestine problem. If the new Arab leadership there offered some possibility of political compromise, pressure from the Arab states implied that no procrastination would be tolerated. In Iraq, public opinion was once again demanding action and prompting top officials to warn of bloodshed unless a unified Palestine was granted independence.[17]

There was little doubt about the passion still aroused by the issue in Baghdad. The man in the street argued from Islamic premises which his leaders placed in Arab nationalist categories. To the common people, Jews were miserly, cowardly, and unclean; the idea of their governing a portion of the Arab world was intolerable. "Palestine," said a January 1945 U. S. intelligence report, "has become more than a remote political problem; it is now a question of personal religion and honor." England's minister to Saudi Arabia spoke in similar terms: "The Palestine problem is the gravest problem occupying the thoughts of Muslims and Arabs today."[18]

The war had suspended the necessity for London to produce some political resolution. With the war at an end, the way out was no clearer than it had been in 1939. The division among British policy-makers was demonstrated by an April 1944 conference held at British Middle East headquarters in Cairo. The White Paper was dead, argued Lampson, and the Arabs would never accept partition. Therefore, Palestine should remain under British control because of its strategic value as well as the lack of any alternative. Other diplomats thought the White Paper still workable; MacMichael thought partition the least of many evils. Churchill was more friendly toward Zionism than were the Foreign Office officials. It was impossible to agree on any major policy change as long as the war continued.[19]

The Zionists were more united than the British, but were equally at a loss to find some strategy which might neutralize Arab leverage. They could decry the influence of the Arab states, as they had done in 1939, but this would not make it go away nor would it convince London to alienate the Arab governments. Ben-Gurion might argue that Egyptian pashas, Bedouin shaikhs, or Iraqi beys had no rights or interests in Palestine, but this was a mere abstraction.

In practice, Zionists could not ignore the effects of Arab anger on Jews in Palestine or in the neighboring countries. One way to break through the circle of hostility was for them to formulate a symbiotic alliance with Lebanese Christian nationalists. In September 1944, Eliahu Epstein of the Jewish Agency arrived in Beirut. His cover story was a survey tour on the problems of Jewish refugees passing through Lebanon, but his real mandate was to forge a political entente. Epstein complained about Maronite leaders' attacks on Zionism in the Lebanese Chamber of Deputies. Rather than join the crowd, he suggested Lebanese Christian political and religious leaders should cooperate against the common enemy: Islamic-oriented Arab nationalism.[20]

With independence imminent, his interlocuters were split on this very question. Were the Muslims an enemy who threatened to sweep away any independent Christian-dominated Lebanon? Or might the Muslims be treated as allies in the struggle against French colonialism? The former idea would make any break with the French difficult; the latter proposal could lead to a post-independence accord with the Muslims to guarantee stability in the new Lebanon. Although Eddé and his supporters dissented, the majority chose the alternative of peace with the Muslims. The compromise they forged, the "National Pact," succeeded in preserving Christian predominance and prosperity for three decades.

Anti-Zionism was a necessary precondition for this arrangement. On August 15, 1944, Riyad al-Sulh, leader of the Beirut Palestine support group, organized a broad meeting which included the Islamic Najadeh party, the Communists, and the Christian nationalist Kataeb. This alliance scuttled the possibility of Jewish-Lebanese Christian collaboration on any large scale. The move toward an Arab League, signalled at Alexandria, frightened some Christians with the specter of absorption into an enlarged Arab state. In this context, Eddé and other Maronites continued to believe in the utility of Zionist assistance.[21]

Six months later, Eddé and other Maronites sent a sealed letter through Weizmann to President Roosevelt. They declared that Arab unity would sound the death knell of all non-Muslim minorities in the region and they pleaded for U. S. aid to prevent this disaster. One of the signers, Patriarch Antoine Arida, sent a similar missive to American Maronites via Tuvia Araza, another Zionist emissary. Arida attacked the Arab League and warned of Arab states' aggressive intentions toward Lebanon. Arida's enemies tried with some success to discredit him by leaking this polemic to the Lebanese press. Yet Arida and a number of Lebanese Maronite politicians took this threat so seriously that they signed a mutual assistance pact with the Zionists.[22]

Tuvia Araza was typical of the young Zionist Arabists who were trying to maintain contacts and gather intelligence in the Arab countries. Born in Palestine, he studied archaeology and Semitic languages in Paris, joining the Transjordan Frontier Force for a year to perfect his

Arabic. In 1938–39, he was liaison officer between the Jewish Agency and Jewish settlement police fighting the Arab rebellion. The following year, he worked in Syria organizing Free French propaganda on assignment for the Jewish Agency and British intelligence.

Pretending to be a tradesman, he sent back valuable information for the Allied invasion of Syria until his capture in the spring of 1941. Tortured by the collaborationist French authorities, he escaped by jumping from a second-story window and, despite a broken ankle, he managed to recross the border into Palestine. After a brief period in the Jewish Agency's Political Department, Araza attended the American University in Beirut, keeping the agency informed on local political developments. He again returned to Palestine in the summer of 1944, to work in the Agency's Arab Affairs section. During his years in the United States, Araza and coworkers helped Arida's Maronite supporters publicize their cause and combat the pro-National Pact faction.

Within Lebanon itself, Archbishop Ignatz Mubarak of Beirut was the most important Maronite contact. Zionist visitors met with him and other high-ranking clergymen. Though he complained about government persecution due to his beliefs, Mubarak gave pro-Zionist testimony before the 1946 Anglo-American Committee of Inquiry and was later one of the very few voices in the Arab world to speak out for partition. Lebanese officials, like Yusuf Harfouche, under-secretary of the Foreign Ministry, privately blamed Lebanon's Palestine policy on pressure from other League members. In their hearts, Harfouche said, most Lebanese (though he undoubtedly meant Maronites) felt some degree of kinship with the Zionists.[23]

Of course, such sentiments, inasmuch as they existed, had little practical effect. Many Lebanese Christians — particularly among the non-Maronites, became sincere Arab nationalists precisely because they saw this as an areligious creed through which Islamic primacy might be neutralized. The rest went along for largely domestic reasons. The only alternative to a pact with Lebanese Muslims was civil war and, since the resulting agreement was quite satisfactory for Christian interests, this posed little temptation.

Lebanese Christians might have been less enthusiastic about the Arab-Israeli conflict than were their Muslim neighbors, but they never thereafter broke ranks. Only in the mid-1970s, when the National Pact broke down into civil war and the long-feared Syrian invasion was upon them did the main Maronite parties accept alliance with Israel. Ben-Gurion's oft-cited dictum, that Lebanon would be the second Arab country to make peace with Israel, was thus realized in a limited sense.

But as a country, Lebanon was too weak and divided to ever take such a risky step.

Aside from Lebanon, Zionist diplomacy was preoccupied with aiding the Jewish minorities in the neighboring Arab countries. Arab governments claimed that Jews were well treated, and indeed Iraqi and Egyptian regimes often protected them from reprisals. Historically, the record is most complicated; Jewish life in the Arab world was neither a litany of unbroken persecution nor a hymn to toleration. From time to time and from place to place conditions varied greatly. Persecution was sporadic, but discrimination and humiliation were never absent. If Jews were active in the cultural, intellectual, and economic life of Baghdad or Cairo in the 1920s and 1930s, there were also many things in which they did not politically or psychologically participate. Palestine was by no means the only barrier to their integration. The ever-present influence of Islam and the shape which Arab nationalism took also tended to set them apart. The Palestine issue merely accelerated and completed the process.[24]

By 1944, only fifty-six hundred Iraqi Jews out of one hundred and twenty thousand, and only two thousand Syrian and Lebanese Jews out of thirty thousand had emigrated to Palestine. Still, these figures are not inconsiderable, given the weakness of Zionist ideology and organizational structure in those countries and the uncertain prospects faced by Jews in Palestine itself. Nor had the region been so insulated from the anti-Semitic atmosphere in Europe. Axis propaganda was intensive, and Jews were denounced in mosques as enemies of Islam. The June 1941 Baghdad pogrom was almost followed by a massacre in Damascus two years later. Traditional prejudice, second-hand Nazi explanations, and anti-Zionism merged to form an acid brew. Sometimes mercenary motives were also present: Yemeni Jews were permitted to leave for Palestine after 1943 on condition that they turn their property over to the government.[25]

When Aden's four thousand Jews prepared to celebrate the war's end by raising British, American, and Jewish flags above their shops and school, Arabs tore down the Mogen David banner. By the time British authorities intervened, Arab attackers were breaking down the gate of the beseiged school. The riot was ended when police persuaded the Jews themselves to lower the flag. "You see," one Jewish goldsmith explained, "the surrender of Germany meant that we were to be free again, but the first manifestation of that freedom here in Aden was bitterly resented by the Arabs."

In places like Aden, rising Jewish nationalism seemed to challenge the established order. Jews were no longer willing to accept the continuous, if rarely fatal, harassment to which tradition subjected them. They were angered when British officials and local Arab police did not provide protection. Events were eroding their centuries-long passivity.[26]

The particularly prosperous Egyptian Jewish community grew from seven thousand in 1800, to thirty-eight thousand in 1900, and to sixty-three thousand by 1937. Heavily urbanized (54 percent in Cairo, 39 percent in Alexandria), many Jews were successful in commerce and industry. Half of them were nominally citizens of European countries, as were large numbers of the Greeks, Italians, and Levant Arabs who dominated modern sectors of Egypt's economy. Some became senators or palace functionaries, like Joseph Cattaui, a minister of finance and member of the Chamber of Deputies in the 1920s. Only a minority openly espoused Zionism (about three thousand activists plus a large number of sympathizers), but the movement was stronger in Egypt than in any other Arab country.

By 1944, the press and politicians were demanding bans on Egyptian Zionist organizations. *Al Balagh* warned they would soon turn Egypt into "a vassal of Tel Aviv." But the authorities were relatively tolerant. When the Department of Public Security asked in February 1945, for the arrest of Zionist leader Leon Castro, its main concern were the novel grounds that to leave him free would damage Egypt's prestige in other Arab states.[27]

There too, however, outbreaks were becoming more common by the end of the war, culminating in the November 2, 1945 riots in Cairo and Alexandria. Demonstrations had been planned on the anniversary of the Balfour Declaration to protest British policy in Palestine. A broad range of organizations, student groups, and political parties endorsed the idea, but their preparations were inadequate. Rather than a peaceful march, the results were mob attacks and looting at Jewish stores and synagogues. Greek and Armenian establishments were also attacked. By 12:45 P.M. twenty thousand people proceeded to the palace, ransacking shops along the way as police watched. Muslim Brotherhood leader Hassan al-Banna finally managed to disperse the crowd, and the Wafd party dissociated itself from the violence. As long as the Jews did not support Zionism, Nahhas told community leaders, they would be safe. Still, even though only 109 of the 500 shops pillaged were owned by Jews, their sense of security was shattered.[28]

Iraqi Jews had already reached this point. Far fewer identified with Zionism, and protection money to the police seemed effective in staving off pogroms. Nevertheless, the Haganah and Irgun undergrounds found new recruits. Some young Jews followed their alienation into the Communist party, where they founded a short-lived Anti-Zionist League. As fiery speeches more and more filled Baghdad's mosques, however, the official communal leadership concentrated on securing promises of protection from the government.[29]

The future status of these Jewish communities was only one of a hundred issues which breathlessly awaited resolution as the war ended. The Palestine question itself must now come out of suspended animation along with other aspects of Middle East politics. Could the Arabs take up where they had left off in 1939? Would the momentum of the London conference and the White Paper be revived?

Surface indications were favorable. The rush of events in 1945 seemed to confirm the Arab cause's ascendancy. The membership of a half-dozen Arab states in the new United Nations promised them an important say in all international disputes. The Arab League pact of March 22, institutionalized Arab state cooperation as a power bloc. The Holocaust, while augmenting Zionism's moral claim, decimated Jewish ranks. The Germans were gone, but London needed Arab help against the Russians. Even the election victory of the historically pro-Zionist Labor party brought to power a British government friendlier to the Arabs than Churchill had been.[30]

Arab confidence was understandable, but more had changed than they realized. Despite all these events, the Arabs had actually lost some ground relative to 1939. In the final analysis, the intrusion of the United States into the region produced an important force which countered Britain's position. The Holocaust had brought not only international sympathy for the Jews but also a whole pool of refugees eager to emigrate to Palestine. Arab unity against Zionism held, but the Arab states could not so easily agree on strategy and ultimate aims. While Jews in Palestine had expanded their settlements and military organization, the Palestine Arabs had recorded few such positive achievements during the war. Finally, the rapid return of the Husaynis to the Palestine Arab leadership was not only a public relations disaster but a strategic one as well. Once again, Arab diplomacy's hands were tied by maximalist and rigid positions.

This last change was not achieved without opposition. Musa al-Alami tried to follow up his success at Alexandria by preventing the Mufti from returning to Palestine. He also courted Jamil al-Husayni, who chose to remain faithful to his cousin, the Mufti, rather than join Musa, his brother-in-law. Some British officials as well as Nuri al-Said had also hoped that Jamil would help formulate a new, more moderate leadership.[31]

The Arab states were not yet ready to give up their enlarged influence over the Palestine Arab movement. Certainly, they wanted no repetition of the 1939 experience, when the Mufti had dictated their response to the White Paper. Yet they also failed to act decisively. Al-Alami had ample reason for his later judgment that the incumbent Arab regimes were too ineffective to build a strong Arab League. A change of government in practically every country would be advantageous for his people, al-Alami thought.

In particular, al-Alami tried to convince Arab leaders to use their leverage in order to mediate conflicts within the Palestinian camp and to help the moderates maintain power. His second objective was to get Arab government financial aid for the Arab information offices in London and Washington and for a land-purchase plan in Palestine (in competition with an Iraqi-backed Istiqlal land fund). Ali Mahir refused to become involved. The Arab League Council instead designated Jamil Mardam, Syria's minister to Cairo, as mediator with the task of unifying six rival Palestinian groups into a new Higher Committee.[32]

Mardam's mission was only a temporary success. After a week of meetings, he was able to organize a twelve-man leadership commission. Although its presidency was left open for the Mufti, his Palestine Arab party held only five of the remaining seats. The others went to dissident groups, including the National Defense party and the Istiqlal, and two independents, al-Alami numbering among the latter. The commission quickly became more of a battleground than a force for unity. Jamil al-Husayni out-maneuvered the smaller groups which had filled the wartime vacuum. Nor would the Mufti himself long be out of the picture. In the closing days of the war, the Germans had tried to spirit him to a neutral country, but he was captured and interned by the French. The following year he escaped under mysterious circumstances, finally reaching safety in Egypt in December 1946. For a man who had supported open rebellion against the British and who had hobnobbed with Hitler in Berlin, it was a remarkable comeback.[33]

Al-Alami could well complain about the Arab League, but it did undertake to focus the Arab diplomatic effort. The old divisions, of course, had not disappeared. Iraq and Transjordan still spoke of their plans for absorbing neighbors, and Egypt made little secret out of its belief that it should dominate the League. "We will play the part in the Arab League that Britain does in the British Commonwealth," boasted Senator Mahmud Abd al-Fath. This claim had to be taken seriously, since the League's headquarters (Cairo) and secretary-general (Azzam) were both Egyptian.[34]

This did not necessarily entail, as al-Alami discovered, generosity toward the Palestinian Arabs. The Egyptian government promised £50,000 for al-Alami's land fund, cut the figure back to £20,000, and finally gave nothing. However, al-Alami was told, if Cairo was allowed to choose the fund's administrators, it would contribute £200,000. Al-Alami angrily refused.[35]

Azzam's energy seemed to make up for some of these faults. Al-Alami considered, with some reason, that Azzam was impetuous and irresponsible, making contradictory pledges and unnecessary accusations which complicated an already difficult situation. Often, his ambiguity and seeming confusion merely reflected conflicts within the Arab camp. His pyrotechnic threats of violence were aimed at frightening the Zionists, Americans, and British into making major concessions. He knew that if challenged, the Arabs would have to go to war, and he sometimes sensed that the overwhelming triumph he frequently predicted could not be delivered. Still, given the state of Arab public opinion, there was little choice.[36]

Neither Damascus nor Baghdad was totally reconciled to working primarily through Azzam. Iraqi leaders distrusted him and tried to play an independent hand in Palestine through their support for the Istiqlal and their subsidies for the Arab information offices. In Syria, the National Bloc beat off an attempt by smaller parties to seize the issue through their own Committee for the Defense of Palestine. The Egyptians and Saudis acted unilaterally (though with support from the other Arab states) to lobby in the United States. In particular, they opposed President Truman's proposal of October 1945, to admit one hundred thousand Jewish refugees into Palestine.[37]

If the Arab states agreed on avoiding a Jewish state, they were not so sure as to the best strategy. A particular difficulty was to estimate British intentions. Many Arabs, like Azzam, believed that London was on their side—the United States was the real problem. It was simply necessary to apply a carrot-and-stick approach to the great powers. As long as Washington and London accepted Arab demands, the Jews could be safely ignored. The Foreign Office encouraged the notion that only American pressure was blocking a pro-Arab solution.

The first step in implementing this analysis was to win confirmation from the United States and reaffirmation from Great Britain that the Arab states had a legitimate special role in Palestine. This was in line with the Alexandria Protocol and the Arab League Pact and constituted the immediate objective of the Arab delegations to the April 1945 founding meeting of the United Nations in San Francisco. Although the Arab states did not win the abrogation of the League of Nations mandate in favor of a transitional trusteeship leading to independence, they amply demonstrated their deep concern over the Palestine issue. While their right to intimate involvement, won at the time of the 1936 general strike, was not enshrined in any international accord, the precedent seemed generally accepted.[38]

Three other objectives would remain at the center of Arab diplomacy over the following two years. First, the Arab states had to coordinate policy with the Palestine Arab movement, preferably in a manner which left them freedom of action. Second, the Arab governments had to demonstrate conclusively to England and America that refusal of their demands would lead to highly dangerous regional instability and to the destruction of those two countries' interests in the area. Finally, a plan for the transformation of Palestine into a unified, independent state under Arab rule must be formulated and accepted by Britain. Jewish opposition would have to be neutralized in this process.

Relations with the Palestinian Arabs were tackled first. The exile and collaboration of the Husayni leadership with the Axis had discredited them. Many Arab politicians did not have fond memories of the Mufti's 1939 policies, and consequently when a vacuum was created within the Palestinian movement an opportunity was created for Iraq and Transjordan to press their plans to annex Palestine.

While the Palestinians were in receivership during the war period, it would be misleading to oversimplify their relationship with the Arab states in the years immediately following 1945. The renewed Husayni leadership played an important role in the 1947–48 developments which very deeply affected the fortunes of the Arab states. In some ways, the relationship was parallel to the friction over the diplomacy of 1939. The Arab governments once more had to take into account the Mufti's charismatic potential and his veto over strategic concessions.

Yet the tensions between the Palestine Arab leadership and the Arab states surfaced more potently in two indirect ways. While Arab governments wanted to keep for themselves the diplomatic initiative, they depended on the Palestinian Arabs to win any military confrontation. Only the failure in battle of the local forces made necessary the intervention of the regular Arab armies. Arab regimes were thus dependent on the Mufti for a victorious military organization and generalship which he could not provide.

Of equal importance, the Mufti's return to the helm ignited once again the sharp rivalry between him and his Transjordanian neighbor. Abdallah refused to accept the idea of Husayni-dominated Palestine. Transjordan's determination to intervene at all costs acted as a first step in a chain reaction which would force all Arab states to follow.

Doubtless, the Mufti had good reason to suspect the ambitions of more than one of his neighbors. The Arab League remembered that the Husaynis had been reinstalled through their intervention, but the Husaynis remembered that the League had more than once tried to checkmate them by establishing a balance of power built on independents and smaller parties. The mediation of Mardam, and a June 1946 mission of Azzam both failed. The League then unilaterally named a new Higher Arab Committee executive, designating it — as they would do with the PLO three decades later—the sole legitimate representative of the Palestine Arabs. Once again, the main figures of the 1930s were dominant even though they, unlike the League's member governments, were neither sanguine about a settlement with the British nor enthusiastic about a White Paper-based solution.[39]

If the personalities involved had changed little since 1939, World War II had vastly altered the political frame of reference. True, the British Empire's retreat was beginning, and this must lead to Palestine's independence, but a wide variety of possibilities were still open. The war's dissolution of accustomed relationships allowed for new blueprints and new ambitions. The Arab League was established as a forum for cooperation, but the legitimization of separate states also validated their rights to different, even conflicting, goals.

The portents seemed to favor the Arabs. The White Paper legacy, Anglo-American desire for Arab friendship, Arab unity, the weight of Arab states in international political councils, and the increased importance of Arab oil were only some of their advantages. There was also an Arab consensus on the centrality of the Palestine question and the necessity that Arab states should fully participate in its resolution. Yet a key question remained: Was the surest way to victory through diplomacy or would only a test of arms suffice?

10
The Failure of Arab Diplomacy: 1946–47

*T*he Arab idea that British Middle East policy gave them much leverage over Palestine was essentially accurate. If between 1937 and 1945 British caution was necessary to prevent an Arab-German alliance, after 1945 the Soviet Union appeared an equally serious threat. On top of all its historical strategic and commercial interests, England needed at least the Arab states' passive acquiescence to the exigencies of the Cold War.[1]

Equally compelling, Great Britain's postwar weakness required a reassessment of strategic and political commitments which necessitated greater Arab cooperation than ever before. London was seeking the best possible terms for the maintenance of key bases and for the continued protection of the Suez Canal. Concessions had to be made because of the changed political atmosphere as the colonial era began to fade into history. Without its past military and economic strength, British policy was more than ever dependent on the carrot rather than the stick. Consequently, new treaties had to be made acceptable to Iraq, Egypt, and Transjordan to adjust their bilateral relations with England.

The escalating cost of the Palestine mandate in terms of Arab antagonisms and of Jewish guerrilla warfare, placed a time limit on this search for an escape route. Annoyed at American support for Zionism, Foreign Minister Ernest Bevin sought to associate Washington in this process through the Anglo-American Committee of Inquiry and, later, the Morrison-Grady plan. When it became clear that no solution was possibly acceptable to both Arabs and Zionists, London dropped the issue into the lap of the United Nations.

Given the balance sheet of British objectives, many contemporary chroniclers overstated the Machiavellian element in British Middle East policy, particularly over its handling of Palestine. London's influence over the Arab League and its member governments should not be exaggerated. Despite attempts to turn events in its favor, British policy was basically on the defensive, retreating before Arab, American, and Zionist pressure, buffeted by no longer affordable expenses and the distaste of international public opinion.[2]

Some policy-makers, probably including Anthony Eden, had believed that creation of the Arab League would facilitate a peaceful solution in Palestine. Yet it also concentrated Arab opposition in the event that London did not find a satisfactory solution.[3] Bevin quickly learned the wider danger: "The repercussions of the conflict have spread far beyond the small land in which it has arisen," he told the House of Commons on November 13, 1945. The Zionists had their supporters in the United States, Great Britain, and elsewhere, he continued, but "the cause of the Palestine Arabs has been espoused by the whole Arab world and more lately has become a matter of keen interest to their 90 million co-religionists in India." Disturbances in Palestine would be reflected elsewhere. Hence London must consider not only the principles "of equity and of humanity but also of international amity and world peace." Such ideas were direct descendants of those expressed at the 1939 London conference.[4]

Bevin, with few bargaining counters and a need for secure bases, had little else to offer the Arabs, who far preferred an end to any British presence on their soil. Transjordan, tightly controlled and in dire need of British subsidies, would make a deal in March 1946, but Egypt and Iraq could not do so. Civilian politicians thought that Palestine itself might make a useful base, but the military men did not agree. It was a liability which could benefit Britain only by its divestiture.[5]

All this took place during the peak of Cold War confrontation with Moscow in Greece, Iran, and Turkey. "The main motive force behind Soviet policy in this area remains the drive toward the open sea," cabled the British ambassador to the USSR. These crises were seen as the first step in a Soviet offensive against the Persian Gulf and the Arab world. British interests, including vital oil fields, stood squarely in the way. Such nightmares were much on Bevin's mind when he warned President Truman in October 1945, that any increase in Jewish immigration to Palestine would bring violent disturbances throughout the Middle East. The U. S. Joint Chiefs of Staff agreed with him.[6]

If Arab pressure over Palestine stirred the British, the Arab government themselves set course on the winds of domestic public opinion. The great agitation and turmoil within Egypt and Iraq during those years were the products of both long- and short-term influences. The rise to intellectual hegemony of Pan-Arabism was no overnight occurrence; for more than three decades Arab nationalism had climbed one rung after another to capture the popular imagination. As time went on, its progress accelerated. The setbacks of 1941–42 had destroyed specific individuals and their strategies, but the essence of their arguments had been widely accepted. While an apocalyptic dissolution of all Arab borders seemed less likely, the formation of the Arab League signalled a new era of intensified state-to-state competition.

This was only part of the background to the unsettled postwar Egyptian political scene. After a quarter-century of promises and musical-chair governments, the country's social and economic problems remained untamed. Egypt was advancing neither in the Western framework of modernization nor in the Islamic framework of a moral and stable order, thought an impatient younger generation. The lingering British influence had been seemingly given new life by the war, which brought in thousands and thousands of foreign troops, and the maintenance of British bases and troops on Egyptian soil after Germany's surrender.

The Muslim Brotherhood grew to enormous size, maintaining, as did other parties, its own paramilitary forces. If the elite tended to overestimate the danger of Marxist revolution, the Egyptian left also reached its high water mark. Given all this, some have been tempted to attribute Egypt's external policy as a mere alibi for internal impotence. Matters were not so simple. Cairo's diplomatic behavior, after all, was a not inaccurate reflection of the *zeitgeist*. As it did not exist in isolation from domestic political culture, it also was reactive toward foreign events. Egyptian governments—even those of the Wafd—had long since defined as dangers the rise of either a Jewish state or a Hashemite super-kingdom to the east. Inasmuch as this concern was a political maneuver, it was in the tradition of the palace's prewar use of Pan-Arabism to undercut the Wafd's appeal.[7]

In October 1944, after Nahhas signed the Alexandria protocol initiating the Arab League's gestation, Farouk found it possible to dispose of his Wafd incubus regime. In 1946, when the king invited neither his prime minister nor his foreign minister to a meeting of Arab leaders on his Inshas estate, it was a further manifestation of such would-be imperial grandeur. "People then understood," wrote the scholarly liberal politician Muhammad Husayn Haykal, "that King Farouk's personal policy had as its aim the establishment of his personal leadership over the Arab states."[8]

Perhaps such an outlet was due in part to the palace's frustration in other directions. Inter-Arab politics offered a relatively free hand for an establishment which could not even call elections for fear of a Wafd victory. As for the more controversial Anglo-Egyptian relationship, this carried with it the most profound dangers. A draft agreement revising bilateral relations fell before the emotional public bitterness against Great Britain. Indeed, when the palace and cabinet were finally persuaded to reopen the battle in 1951, events were set in motion which led to the complete collapse of the monarchy and parliamentary system. Palestine as an immediate issue which demanded quick response and Pan-Arab politics which promised high (if intangible) rewards at little cost, seemed better opportunities for government activism.[9]

The differences between Iraq and Egypt, on one hand, and Transjordan and Saudi Arabia, on the other, were similar in the second half of the 1940s to what they had been in the second half of the 1930s. Abdallah and Ibn Saud, both still in power, embodied the continuity in the two states' policies. Abdallah promoted his Greater Syria federation at every possible opportunity. The Saudi response was to move toward a de facto alliance with Egypt. Transjordan's emir did not try to hide his contempt for this dangerous new factor. To him, the Egyptians were not even legitimate Arabs, and King Farouk was a mere political parvenu.

Nor was his old quarrel with the Mufti forgotten. While Abdallah tried to stir up anti-Mufti sentiment among the Palestine Arabs, the Mufti supported the Jordan Arab party which opposed the emir. This party, among whose leaders was Sulayman al-Nabulsi, demanded political liberalization and attacked Anglo-Transjordan amity. There were particular complaints about a concession for mineral exploration given to a group of Zionists. Abdallah counterattacked, winning over many oppositionists, including al-Nabulsi. He also encouraged a party of Hejaz exiles who wanted to overthrow Ibn Saud.[10]

Abdallah's greatest success was in London, which granted Transjordan independence in May 1946. Freed from these last fetters, the emir made his Greater Syria plan official government policy. Since Syria itself, now independent from the French mandate, was strenuously opposed to any Transjordanian takeover, Damascus was added to his enemies' list. The same thing happened in Palestine, where al-Alami's efforts to unseat the Mufti were going down to defeat. Thus while Abdallah had gained limited British favor, he managed to line up against him Egypt, Saudi Arabia, Syria, and the majority of Palestine Arab leadership. The accumulation of so many rivals would eventually cost Abdallah his life.[11]

Outside of Abdallah, few Arab statesmen were left by mid-1946 who thought concessions—or even negotiations—with the Jews might still be useful. Emir Zaid, another of Sharif Husayn's sons, might quietly comment that the Arabs must adjust to the Jewish presence in Palestine, and similar views might be expressed by a social-democratic modernist like Kamil al-Chadirchi, but both men were outside the mainstream. As late as January 1947, Muhammad Husayn Haykal suggested Arab-Zionist cooperation against the British who, he maintained, provoked tension over Palestine so that they themselves could keep it. Yet his belief that Egyptian Prime Minister Nuqrashi or the Arab League might accept such a plan was clearly chimerical.[12]

Even economic contacts between the Zionists and the Arab world were beginning to disappear. The Arab League decision to boycott Zionist goods cut Palestine's exports in the first quarter of 1946 to 31 percent of their value twelve months earlier, despite Egyptian officials' lack of enthusiasm. Haykal, at the time president of the Senate, complained that the embargo was difficult to enforce and might hurt Egypt's relations with the West. Actually, while ending direct trade with the Jews of Palestine (and after 1948, Israel) it had little broader effect until the Arab oil boom of the 1970s.[13]

By dealing directly with Great Britain, Arab leaders reasoned, they would circumvent any need to reach agreement with the Zionists. Cooperation with London would be coupled with a continuing demonstration of Arab unity. Sometimes, however, the latter precluded the former. An example of this last point was a January 1946 British request to allow transport to Palestine of fifteen hundred Jewish refugees in order to reunite families. This was an interim measure, the Foreign Office explained, made necessary by the exhaustion of the 1939 White Paper quota. Egypt agreed at first, but after the Arab Higher Committee rejected the proposal all the Arab states fell into line. England announced it would extend the limited quota anyway.[14]

More serious was the escalation of rivalries between the Arab states. In January 1946, a joint declaration of Kings Ibn Saud and Farouk brought their country into an alliance. A Hashemite bloc of Transjordan and Iraq formed in response. Rumors of a British-supported Transjordanian plan to take over Palestine, though without foundation, stirred further Egyptian and Saudi anger. "The defense of Palestine is imposed on me by my religion, my honor, my children, my people, and by you people of Palestine," Ibn Saud told Jamil al-Husayni. If necessary, Saudi Arabia would go to war over the Palestine question.[15]

The Anglo-American Committee of Inquiry came as the first test for Arab strategy on Palestine. Two months after President Truman called for granting Palestine immigration certificates to one hundred thousand Holocaust survivors, Bevin responded on November 13, 1945, with the suggestion of a joint committee to examine both the refugee question and Palestine's future. The Jewish Agency and the Arab League agreed to give testimony before the twelve-member committee, evenly divided between Americans and Britons, but refused to be bound by its recommendations. In particular, the Arab side doubted that American participation would be helpful to them.[16]

Nevertheless, spokesmen representing all sides testified before the committee, which travelled to Arab capitals as well as to Palestine. Dr. Muhammad Jamali, director-general of Iraq's Foreign Ministry, invoked the close relationship between his country and Palestine, whose coastline represented Iraq's seaboard and whose road and pipeline connections were economically important to Baghdad.

A Palestine solution, he continued, was also vital for the protection of Iraq's large Jewish minority. Iraq could not abide the loss of any part of the Arab world; Palestine's location made it especially inseparable. Without it as connecting link between the Fertile Crescent and North Africa, he concluded, Arab unity was impossible.

Ibn Saud's testimony stressed his characteristic Islamic view, rather than such a realpolitik interpretation. "Jews are our enemies everywhere," he explained, and the conflict went back thousands of years. The Jews lived in luxury while Arabs suffered in poverty and misery. The Arabs were friendly to the West, Ibn Saud concluded, but they were willing to go to war over Palestine.

The committee's report, issued May 1, set off an explosion equal to that produced by the Peel proposals nine years earlier. Since Jewish survivors in Europe did want to go to Palestine, the report concluded, the White Paper should be rescinded and one hundred thousand of them admitted. At the same time, Palestine should be neither Jewish nor Arab: a united binational state might be preferable. Until a settlement could be worked out and Palestine granted independence, the country should remain under British control through a United Nations trusteeship.

These suggestions pleased no one. Truman endorsed the immigration proposal, but gave no indication that the United States would help implement the other recommendations. The British government rejected the report as unworkable. Azzam, Iraq, Egypt, and other Arabs attacked its provisions on immigration and on a continued period of foreign control. In Iraq, this reaction — which included a symbolic general strike — restarted mass agitation over Palestine. Most active were Sami Shawkat's National Revival party and the Istiqlal party, led by Muhammad Mahdi al-Kubba, a Muthanna Club founder, and others who had backed Rashid Ali's junta. The lines of 1930s politics seemed to once more dominate Baghdad.[17]

In Palestine itself, public order was well on the way to a breakdown. The extremist Irgun and Stern groups had started anti-British terrorist campaigns as soon as it was clear that the war was won. The Haganah and Jewish Agency generally opposed their operations, but they were deeply involved in "illegal" immigration and in building their own underground army. They accused Britain of appeasement, betrayal, and anti-Semitism because of the Labor government's pro-Arab policy. The murder of British soldiers in Palestine further inflamed Bevin and British public opinion. To retaliate, the mandate government suppressed the Jewish Agency in June, arresting many of its leaders. One month later, the guerrillas carried out their biggest coup: the bombing of the King David Hotel in Jerusalem, the site of British government offices.

While London grew more and more impatient at finding some solution which would allow British withdrawal, the search was unsuccessful. Bilateral talks between Assistant Secretary of State Henry Grady and Lord Herbert Morrison (the Morrison-Grady plan) produced a canton arrangement rejected by both sides. Arab-Jewish talks organized in London were also a failure.

Meanwhile, the Anglo-American Committee report spurred a major reappraisal among the Arab states. Summit meetings at Inshas in May and at Bludan in June tried to formulate the available options and strategies. At Inshas, Arab leaders stuck to general principles: upholding the White Paper and condemning the new suggestions. Ultimately, confirmed the heads of state from Egypt, Syria, and Yemen, along with Saudi Arabia's crown prince, cooperation with the United Nations was the best way to achieve peace.[18]

The Bludan meeting was dominated by far more militant elements, particularly Iraq's fiery delegation. There were really three Arab positions. Iraq spoke for immediate strong action against Britain and America: "The time for talking has passed," thundered Jamali. "The Americans understand only the language of force." Behind the scenes, Iraq's regent admitted the domestic motivations. The army was hard to control because of the officers' passion over Palestine. Unless Iraq was out in front of the other states, he feared the civilian radicals and the army might revolt.

Egypt and Saudi Arabia, who would have been asked to bear most of the costs of confrontation, along with Lebanon, were less eager for a fight. "If we tell the Palestine Arabs to 'fight with all the arms at your disposal,'" countered Egyptian delegate Makram Ubeid, "we shall only be responsible for inflicting heavy casualties on them; for the Jews are much better armed than the Palestine Arabs." Saudi diplomat Yusuf Yasin emphasized the need to use political tools and to be realistic about Arab capacities.

The third group consisted of Syria, Transjordan, and the Palestine Arabs themselves, for whom the question of timing was all-important. Violence would be necessary, they argued, but it could only be practical after a British withdrawal. The Mufti wanted the help of the Arab states without their political interference. He was confident his forces could defeat the Zionists with Arab aid. Abdallah hoped to win British support for Transjordan's occupation of Haifa, the Negev, and central Palestine. Then he could reach a settlement with the defeated Jews. These rivals with opposite objectives both had reasons to counsel patience.

The resulting resolutions reflected their views. The time would come for Arab states to furnish money, arms, and soldiers for Palestine, but this still lay in the future. An economic and political confrontation with the British and Americans should be avoided if possible, but they were threatened with sanctions if any attempt was made to implement the Anglo-American Committee proposals. Although those present did not realize it, Bludan was a first step toward the 1948 war.[19]

A stiffening Arab position did not help British diplomatic efforts. In September, an Arab League meeting in Alexandria decided that further negotiations with the Zionists were worthless. They demanded independence for Palestine by the end of 1948 and an immediate end to Jewish immigration. The Zionist leadership only wanted talks which considered partition, while the Arab Higher Committee refused to talk to the British unless they dealt directly with the Mufti. Faced with all these conflicting conditions, Bevin was stalemated.[20]

This placed Abdallah in the advantageous position of being the only Arab leader conducting serious talks with either the Zionists or the British. He took full advantage of these opportunities through contacts with Moshe Sharett, Arabic-speaking director of the Jewish Agency Political Department, and Eliahu Sassoon, the agency's Syrian-born Arab Affairs expert. As early as August 1946, he told them that Palestine would eventually be partitioned and that Transjordan would annex the Arab portion. It was a remarkably prescient analysis of what would happen two years later.[21]

The Jews followed up their talks with Muhammad Husayn Haykal in

Egypt with a proposal that Cairo support a partition of Palestine, but Egyptian leaders had been hesitant. Azzam and Ibn Saud were dead set against any such plan. Abdallah, however, thought such a solution not only possible but absolutely desirable.[22]

Taking his case to the British through Transjordanian Prime Minister Samir al-Rifai, Abdallah suggested partition as the only solution. A fallback position could be to join all Palestine to Transjordan with provincial autonomy for the Jews. The English were not yet ready for such a plan, one which they knew was unacceptable to the other Arab states.[23]

Already these governments were moving to the next stage of escalation: increasing pressure on America and Britain; increasing aid to the Palestine Arabs. After Truman called for the admission of one hundred thousand Jews to Palestine in October 1946, Syria and Lebanon began to harass construction of the American oil companies' "Tapline" pipeline project. Ibn Saud accused Truman of violating his and Roosevelt's earlier promises, but Truman accurately replied that only continued consultations were pledged. Such talks had already taken place.[24]

While Arab governments were willing to clash with great powers or even go to war for the Palestine Arabs, their material aid was not always generous. Iraq, most militant in rhetoric, was particularly stingy. The aid given was more often paid to the Istiqlal or al-Alami rather than the Arab Higher Committee. Baghdad paid for Arab information offices in Washington, London, and New York on the stipulation that al-Alami would run them without Husayni interference.[25]

Syria gained its own foothold in the Palestine Arab movement through its subsidy to Fawzi al-Qawukji. The former commander of the 1930s guerrilla bands returned to Damascus from his Berlin exile. The Syrian Defense Ministry gave him a home, offices, and a thousand Syrian pounds a month.[26]

King Farouk put Egypt squarely behind the Mufti, although supplying little money. By granting al-Husayni political asylum, however, Cairo was providing him with a valuable base of operations. After August 1946, the Mufti once again openly assumed leadership of the Arab Higher Committee. When one adds to this list Abdallah's backing for the Nashashibis, the sum shows four Arab countries supporting four different Palestine Arab factions.

Egypt's choice—and general Arab strategy—were deeply affected by suspicions over Abdallah's plans. There were no end to rumors and stories about an impending Transjordanian military occupation of Palestine and Syria. Abdallah's troops were "massed at the borders of Palestine,'' reported *Akhbar al-Yawm* on February 1, 1947, to implement the Greater Syria plan. Despite Amman's denial, the headlines continued. The Arab states insisted on Palestine's independence as soon as possible to avoid any such Anglo-Abdallah collaboration.[27]

This factor and Arab opposition to any transitional period to independence led to the collapse of Britain's last attempt at a settlement. When a London conference was convened on January 27, 1947, the Arab Higher Committee was in attendance while the Jewish Agency stayed away. This was a fundamental sign of the expected outcome. Indeed, the British proposals were relatively favorable toward Arab objectives. There would be no partition, but there would be local self-government. Palestine would remain under British rule for five years in preparation for independence as a united state. The high commissioner would remain supreme during this time, advised by a Jewish-Arab council. The Jewish Agency would be dissolved, and during the first two years one hundred thousand Jews would be admitted. After that, the Arabs would have a voice in immigration policy, but the final word would lie with the UN Trusteeship Council. At the end of four years, a constituent assembly would be established to draw up a constitution, with the Trusteeship Council retaining a deciding vote if disagreements arose in this process.[28]

As in 1939, this plan did not represent a total Arab victory, yet it certainly provided the raw materials for such an outcome. London was willing to undertake a program which would never be accepted by the Jews. Could there be any doubt that the state which would emerge would be dominated by the Arabs? The Jewish Agency certainly thought so; the Arab states nevertheless rejected the offer.

English efforts were now at a dead end. A decade of meetings, secret consultations, proposals and counter-proposals, investigations, commissions, and committees had produced nothing. London had ignored Jewish demands, but its maximum offer was below the Arabs' minimum position. Palestine was a political and economic liability to an England in full retreat from empire and fiscally prostrated by World War II. On February 18, Bevin announced Britain's abdication of responsibility—let the United Nations try its hand if anyone else thinks it can do better, Bevin seemed to say with some bitterness.

The Arab governments were not in principle adverse to using the United Nations as a forum to settle the Palestine question. In fact, Bevin had once predicted that if London tried to establish a Jewish state, the Arabs would immediately seek a redress of grievances there. The issue was the way in which Palestine was presented. The Arabs wanted a prearranged agreement with the British or at least an understanding which would lead to a directed verdict. While London continued to advocate a transition period, the Arab states' agenda proposal called for the termination of the Palestine mandate and the declaration of its independence: the sooner, the better.[29]

Iraq still faced enormous political pressure from within to take the most extreme possible stand. Five parties, including the Istiqlal and the National Revival group, called for immediate armed intervention. Nuri al-Said's regime was under attack on a number of issues, and he responded with emotional appeals over Palestine. The Arab League did not like either the Iraqi or the Transjordanian approach. Some people, said Saudi diplomat Yasin, at the time president of the League Council, were trying to "obstruct" unity and that made them "enemies of the Arabs."

Essentially, the lines along which the Arab states split at Bludan still held. Egypt and Saudi Arabia continued to prefer diplomacy. Military aid or intervention in Palestine remained possible, but such measures were auxiliaries for convincing Britain and America of Arab seriousness. Yet by refusing to make concessions on the British proposals, these states undercut their own strategy. Maximal demands would have to lead to maximal action. Besides, could the Arabs possibly have as much leverage with the United Nations as they possessed when confronting Britain alone?

When Nuri al-Said threatened, "There no longer will be an Arab League" unless it took a stronger stand or when Transjordan claimed that its own proximity to Palestine carried a right to "independent action" no matter what its colleagues decided, they were making war inevitable. Egypt and Saudi Arabia were no less patriotic than Iraq or Transjordan, their interests simply dictated different approaches. Yet the more vocally militant the two Hashemite states became, the more Egypt and Saudi Arabia would have to compete with them. It was no longer merely a question of prestige and Arab leadership: the latter two could not afford to let their enemies take over Palestine.[30]

Iraq and Transjordan, of course, were not really close allies—their interests fundamentally conflicted. Each wanted Palestine for their own sphere of influence. While Transjordan's hope lay in British support, Iraqi Pan-Arab politicians hated England. Domestic politics were central to al-Said's behavior; tactical problems dictated Abdallah's dissension from the Arab mainstream. The other Arab states might well pool their delegations' efforts in the United Nations; Transjordan, not yet a member, was excluded there. Transjordan's greatest asset — its long-cultivated special relationship with Britain — was side-stepped when direct negotiations were abandoned.

Undiscouraged, Abdallah could also point to some bright spots in the spring of 1947. Transjordan's own independence gave him considerably more freedom of action, and the April Treaty of Brotherhood and Alliance with Iraq further strengthened his position vis-a-vis Egypt and Saudi Arabia. The accord pledged mutual military cooperation against "aggressors," which might include other Arabs as easily as the Zionists. Although al-Said and Jamali hardly sought involvement in Abdallah's various feuds, this agreement was a commitment which other Arab states took very seriously.[31]

Nor did Abdallah keep his intentions over Palestine a secret. When U. S. Ambassador George Wadsworth visited him in the company of Iraqi Foreign Minister Jamali, Abdallah spoke freely about partition as the only solution to the Palestine problem. Eighty percent of the Palestine Arabs agreed with him, he claimed, and held back only out of fear of the Mufti. Transjordan would support partition with two reservations: the Jewish state should only include areas with a Jewish majority, and the remaining Arab portion should be joined with neighboring countries. Obviously, this was a formula similar to that proposed by the Peel Commission.

Jamali remained silent during the entire discussion, but during the ride home he could no longer restrain himself. Iraq could not agree with Abdallah's estimate of Palestine Arab opinion, which ran in quite the opposite direction. Moreover, he continued, the Arab states would never accept partition. While Jamali was correct in the short run, events would follow Abdallah's prescription.[32]

As shown in the Egyptian newspapers, other Arab governments were equally well aware of Abdallah's plans. Musa al-Alami hinted that a coup was being planned against Abdallah and that he would never survive partition. Such a plot was apparently being organized under Syrian sponsorship, but Transjordan's intelligence easily broke it up.[33]

Transjordan was by no means the sole or even the major preoccupation of the Arab states in mid-1947. Most important was the struggle waged in the United Nations for Palestine's immediate independence. Working together, the Arab delegations — particularly those of Syria, Iraq, and Lebanon (Egypt and Saudi Arabia were less active)—fought to avoid any new investigation into the issue. When the vote came, they lost by an overwhelming margin. Instead, the General Assembly established a Special Committee on Palestine (UNSCOP) to hold hearings and recommend a solution.[34]

Like so many other attempts at mediation, UNSCOP did not win the trust of either Arabs or Jews. The Arab League and the Jewish Agency agreed to cooperate anyway, but the Arab Higher Committee retreated to its preferred abstentionist policy. In Palestine, UNSCOP glimpsed ample proof that the fuse was quickly burning toward explosion. Arab protest strikes and mass demonstrations were daily occurrences, matched by Jewish terrorism against the British and "illegal" immigration activity. With Palestine so obviously on the verge of intercommunal war, even the most pro-Arab members of UNSCOP were hard-pressed to suggest the possibility of maintaining a united state. Britain's inability to produce any mutually acceptable solution furnished additional arguments on this point. Arab rejection of Bevin's January 1947 plan doomed any hope for keeping Palestine united.

Yet the Arab states refused to consider any form of binational structure. The verdict of Arab state leaders was unanimous during their July testimonies before UNSCOP. Camille Chamoun, Lebanon's chief delegate, said that partition or continued Jewish immigration was unacceptable; at most, the Jews would be assured of minority rights. Foreign Minister Hamid Frangieh undermined even this offer by calling all Jews who had entered Palestine since the Balfour Declaration "illegal immigrants." Under such a definition, as many as four hundred thousand might be deported from an Arab Palestine.

Saudi Arabia's Ambassador Hamza warned that creation of a Jewish state would mean war. Speaking for Iraq, Jamali declared, "We have not come to the United Nations to ask for a compromise between just and unjust, we want just solutions and just solutions are not always based on compromise." Even Abdallah endorsed the Arab consensus.[35]

The results equalled the worst Arab nightmare. The UNSCOP majority report, supported by seven delegates, called for Palestine's partition into independent Arab and Jewish states. The Arabs would receive western Galilee, the hill country of central Palestine (with the exception of Jerusalem, which would be under a permanent trusteeship), and the coastal plain from Isdud to the Egyptian border. The Jews would hold most of the Negev, the northern coastal strip, and eastern Galilee. A minority position endorsed by three members, advocated a federal solution, a political confederation of the two states each with a wide measure of autonomy. The majority stand envisioned an economic union; the minority view gave the Arabs a more favorable territorial settlement. Predictably, the Zionists were pleased by the partition plan, while the Arabs were outraged by both proposals.[36]

Shortly thereafter, Azzam met with two Jewish Agency officials,

David Horowitz and Aubrey (Abba) Eban, to discuss the post-UNSCOP situation. "The Jews are a *fait accompli* in the Middle East," argued Horowitz, and the Arabs would eventually recognize this. Wouldn't it be better if this could be done without bloodshed? It was still not too late for an agreement between the Zionists and the Arab League. This might include plans for economic cooperation and guarantees against any Jewish expansionism.

"The Arab world is not in a compromising mood," Azzam accurately replied. Horowitz's suggestion might be rational and logical, but such was not the way international affairs were conducted: "Nations never concede; they fight. You won't get anything by peaceful means or compromise." Only force of arms could settle the conflict. The Arabs might lose, Azzam mused, but it was too late to make peace.

Azzam's own son represented this new Arab spirit. "When he came back from one of the more violent student demonstrations against the British," Azzam recounted, "I told him that in my opinion the British would evacuate Egypt without the need for his demonstrations." The boy asked in surprise: "But, Father, are you really so pro-British?" This newly militant mood engendered its own set of tactics. Battle was cathartic, necessary to revive damaged Arab pride. Nothing could stand against the force of this impatient nationalism.

Horowitz thought Azzam's seeming admiration for force and violence marked him as a fanatic and near-fascist, but his remarks had only mirrored Arab political realities. No Arab leader, Azzam had noted, could compromise with the Zionists and hope to keep his life, much less his power. Even the Mufti could no longer control "The Street." The same could be said of the Arab governments.[37]

Yet Azzam's fatalism was also less than candid. While the anger of Arab public opinion may have been predetermined by its most basic religious and political principles, the magnitude of response was not altogether spontaneous. Azzam and his friends had worked hard to stir such sentiments. They may have repented in office for that which they helped create in opposition, but equally they had shown no great reserves of persuasion and creativity in resolving the dilemma. After 1948, many of them became victims of the furor over their Palestine failure; this did not make them innocent bystanders who, like Azzam, could bemoan the hysteria and fanaticism of the masses.

Due to their failures, the national leaders of the era of Arab parliamentary experiment were perhaps excessively condemned by the new radical military regimes of the 1950s. They ably gained independence for their respective countries, but with that accomplished they seemed to lose direction, their energies concentrated exclusively on obtaining or maintaining power. Neither the kings nor men like Jamali, Mardam, al-Quwatli, Riyad al-Sulh, Nuri al-Said, or Nuqrashi had any social program or development plan.

Their forté was political intrigue rather than charismatic leadership. Possibly this was due to the tortured exigencies of their personal histories and their hegemony at a time when the Arab world was only beginning to once again become a subject rather than a mere object of events. Riyad al-Sulh had worked, for example, with the Turks, the Hashemites, the French republic, the Vichy French, and the Axis, as well as the British. At various times, he had befriended the Zionists or led anti-Zionist forces.[38]

Mardam, Syria's prime minister, had an equally convoluted past. His career was often cited as the outstanding example of opportunism in contemporary Syrian politics. It was usually impossible to cite what his views actually were on any given subject. Corruption was so profound that it tainted even the most sacred Arab causes. Mardam had to absent himself from parliament to avoid debates on the disappearance of funds collected for Palestine. Scandals over the purchases of military supplies would convulse Lebanon and Egypt in later years. Even the Muslim Brotherhood siphoned off money raised for use in Palestine for its own operations. Persistent factional warfare based on personal conflicts made cooperation between parties (and even within parties) extremely difficult.[39]

The resulting weakness of the various governments severely limited their ability to negotiate international issues. This did not apply only to Palestine, as demonstrated by the frustrating experiences of Egyptian and Iraqi statesmen in updating their relations with Britain. Neither government could hope to win a favorable enough treaty to satisfy domestic critics, and their attempts to do so led to the 1948 Baghdad riots and the 1952 Egyptian military coup. Intransigence may have been justified by British offers, but it was also made attractive as the line of least domestic political resistance.

Nor did the Arab states hold the fraternal respect for each other which they so often invoked publicly. If the British shut their eyes for five minutes, Yasin said, the Iraqi government would be swept away. Many other Arab leaders evinced similar sentiments. With rare exception, the Arab League was riven by strife and mistrust, with conflicting interests and colliding ambitions. Nevertheless, despite the undemocratic nature of Arab leadership, there is no reason to accept the Zionist argument that more responsive and representative regimes would have been more conciliatory. If anything, greater faithfulness to "The Street" would have created a greater degree of militancy.[40]

As it was, Arab rulers were not so reckless over the possibility of war as might have appeared from their public statements following presentation of the UNSCOP reports. There was still an escape hatch: whether through fear of Middle East chaos or from a true appreciation of national interest, Arab leaders believed, Britain would be on their side. The threat of war would likely convince the United Nations and the great powers of Arab determination. In turn this would lead to a retreat from partition.

Britain's announcement that it would withdraw from Palestine no matter what happened seemed a positive step in that direction. The Arabs need no longer fear a conspiracy to maintain the mandate. Further, they concluded, without Arab cooperation the whole United Nations scheme would soon collapse. This declaration abolishing the mandate, said Lebanese Prime Minister Riyad al-Sulh, "frustrates all hope of establishing a Zionist Jewish state, and solves the Palestine question justly in favor of the Arabs."

Arab leaders believed that the Jews could not survive without British protection. Faced with a British withdrawal, the Zionists would either have to surrender their objective or be defeated by Arab forces. At worst, Azzam thought, Palestine would pass through a period of UN control and emerge as an independent state under Arab majority rule. Since no force could impose a settlement without British support, the Arab cause would triumph.[41]

The Foreign Office substantially agreed with Azzam's reasoning. Arab threats and British withdrawal would likely force abandonment of plans for any Jewish state. Concessions, however, would be mutual: as all-out war approached, the Arabs too would recoil and moderate their demands. A collision would either be avoided or quickly settled.[42]

Thus concluded the British cabinet's September 18 report on UNSCOP. Not only was the majority plan unfair to the Arabs, English analysts concluded, but any British attempt to coerce acceptance would antagonize the Arab states at a time "our whole political and strategic system in the Middle East must be founded on cooperation with those states." Good relations with a Jewish state "would be poor compensation for the loss of Arab goodwill." In short, partition might destroy Great Britain's "firm strategic hold on the Middle East which is an indispensible part of Commonwealth defense policy."

It was doubtful if time would heal these wounds. Conflict over a Jewish state would create constant regional unrest and would damage

Anglo-Arab relations. Rather than carry out such a costly resolution, His Majesty's Government would withdraw. Such a step would lead to the involvement of some or all Arab states in a war against the Jews, but it would also spare British lives, resources and interests. Withdrawal might also "induce a sense of realism" in both sides to avoid such a battle. Perhaps they would compromise and ask Britain to remain in Palestine for a limited time to help implement their agreement.[43]

The Arab states' hope that threats of violence would impress Great Britain and the United States came close to success in the spring of 1948. Yet neither the Jews nor the Arabs would back down in the face of confrontation. While Arab statesmen still privately hoped for diplomatic solutions, the mood of the Arab world was increasingly intent on a test of arms. Arabs were convinced that they would win any military struggle and, at any rate, this seemed a lesser risk to Arab politicians than standing against the tidal wave of public opinion.

Although the Arab states had correctly estimated their leverage over Britain in the postwar period, they were unable to make the concessions necessary to reach an agreement. Their strategic decision to ignore the Zionists led them to underestimate their political and military staying power. Bevin's turn to the UN was a disaster for the Arabs' position. If the Arabs felt, to paraphrase Jamali, that the only acceptable outcome was the UN's complete endorsement of the Arab position, their disappointment was likely. Domestic agitation and fear of Abdallah hardened the Arab position at a time when the range of proposed settlements were becoming increasingly unfavorable. If the UN voted for partition could war be far behind?

11
The Perils of Partition: 1947—48

In reacting against UNSCOP's report, most Arab governments hoped that the fruits of victory could be harvested without war. Yet all agreed that preparation for battle was a necessary concomitant to pressuring the UN to back down. The actual UN vote for partition in November thus came as objectively something of an anticlimax. Over the following months, the Arab states supported guerrilla and volunteer forces within Palestine hoping that this could decisively defeat the Jews or force a withdrawal of the UN plan. This was the Arab states second line of fortification. The third—direct intervention of Arab armies—was still held in reserve.

Though Arab diplomatic efforts did not end in November 1947, they never really recovered from the setbacks caused by the British abdication of responsibility to the United Nations. Moreover, at this stage the roots of the coming Arab defeat were already in place. The politicians were convinced that it was up to the generals to prepare for a military option, but all the decisions continued to be made by the political leaders. Blinded by their belief in the inevitability of Arab victory, by their own propaganda about the unlikelihood of effective Jewish resistance, and unable to admit any hesitancy or weakness (for political as much as psychological reasons), Arab leaders marched their countries straight into a costly and humiliating disaster.

Even on the most basic decisions, Arab unity was often lacking. While all of them agreed on the importance of keeping Palestine Arab, their objectives differed widely. Iraq's fluent hawkishness was advanced more for domestic reasons than from any real willingness to sacrifice.

Transjordan was most anxious to invade, but looked on the involvement of its compatriots as a nuisance which might rob it of a great prize. Egypt and Saudi Arabia were half-hearted in their advocacy of militancy, hoping the Arab Higher Committee's forces would spare them the trouble.

More than one Arab statesman or general who publicly declared unflinching confidence in victory was more candid in private. Yet even if fatalism ruled one part of their minds confidence was the dominant note. They could scarcely reconcile the two in their consciousness both because such views would be branded defeatist by hostile public opinion and because any such break would damage the prospects of intimidating the Jews, UN, and United States. This intellectual conflict seemed to accentuate the carelessness with which plans and assessments were laid down, helping to make their misgivings into a self-fulfilling prophecy.

One of the few Arabs who had extensive military experience against the Jews, al-Qawukji, was a prime example of this phenomenon. In print, he boasted, "We will murder, wreck and ruin everything standing in our way, be it English, American or Jewish." The Western press which criticized the Arabs would change their tone when they triumphed and would loudly trumpet, "'The Arab nations advance on all fronts' or 'The Arab cause is a just one.'" When a correspondent expressed doubt as to whether the Arabs could conduct a modern war without proper equipment and a unified command, he replied, "More than the arms I value the people who will be conducting this holy war."

In private, however, he admitted that Arab armies were ineffective, divided, and could never efficiently coordinate their operations. Guerrilla warfare would have to be the Arab tactic, but nobody in the regular national armies had any such experience. As for the Mufti, al-Qawukji bemoaned his leadership as more dangerous for the Arabs than for the Jews, saying al-Husayni was "universally disliked."[1]

Nor was Abdallah particularly sanguine about Arab military prospects—a position which made him advocate the need for agreement with the British and the Jews. In October, he told Azzam and Iraqi leader Salih Jabr that it was folly to talk of ejecting the Jews from Palestine. The Arabs were not capable of doing so and the civilized world would not permit it. Consequently, an Arab-Jewish accord should be made limiting the Zionists to the smallest possible part of Palestine.[2]

Abdallah practiced what he preached. As master of the Arab Legion, the most formidable fighting force in the Arab world, and in control of his own country, Abdallah had far more maneuvering room than did his colleagues. His small though well-disciplined force of tough Bedouin soldiers and experienced British officers was far more capable than its rag-tag allies of capturing and holding large portions of Palestine. Abdallah's very strength and ambitions tended to add to the division and mutual suspicions that plagued the Arab League.

For example, Abdallah told his friends that the British were not only increasing his arms supplies but were also supporting his plans to seize as much of Palestine as possible. Otherwise, Abdallah maintained, he would be trapped between Syria and a Mufti-ruled Palestine, "encircled on almost all sides by enemies." If the Jews moved against his forces, he would attack them. Then, once peace and order had been established, he would reach an understanding with the Zionists. Abdallah's claims of British endorsement in October 1947 were apparently quite false, but they added to Arab confusion.[3]

His next step was equally unsettling. He hinted that Transjordan might permit Syria and Lebanon to occupy a narrow strip of northern Palestine but he would block any extension of their zone by capturing Acre on the Mediterranean. This threat was also credible since the Arab Legion still had units stationed all the way up the Palestine coastal plain, from Gaza to Haifa.[4]

Abdallah's domestic actions also represented the battening of hatches before a major confrontation. The sole legal political party, Al-Nahda, which supported Abdallah and his Greater Syria plan, received most of the seats in elections for Transjordan's National Assembly. The Mufti, who wanted to move his headquarters closer to the coming action, was barred from Amman and moved his base of operations to Lebanon instead.[5]

Azzam also had doubts about the Arab military position, but his private statements were quite contradictory. He could accuse the Mufti of underestimating the Jews and then, a few minutes later, could claim that without outside interference the Arabs would settle the Palestine problem in six months. Azzam, like Nuri al-Said, was more moderate talking to the British in London than he was in speaking to fellow Arabs in Cairo. Yet his cynicism and despair came out in his conversation with Eban and Horowitz. He was clearly depressed by the need to rally the Arab League through the most extreme and uncompromising statements. Despite the attempt to exercise leverage for a diplomatic solution, he believed war and the declaration of a Jewish state were unavoidable.

When the British withdrew and the Jews claimed independence, the Arab countries would help their Palestinian Arab brethren with volunteers, arms, and money. It would be a long, bitter, and bloody battle like the Spanish Civil War, Azzam commented. Anti-Jewish pogroms in the Arab countries, horrible chaos, and bloodshed would follow. The Arabs would triumph in a relatively short time, he thought, but the price would be high. It was a gloomy vision. Even if victory were assured, how many would survive to enjoy it?[6]

In short, the dangers of war were sometimes recognized but could not be taken into account in the decision-making process—Arab leaders had no political or emotional choice other than to make military preparations. The best that could be hoped was either an easy Arab military victory or the frightening of the United Nations, the British or the Jews into making concessions. No serious consideration was given to any giving of ground by the Arabs. The same public opinion which made militancy a necessity would not allow for such considerations. Predictions of chaos and a regional power vacuum might be enough to sway London and Washington, preoccupied as they were with concern over regional instability and Soviet penetration.

All of these points set the tone for the mid-September Arab League meeting in Sofar, Lebanon. Once again, the Iraqi delegation led by Prime Minister Jabr, took the lead. A few days earlier, Jabr and the recently returned Rashid Ali al-Gailani attended a large Istiqlal protest meeting in Baghdad. They demanded an independent Arab Palestine, a blockade to prevent Jewish infiltration, and the ejection of all Jews who had entered Palestine — or any other Arab state — since 1914. All Arab military volunteers should be given full soldiers' benefits, and recruiting offices should be opened to raise troops, the rally's demands continued, and all British and American goods should be boycotted.[7]

Jabr presented this ambitious program at the Sofar conference. Saudi Arabia and Egypt particularly rejected the anti-Western boycott or other economic measures, complaining that Iraq was simply scoring propaganda points with the Arab public. Jabr responded that Britain and America would hesitate to support partition if they knew it might cost them their oil concessions. Neither country would take it lightly if their Middle East petroleum was cut off, he concluded. Yet there was no sign of serious willingness to take such a serious decision.[8]

The meeting's communique was thus couched in more moderate terms, but it was sharp enough to serve as the occasion for British rejection of UNSCOP's report. Since the Sofar declaration warned that establishment of a Jewish state would lead to an unavoidable outbreak of violence in the Middle East, clearly partition was not acceptable to the Arab side, Bevin explained. On the other hand, despite Jabr's arguments, the league had not yet decided on implementing practical measures of military preparation.[9]

The reaction to the UNSCOP plan was universally negative in the Arab world. In Lebanon alone, the U.S. embassy received 150 telegrams of protest in only two days. "The Palestine Arabs will launch a relentless war to repel this attack on their country," proclaimed *Al-Ahram*, "especially as they know that all the Arab countries will back and assist them, supplying them with men, money, and ammunition."[10]

This was the beginning of an Arab campaign to affect the General Assembly vote on the UNSCOP proposals, an effort matched by an equally vigorous Zionist campaign. Whether or not the Saudis would go along with Iraq's proposal on oil concessions was a matter of much concern to American policy-makers since Saudi Arabia was the only Middle East country where American companies dominated production. While the United States successfully negotiated air transport agreements with Egypt, Lebanon, and Syria, Iraq blocked any accord because of the Palestine issue.[11]

At the second UN session, Arab League members tried a variety of tactics to swing votes against the UNSCOP recommendations. These included threats to U.S. oil interests, challenges to the General Assembly's competence to deal with a mandate originally issued by the League of Nations, and suggestions that the whole question be put before an international court.

American State Department officials like Loy Henderson were worried that U.S. support for partition would undermine relations with the Arab states. The United States would be "held responsible" if partition was implemented, Iraqi UN delegates warned, and a joint Arab group which came to see Secretary of State George Marshall on September 23, carried a similar message. Ten days later, American representatives at the United Nations were told that the Arabs might make a deal with Moscow, in which Soviet support over Palestine might be traded for Arab votes on other issues.[12]

Middle East chaos might also hurt broader American and Western interests there. Syria's Faris al-Khuri and Lebanon's Charles Malik claimed that peace all over the world might dissolve into a growing international conflict. Jamali declared that support for the Jews constituted a "declaration of war" against the Arabs.[13]

Yet in early October, when the Arab League Political Committee gathered in Aley, Lebanon, to assess their progress, diplomatic prognostications seemed gloomy. Delegates agreed that the UN would probably vote for partition. Following earlier discussions, Iraq, Lebanon, Palestine, Syria, and Transjordan agreed to establish a military committee — from which Egypt significantly absented itself. Cairo was not yet ready for such a commitment. Nevertheless, the conference proceeded to agree on formation of a general Arab headquarters, mobilization of Arab armies on Palestine's borders, the supply of ten thousand rifles to the Palestine Arabs, and the purchase of fighter planes abroad.

The financial burden for all this was divided in proportions relative to each country's wealth and population: Egypt 42 percent, Saudi Arabia 12 percent, Syria 12 percent, Lebanon 11 percent, Iraq 7 percent, Transjordan 5 percent, and Yemen 3 percent. Arab military experts recommended leaving the Palestine Arabs themselves with responsibility for their defense. The local people, after all, knew their own requirements and were more committed to the struggle; besides, such a plan was far cheaper than direct Arab involvement. Therefore the conference recommended: "The Arab armies shall remain stationed on the borders of Palestine and shall not enter Palestinian territory unless the Jews received outside help."[14]

Both the wishes and thinking of Arab leaders was that the Palestine Arabs could win victory without involving the Arab states in a full-scale war. Further, there was no interest in marching into Palestine while British troops were still there. Not only would this destroy chances for surreptitious British support for the Arabs, but it might also put several states into confrontation with an ally which supplied them with economic aid and military hardware. At the same time, despite this dependence on the Palestine Arabs, there was not universal support for the Arab Higher Committee. When the Mufti appeared at the closing session and demanded immediate establishment of an Arab Palestine government, Syria and Lebanon wavered while Transjordan and Iraq were outspokenly opposed.

Delegates then moved on to Amman to convince Abdallah to relent. They found him adamant: Transjordan would neither abandon the Greater Syria plan nor would it help create a neighboring government headed by Abdallah's old enemy, the Mufti. Abdallah argued that this was all a moot point—only direct intervention by the Arab armies could save the day.

Almost immediately, this last view received support from an unexpected quarter. Iraqi General Ismail Safwat, chairman of the just-established joint military committee, reported that the Zionists were much better organized than the Palestine Arabs. Urgent recruiting campaigns and arms purchases were necessary, he warned, Arab armies must be moved near the border and a land-and-sea blockade would have to be established to prevent aid from reaching the Jews.

The Arab League's response was disappointing. Sloth, disunity, confusion, and weakness were making their first costly appearance.

While Syria ordered a partial mobilization on October 9, Damascus was daunted by a British warning against interference in Palestine. Meanwhile, Haganah units were crossing into Syria on reconnaissance missions and, despite all the talk of Arab solidarity, Syria was reluctant to allow Iraqi troops on its soil. What assurances were there that Baghdad would not use these military forces to annex the country? Once the Soviets decided to endorse the partition of Palestine, the regime was frightened about the possibility of Communist party subversion. To round out this series of problems, al-Qawukji—who had a real following in Syria—openly attacked the Mufti.[15]

The Mufti's most reliable—perhaps sole reliable—foreign ally was the Egyptian Muslim Brotherhood, whose world view was fairly similar to his ideology. Without waiting for action from the reluctant Egyptian government, Hassan al-Banna, the Brotherhood's revered leader, opened recruiting offices and began raising ten thousand volunteers to fight in Palestine. Otherwise, al-Husayni was cynical about the Arab states' promises. He did not really believe, the Mufti told friends, that Saudi Arabia, Egypt, or Lebanon would actually order their armies across the border. If asked by a foreigner, he would refrain from such criticisms and aver that Arab unity was complete, but he could tell the truth to brother Muslims. Ironically, his greatest friction came with Iraq, whose gap between words and actions was particularly wide.[16]

Most of all, the Mufti must have had Transjordan in mind. Unlike the other states, Abdallah was all too eager to intervene and had no intention of subordinating his army to any joint command. The Mufti was so suspicious of possible collusion between Britain and his own Arab allies that he rejected High Commissioner Alan Cunningham's proposal to ensure peace until the British withdrawal. He preferred to have Palestine firmly under his control before any foreign Arab armies entered it.[17]

Since these antagonisms were paralyzing Arab cooperation, Ahmad Hilmi and Abd al-Hadi undertook the unenviable task of reconciling Abdallah and the Mufti. Abdallah's reaction to the idea was so passionately virulent that they feared to speak further with him. "Why couldn't the two leaders work together?" they asked Abdallah key adviser, Prime Minister al-Rifai. The answer was simple, he answered. The Mufti was identified with Transjordan's enemies, Syria and Saudi Arabia, and was antagonistic toward the two Hashemite states. But the Mufti was also alienating other Arabs through his threats and extortions. When the British left a vacuum, al-Rifai continued, the first requirement would be to restore order within the Arab areas—an act taking precedence over an offensive against the Jews. Since the Mufti was incapable of doing this—

and thus incapable of defeating the Jews—the administration of liberated lands must be under Amman's control.[18]

Soon, a dramatic if not unexpected event would jolt all these debates from the realm of abstraction. Despite Ibn Saud's last minute efforts at preventing American support for partition—"the results of this decision will lead to a death-blow to American interests in the Arab countries"—Truman did not flinch. After making last-minute offers of concessions, the Arab states lost their long diplomatic battle on November 29, 1947. The General Assembly voted 33 to 13 for the UNSCOP majority plan. The partition of Palestine was now accepted UN policy.

As in 1929, 1937, and 1946, a wave of anger, demonstrations, and violence swept across the Arab world. On the General Assembly's floor, Arab delegations attacked the vote as anti-democratic, illegal, impractical, and contrary to the UN Charter. Delegates warned that their countries would never accept it: they would overturn it. Arab diplomatic fortunes had declined with remarkable speed given their continuing geopolitical importance. In 1939 and in 1946, they had been offered a united Palestine on far more favorable terms, yet they had blocked these proposed solutions. Now, the most detrimental settlement ever proposed had been internationally endorsed during the era of the greatest level of cooperation and unity ever seen in the Arab world! Only two options were left for the Arab states: either the Jews would be militarily defeated or Arab pressure would force reversal of the scheme.[19]

On either count, the time had come for mobilization and the venting of Arab passions. The first victims were Jews in Baghdad, Aleppo, where more than 300 homes and synagogues were sacked and half the city's 4000 Jews fled, and Aden, where the official death toll was set at 76. In Damascus, police looked on with indifference while a demonstration of ten thousand people turned into a riot. They broke into the U.S. and Belgian legations and the Soviet cultural office. Four communists were killed when their party headquarters was stormed and destroyed.[20]

The following day, December 1, President al-Quwatli told Syrian troops on parade, "We are ready with our forces, small in number and equipment, but strong and great in faith and honor to defend with our lives our unquestionable rights." While apologizing to Washington for the destruction of American property, he warned about years of bloodshed and the growth of Soviet influence which would follow the partition resolution. Within a week, Syria instituted compulsory military training and set $2 million for arms purchases. Thirty parliamentary deputies immediately volunteered for military service in Palestine — though only two of them ever fulfilled that pledge.[21]

Like the firing of a pistol to start a race, the passage of the UNSCOP majority proposals began the sprint toward war. The Arabs, like runners who had spent years in training, were finally being called for the decisive event. Perhaps some had been enervated by that strange combination of overconfidence and pessimistic fatalism which tortured several leaders, but much of this was stilled through the filter of crisis. Not only in Palestine but throughout the Arab world, the conflict seized full attention.

Various splinter parties in Damascus, including the small Syrian Muslim Brotherhood and the then-obscure Baath Party of Michel Aflaq, quickly formed a Society for the Liberation of Palestine. With the support of Prime Minister Mardam, they organized a "Popular Army," compared locally to the foreign volunteer units in the Spanish Civil War. Though logistics lagged behind rhetoric, Syria's defense minister openly boasted of the effectiveness of these forces.

Three recruiting stations and two military training camps opened in the capital. Young men over eighteen years of age could sign up for combat duty; those younger could join as supply troops or stretcher-bearers. As al-Qawukji took over command of these units, the pace of preparation quickened. While supporting the Popular Army, al-Quwatli and Mardam wanted to avoid confrontation with Britain. They told Bevin that they were only trying to ensure Britain's neutrality and London's refusal to further partition. Anglo-Arab relations should not be prejudiced.[22]

Whether Syrian leaders looked upon the Popular Army as a means of extending their own influence into Palestine was not entirely clear. Certainly, Pan-Syrian feeling was by no means dead, and the Damascus government preferred to deal with al-Qawukji rather than with the Mufti himself. Abdallah not only refused to admit any Syrian or Iraqi troops into Transjordan, he also complained to the Syrian government about the Popular Army. Since many of al-Qawukji's soldiers were Syrian, the element of national interest could not have been entirely lacking in Syrian calculations. By supporting the Popular Army, Damascus had a headstart over Transjordan's Arab Legion in the race to control Palestine.[23]

Abdallah made no secret of his own ambitions. If his execution was audacious, his analysis of the political situation was remarkably cool headed. The combined power of the United States and Russia would hardly be deterred from implementing partition, he argued, and it was his duty to face the facts for the benefit of his family and country. With six thousand Legionnaires already stationed in Palestine, Transjordan could easily capture a great deal of the territory.[24]

On November 27, two days before the General Assembly vote,

Abdallah had met Golda Meir at the home of Avraham Rutenberg of the Palestine Electric Corporation, near the Palestine-Transjordan border. Abdallah made no particular efforts to keep the meeting secret. Although only a limited number of people knew about it, such unconcern, as with Abdallah's discussion with Ambassador Wadsworth, was a sign of either political recklessness or contempt for the power of the other Arab states.

He had no plans to infringe on the partition plan, Abdallah explained, but he thought its prospects would be improved if the Zionists would give up some of their projected territory. Meir refused. He then tried his maximal plan: Palestine would remain united under his rule, and he would protect the Jews. Again, Meir was not enthusiastic. Finally, he moved to his minimal aims: Transjordan would only annex the Arab part of Palestine without attacking the Jews. After all, he argued, the Jews and Transjordan had several things in common. Both had the Mufti as enemy and both opposed internationalizing Jerusalem. Once again, Meir would make no commitments.[25]

Thus by November 1947, Abdallah's efforts had neither neutralized the Jews nor won over the British. In fact, London was not operating at all to Transjordan's advantage. At that point, British tactics were more concerned with an efficient withdrawal than with Palestine's future disposition. Iraq was informed of London's timetable even before the House of Commons and was provided with valuable details on the pull-out of British units. The plan was to remove troops from south to north—the reverse would have been more advantageous for Transjordan —with the utmost speed, even if it proved necessary to leave behind supplies. There was no particular favoritism toward Amman.[26]

Next to Syria, passage of the partition resolution provoked the most turmoil in Egypt, whose domestic and foreign policy already faced more than its share of crises. The demand for unity with Sudan and for British military evacuation of Egypt stirred equal passion. So many demonstrations and strikes took place that *Al Ahram* started a special second-page feature ("the situation in the country") to cover them.

The Muslim Brotherhood was larger and more active than ever before. As early as October 8, Hassan al-Banna called for ten thousand volunteers to fight in Palestine. The UN decision stepped up this campaign. Muslim religious leaders at Al Azhar even declared a *jihad,* a holy war, against the Zionists.[27]

The Brotherhood's agitation was often conducted on a chillingly demagogic level, designed to recall the Muslim spirit of earlier centuries. One of al-Banna's December speeches even claimed: "God has allowed this decision to be taken by the UN in order to give you a chance to enter Paradise as well as enrich yourselves in this world. You have always yearned for this chance and now you have it, so do not hesitate. A wind is blowing from Paradise, sweet with the smell of martyrdom!"

Volunteers for Palestine were "the battalions of Allah," al-Banna added. Egypt faced clear and immediate dangers, for if Palestine were taken over, "all the Arab countries will fall." *Al Ikhwan* editorialized on December 10, "The sons of Israel were kicked out of Egypt by the Pharaohs, but the Zionists continue to dream about their lost empire."

Such rhetoric not only made the Egyptian regime quite nervous, but it also understandably terrified Egyptian Jews. While progovernment newspapers insisted that Egyptian Jews were entitled to the same rights and protection as other citizens, the Muslim Brotherhood accused them of supporting Zionism and demanded that they be forced to give money to support the Arab armies. Fantastic sums were cited as having been contributed by them to the Zionists. These provocative stories were not restricted to Brotherhood organs. *Misr al Fatat* called for mass arrests while *Al Kutla,* controlled by Makram Ubeid's Wafd split-off, merely wanted them registered and "disarmed" by police.

Al Assas, a newspaper identified with Prime Minister Nuqrashi, spoke in quite different tones. "It is at once illogical and unfair to expect a Jew to help fight another Jew who is trying to establish a national home to which he can immigrate if he had to," said one article. "Every Jew is in favor of a Jewish state," but as long as they stayed within the law they should not be embarrassed or harassed. "These words sound very much like the jingling of Jewish gold," jeered *Al Ikhwan.* Still, the Nuqrashi government stood fairly firm on protecting the Jews despite the Brotherhood's attacks.[28]

One factor in Arab leaders' preference for volunteers and dependence on indigenous Arab forces was knowledge of the deplorable state of their own armed forces. British observers noted that the Iraqi army's chief of general staff "is completely ignorant of modern warfare and all that implies." The British military mission to Saudi Arabia informed London that the Saudis possessed neither forces nor arms for more than a token intervention, a view confirmed by the Saudi finance minister.[29]

As for the Syrian army, Sheikh Yusuf al-Atrash, a veteran leader of the martial Druze, explained why his people would not volunteer to fight in Palestine: "The Jews are well-prepared. Should they come to a clash with the Syrian Army, they would be more than a match for this miserable force." "That," he accurately prophesied, "would be the end of this regime in Damascus."[30]

Most British and American military experts nevertheless believed that the Arabs would win in Palestine. In the words of an American intelligence report, "The loosely organized, ill-equipped armies of the Arab nations do not have any capabilities against a modern opponent, but they do have the strength to overrun Jewish resistance in Palestine." Within the country, there might be three times as many soldiers in the Jewish underground army as in the local Arab forces, despite the presence of twice as many Arabs as Jews in the general population. The Haganah was also far better armed and trained — many of them in the British army during World War II — than the Arab forces. But high-ranking officers had more faith in the regular armies of the Arab states than they did in a group of guerrillas and self-made underground units on the Jewish side.

The raw figures were not unimpressive. The combined armies of the Arab nations numbered one hundred and thirty thousand men, with an additional one hundred thousand armed tribesmen and militarized police. Already, by the end of 1947, three thousand troops of the Syrian First Brigade were stationed at Kuneitra, only fifteen miles from the border, and the Egyptians were conducting training operations in Sinai. Yet two factors seriously undermined these numerical advantages: their low state of efficiency and mobility plus the need to retain the bulk of these forces at home for the maintenance of internal security. Ironically, the very growth of the radical groups in Iraq, Egypt, and Syria reinforced that latter problem.

When coupled with the lack of coordination and cooperation between the states, these shortcomings would lead to the surprisingly thorough defeat suffered by these forces. By the end of 1947, only Iraq and Transjordan were really committed to send troops. The former could muster one brigade with a total strength of under five thousand (out of a three-division force of thirty-one thousand). The more effective Arab Legion could send the same, though as many as five thousand more could be added from the Transjordan Frontier Force and other sources. However, it was widely expected—by Abdallah among others—that the able commander of the Legion, General Glubb, would resign at the outset of any invasion. This was another sign that the British had still not accepted Transjordan's plans.

Finally, al-Qawukji might raise another seven thousand men for his volunteer forces. Since he was still feuding with the Mufti and could not expect cooperation from Abdallah, al-Qawukji was caught in still another of the many breakdowns in Arab coordination. This very issue was also bedevilling the Arab states on the political side.[31]

A secret October 1947 analysis by the Syrian government pointed out a number of these damaging conflicts. Saudi Arabia was restrained through fear of losing vital American aid, while Egypt wanted UN support for its attempts to force out the British. Nuqrashi was dragging his feet on every move toward military preparations.

Syria was also disillusioned with the Mufti. He had demanded that the league move even more quickly, even before the partition vote. If the Arab states only did their part, the Mufti argued, the Jews could be defeated in a few days. When Arab governments disagreed, he called their leaders cowards blinded by American dollars. Neither could he be satisfied with his two strongest "supporters" for greater Arab state involvement, Iraq and Transjordan, whose goals were not necessarily the same as the Mufti's.[32]

Such dissatisfaction did not go in one direction only. Even Azzam concluded that al-Husayni had learned very little since going into exile a decade earlier. He did not understand the difficulty of destroying the Jews, the Arab League secretary-general explained, and this is why the neighboring governments resisted the Mufti's call for an interim Arab government. This might interfere with necessary diplomacy and intervention on a state level. So irresponsible and troublesome was the Mufti, Azzam added, that he was for the Arabs the equivalent of what the Irgun or Stern Gang were for the Jews.[33]

Egypt and Saudi Arabia's dissatisfaction with the Mufti was rather different from the complaints of Iraq, Syria, and Transjordan. To the last three, the Mufti was in varying degrees a potential competitor for power. Their militancy was dictated by both domestic considerations and by the desire to intervene for their own ends. To Egypt and Saudi Arabia, in contrast, the Mufti was a tactical extremist who might destroy the chance to achieve Arab aims by a diplomatic process. These relations also furthered a curious reversal: the Egyptian and Saudi governments, less willing to go to war, were far more eager for the Mufti to win on his own than were the Iraqis or Transjordanians. Thus the Mufti's closest friends in a showdown were also those states which were less "militant" over direct military participation in the fight.

Azzam, like the Egyptian government, preferred a military strategy based on Palestinian Arab guerrilla warfare. By disrupting Jewish social and economic life, the Arabs could prevent any Zionist state from being organized or from functioning. A protracted low-level war could succeed through attrition without the need for foreign Arab forces because of demographic factors. Even if the local Arabs lost five times as many men as did the Jews, Azzam argued, they would eventually win.[34]

Such estimates were in the tradition of Arab failures to properly evaluate Zionist determination. The Jewish Agency's chief Arabist, Eliahu Sassoon, warned Azzam on this point in a December 5 letter: "A people which after seventeen centuries of exile and ceaseless persecutions still has the spiritual strength to build a new civilization is not a factor which can be treated with contempt." Certainly, Sassoon noted, it was not a movement easily destroyed by brute force.[35]

Since neither side was willing or able to offer new concessions or dramatic and creative solutions, the time was past for such initiatives. Preparations for war moved forward on both sides. The heady Arab League Cairo meeting of December 8–17 marked major aid commitments on the Arab side. Those present believed that the Arab League would collapse and individual governments would topple if they could not fulfill their promises to stop partition. Samir al-Rifai and Yusuf Yasin even claimed that the lives of their respective kings would be endangered unless they took effective action against the proposed Jewish state.

On the other hand, a full-scale international war would bring immense chaos and destruction to their own countries. Caution was also needed to avoid any clash with Great Britain and to prevent the dispatch of United Nations or American troops to Palestine. (Washington never seriously considered such an option.) Nuqrashi was well aware of the Egyptian army's weakness; perhaps he was not the only Arab leader with such doubts in mind.

If any reinforcement was needed on these points, British General I. N. Clayton, who had helped Syria and Lebanon win their independence from France, urged the Arab states to withhold their troops until Britain withdrew from Palestine. He even pointed out that sending Arab armies abroad might encourage subversive or dissident elements to seize power at home.

Despite their earlier feuds, the sense of impending crisis forced cooperation among the Arab states. At one point when a session was hopelessly bogged down, Azzam recounted, news bulletins were brought into the room quoting Golda Meir as saying, "We are better organized and equipped than you Arabs. In any case you are going to be beaten. Surrender now and save yourselves bloodshed." The effect on the meeting of this story, genuine or not, was electric. The atmosphere cleared, and the discussion progressed toward agreement.

Abdallah had given strict instructions to Transjordan's representative Omar al-Dajani not to agree to the passage of foreign Arab armies through Transjordan or to give the Mufti a free hand in political or military affairs. The meeting's secret resolutions were not inconsistent with these objectives.

The Arab League reiterated its decision to have the irregular Palestine Arab and volunteer forces carry the brunt of the fighting. They would attempt at all costs to avoid any clashes with the British. Nuqrashi opposed the presence of armed volunteers in Egypt, obviously fearing they would be used by the Brotherhood to overthrow the government. The main headquarters therefore would be located in Syria, with the volunteers to concentrate near the Palestine border. The Syrian and Lebanese defense ministers would represent the League in day-to-day consultations with al-Qawukji.

Arab governments would facilitate the supply of weaponry and hospital facilities. A quota was given to each state for the raising of three thousand volunteers and ten thousand rifles. Eight battalions would be organized under General Safwat, with al-Qawukji as the field commander.

Military tactics were also discussed at length. The guerrillas would attack on numerous fronts, spreading the Jewish defense forces as thinly as possible. The best time for a concerted offensive after this wearing-down process would be in April or early May. If the irregular forces failed, regular armies might be sent in August, but this would be decided by later Arab meetings. The Arab armies would not march, however, if British troops or an international peace-keeping force was in Palestine. Thus while the Arab governments would send in troops if necessary, they continued to hope it would not be required. With any luck, local forces would smash the Zionists even before Britain's May 15 withdrawal deadline.

The hottest debate came over the question of the leadership of these efforts. Reception of the Mufti, as at the previous meetings, was not exactly warm. Nor did the Mufti trust al-Qawukji as field commander of the Popular Army, he preferred his own cousin, Abd al-Qadir Husayni, who commanded guerrilla forces in the south. The all-important question of daily political administration in the Arab areas of Palestine was virtually ignored, and the decision not to establish any civil administration there was a dangerous error. Bereft of leadership, many Palestine Arabs would flee their homes as the economy and social services broke down and no political discipline or organization was there to rally them. More immediately ominous for the Arab Higher Committee's cause was the Arab decision not to determine Palestine's future status until after victory was achieved.[36]

Further, despite the conference's resolutions, Nuqrashi remained reluctant to use regular troops except in an emergency. Regular army officers like Gamal Abdul Nasser who volunteered to train irregular troops were denied official permission to do so. Like the Saudis, Nuqrashi still thought possible a diplomatic alternative to partition. Perhaps, he concluded, the Arabs might be better advised to seek something along the lines of the Morrison-Grady proposals or the UNSCOP minority report. Negotiations with the United States would soon show that such an escape route might still be open.[37]

Public communiqués from the Cairo meeting nevertheless continued to project Arab unity and militancy. "The world will see," they confidently announced, "it is impossible to beat Arabs by force." Abdallah had doubted such hopes longer and more adamantly than Nuqrashi or any other Arab leaders. For months before the Cairo meeting, he had not believed that guerrillas could defeat the Jews. At every opportunity, he and al-Rifai pressed their Transjordanian solution on the British. Even at the Cairo meeting, al-Rifai approached General Clayton: What would the British think, he asked, if the Arab Legion marched in as the British soldiers marched out?

He outlined the plan on December 12. The legion already had units stationed in Palestine as part of the British army. Bevin had just announced in the House of Commons that these men would be withdrawn along with British forces. As far as Transjordan was concerned, a few days after the legion's May pull-out from Palestine, they would turn around and come right back. Transjordan had no intention of leaving Palestine for the Iraqis to seize, said al-Rifai. Instead, Transjordan would gain control of Palestine, hold on for a year or two, and then would negotiate with the Jews. Abdallah would offer the Zionists internal autonomy and some share in governing an enlarged Transjordan. "With the support of the Jewish economy," the prime minister concluded, Abdallah's domain "would become the most influential state in the Arab Middle East."

Would the Jews accept such a program? Yes, al-Rifai claimed, enough of them would to put together an agreement. Such plans should be kept secret from the other Arab states, although they would not ultimately pose a problem. The British were not easily convinced. Clayton was skeptical; the Foreign Office was noncommittal. Alec Kirkbride thought Abdallah's real aim was more modest—the absorption of the proposed Arab state in Palestine. No such decision was necessary at that point: Abdallah could allow the military outcome to determine the extent of his territorial claims.[38]

Actually, the Arab Legion was already involved in the violence which broke out in Palestine after the partition vote. Transjordanian soldiers were involved in murders and ambushes against Jews as early as December 1947. Others began to help armed bands of volunteers across the border. Despite the Jewish Agency's numerous requests, legion units were only removed in May 1948. As al-Rifai had predicted, they were then concentrated just east of the Transjordan-Palestine boundary in the Jericho valley and in the hills just east of Jerusalem.[39]

Meanwhile, al-Rifai and Abdallah continued their political campaign. Toward the British, they implied that Transjordan's plan was certain of success and was both the sole and best available option. To others, they hinted that British support had already been granted. While Britain's high commissioner to Transjordan, Kirkbride, assured Zionist representatives that this had not yet been decided, he was impressed by their comment that Abdallah would make a preferable neighbor.[40]

Kirkbride spoke truthfully. Only as late as January 10, 1948, was the British government beginning to transform its policy toward acceptance of Abdallah's minimum plan. On that date, the Foreign Office warned him of the dangers involved: "We feel sure that Your Majesty will not have underestimated the difficulties of the task or the risks which would ensue if Transjordan were to take steps which isolated her from the other Arab states or which caused the [UN] Security Council to consider actions against her."

All these problems were not lightly dismissed. Therefore, Kirkbride was instructed, "We do not feel that we can give him any encouragement to act alone." Not only would Abdallah become a target for Arab anger, it might also "give rise to the accusation that we are using him to engineer our re-entry into Palestine."

On the other hand, Abdallah's annexation of only the projected Arab areas in Palestine might hold positive advantages. Transjordan could provide them with a stable government and avoid endless local warfare. If he stuck to the partition lines, it would be harder for the United Nations to condemn him. Possibly, some way could be found to do this without alienating the other Arabs or contributing to anti-British sentiments among them. Such a balance sheet was far from discouraging to the Amman government. Rather, it marked a gradual swing in Abdallah's direction. One month later, Bevin would finally provide complete endorsement.[41]

Abdallah's plans were certainly no secret among the other Arabs by December 1947, but Egypt and Saudi Arabia were equally suspicious and resentful over Iraq's behavior. Ibn Saud was convinced that Baghdad was using its militant posture as a cover for plots against him.

Iraq's constant calls for breaking economic ties with the Americans directly threatened Saudi Arabia's main source of income. Such moves would cost Iraq nothing, the king angrily told Iraqi leaders, "You have no cooperation with Americans to sacrifice." Before they made such suggestions to him, the Iraqis might first cancel their own oil concessions to Great Britain as a demonstration of their seriousness.

Why should Saudi Arabia so weaken itself at the demand of such questionable friends? "The king is no fool," said his old friend Philby. Thus Ibn Saud sent word to the Iraqi government: When they were prepared to advance him $300 million to recompense for the loss of oil royalties he might be more responsive to economic warfare against the United States.[42]

There was no rift in public opinion to match these private disagreements and conflicts. No matter what the Arab country, the newspapers, political parties, mass organizations, religious officials, and university students all echoed the cry to arms over Palestine. The UN vote for partition raised the long simmering concern to an angry boil. As always, the Palestine question coexisted with other issues, but between November 1947, and May 1948 it was never absent from discussion.

Syria well represents these moods at the end of 1947. Newspaper editorials called the UN delegates who supported partition "fools and dopes" because they did not understand that "every Arab and every Muslim will fight for and defend the holy shrines in Jerusalem.... We are ready for a new crusade." On December 17, the League of Ulema of Syria indeed did proclaim a holy war. Two days later the first volunteer units crossed into Palestine.

Fund-raising was equally a priority. The minister of interior appointed an official committee to collect money; the League of Ulema called on the faithful to contribute, suggesting a special Palestine tax on clubs, theaters, and recreation in general.

Hysteria also developed against the local Jewish communities. Four different newspapers accused them of, respectively, espionage, treason, collaboration with Zionism, and the spreading of cholera. The suggested range of punishment varied from banishment in remote areas to mass round-ups and concentration camps. The Damascus city government dismissed seventeen Jewish telephone switchboard operators and a Jewish engineer. The national government also fired Jewish employees. Many families were reduced to begging; some changed their names in order to get jobs. As in Egypt, such measures were pushed through by a minority, but unlike Egypt there was no one in power willing to stand up to them.

Still, Syrian Arabs had no doubts as to the outcome of the conflict. The Zionists would easily be defeated, and Palestine would be saved. The Jews in Palestine were not a very worthy foe and, after all the Syrian newspapers explained, were only "following orders from New York, the Jewish world capital." In contrast, al-Qawukji explained, the Arab was a natural born soldier.[43]

All the Arab states were equally angered and dismayed by the UN decision to implement a plan to partition Palestine into Jewish and Arab states. There could be no question of accepting such a solution, not on technical grounds such as the size of the Jewish state but on intensive opposition to any such entity. There was also broad agreement on the need to aid Palestine Arab guerrillas and to hope that such indirect measures would suffice. Arab quarrels should not be overestimated since they did not prevent a broad range of cooperation on these issues. Little difference could be found on the ways in which the general Arab public reacted to partition.

Yet these differences on a leadership level did affect the ways in which the various Arab states responded. Such conflicts between states weakened and ultimately helped to defeat Arab efforts. Essentially, this division focused around a Saudi-Egyptian and an Iraqi-Transjordanian bloc, but this model alone would be far too simplistic. The latter group was far more eager for Arab state intervention and far less friendly to the Mufti's leadership of the Palestinian Arabs. To Saudi Arabia and Egypt, their rivals seemed part of an undifferentiated Hashemite conspiracy to control Palestine's future and to threaten Saudi security.

Egypt and Saudi Arabia had had a long history of rocky but ultimately successful diplomatic negotiations with the West. Both were conscious of their relative fragility—Egypt in terms of domestic politics, Saudi Arabia through its economic dependence on the West—and the demands which a war would place upon them. Neither was in a position to compete for direct control of Palestine. They therefore backed the Mufti as a leader independent of Hashemite entanglements. Either a victory by his forces or continued pressure on Britain and America might provide an Arab triumph without a full-scale, international war.

While the two Hashemite states might have been individually planning to dominate the Arab east, there was no "Hashemite conspiracy" because of the sharp differences between the objectives of Iraq and Transjordan. By choice, Abdallah stood against all the other Arab governments, including Syria and the Arab Higher Committee. His plan sought the culmination of his two-decades-long attempt to add Palestine —or as much of it as possible—to his kingdom. He did not fear his Arab colleagues as he did not believe in their power to defeat the Jews. If Egypt and Saudi Arabia sought to enlist the British and Americans for a negotiated rejection of partition, Abdallah wanted to win them to his annexationist proposal. Though eager for Arab intervention into Palestine, Abdallah wanted a particular kind of direct invasion and would allow neither Syrian nor Iraqi troops onto his territory.

Syria occupied an intermediate position. Of all the Arab states, its emotional ties to Palestine ran the deepest; it was the natural base for a volunteer liberation army. Was their backing for al-Qawukji a loyal effort to aid the Mufti or an attempt to set up an alternative leadership beholden to Damascus? This is not entirely clear, but conscious of the Greater Syria and Fertile Crescent unity plans, Syrian leaders would not allow either Transjordanian or Iraqi troops on their soil. Could Damascus countenance a third unfriendly neighbor in Palestine?

As for the Mufti, he seemed to distrust all the Arab regimes. His differences with them in 1937 and 1939 could not be forgotten, nor could he ignore their attempts to support rival Palestine Arabs during his long years of exile in Europe. Abdallah was an old enemy and al-Qawukji a more recent critic. The dominant Iraqi politicians had all sided with the British against the Rashid Ali coup. He must have had an ambiguous feeling toward Arab state military intervention. He surely would not forego such troops if needed against the Zionists, yet could he really trust them to leave him in control of an independent Arab Palestine? The Arab League's repeated refusal to accept the establishment of an Arab Palestine government did not bode well.

The unanimity of Arab feeling over Palestine left a great many important issues unresolved. Most of them would have to be straightened out in the remaining five months before the deadline for partition. Events in the fateful year 1948 would accelerate accordingly.

12
The Slippery Road to War: January–May 1948

*A*s the year 1948 opened, talk in and about the Arab world increasingly turned to military matters. The Palestine Arabs and the Arab states were pledged to resist partition at all costs; the Jews were equally determined to declare their own state on the territory assigned to it by the United Nations. Great Britain, refusing to be caught in the middle of this collision, declared the complete withdrawal of its forces and abdication of the mandate by May 15, 1948.

Fighting in Palestine started immediately after the UN vote for partition. The guerrillas of the Arab Higher Committee and al-Qawukji's liberation army were making an all-out effort to shred the Zionist forces before Israel could be established. Volunteers and material aid from the Arab countries was steadily flowing into Palestine. Yet if those troops already in the field were insufficient to deliver an Arab victory, could the neighboring countries avoid direct intervention by their own regular armies?

King Abdallah, his royal title elevated by Transjordan's independence, hoped for and expected such an eventuality, since he had long planned to annex Arab Palestine—and the Jewish parts, too, if possible. Iraq, pressed by tremendous internal pressures, also professed itself eager for the fray. Syria cheered on al-Qawukji, its favorite son in the battle for Palestine. Egypt and Saudi Arabia aided the Mufti, preferring an outcome which did not require their own direct involvement.

Most of these expectations were shattered on the battlefield. Far from folding under the guerrilla assault, the Zionists held all their settlements against the irregular forces. The Haganah, with its long years of underground experience and its many veterans of the British army, was more than a match for the local opponents, though the margin of Jewish victory was far narrower than is often thought. Social and political organization was one key difference: the Arab Higher Committee's failure to set up local infrastructures and to mobilize their own people was to cost dearly.

In April 1948, a Zionist counteroffensive advanced into the territories earmarked for the Arab state. The Arab strategic plan had called for stretching the Zionist forces thin, then striking hard at the weak points. Instead, the poorly coordinated Arab units were forced onto the defensive and were not properly deployed to defend their own rear areas. Weeks before May 15, although the Arabs still threatened to cut off Jewish Jerusalem and the Zionist position was far from strong, it was clear that guerrilla forces alone would not suffice to sweep the Jews into the sea.

This reduced the Arab states' options to two: a last-minute diplomatic miracle or all-out war. For one brief moment it seemed that the United States might rescue the former alternative. American policymakers were horrified by Arab threats of regional chaos and the decimation of U.S. interests. The appalling violence in Palestine coupled with Britain's rejection of responsibility made orderly transition seem unlikely. Therefore, the State Department signalled a retreat from partition in late February, thinking to prevent a massacre of Jews as much as avoiding a lynching of American petroleum concessions. One goal of militant Arab rhetoric, of course, had been to produce just such a reaction.

A peaceful solution was not possible any more than an exclusively internal one. Truman's return to the helm—or at least his return to the original course—meant a continued American commitment to partition, but the diplomatic breakdown was not simply an American responsibility. When provided an opportunity, Egypt and Saudi Arabia found that it was too late to brake the acceleration toward war. Arab public opinion and the determined interventionism of Transjordan and Iraq forbade such a solution.

On May 15, 1948, after the British withdrew their last detachments, the mandate ended and the state of Israel was born. Regular Arab armies crossed into Palestine at the same moment. Thirty years of Arab debate and protest, it seemed, would culminate in this single, decisive contest.

Arab politics between January and May 1948, is the story of a crisis growing toward the boiling point. Nowhere was this more apparent than in Damascus. "Syria unofficially went to war in December," wrote U.S. Minister Robert Memminger on January 2, 1948. Many Syrians demanded that this be made official even before May. The government responded by doing everything short of giving its own army marching orders.

Parliament quickly declared the UN partition plan not binding on Syria, voted $1 million for a Palestine Liberation Fund, and passed a compulsory military training law. The minister of national economy took control of all exports to Palestine; the minister of defense opened recruiting centers in schools and government buildings, quartered volunteers on army bases, and chose regular officers to train them.[1]

Even General Safwat's headquarters for the Popular Army was located in a Syrian military camp just outside of Damascus. One of his top aides was Syrian Colonel Adib al-Shishakli, who would emerge as the country's dictator the following year. Another future coup-maker, Colonel Husni al-Zaim, was promoted to director-general of police to prepare security measures for the coming war.

There was much to keep them busy. As early as December, sizeable bands were being sent across the border and on at least one occasion a hit-and-run raid was staged from Syrian soil. By mid-February, about thirty-eight hundred men, mostly Iraqis, Syrians, and Palestinian Arabs, had received basic training. At the peak of military operations, al-Qawukji was able to field about five thousand men, including about one thousand Palestine Arabs.

The military course of the war would cast considerable doubt on al-Qawukji's skills as commander, but this could not be blamed on lack of experience. Born in Aleppo, Syria, he fought in the Ottoman army during World War I and with the French against Faysal's short-lived Syrian kingdom. Such a record did not seem likely to produce a dedicated Arab nationalist. Nevertheless, in 1925 he changed sides and joined an anti-French revolt. From this point on, his life became a series of defeats and flights. After the French crushed the uprising, al-Qawukji became military adviser to Ibn Saud and later joined the Iraqi army. In 1936 he resigned to lead guerrilla forces during the Palestine general strike. Under British pressure, he retreated to Iraq and, when Rashid Ali fell, to Germany where he sat out World War II. This career sadly illustrated the trail of Arab disappointments during those decades.

Now the Palestine war offered one last great opportunity for vindication, not only for al-Qawukji personally but for the long-trampled pride of all Arabs. Syria did not skimp on the aid needed to fulfill this vision. Active-duty officers and artillery were provided to help. When al-Qawukji's first 700-man battalion crossed into Palestine, they rode in Syrian army trucks and followed its guides.

This was still only January 1948, and the British were unprepared to countenance such direct foreign intervention. After a stiff British protest, al-Qawukji was urged to route his infiltrations through Lebanon or Transjordan. The latter country provided a far better access to his advanced base at Nablus, but the political obstacles were somewhat daunting. To Abdallah, these volunteer forces were a "menace" to his own plans and possibly the internal security of his kingdom. When the vanguard of al-Qawukji's forces reached Deraa in Transjordan on January 22, the local commander refused to let them pass. Taha al-Hashimi advised them to cross the border by force, but General Safwat wisely chose a private meeting with King Abdallah in Amman. After Safwat gave assurances, the men were escorted through Transjordan and across the Allenby bridge into Palestine.[2]

In addition to such willing or unwilling logistical aid, Arab states also donated a variety of weapons to the Mufti's forces. A February 8 Arab League military committee report counted more than forty-five hundred rifles, more than a million rounds of ammunition, and large amounts of small arms provided mostly by Egypt and Iraq.

International political developments also seemed to move in the Arabs' favor. While a December 1947 American arms embargo made it difficult for the Zionists to purchase military equipment, British weapons continued to flow into the Arab states. British treaties with Egypt on January 5, and with Iraq five days later provided additional benefits. The former accord ended the wartime blockage of Egyptian sterling accounts, allowing $25 million and £25 million in foreign exchange for immediate use. The Anglo-Iraq Portsmouth treaty gave Iraq the opportunity to draw on British military equipment with a high priority.

As if this were not enough, the British sea blockade against Jewish immigrants seeking to enter Palestine was tightened at the very moment when al-Qawukji's forces were passing unhindered across the border. London informed the United Nations on January 21, of the impossibility of opening a port for Jewish immigration. Only on May 15, did this naval embargo end.[3]

Particularly generous was the £2.5 million annual subsidy for Transjordan's Arab Legion, with thirty-seven British officers seconded as advisers. A forty-five-man British military mission had been established in Saudi Arabia and, though Egypt had already dismissed its British training mission, Cairo received 40 war planes, almost 300 troop carriers, and other equipment over the two years ending in June 1947. Needless to say, such assistance was not intended for use in Palestine, but the Arab armies' increased strength became an important factor in the crisis.

England and the United States tread cautiously in further endangering their relations with the Arab world. Britain's minister of state told Parliament on February 16, that there was still no evidence that military equipment supplied Arab governments under London's new treaties was being forwarded to Palestine. Two days later, the cabinet announced continued deliveries to Iraq of aircraft, artillery, antitank guns, antiaircraft batteries, and armored cars. Export licenses were not withdrawn until June 3, two weeks after the overt invasion by the neighboring states. When U.S. Secretary of State Marshall met Jewish Agency representatives on March 26, he denied knowledge of any foreign Arab troops in Palestine.[4]

No wonder that Nuri al-Said could later tell Iraq's parliament, "It became clear to us that Britain viewed with favor the Arab aims regarding Palestine." So intoxicating was the atmosphere after the successful Portsmouth talks that Foreign Minister al-Jamali claimed Bevin's agreement on the spot for an Iraqi invasion of Palestine to destroy the projected Jewish state.[5]

Some of these hindsight declarations were apparently untrue, since by that time establishment politicians were defending themselves over the unpopular Anglo-Iraq treaty and the disastrous military campaign in Palestine. Bevin's deal was with Transjordan, not Iraq, and for Abdallah's limited conquest, not the obliteration of the Jews. As always, Abdallah sought to complement an accord with the British by an agreement with the Zionists. While he lobbied in London for his occupation of the Arab portion of Palestine, the king also met with Golda Meir and other Jewish Agency delegates. Their code name for him was also "Meir," an anagram of "emir," his traditional title.

Abdallah's ambiguity, however, fed Zionist suspicions. Was he only seeking to occupy the territory set aside for the Arab Palestine state or did he still wish to be monarch of the whole country? Did he plan to attack the Jews or could a settlement be resolved without war? Were the Palestine Arabs or the other Arab states likely to accept such a Transjordanian solution?

Ben-Gurion, by now the Zionists' unchallenged leader, wavered. His chief Arabist, Sassoon, told him that the Mufti monopolized the Palestine Arabs' loyalty. Abdallah was "completely isolated" and "cannot be relied upon," Ben-Gurion wrote. The king was not so easily written off. He would not accept the Mufti's rule, Abdallah told his Jewish contacts, and would not let Iraqi troops enter Transjordan. He was willing to make an alliance with the Jews, perhaps bringing in Druze leaders as well. Ben-Gurion decided to wait and see: "If he'll stay until the end isn't clear to me," he wrote Shertok, "but there's a chance."[6]

The British, who were moving toward acceptance of Abdallah's offer, urged the Jews to agree. Officers at British Middle East headquarters described Abdallah's plan to annex Arab Palestine as "the one possible policy offering some chance of averting chaos." They realized that the Arab League, Syria, Saudi Arabia, and the Mufti's men would not be pleased, but they doubted the viability of any Arab Palestine state. Certainly, the Mufti would not prove friendly to British interests. Perhaps war might be avoided.

Zionist leaders understood the advantages of a Transjordan solution for Britain, but were not so sure of how it would affect them. After all, Abdallah spoke of Jewish territorial concessions, including the granting of an Isdud-Jaffa corridor to provide his kingdom with an outlet on the Mediterranean. Abdallah's pursuit of a Greater Syria unity might also encourage his rivals to overthrow him, tearing up any contract he had made. Moreover, they did not believe that Abdallah could restrain the other Arab governments from a full-scale invasion. On the other hand, if Abdallah could reach an acceptable agreement, the Jewish state might give him a large loan on favorable conditions. There were also indications that al-Alami and other Palestine Arabs might rally to Abdallah's annexation of the Arab area.

British Secretary of State for the Colonies Arthur Creech-Jones also argued on Abdallah's behalf. The Mufti's influence was declining, he claimed, and he did not believe that the Arab states, except for Syria, would really go through with a general offensive. Under no circumstances would the Arab Legion attack the Jews, he explained. The whole matter would be broached to Abdallah's representatives in February, when they came to London to discuss updating the Anglo-Transjordan treaty.[7]

As the moment of truth approached, Transjordan showed an unaccustomed caution in its inter-Arab relations. Abdallah promised to cooperate with his fellow Arab League members and to carry out their joint decisions. Syria's Jamil Mardam was unimpressed. Abdallah might want to annex Palestine, Mardam explained, but if he tried to do so he would be assassinated. This was the ultimate Arab sanction against any breaking of ranks.[8]

Abdallah had long since become hardened to such threats. He carefully laid the groundwork for his negotiations with Britain and a new relationship with Palestine. He named a Palestine-born prime minister, Tawfiq Abu al-Huda, and a new foreign minister, Dr. Fawzi al-Mulki. As minister of communications, the king chose Baha al-Din Tuqan, a member of an important Nablus family who had served as Transjordan's consul-general in Jerusalem.

These men still could not settle on a single plan. Abdallah, al-Rifai, and al-Mulki all told American diplomats that they would prefer to take all of Palestine, giving the Jews a small territory within a federal system. When the Zionists heard this, their doubts about the value of an accord with Abdallah were reinforced.

All this made for a most dangerous game. Mardam's prophecy might still be fulfilled. The Mufti's agents were trying to subvert the Arab Legion troops, to turn them against their king. Abdallah was risking everything on this last chance to win additional territory for his kingdom. Abdallah was brave enough, impetuous enough, and perhaps foolish enough to accept the challenge.

Such dangers might have seemed considerably diminished after Bevin's talk with Abdallah's new prime minister and foreign minister. They had gone to London, along with General Glubb, ostensibly to discuss modifications of the 1946 Anglo-Transjordan treaty; the mission's real purpose was to explain Abdallah's intentions over Palestine.

Abu al-Huda stated the problem from Amman's standpoint: The Jews would establish their state on May 15, but their Arab counterparts were not so well organized or prepared. Therefore, either the Jews would take over the Arab state or the Mufti would make himself its master. Only the Arab Legion could avoid this, but Transjordan would only occupy those Arab areas contiguous to its borders. Gaza and western Galilee would not be seized.

Bevin had already made up his mind. "It seems the obvious thing to do," he replied in a matter-of-fact manner, "but do not go and invade the areas allotted to the Jews." Abu al-Huda agreed. On this note the meeting ended. After thirty years of seeking some way out of Palestine, the British government had made its commitment. After equally long decades of effort, Abdallah's prize seemed within reach. His diplomatic coup might change the whole situation at a single stroke. The Arab states would protest at first, but it would not be long before they would accept this outcome—so Bevin and Abdallah thought.[9]

Matters were not, of course, so simple. The other Arab states had not reconciled themselves either to the creation of a Jewish regime or to Abdallah's inheritance of Arab Palestine. Their own public opinion and political factions were pressing them onward to war. Abdallah's defection would only accelerate these trends.

In Egypt, for example, Prime Minister Nuqrashi sat atop a political powder keg. Like many palace politicians, he had started as a militant Wafdist: charter party member, head of the student section, tried and acquitted of involvement in the murder of the British commander of Egypt's military, Lee Stack. Nuqrashi even married a niece of Zaghlul's wife. Nevertheless, the party expelled him after a 1937 factional struggle. With Ahmed Mahir, he founded the conservative Saadist party and served in Ali Mahir's and Mahmud's cabinets. When the king threw out the Wafd in October 1944, Nuqrashi became minister of foreign affairs, and when Prime Minister Ahmed Mahir was assassinated because of his declaration of war against Germany, Nuqrashi succeeded him.

The sixty-year-old prime minister, nicknamed the "timid sphinx" and "the village schoolmaster of Egyptian politics," faced a most untimid Muslim Brotherhood. Closely allied with the Mufti, the Brotherhood had already placed two thousand volunteers in the field. After the Palestine war, Nuqrashi would finally have his showdown with the group, a collision which would lead to his assassination. Yet in the spring of 1948 he knew his political position was too weak to challenge them. The Wafd also criticized his regime for insufficient militancy, and there could be no doubt that any free election would bring that party to power.

Quick to seek leadership on such an essential issue, the Wafd helped organize the Nile Valley Higher Committee for Palestine and tried to raise its own volunteer fighters to compete with the Brotherhood. As in Syria, there were mass meetings and fund-raising campaigns. Propaganda intensified against Egyptian Jews, who were accused of contaminating water supplies, smuggling gold, flooding the country with counterfeit banknotes, training terrorists, and spreading cholera in Syria. (The "war of microbes," in the headlines of the pro-Wafd *Al Misri*.) Other newspapers warned that the Jews might try to sabotage Egypt's factories and water supplies. The pro-Wafd weekly *Al Nida* spoke of 7000 Zionist agents with 500 hidden wireless radios in Cairo alone.[10]

Similar things happened in Lebanon, where the government took over supervision of money-raising efforts and the collection of weapons and volunteers. Yet public opinion and leading newspapers disapproved of the bombings against Jewish schools, shops, and homes. In a country resting on a complex web of intercommunal relations, the spread of such hatreds might be impossible to stop. Many Jewish merchants were, however, frightened into giving substantial sums for the Arab cause: the newspaper *L'Orient* shamed slackers by noting that a leading Jewish banker donated more money than Lebanon's richest Muslim landlord.

Government protection was provided the Jewish community in

Beirut's Abu Jamil quarter, but foreign—particularly Palestinian—Jews were deported. The American University of Beirut refused the government's order to expel its 100 Jewish students, but it did furnish a list of those non-Lebanese nationals who might be deported. True to Lebanon's tradition of hospitality, most were allowed to finish their courses first.[11]

Underneath the confident surface, Lebanese and Syrian politicians began to evidence their first signs of doubt over Arab planning. Mardam predicted victory "within a few years" and promised that al-Qawukji's army would soon "teach the treacherous Jews an unforgettable lesson." At the same time, he quietly accused the Arab Higher Committee of political and military incompetence. Lebanese Finance Minister Muhammad Abbud spoke of a small selfish group which ran the Arab League, and would fall apart without the Palestine issue. The Jews had done the work of building up Palestine, Abbud complained, but the Mufti, al-Qawukji, and Ghuri would take it over in order to feather their own nests.[12]

The turbulence in these countries was as nothing compared to Iraq, where the Anglo-Iraq Portsmouth treaty had unleashed a hurricane of protest. The winter of 1947–48 had already seen a wild round of inflation, a plague of locusts, poor harvests, and violent street demonstrations. On top of this, the treaty set off student rioting and a march of tens of thousands in downtown Baghdad. When police and dissidents opened fire on each other at the "Battle of the Bridge," dozens were killed and the unpopular government fell.

It was like the late 1930s all over again. The new regime was anti-British and included the Pan-Arab Istiqlal party, the main agitator over Palestine. By March 1948, Baghdad was again in a militant mood. Soldiers deserted the Iraqi army to join al-Qawukji, while the newspapers carried daily reports of Arab successes and of heavy Jewish casualties. Reuter's dispatches which were less sanguine could be edited to taste through the government monopoly on news dissemination. Such misinformation made it particularly difficult for the government in later years to explain the unexpected Arab defeat.

Safwat knew better, but it took him six weeks to arrange a conference of Arab military commanders to discuss their previous lack of coordination. The February meeting of the Arab League Political Committee did not provide any improvements. Syria and Iraq failed to win Saudi support for economic sanctions against the United States. The Egyptians and Saudis had hoped for some diplomatic solution. With the problems plaguing the Arab irregulars in the field and the cooperation of the Arab states, such initiatives were more welcome than ever.

By fortunate coincidence, these statesmen were not the only ones who felt events slipping out of control. American diplomats were also becoming fearful of a Middle East disaster. They would seek to knit together a last-minute accord to avert this danger.

As early as January 1948, the State Department's Policy Planning Committee was warning that partition, originally adopted as a pragmatic solution, might be unworkable. The Palestine civil war and British noncooperation would doom the complex UN plan. A Jewish state could not survive, and the United States would dare not forcefully intervene to save it, lest America find itself at war with the Arab world. Washington might best follow Britain's decision to have nothing to do with partition. They recommended the return of the issue to the UN Security Council for a new investigation.

Truman was worried. The deepening of the Cold War raised U.S. strategic interests in the region: a new crisis was the last thing needed by the White House. The barrage of State Department arguments continued: Palestine was not ready for self-government, and an extended trusteeship period might be necessary to sort out these problems. Exactly who made the next key decisions has never been entirely clarified, but suddenly American policy was dramatically altered. On February 24, American UN Ambassador Warren Austin hinted at the new stand; on March 19, Austin recommended that partition be suspended. Truman was angered at this latter speech, accusing the State Department of distorting his orders. Nevertheless, the United States did not completely return to its original enthusiasm for partition until Truman's recognition of Israel on May 15.[13]

The extensive controversy over these events has always focused on American relations with the Zionists, attributing Truman's actions to moral considerations or to the pursuit of liberal votes in the upcoming elections. The State Department's behavior is explained either by the officials' dedication to the long-range national interest or to their visceral opposition to Zionism. Yet almost all of these debates have ignored the bilateral U.S.-Arab diplomacy involved in the twists and turns of that period. American policy seemed motivated by the belief that some sort of peaceful settlement with the Arab states was still possible. When this hope faded and no imaginative alternative any longer presented itself, Washington's best remaining option apparently was a return to support for partition.

Austin's reversals were the answer to Egyptian and Saudi prayers. Arab delegates to the UN had already suggested a reconsideration of partition. Egypt's foreign minister read Austin's first speech with considerable relief, and official Arab reaction elsewhere was guarded but favorable. If plans for a Jewish state were abandoned, the Egyptians suggested, they would be willing to discuss a federalized or cantonized Palestine with limited Jewish immigration. If Cairo would only serve as an example to its allies, U.S. Ambassador S. Pinkney Tuck hoped, war might still be avoided. The task was difficult, but Cairo was willing to try.[14]

At first, prospects for an agreement seemed extremely hopeful. When Secretary of State Marshall explained that the American position sought to preclude Arab military intervention, Azzam agreed. Chamoun and Malik from Lebanon. Mahmud Fawzi of Egypt, and Syria's al-Khuri, suggested three possible plans on which a settlement might be based.

The first was a unitary state with explicit minority guarantees, a bicameral legislature with equal Jewish representation in the senate, municipal autonomy, and admission of up to one hundred thousand Jews over two to three years. Second, similar principles could be applied within the framework of a federal or canton organization for the state. Third, the least likely alternative would be a continued trusteeship with a larger measure of self-government. Underlying these suggestions were two preconditions on which the Arabs would not compromise: partition must be abandoned and any trusteeship must be a transitional one leading to independence.

King Ibn Saud, Azzam, and Nuqrashi were especially enthusiastic over this program. When the Security Council voted to support a truce on April 17, Azzam voiced league acceptance in principle if these two last points were satisfied. The Arab states—or at least some of them—had finally made concessions along the lines of the postwar British proposals, the Anglo-American Committee of Inquiry report, and the UNSCOP minority plan. Such initiatives a year or two earlier might have saved victory for the Arab side. Had events gone too far by the spring of 1948 to still reverse the partition process?[15]

The State Department refused to take a fatalistic approach, but one obstacle after another blocked progress. The Arab states were not entirely secure about their own three proffered options. Besides, as in 1939 Egypt could not guarantee delivery of its hawkish allies. Further, the implementation of any new program for Palestine required the restoration of order there, but the British refused to consider staying on beyond May 15, would not use force against either side, and had little faith in any truce agreement. They had already settled on Abdallah's proposal. The United States itself was not eager to send American troops under any conditions. When the State Department's Dean Rusk, suggested an international peace-keeping force to police the truce and trusteeship, the Arabs were not enthusiastic. Even his remarkable suggestion that Egypt, as a leading Arab League member and a relative moderate, might participate in this multinational unit did not change Cairo's mind.[16]

Though some Zionist leaders seemed to bend under American pressure to stand down from partition, Ben-Gurion and the majority remained adamantly for creation of a Jewish state on May 15. They were loathe to sacrifice an opportunity which might not come again for centuries. Contrary to the warnings of Western military experts, they believed it was possible to turn back the inevitable Arab invasion. Weizmann urged President Truman to live up to American pledges in support of partition.

But the fatal blow to American efforts was dealt by the disunity of the Arab League members and by the continuing pressure of public opinion in the neighboring states. Further, as in 1939, the Mufti was not willing to accept such half-loaf or even three-quarters-loaf ideas. Nor did Abdallah intend to lose his prize at the last moment. Internal conflict in Baghdad and Cairo also discouraged those regimes from following through on any personal preferences for a diplomatic settlement. The locomotives' boilers had been too highly stoked to respond to their own engineers. Political brakes no longer functioned.

Saudi Arabia, where religious passion mingled with the desire for empirical success, was particularly in favor of the truce idea. Prince Faysal wanted to ensure that a new trusteeship would bar immigration and land sales. The whole mechanism made him apprehensive — foreign-controlled mandates had not proved congenial to the Arabs before — but anything was preferable to a Jewish state. As long as that could be avoided, there would be no Saudi problem with "public opinion."[17]

On the other hand, growing political violence in Egypt undermined that keystone of any settlement. The emotions of the masses and of most of the political elite were too deeply engaged. A proliferation of organizations, many with interlocking directorates, others with only paper existences, proclaimed their devotion to an exclusively Arab Palestine. The Muslim Brotherhood, the Nile Valley Committee for the Defense of Palestine, the Al-Azhar religious notables, the Mufti, Young Egypt, the Young Men's Muslim Association, the Arab Land Committee, and the Arab Union, poured out exhortations and denunciations.

Behind the ad hoc groups stood powerful political forces from across the ideological spectrum. They eagerly awaited the least sign of government weakness or moderation. "If Rommel had won," said Salih Harb, a veteran politician and director of the Young Men's Muslim Association, "we would be independent now." Was Nuqrashi, in view of Rommel's failure, to be considered a mere lap dog of the British? Could the activity of Ali Mahir and Makram Ubeid in the Nile Valley Committee be viewed as completely separate from their attitude to the government? What about the thousands of Muslim Brothers and the hundreds of Young Egypt members being drilled for service in Palestine? In the face of all this, with the undaunted belief in a quick and glorious victory, was there a real chance of Nuqrashi imposing a truce and urging a new trusteeship arrangement?

Cairo was full of guns and ammunition: rifles stolen from the British or left over from the war; equipment from America, Italy, Germany, and other countries. The Brotherhood was telling Egyptian soldiers to desert, taking their weapons with them. Egyptian officers were filling the lobby of the Arab League office in their rush to volunteer. One truck being loaded with weapons exploded only fifty yards from the Mufti's villa, but the convoys to Jerusalem rolled onward as the weeks went past. The momentum could not have been greater. Nuqrashi would not forget that a change in policy might turn all those guns against him.[18]

Moreover, the martial energy and easy confidence were deceptive. The impressiveness of the armed forces' planes, armor, and artillery concealed a frightful lack of preparation. Only four battalions were really fit for battle, General Muhammad Naguib, the expeditionary force's second-in-command, warned his superiors that the available men and materials were inadequate for the mission assigned them. Nuqrashi could not have been entirely ignorant of these facts. If an Egyptian invasion of Palestine were defeated by the Jews, the country's prestige would be severely damaged. For the incumbent regime, the results might be fatal. As rumors of a planned coup swept Cairo following an assassination attempt against Nahhas, Nuqrashi preferred the army stay at home to protect the government. Wisely, Iraq and other hawkish regimes concentrated their persuasive powers on King Farouk instead of his prime minister. Egypt would lose face if it did less for Palestine than the other Arab states, they told him. When the time came, Farouk would override Nuqrashi's hesitancy.[19]

Chaim Weizmann, the Zionist leader, was asked at this time how a few hundred thousand Jews could hope to stand up against millions of Arabs. Numbers were not necessarily decisive, he replied: "The trouble with the Egyptian army is that its soldiers are too lean and its officers too fat." This assertion also applied to other Arab armies. Many officers were neither competent nor courageous—though there were no lack of exceptions — and social distance between officers and enlisted men lowered military effectiveness. Many of the worst commanders received their positions through political influence. Wholesale munitions profiteering on the home front meant inferior or inadequate weaponry for front-line units—a cause of dispiriting scandals particularly in Egypt. These conditions encouraged many young officers to join revolutionary groups or mount antigovernment conspiracies in later years in order to avenge these shameful shortcomings.[20]

The discouraging news from Palestine was responsible for calling the Arab states' hand. The Jewish offensive was meeting with success, Safwat warned, and the guerrilla forces might not hold out for long. Dispatch of the regular armies was a necessity, the general told the Arab League Political Committee's April 10 meeting in Cairo.

Then came a bombshell: Transjordan would send the Arab Legion into Palestine as soon as the mandate ended, its delegate announced, and he requested the league to issue orders to that effect. The Egyptians and Riyad al-Sulh, who had been working on a diplomatic solution, argued against a formal invasion. The meeting dissolved in confusion and consternation. They had for so long talked about sending in their armies, but now that the idea was actually on the table there was perceptible hesitation. Equally controversial was the invasion's political objective.

Two days later, Farouk suggested some conciliatory language. Any Arab intervention in Palestine would be considered a purely temporary expedient; under no circumstances would it constitute a conquest or partition of Palestine. After its liberation, Palestine would be returned to its inhabitants who would choose their own government. This compromise pleased everyone and was incorporated into the Political Committee's resolution.

Ostensibly, this decision seemed aimed at Transjordan, but in practice it was a material victory for that country. Despite the paper declaration pledging eventual withdrawal from Palestine, Abdallah now had Arab League agreement to enter the country. Once the Arab Legion was in, he knew, it could not be easily dislodged by the League. Thus Amman quickly reiterated its own independent position: "Palestine and Transjordan are one, for Palestine is the coastline and Transjordan the hinterland of the same country." If the other Arab states chose not to order their armies across the border, Abdallah would be all the happier. Sometimes he actually seemed to believe that other Arab states might actually allow him a unilateral invasion and a free hand.[21]

This dream became less likely with each passing week. In every country, April saw the pressures for war intensified. A student hunger strike in Baghdad urged the army's dispatch to Palestine. The Iraqi government closed its oil pipeline to Haifa and began full military preparations. The regent, Abd al-Illah, took his ministers of defense, finance, and foreign affairs to Amman and Cairo for consultations. Shortly thereafter, on April 27, the army's Second Motorized Brigade left for Transjordan on its way to the Palestine border.[22]

A citywide general strike rocked Beirut on April 16, calling for an end to the official nonintervention policy. "You have been stingy in providing the warriors with arms and ammunition," *Al Hayat* taunted the Arab leaders. Other newspapers criticized government officials' meager contributions to the Palestine fund. One daily remarked, "Among the young men who shouted 'Long live Arab Palestine!' we did not see a single one get a gun, put on a uniform, and say 'On to Palestine!'" To avoid such criticism, and to shield military activities, the government imposed censorship on April 29, over all news concerning Palestine.[23]

After a Jewish offensive captured the port city of Haifa, a Damascus general strike demanded Syrian intervention. Mardam responded with a promise to "fight on land, at sea, and in the air until we achieve victory," in phrases reminiscent of Winston Churchill's Battle of Britain speeches.[24]

All of this activity apparently convinced Abdallah that his idea of a preemptive deal with the Zionists was impossible. His April 10 challenge had been accepted by the other states. Through no fault of the State Department's, their last-minute effort had also failed. By April 24, the last day of the Arab League's Cairo conference, the invasion of Palestine had been decided. Two days later, Transjordan's king acknowledged this to a visiting journalist: "The only way left for us is war. I will have the pleasure and honor to save Palestine."[25]

The British reacted to all this with cynical blindness; the Americans evidenced frustration. Only two days after Abdallah's battle cry, Bevin told Parliament, "There are no signs that King Abdallah intends to take any warlike acts." U.S. Secretary of State Marshall appealed one last time to Azzam: Washington was sincere in its new trusteeship proposal. America wanted to help the Middle East with political and economic aid, he cabled, but such efforts would be useless if the Palestine crisis escalated to war.[26]

As for the Jews, these events confirmed them in their earlier decision not to make an arrangement with Abdallah. The Zionists would oppose all Arab intervention into Palestine, Shertok wrote, "including and primarily Transjordan." Sassoon and other Jewish Agency Arabists thought negotiations would only prove viable after the Jews had proved their mettle on the battlefield. Even then, they preferred an independent Arab Palestine state to the expansion of Transjordan.[27]

Yet even then the Arab states had not entirely burned their bridges. True, trains carrying Egyptian infantry and artillery battalions were beginning to chug eastward from Cairo and Alexandria and, on April 27, the Egyptian navy began patrols along the south Palestine coast, but Nuqrashi had not given up hope. When the Arab League met in Amman on April 30, it was suggested that the mere mobilization of Arab armies on the border would cause the great powers to intervene, forcing the Jews to accept Arab peace conditions.

Overweening confidence made this possibility seem irrelevant. When military commanders warned that the war required five fully equipped divisions and six air force squadrons under united command, the Political Committee rejected this as exaggeration. Arab armies still lacked joint leadership, but unless the invasion was carried out on schedule, Azzam warned, the Arab League might dissolve into warring factions. Any government resisting a march on Palestine might be overthrown by its own people.[28]

Azzam's sad reference to "warring factions" acknowledged the pressure from Transjordan, Iraq, and Syria for quick military action. But King Abdallah did not neglect necessary political preparations either. General Glubb and other Arab Legion officers briefed Palestine Arab mayors and notables on their military plans at special social gatherings. They enjoyed some real success in winning new adherents for Transjordan's annexation program. The king also raised contributions to help the first outward wave of Palestine Arab refugees fleeing the fighting. Some of them were put to work spreading Amman's propaganda.

"The Zionist fortress will fall after the first attack," Abdallah told a journalist, "and the Jews will stretch out the hand of peace to the Arabs." Here was the essence of Abdallah's new dual strategy. With the inevitable invasion by all the Arab states, he could no longer offer the Zionists a *de facto* partition of Palestine between them along the borders set down by the United Nations. His offer to Meir the previous November was now obsolete. However, he could once again promise the Jews fair treatment when his kingdom took over Palestine. After the Zionists were defeated, they would remember his generosity and accept his annexation. Their cooperation would strengthen his new realm and provide legitimacy for its expansion. Coupling this support with that of favorable Palestine Arabs, Abdallah could displace the Mufti and solve the Palestine conflict once and for all. Jews and Arabs might live side by side in peace under his rule.

Such were the circumstances around Abdallah's second meeting with Golda Meir. She was conveyed to him dressed in Arab garb in the automobile of one of his trusted men. Meir found the king depressed, preoccupied, and anxious. After all, the need to deal with a half-dozen other Arab armies on Palestine's soil scarcely simplified his plan. Perhaps it would be better to gain some more time. The king therefore proposed that the Jews postpone declaring independence for one year, after which Palestine would merge into Transjordan. The Jews would receive 50 percent of the seats in the united kingdom's legislature, and the other Arab states could not invade. He explained, "I am no longer alone, but there are five of us now, and I am committed to the struggle." Meir refused his offer: the Zionists would take their chances. Ezra Danin of the Jewish Agency, who was also present, advised the king to tighten his own security—there would be dangerous days ahead.[29]

Abdallah's urgency was understandable. Earlier that day, May 11, the invasion plan was approved by the Arab League's Political Committee. Each country's army was assigned a particular mission. Transjordan would move through Jenin to Afuleh, Syria should march into the central Galilee through Safed and toward Nazareth, and Iraq would advance through Afuleh. The Lebanese army would drive along the coast through Acre. All four would link up to attack Haifa. The Egyptians would divert Jewish forces away from Haifa by besieging Tel Aviv. This was impressive in theory, but the Arab armies lacked the skillful coordination to implement the plan. The Zionist forces were able to defeat them one by one.[30]

Even after all of these decisions were made, Egypt awaited the last possible moment to commit itself. Only on May 12, did Nuqrashi ask a secret session of parliament to authorize the invasion. Farouk refused to abide this delay and ordered in the army himself. Already, knowledgable people in Cairo knew that things in Palestine were not going well. The generals protested that their troops were untrained. If the Jews defeated the Egyptians, the result might be as disastrous as any refusal to declare war. Nuqrashi still believed that the United Nations would intervene before the fighting went very far. Egypt was not really going into a full-scale conflict, he reassured his commanders, the decision was really more in the nature of a political demonstration.[31]

Martial law was declared at 6 P.M. on May 14. Reservists were mobilized; censorship of mail, radio, and the press was imposed. Across the country, prayers in the mosques urged peace at home and Arab victory. Farouk received Jewish leaders and promised them protection. Foreign diplomats were called in and told that the Egyptian army would cross the border at midnight. *Al Ahram* predicted an Arab triumph: "The history of the Egyptian army is one long list of victories."[32]

These final days were as frustrating for Glubb as for Nuqrashi. Transjordan's Prime Minister Abu al-Huda could not give the legion more money because there were no reserve funds in the treasury. During the last few days of the mandate, however, the British army transferred large amounts of supplies to the legion. Gasoline and ammunition had also been sent through Suez to fulfill Bevin's promised support. The legion attacked Jewish settlements even before May 15, taking Kfar Etzion twenty-four hours before the mandate's official end.[33]

The Arab League's May 13 meeting was sadly disorganized. Azzam apparently had little knowledge of Arab and Jewish military strengths, instead he felt that Arab spirit and enthusiasm would be sufficient. Formation of a joint command was handled with particular offhandedness. Glubb turned down the suggestion that he become overall commander, a gesture he saw as designed to furnish a prefabricated scapegoat. The Egyptians then pressed the commander-in-chief designation on Abdallah, but never sent him an order of battle. Cairo's soldiers even seized ammunition being shipped to the legion through Egypt. Many young officers must have echoed Glubb's complaint: "The politicians, the demagogues, the press and the mob were in charge — not the soldiers. Warnings went unheeded. Doubters were denounced as traitors."[34]

Yet ready or not, the Arabs must face the deadline. King Abdallah dramatically announced to the British representative in Amman that the Arab armies would march into Palestine at midnight May 14. When asked about the Jewish forces, the king waved his hands and said, "It does not matter how many there are. We will sweep them into the sea!" Abdallah seemed both utterly confident and acutely anxious. He had not slept the night before.[35]

No one could fail to see that the decisive moment had at last arrived on that sultry May day. People wildly cheered the legion units as they drove westward down the dusty roads. Some of the troops joined them, waving and laughing. Glubb recounted, "The procession seemed more like a carnival than an army going to war." But the Arabs were flushed with pride. An Arab Legion officer spoke in wonder of that beautiful day "when the whole world held its breath anticipating the entry of seven Arab armies into Palestine to redeem it from the Zionists and the West." The Arabs "stood as one man to demand justice and to please God, conscience and the sense of duty."[36]

Abdallah and his staff stood at the eastern end of the Allenby bridge across the Jordan river as the clocks edged toward midnight on May 14. At 12:00 A.M. exactly, the king drew his revolver, fired into the air, and shouted "Forward!" The long line of vehicles moved off, across the bridge toward Jericho. By dawn, they were in the central Palestine hills: four bedouin mechanized regiments (many of their soldiers recruited from Saudi tribes), seven infantry companies, and eight light artillery pieces, forces totalling forty-five hundred men.[37]

Three thousand Syrian soldiers crossed into Palestine and occupied an abandoned Transjordan Frontier Force camp near Semakh on the Sea of Galilee. A thousand Lebanese troops edged across their border to the north. Three thousand Iraqi troops already in Transjordan crossed the river to take up positions near Nablus. Their commander quickly claimed the capture of a power station despite the fact that its departing Jewish staff had already turned it over to Transjordanian authorities. While ten thousand Egyptians prepared to enter Palestine from the eastern Sinai, Cairo's air force was bombing Tel Aviv.[38]

To the Arab peoples and regimes, May 15 must have indeed seemed a day full of glory and hope. The assembled Arab armies along with the Mufti's guerrillas and al-Qawukji's volunteers would easily defeat the Zionists. The issue so long debated in speeches and tedious diplomatic memoranda could be quickly solved at last. Could anyone have doubts on such a day? "This will be a war of extermination and a momentous massacre which will be spoken of like the Mongolian massacres and the crusades," Azzam told a press conference. So clear was the preponderance of Arab power that the enemy might be frightened into submission!

Yet censorship had done its job all too well. The Arabs' best chance had already flown. By May 15, the Jews held all of western Galilee, Haifa, and Safed. The mandate's termination meant the end of the British blockade. Military equipment and fresh, if untrained, reinforcements could now be landed. Fighting with their backs to the wall, the Jews showed remarkable spirit and ingenuity. Shortcomings of the Arab armies — particularly the lack of an overall coordinating command — which had not been resolved in peacetime could not be finessed in the heat of battle.[39]

Ben-Gurion, who never doubted the need of the new state of Israel to secure its independence against the Arab armies, clung to the hope of eventual conciliation: "We extend the hand of peace and good-neighborliness to all the states around us and to their peoples, and we call upon them to cooperate in mutual helpfulness with the independent Jewish nation in its land."[40]

Since the British mandate over Palestine "has come to an end without there being a legitimately constituted authority in the country,'' the Arab League replied, chaos and anarchy might ensue. This state of affairs, ''threatening to spread to the neighboring Arab countries,'' necessitated their direct intervention.[41]

The battle officially begun on that day has still not ended.

13

Abdallah's Perilous Peace-Making: 1948–51

*A*bdallah's efforts to annex the Arab portion of Palestine and to reach a bilateral settlement with the Jews continued after the Arab defeat in the 1948 war. Since this constitutes a continuation of his activities during the mandate period, the story will be briefly recounted here.

Nearly every Arab leader who had negotiated with Israel—even as part of the postwar truce talks—had been murdered, said Israeli Ambassador Abba Eban in July 1951. The list included Egypt's Mahmud al-Nuqrashi, Syria's Husni al-Zaim, and Lebanon's Riyad al-Sulh. Most important had been the latest addition, King Abdallah himself, struck down by assassins on July 20, 1951. Eban noted that this record would obviously discourage other Arab politicians from seeking detente with the Jewish state.[1]

Five years later, when U.S. Secretary of State John Foster Dulles was encouraging secret Egypt-Israel talks, Egyptian President Gamal Abd al-Nasser cited Abdallah's fate in refusing to meet Israeli Prime Minister David Ben-Gurion.[2] Thirty years would elapse between Abdallah's near-success and Anwar al-Sadat's dramatic trip to Jerusalem. Abdallah's failure and his subsequent assassination cast a long historical shadow on the Arab-Israeli conflict.

Another element of continuing interest was the Arab battle over control of the "West Bank," the portion of Palestine still held by the Arab Legion at the end of the 1948 war. Abdallah and his descendants would rule this land as an integral part of their kingdom until they were driven from it in the June 1967 Middle East war. Political difficulties arising from the West Bank's annexation provided the impetus for Abdallah's negotiations with Israel. Its disposition is once again a central issue in regional politics.

As early as the 1920s, Abdallah sought to expand his thinly populated, largely desert kingdom of Transjordan by taking over neighboring Palestine. He could only succeed by winning over a disparate set of allies. As mandatory power over both Palestine and Transjordan, London's support was indispensible. Dependent on British subsidies, Abdallah constantly courted Great Britain.

Abdallah also conducted on-and-off negotiations with Zionist leaders during the 1920s, 1930s, and 1940s. He also tried to build a base of support among Palestine Arabs through including some of them in his government and by supporting the Nashashibi faction against the Husayni party in Palestine Arab politics.[3]

Other Arab states were aware of and hostile to these plans. Saudi Arabia worried about a resurgence of its old Hashemite enemies, while Egypt learned to project its own ambitions toward Arab leadership. Abdallah's desire to annex Syria and Palestine added the Damascus regime and the Mufti to his list of enemies. These forces blocked the 1937 Peel Commission proposal to give Transjordan rule over most of Palestine.[4]

Abdallah's second chance came in 1948 when the British, desperately seeking some solution to the coming crisis over partition, decided to approve Transjordan's takeover of the projected Arab Palestine state. The meeting between Foreign Minister Bevin and Prime Minister Abu al-Huda sealed this agreement.[5] This plan, of course, was against the Arab League position. If Abdallah broke ranks, warned Syrian Prime Minister Mardam, he would be assassinated. Nor would the Jews agree to the king's program. The risks for Transjordan in this endeavor were therefore quite high.[6]

The course of the war, however, closely followed Abdallah's earlier predictions. Only the Arab Legion was able to save much of Arab Palestine while its military colleagues were badly beaten. Israel not only survived the war, but expanded its boundaries beyond the lines originally envisioned by the United Nations.

Despite this, the other Arab states were unwilling and perhaps politically unable to recognize the new situation. Not only did they continue to oppose Israel, but they also still preferred the Mufti to a strengthened Transjordan. In September 1948, after years of resisting the establishment of an Arab Palestine regime, the Arab League transformed the Husayni-led Arab Higher Committee into an all-Palestine government headquartered in the Egyptian-held Gaza Strip.

Naturally, Abdallah opposed this, and he organized a countermeeting of his own Palestine Arab supporters. In December, a second such gathering, supported by the legion and Transjordan's military administration on the West Bank, called for unity with Transjordan. The legion forcibly blocked attempts by the Mufti's supporters to form their own army hostile to this proposal.

By the end of 1948, then, the king's army occupied a large portion of eastern Palestine including Hebron, Nablus, and the old city of Jerusalem. Hundreds of thousands of Arabs in this territory possessed skills beyond those of native Transjordanians and promised to add to his state's wealth and strength.

At the same time, the territorial and demographic changes represented by these developments posed two major threats to the kingdom. The hundreds of thousands of Palestinian refugees east of the river, housed in camps around Amman and other towns, had no particular loyalty to the king or his state. Successfully integrated they would be a definite asset; otherwise, they might form a base for opposition movements. Would they come to hail Abdallah as their liberator or curse him as a traitor to their cause?

Israel's existence also represented both threat and opportunity. Transjordan's access to the Mediterranean was now cut off, its trade subject to the goodwill of Arab neighbors. Some way need be found to carve out an alternate route through Israel. Moreover, Israel's demonstrated military might could destroy the Arab Legion, the foundation of the king's power, in any renewed conflict. Peace with Israel would not only preserve this army and enhance Transjordan's security, but would also allow Abdallah to pursue his ambitions with regard to Syria.

Abdallah's reasoning was built on a belief in his own unchallenged political might. For decades, he had ruled the country without significant internal interference. He *was* Transjordan, and the country responded to his will. The political elite was composed of those he chose to hire, and they ceased to have influence when he decided to remove them. If a settlement with Israel was required for his realm's peace, prosperity, and access to the outside world, he would make an agreement with Israel. If this was to be the precondition for avoiding heavy military losses and for keeping his newly acquired territories, he would pay that price. No one would be able to stop him.[7]

Yet this man whose analyses of political relations abroad were so often profoundly astute seriously miscalculated the most obvious changes in his own country. The post-1948 atmosphere in the Arab world, the underground plots presaging the coming wave of military coups, the fears of his own ministers, and the new demographic weight of the Palestinians in his kingdom all combined to upset these estimates.

Israel had its own reasons for wanting permanent peace with its eastern neighbor. Such an accord might break the ring of Arab hostility and encourage other Arab states to accept Israel. The young country faced economic and social problems formidable enough even without the need to maintain a large army. There too, however, domestic political considerations limited the negotiators' options. Right-wing parties would surely make much political capital out of any major concessions made by Ben-Gurion. The Holocaust experience and Anglo-American vacillations over Palestine had made the Jews distrustful toward paper promises. They were determined to base Israel's security on military strength and defensible borders. Ben-Gurion's determination to obtain the most favorable possible agreement in this regard tended toward an inflexible bargaining position. This, in addition to Israeli insensitivity on the effects of border incidents, helped narrow Abdallah's margin of maneuver from the difficult to the impossible.

Ben-Gurion and the Israelis also tended to overestimate British opposition to the idea of a bilateral Israel-Transjordan agreement. London's caution was not motivated by hostility to Israel but by fear that Amman would become dangerously isolated. On the other hand, the refusal of England and America to more actively support such a treaty denied Abdallah encouragement at a key moment in the negotiations.

The Israel-Transjordan talks began at Ben-Gurion's suggestion in December 1948. In the first, exploratory stages, the Israeli prime minister cautioned Moshe Dayan, military commander in the Jerusalem area, and Reuven Shiloah of the Foreign Ministry to make no commitments to accept Amman's annexation of the West Bank or to give up any territory in the Negev. Their mission was to find out what Transjordan wanted as part of a peace settlement.

Amman's demand for the return of Ramleh and Lydda to the Arabs —towns destined for the Arab Palestine state which had been captured by the Israelis in the war—and Arab access to Jaffa, convinced Dayan that further meetings were a waste of time. Ben-Gurion disagreed: "We must probe every possibility of achieving peace. We need it probably more than the Jordanians." King Abdallah was also eager for a settlement which would, he said, "relieve me forever of the Palestine headache."[8]

After Egypt reached a military armistice with Israel on February 24, 1949, public talks between Israel and Transjordan began to discuss a purely interim truce. Israel's occupation of the southern Negev demonstrated their military superiority and ability to punish Transjordan unless the military fronts were stabilized. Consequently, the status-of-forces accord was signed in early April. In contrast, despite the king's persistent optimism, the secret talks dragged on with little progress.

With good reason, Abdallah said that he was more worried about the other Arab states than about any Israeli threat. British intelligence and the Central Intelligence Agency independently discovered an assassination plot against Abdallah in January. The plotters included the Mufti, Syrian President al-Quwatli, and the Muslim Brotherhood. The trigger-men, two veteran Palestinian guerrilla leaders, first intended to shoot the king in a mosque, but eventually chose to mine a road he was expected to use. This information allowed Transjordanian police to arrest them in time. Others on their death list included Ahmad Khalil, military governor of Ramallah, and other Palestinian supporters of the king.[9]

The foiled assassination attempt did not discourage Abdallah's plan to annex the West Bank. The king's visit to London in September secured Bevin's approval while a successful tour of the area convinced Abdallah that the local population was amenable. January 1, 1950, was set as the date for permanently joining the West Bank to Transjordan. Since the kingdom would now extend along both shores of the river, it would be renamed Jordan.[10]

Abdallah quickly accepted a November 11 Israeli proposal for direct negotiations toward a permanent settlement. This would protect his flank during the difficult transition period. The king exuded confidence: all his goals would be fulfilled at the same time. Even the other Arab countries would be forced to accept his initiatives. "They wanted us to take the lead in war," Abdallah remarked, "and now wish us to be the first to make peace." He was contemptuous of the "stalling and obstructive attitude" of these states and the snail's pace of the UN Palestine Conciliation Commission. He might even visit America to convince Jewish leaders there of his moderate attitude.[11]

The Israelis were equally elated. Dayan and Ben-Gurion knew that Abdallah's relations with the rest of the Arab League could not be worse and that their demands for the internationalization of Jerusalem threatened Jordanian as well as Israeli interests. In exchange for some territorial concessions, a Haifa free-trade zone, and duty-free transit for Jordanian goods, Israel might finally make peace with one of its neighbors.[12]

Roadblocks at the December meetings, however, threatened to upset these high hopes. Two of them were quickly solved. When Jordan demanded the southern Negev in order to have a land passage to Egypt,

Israel declared it would rather end the talks than cede Eilat. When Israel expressed concern over the possibility of British military bases on the West Bank, London agreed to forego this option.

The more serious conflict was over Jordan's corridor to the Mediterranean. Shiloah offered a road from Hebron to the coast. The Jordanian negotiator, al-Rifai, termed this suggestion worthless. Substantial amounts of territory must be turned over to justify a peace settlement. Shiloah's colleague Sassoon replied that such major concessions could only take place in a comprehensive Arab-Israel peace treaty. Israel had its domestic politics too and could not yield a wider corridor. Shiloah asked why more land was needed if Jordan simply required a trade corridor to the sea? Differences over the projected corridor's width continued for some weeks: Israel proffered 200–300 meters; Jordan wanted 8–10 kilometers.[13]

These differences could not be insuperable. UN negotiator Ralph Bunche predicted in February 1950, "I cannot believe that with a little goodwill and some useful third party assistance at the right time at least Jordan and Israel and possibly Egypt too could be boosted over the hump." This was more likely to happen in direct, on-the-spot talks than through foreign intermediaries. But these foreign well-wishers could help. Shiloah, MacDonald, and David Fritzlan, U.S. chargé d'affaires in Amman, all recommended that some American involvement would be useful in encouraging both sides to make a breakthrough. Fritzlan warned that at some critical point this might make the difference between success and failure, helping the king overcome the objections of his own cabinet.[14]

While Fritzlan's view would soon prove accurate, the February 17 meeting marked a major step forward. The king suggested a five-year renewable nonaggression pact as an interim step toward final settlement. Jordan would gain guaranteed transit rights across Israel and a free-port zone in Haifa. Committees would explore more difficult issues including trade, protection of the holy places, and the disposition of Arab refugees' land in Israel. Certain Arab quarters would be returned in Jerusalem and compensation paid for confiscated property. Israelis would be provided guaranteed access to Mount Scopus and the Western Wall.

A week later, Israeli negotiators accepted these terms. The pleased king pledged he would not go back on his word: if his current government would not approve the agreement he would get a new government which would do so. After three hours of conversation and a pleasant social dinner, both sides initialed the pact. "It is not yet in the bag," reported an ecstatic Shiloah, "but we are optimistic." Abdallah made a radio broadcast promising greater democracy in Jordan as soon as the negotiations with Israel were successfully concluded.[15]

At this point, everything began to go wrong. Pressure against any such agreement increased from the other Arab states and within Jordan itself. Britain did not want to endanger its relations with the rest of the Arab world by appearing to sponsor a bilateral settlement. The United States hesitated for the same reason as well as a distrust of Abdallah's future ambitions toward Syria and elsewhere. Most fundamentally, Abdallah began to sense that an open accord with Israel might make it harder rather than easier to annex the West Bank.

The first cause for alarm was provided by attacks on the king from Abdallah al-Tall, an exiled Jordanian officer in Cairo. Al-Tall, a native Transjordanian, had joined the Arab Legion during World War II. He became a battalion leader during the 1948 war and so impressed the king that Abdallah personally promoted him to lieutenant-colonel, military governor of east Jerusalem, and the city's civilian governor within one year. Despite this royal patronage, al-Tall, who had watched Syrian colonels overthrow their own regime in the aftermath of the war, began to explore coup possibilities.

During 1949, al-Tall visited opposition leaders including Sulayman al-Nabulsi, as well as Egyptian officials and Syrian dictator Colonel Husni al-Zaim. Abdallah's enemies began to pay him subsidies. After failing to convince General Glubb to make him a brigadier general, al-Tall resigned his position and went to Egypt in October 1949.[16]

He took with him documents about the early stages of the secret Israel-Jordan talks in which he had participated. Al-Tall held a series of press conferences in January 1950, and began to publish materials attacking the king in March. These actions led to further denunciations of Abdallah in the Arab press. *Al Misri* called for annulment of the Anglo-Jordanian treaty and the king's abdication. Others advocated expelling Amman from the Arab League.[17]

More immediate threats were posed by Syria and Saudi Arabia, which promised to seal their borders with Jordan if it signed any agreement with Israel. In that event, said Saudi diplomat Yusuf Yasin, Jordan would be considered an enemy. Another retaliatory act was the invitation of the Mufti's shadow All-Palestine Government to the March 1950 Arab League meeting, which became an anti-Abdallah rally. The league confirmed its 1948 resolutions pledging that Arab states would not seize Palestine for themselves. If Jordan ignored this, diplomatic and economic sanctions could be directed against it.[18]

At the same time, an escape hatch was offered to Jordan by Iraqi Prime Minister Tawfiq al-Suwaydi. Annexation might be accepted if Abdallah would abandon negotiations with Israel. This option undoubtedly hardened opposition for a peace pact among Jordanian politicians. Jordan's cabinet had already decided to oppose the king's plan during an extraordinary all-day session March 2. When they failed to convince the king, Abd al-Huda and the other ministers resigned. So strong was their feeling on this issue that al-Rifai failed to form a new government.[19]

This turn of events worried Israeli Foreign Minister Moshe Sharett. The crisis in Amman was "more than a local test of strength" between king and opposition, he explained: "Now Amman is the crossroads of the Middle East. Decisions there will affect the whole course of history for the next few years." The king needed Anglo-American encouragement to counter existing pressures and economic support in case of an Arab League boycott. America might pledge to supply sugar and other items Jordan imported from Egypt if necessary. Ambassador Mac-Donald agreed and appealed to President Truman for such an offer.[20]

The State Department agreed in the abstract that a chance to improve the unstable *status quo* was worth some risk, but American diplomats and the Saudi government warned that deeper involvement might endanger Washington's other regional interests. To side with Jordan and Israel would be to stand against the rest of the Arab League. Secretary of State Dean Acheson refused any new commitment.[21]

The king had earlier decided to postpone annexation until new parliamentary elections were held. These resulted in a victory for Abdallah's men. The resolution annexing the West Bank was therefore passed, over the opposition of some Palestinian deputies, on April 24. Britain quickly recognized this step, providing Abdallah with an additional lift, and at the same time opened diplomatic relations with Israel. A cheerful and optimistic king affirmed loyalty to his preliminary pact with Israel and promised to successfully conclude the secret talks.[22]

Arab states were at a loss as to how to deal with this *fait accompli* of annexation until Iraq suggested a face-saving solution: the Arab League approved Jordan's holding the West Bank in trust pending final settlement of the Palestine question. Abdallah hailed this as a personal victory over the Egyptian and Saudi "snakes and scorpions." After thirty years of competition, Abdallah ruled most of the remaining Arab Palestine. The Mufti's forces were politically dead, but they might still gain revenge — they began to form terrorist groups in Jordan, and they received foreign Arab support. The king was their prime target.[23]

Like its predecessors, Abdallah's new cabinet of Prime Minister

Said Mufti opposed any resumption of negotiations with Israel. Why take further risks when the West Bank was now safely in hand? The politicians tried desperately to prevent any more talks. When the British refused to help him, Prime Minister Mufti tried outright sabotage. Sent by Abdallah on an information-gathering trip in the West Bank, the prime minister and foreign minister incited local leaders against Abdallah's plan. They circulated petitions against any bilateral agreement, and these were signed by some of the king's most faithful past supporters. Abdallah was furious.[24]

Yet what action could he take? He could find no politicians who would dare implement any pact with Israel. Annexation had worked against him by strengthening the forces of opposition. An attempt to continue serious negotiations might provoke a major domestic crisis. His own cabinet "sang Egypt's tunes," Abdallah complained to Walter Eytan of the Israeli Foreign Office on October 1. They were even systematically withholding information from the king. Power was slipping from his hands.[25]

Problems were accentuated by a series of border clashes which erupted at the end of 1950, including an Israeli raid on a village near Bethlehem and disputes over key roads. The king blamed Israel's actions and his own ministers' provocations for this new set of difficulties. It was too late for any diplomatic way to peace.[26]

On February 13, 1951, Shiloah met Abdallah for the last time. The king seemed a lonely, weary old man increasingly aware of his declining power; even long-faithful al-Rifai was only playing for time, keeping up the appearance of complying with the king's desires. Shiloah himself was tense and tired in the fading of his hopes. He could only hand Abdallah a list of Jews killed by terrorist attacks originating from Jordan, suggesting measures to better maintain the armistice. Shiloah's border-crossing back into Israel came closer to disaster than any of his previous secret journeys, as if to symbolize the clanging down of barriers between the two countries.[27]

Thus came to an end the attempt to make a permanent peace between Israel and Jordan. Four months later, the murder of the king himself would definitively end the first period of Arab state intervention into the Palestine conflict.

The assassination conspiracy's background remains murky even today, but there is strong circumstantial evidence connecting the plot to the Mufti. The central figure, Musa Abdallah al-Husayni, was a cousin of the Mufti and an aide who had accompanied him to Germany during the war. Musa later became an adviser to Jordan at the May 1949 UN

Palestine Conciliation Commission conference. After failing to win election to parliament, he dropped out of politics to start a tourist agency. Abdallah had given him a house in Jerusalem as a reward for having joined his side.

According to the best available information, Musa had contacted al-Tall in April 1950, to begin planning Abdallah's removal. Al-Tall has, however, always denied involvement, attributing the plot exclusively to the Palestinians. King Husayn, Abdallah's grandson, later accepted this view. The conspirators apparently hoped that Prince Tallal, Abdallah's son and heir apparent, would adopt a drastically different policy.[28]

A timely coincidence almost saved Abdallah's life. On July 16, 1951, Riyad al-Sulh, former prime minister of Lebanon, was killed by terrorists during a visit to Jordan. The assassination was in revenge for his ordering the execution of Syrian Social National Party leader Anton Saadeh some years earlier. This ambush against Abdallah's own car had nothing to do with Jordanian politics, but it intensified the atmosphere of tension in Amman.

British Ambassador Sir Alec Kirkbride begged the king to abandon his custom of praying every Friday in Jerusalem's Al-Aqsa mosque, since that city — a center of Palestinian nationalism — was particularly hostile to the king. The American Minister Gerald Drew also urged caution, since al-Sulh's assassins were still at large. Again, the king brushed aside the warnings with a fatalistic shrug. He would not be intimidated.[29]

After leaving Drew, Abdallah and his grandson Husayn visited Amman's airfield for a graduation ceremony of Arab Legion pilots. From there they flew to Jerusalem where the mayor of Nablus begged the king to pray in his city instead of at the Al-Aqsa mosque. Again, Abdallah refused.

At noon the following day, July 20, the king arrived at the mosque. "Don't imprison me," he told the commander of his guard as he walked up the steps. The crowd was allowed to move closer. Suddenly, Mustafa Shuqri Asha, a nineteen-year-old veteran of the Mufti's shock troops, fired point blank, instantly killing the king. As Husayn bent over his dying grandfather, the guards gunned down Asha.

Soldiers in full battle dress quickly filled Jerusalem streets, sealing off the city. Loyal Bedouin troops roughed up Palestinians, who they blamed for their beloved king's death. The French consul in Jerusalem concurred, "There are 600,000 Palestinian Arabs who are delighted with the death of Abdallah." so did Ahmad Khalil, now governor of Arab Jerusalem: "It is not possible that a young man without backing would kill the king. ... Unless we discover who are the persons behind the murder, Jordan is through.''[30]

This most dire prediction was not fulfilled. Talal succeeded to the throne though his chronic mental problems shortened his reign. He was not the militant Arab nationalist nor the anti-British leader that some foreign Arabs had hoped for, but his government quickly declared that there would be no further talks with Israel. He rode out Iraqi and Egyptian eagerness to make the West Bank an Arab League mandate. The Mufti himself gained nothing. He succeeded in raising funds in Pakistan, but he could find little support among the Arab states. Already he, like Abdallah, was a figure of the past.[31]

Ben-Gurion sent private condolences but refrained from a public statement on the king's murder lest it be used by Abdallah's enemies. Dayan and Ben-Gurion blamed British indifference for the failure of negotiations. Nevertheless, they added, London and Washington might still keep Jordan out of the hands of hard-liners. Some day the talks could be renewed.[32]

Changing objective circumstances had more to do with the failure of negotiations than did American and British passivity. Still, both could have done more to encourage a settlement. John Foster Dulles would expend far more political capital three years later on far thinner opportunities for peace. Most important, however, was the internal Jordanian situation. The abandonment of bilateral solutions became the price for the West Bank's successful annexation. The resulting situation, with Palestinians outnumbering Transjordanians two-to-one, changed the country's political face. The king had failed to adjust.

Pointing out these objective difficulties does not mean that options did not exist. A bit more effort might have pushed negotiations to a successful conclusion. Such an analysis also applies to the much broader history of the Arab-Jewish conflict over Palestine. Hindsight often makes the final result seem inevitable. Yet there are often moments when alternatives appear—brief, perhaps, but holding immense promise. This is the tide which when taken at its peak leads on to fortune; when missed leads on to shallows and to miseries.

14

Egypt's Revolution, Israel, and America: 1950-56

America's entanglement with Gamal Abdul Nasser's revolutionary regime is one of the most interesting—and hitherto mysterious— chapters in the history of U.S. Middle East policy. During the early years of his rule, many American observers thought the charismatic colonel a potential ally. Yet by the end of the 1950s he was the key force behind political upheaval and anti-American feeling in the Arab world.

Events belied American expectations. Hopes for Egyptian support in an anti-Soviet collective security network were dashed when Cairo became Moscow's ally and tried to destroy the region's remaining pro-Western regimes. Washington hoped that Egypt would become the first Arab state to make peace with Israel, instead it played a central role in intensifying the Arab-Israeli conflict. Nasser's leading position among the Arabs was fulfilled at the expense of, rather than in conjunction with, Western objectives.

Could the outcome have been a different one? Why did the seemingly promising relations between Washington and Nasser's Free Officers group break down? Was this due to internal Egyptian conditions or to domestic American pressures? Was it caused by some ideological inflexibility on the part of Nasser or of U.S. Secretary of State John Foster Dulles? Did an unbridgeable Arab-Israeli conflict make the break inevitable? And what role was played in all this by secret State Department and covert CIA operations?

The answers to these questions reveal much about U.S. foreign policy-making, the role of ideology in the two countries, Anglo-American political relationships in that era, and the nature of U.S. and

216

Egyptian national interests. They also add a new dimension to an understanding of Dulles' foreign policy and to the development of Middle East history in that dramatic time.

"It's hard to put ourselves back into this period," recalled Raymond Hare, a State Department official who became U.S. Ambassador to Egypt in 1956. "There was really a definite fear of hostilities, of an active Russian occupation of the Middle East physically, and you could practically hear the Russian boots clumping down over hot desert sands."[1]

Given this perceived threat and the growing importance of Middle East oil for the Western world, the United States was interested in strengthening and stabilizing Arab countries. Washington still recognized British and French political predominance in the region but, particularly during the Truman administration, also appreciated the justice and future importance of indigenous nationalism.[2]

American policy-makers did not see these two concerns — Western defense requirements and local demands for independence and development — as being innately contradictory; on the contrary, the maintenance of peace and the fulfillment of Western interests required their reconciliation. In this context, Washington also sought a settlement of the Arab-Israeli conflict. Since many Arabs blamed Israel's creation on the West, continuing tensions on this issue was deemed one factor undermining U.S.-Arab relations.[3]

Washington was well aware that many Arab regimes were quite shaky. In Egypt, a dissolute king, quarrelling politicians, extreme poverty alongside a complacent elite, popular dissatisfaction, and the growth of extremist leftist and Islamic groups, combined to create a volatile situation. "Talk of coup d'etat is in the air," wrote U.S. Ambassador Jefferson Caffery in November 1950.[4]

The West's prime security interest in Egypt was the preservation of the sprawling British base near the Suez Canal for use in time of crisis or war. Secretary of State Dean Acheson urged Anglo-Egyptian cooperation rather than confrontation in determining the base's future. The Pentagon supported London's September 1951 proposal for a joint Middle East command, including Egyptian officers, under a British supreme commander. But Egypt, stung by past British interference in its internal affairs, preferred the departure of British troops and the transfer of the base to its own control. When Cairo abrogated the 1936 Anglo-Egyptian treaty in October 1951, Washington supported Britain but urged that country toward a compromise solution.[5]

Acheson was appalled at Prime Minister Winston Churchill's thought that a "splutter of musketry" would resolve the issue. On the contrary, British military actions against Cairo-supported guerrillas led to massive riots and to the burning of Cairo in January 1952. Washington refused Churchill's request to send ships and Marines to help squelch the unrest. Acheson replied that it would be impossible to maintain the base against Egyptians' wishes.[6]

During the first half of 1952, Washington also worked for a compromise in the Anglo-Egyptian dispute over the Sudan's future. The State Department also agreed to a confidential Egyptian request to equip and train three special police divisions organized to maintain order.[7]

To solve the impasse over the base, the United States suggested a Middle East Defense Organization (MEDO), designed to remove Britain as an imperial power and to transform the Suez base into a cooperative effort. The fall-back position for containment of the USSR was a Northern Tier pact, to be based on the non-Arab states along the Soviets' southern border. Continuance of the existing Anglo-Egyptian stalemate, warned Assistant Secretary of State for Near East Affairs Henry Byroade in July 1952, "would lead to riots and disorders which the Egyptian authorities might not be able to control." American influence, he urged, must be used to produce a compromise.[8]

Just forty-eight hours after this analysis was completed, Nasser's Free Officers group overthrew the Egyptian monarchy in an almost bloodless coup. The course of Egypt's history was sharply altered. There has been much speculation over the role of the United States—and more particularly that of the CIA—in this event.[9]

Kermit Roosevelt, CIA's director of covert operations in the region, visited Cairo shortly after the January riots to assess the country's future; he met a variety of political figures, though not Farouk himself. Washington hoped in vain that some strong prime minister, perhaps Naguib Hillali, could face down the king. But in late March, Roosevelt, then in Baghdad, received a cable from an Egyptian friend requesting a meeting in Cyprus. There, Roosevelt was told of the planned revolution and of Nasser's leadership, but he refused to come to Egypt to meet the plotters.[10]

The U.S. embassy also had some, though more diffuse, hints of what was to come. Although there was speculation about the intentions of the Free Officers, it was generally considered a purely reformist group concerned only with military affairs. Major Ali Sabry, an Egyptian air force officer who was friendly with an American military attaché, Lt. Col. David Evans, reported in mid-July that an ultimatum would soon be presented to the king.[11]

On the night of July 22, Evans' suspicions were raised by the deserted streets in downtown Cairo. He unsuccessfully sought to contact his acquaintances among the Egyptian officers by telephone. Finally, he reached Sabry's wife. Her husband, she said, had dramatically strapped on his .45 pistol, kissed her, and left, explaining that he might never return.

At 3:30 A.M., Sabry himself knocked on Evans' door. He carried a message from the revolutionary council which now ruled Cairo: The new rulers declared themselves pro-Western, seeking a more responsible government and a higher standard of living for their countrymen. Sabry asked Evans to contact the British and to ask them not to intervene.[12]

A few hours later, Farouk personally called the American and British embassies and asked them to send ships to his aid. Both refused. The revolution had triumphed.[13]

In his first evaluation of the new regime, Ambassador Caffery considered the Free Officers to be an amorphous group without any program, "bound together by common disgust with their superiors." Their figurehead chief, the popular General Muhammad Naguib was not "a particularly strong or intelligent leader."[14]

Nevertheless, the officers seemed friendly to the United States and expressed a desire to take part in the Middle East's defense. Britain quickly offered military aid in exchange for settling the base issue. Caffery was generally optimistic: the United States should not rush Egypt toward an acceptance of MEDO, he suggested, but it should help Cairo build an effective and inexpensive military force for protecting the country.[15]

As predicted, the new Egyptian government began to court the United States. Naguib promised that American arms would not be used against Israel and voiced willingness to compromise on the Sudan. Two Free Officers' emissaries told Caffery in mid-August, "Egypt is a weak nation and needs a strong friend. We would like the United States for a friend." Their proposed agricultural and social reforms, they suggested, were the best means for combatting communist subversion, a view shared by the Truman administration.[16]

Caffery praised the revolutionary regime's performance as clearly good from the standpoint of U.S. interests. Eager as the new rulers were to attack corruption and social injustice, Caffery noted, they lacked experience, organization, and a popular base of support, but Naguib wanted to turn first to the United States for help in overcoming these difficulties.[17]

The Israelis were also hopeful. Their secret approach through Paris brought a response from Cairo that the Free Officers would focus on internal affairs and had no aggressive designs against Israel. Prime Minister David Ben-Gurion made a conciliatory speech and privately offered technical aid.[18]

Encouraged by these developments and by the officers' reform program, Acheson persuaded President Truman to make a favorable statement on the Naguib regime. Despite British reservations, such a declaration, hinting at future American aid, was made on September 3, and was well received in Cairo.[19]

The American position in the midst of a dispute between two friends, Britain and Egypt, allowed Washington to work as a mediator, but it posed the danger that both might be antagonized against the United States. The first step, U.S. policy-makers decided, was to build a bilateral relationship with Cairo. Only then could they seek to solve the Suez base problem and advance toward establishing MEDO. American aid and support for Naguib and the Free Officers was considered the best approach toward these ends.[20]

As expected, Naguib requested American military supplies and financial assistance, offering in exchange secret commitments to join MEDO. If tank parts, armored cars, ammunition, radio sets, and other equipment was provided, Cairo would give guarantees that they would not be used against Britain or Israel. Caffery and Acheson agreed on the importance of quick American assistance, but they wanted more definite Egyptian pledges and public gestures.[21]

For their part, Egyptian representatives said they must be cautious in the face of extremist — particularly Muslim Brotherhood — pressure; they were nevertheless willing to enter a defense pact if Britain evacuated the Suez base. Caffery raised the obvious question with Acheson: Which would come first: British evacuation or Egyptian acceptance of MEDO? Military aid or evidence of nonaggressive intentions toward Israel?

Equally serious was the Free Officers' ignorance of American aid procedures and Naguib's limited power within the junta. Nasser was more skeptical about an American alliance. He needed arms to ensure the military's loyalty, he said, but was not prepared to alienate supporters by making concessions without firmer prospects of aid. Washington's dispatch of some equipment originally promised to the royal government was not enough to quell Cairo's increasing signs of impatience.[22]

The Truman administration's lame duck status further delayed matters. In November 1952, Deputy Secretary of Defense William Foster visited Egypt and unilaterally invited an Egyptian mission to discuss arms aid. Nasser quickly sent Sabry to Washington. Unfortunately, the U.S. government would make no decision until the newly elected Eisenhower White House organized itself. Sabry returned to Cairo in January, empty handed and personally embittered. This failure "hurt us a great deal," wrote Free Officer leader Anwar al-Sadat years later, and increased doubts about the sincerity of American promises.[23]

Caffery saw the danger. Naguib, "more cautious and pro-Western" than the younger officers, was slipping, he cabled, and any delay in furnishing aid might destroy his remaining influence. Naguib himself complained he was being "suffocated by the smell of roses" from America while he preferred the whiff of its gunpower. By January 1953, Anglo-Egyptian talks over Sudan and Suez were not going well. Egypt refused any prior commitment to participate in Middle East defense; London warned Washington that U.S. aid for Egypt might jeopardize Anglo-American links.[24]

The new secretary of state, John Foster Dulles, decided to take his time in reviewing the aid issue, despite CIA and State Department requests for speed. The achievement of a solution on Sudan, a U.S. loan for wheat purchases, and steps to declare Egypt eligible for U.S. military training programs would have to suffice for a while.

Nasser's frustration led him to his first outspoken public attack on the United States on March 1. America was losing its prestige as a champion of liberty and self-determination, he declared, through its support for "imperialistic powers." Any opposition to rapid evacuation by the British troops would convince Egypt to side with the Soviet camp "as an act of revenge for the humiliation which we suffered over seventy years." The Muslim Brotherhood and left-oriented nationalists took similar positions.[25]

Muhammad Hussanayn Heikal, Nasser's trusted advisor, explained that the Arabs wanted a defense against America's friends as well as against its enemies. "You will never be able to get the oil of the Middle East if its people revolt against you, and you will not be able to defend the Middle East if its people do not side with you. ... Either you win us forever, or you lose us forever."[26]

One way of winning friendship, suggested World Bank President Eugene Black, was American aid for building the Aswan Dam. Byroade agreed. For Egypt to serve as Washington's wedge in reconstructing its position in the Arab world, he wrote, the Aswan project could provide "the greatest political and psychological, as well as economic effect."[27]

Dulles decided to see for himself by travelling to the Middle East.

British positions were deteriorating, State Department briefing papers told him, and London's "colonial and imperialistic policies are millstones around our neck." America must convince Middle Easterners that it sympathized with their aspirations and must press Britain and France toward orderly change. Naguib believed, Dulles was informed, that once the Suez base issue was solved he could move toward agreement with Israel, as long as Egypt gained a corridor through the Negev to Jordan.[28]

Obviously, Dulles accepted these premises. On meeting Nasser, he stressed the importance of an Arab-Israel settlement, while the Egyptian leader explained his view that British domination was the main obstacle.

Naguib did tell Dulles, "After the British get out, I am pretty sure I can reach an agreement" with Israel. For his part, Dulles said he would like to help Egypt take the leading role in the Arab world through American assistance.[29]

When Dulles returned home he abandoned the MEDO plan and adopted the Northern Tier option, a pact aimed at blocking any Soviet advance through the bordering non-Arab states. Dulles also increased efforts to win British concessions on the Suez base and promised U.S. aid to Egypt as soon as a treaty was signed to resolve that matter.[30]

While Anglo-Egyptian negotiations dragged, covert Egypt-Israel contacts moved even more slowly. Nasser's speeches on the subject became sharper, but Foreign Minister Muhammad Fawzi, speaking to UN official Ralph Bunche, suggested that "Egypt can accept one partition but not two," explaining why Cairo wanted a Negev corridor to link it with the eastern Arab states. These feelers were abandoned when they leaked into the press, yet Bunche and the State Department agreed that an Arab-Israeli settlement might be within reach.[31]

By the end of 1953, however, Egypt had gone fourteen months without any significant American aid. "America will not please us to infuriate Britain," Nasser complained in a November speech, privately adding that Egypt might adopt "positive neutralism" in the East-West conflict. Another secret request from Naguib seeking badly needed economic assistance, met with little response from Washington.[32]

Better contacts were maintained through back channels. Kermit Roosevelt first met Nasser in January 1953, and from that time on CIA officers kept in close contact with him. At one point, the CIA passed $3 million to Nasser, a grant he saw as a bribe attempt. The money was used to build a tower in Cairo, as a sign of Nasser's contempt for the bid. According to one participant, Miles Copeland, the CIA gave the Free Officers a great deal of organizational, logistical, and even ideological advice through 1953 and 1954. Several first-hand sources play down the extent and importance of these covert operations. Still, the effect of this special relationship was to feed American hopes that a de facto alliance was within reach.[33]

Yet with Anglo-Egyptian negotiations dragging on into 1954, this covert relationship could lead nowhere. Ostensibly, only minor issues separated the two sides, but intransigence was prompted by Egyptian domestic pressures against concessions and by British confidence that Cairo would soon yield. Nasser increasingly complained that America had joined with Britain to squeeze him, a view reinforced by Washington's sloth in meeting even his requests for economic aid.[34] "It is all very well to speak of extending aid in conjunction with the Suez Base agreement," explained Egyptian Ambassador Ahmad Husayn, "but are we to delay all our plans indefinitely because the British are not prepared to make an agreement at this time?"[35]

While Britain's friendship was a higher priority for American foreign policy than was Egypt's favor, the United States did not want to see Nasser weakened, even after he displaced Naguib from power. "Nasser is the only man in Egypt with strength enough and guts enough to put over an agreement with Britain," wrote Ambassador Caffery on March 31. He was quite right. Despite continued opposition from the Muslim Brotherhood, Nasser finally cleared the last barriers to an agreement. On July 27, the Anglo-Egypt treaty was finally initialed. The moment seemed ripe for the long-awaited and long-promised American aid program to begin.[36]

Once again, Egyptian hopes of American assistance soared. In an August 1954 interview with an American magazine, Nasser gave a very shrewd assessment of U.S. foreign policy and suggested a basis for U.S.-Egypt cooperation. Like Naguib, Nasser argued that alignment with the West must proceed slowly. He favored an independent Arab bloc which would receive Western arms alongside a separate Northern Tier pact without any Arab members. In a bow to American sensibilities, he promised not to recognize the Peking regime in the near future and to consult Washington before taking any such step.

Past imperialism had made the Arabs suspicious of the West, Nasser explained, and defense must be mainly implemented by the area's own people. Too close an alliance would give the communists the chance to take an ultranationalist line and to overthrow existing governments. Foreign bases symbolized occupation, foreign occupation caused hatred, and hatred meant noncooperation. This is why he could not accept an American military training mission in Egypt, Nasser added, though he was willing to send officers abroad for instruction.

America's handling of the Cold War, Nasser concluded, helped the

USSR penetrate countries which only accepted its aid to win independence; Western flexibility could avoid this problem. He cautioned against confusing Arab and African nationalist movements with communism. He complained that Americans saw freedom from foreign domination as "the inalienable right of every man, yet balk at supporting these nations for fear of annoying some colonial Power that has refused to move with the times." This view was similar to that of liberal State Department analysts.[37]

Even Caffery thought Nasser's policy "well balanced and reasonable." So close was their relationship that Nasser told him, in strictest confidence, of his plan to liquidate theMuslim Brotherhood in the near future. A week later, after an attempt on Nasser's life, that group's leaders were arrested and its organization was destroyed.[38]

With the treaty signed and Nasser's control secured, Washington began to move toward fulfillment of its aid promises. In early August, $20 million in economic assistance and an equal amount for military help was set aside. President Eisenhower, Allen Dulles, and Henry Byroade all called for quick action. Although it would be hard to give arms to the Arabs and not to Israel, agreed the secretary of state, he was willing to try.[39]

Yet nothing happened despite all this determination. The reason was that Secretary of State Dulles decided that aid used as leverage to gain an Anglo-Egyptian treaty might continue to be dangled as inducement for an Egypt-Israel settlement. This idea had been planted in his mind by a number of State Department reports over the previous year as well as by his belief that removing this source of friction would eliminate an opportunity for Soviet meddling and would simplify the matter of regional defense.

There was another incentive for solving this problem: the Anglo-Egyptian treaty removed the buffer of British troops along the Suez Canal and this, along with the prospect of Western aid for Egypt, heightened the possibility of an Arab-Israeli confrontation in the Sinai peninsula. Byroade suggested to the worried Israelis that a settlement might be worked out involving an Egyptian denial of aggressive intentions and a detailed Western guarantee for Israel's borders. If Nasser did not act soon on Israel, replied Israeli Minister Reuven Shiloah, during the "honeymoon period," he would certainly not do so in the future.[40]

Byroade's suggestions were soon incorporated in U.S. policy. A few days later, on August 3, Dulles warned that Israel's insecurity might lead it to a more militant policy. "We have considered Egypt afforded (the) best prospects (of) moving on Arab-Israeli issues not towards formal

peace at this time but towards practical arrangements to improve relations," he wrote Caffery, recalling Egyptian hints of such aims. Great
expectations had been aroused in Washington.[41]

Thus two weeks after the Anglo-Egyptian treaty, Dulles and British
Foreign Minister Anthony Eden agreed to work toward a relaxation of
Arab-Israeli tensions. Eden appointed Evelyn Shuckburgh, his Middle
East affairs director, and Dulles asked Frances H. Russell, a foreign
service officer, to head the State Department's equivalent "Alpha"
group.[42]

This ambitious goal was not the only thing holding up U.S. military
aid to Egypt. The Mutual Security Act of 1954, under which aid was
administered, required recipient countries to accept a U.S. military
mission (MAAG). Nasser refused because of potential domestic opposition and as an affirmation of Egyptian sovereignty. He "wanted military
assistance without any conditions," Caffery later complained, but Caffery himself had agreed to an Egyptian proposal at the end of August 1954 to increase economic aid to free Cairo's funds for military
purchases.[43]

Nevertheless, direct efforts to reach some compromise failed. Two
American colonels, dispatched to convince Nasser to accept the
MAAG, could not move him. At about the same time, Caffery retired
and was replaced by Byroade, a former general and a State Department
holdover from the Truman administration. Dulles hoped that Byroade
would get along well with the Egyptian leader, since they were about the
same age and were both military men. Cairo's refusal to accept the
MAAG and his own continued hope of solving the Arab-Israeli conflict,
however, produced Dulles' decision on December 31, 1954, against
selling arms to Egypt.[44]

As Dulles predicted, 1955 was to be a decisive year both in Arab-
Israeli relations and in Moscow's use of regional conflicts to gain a
Middle East foothold. The Lavon affair, alongside Israel's raid against
Egyptian forces in Gaza and the dovish Moshe Sharett's replacement by
activist Ben-Gurion as Israeli prime minister in February 1955, all raised
the level of tensions.

The Lavon affair concerned the activities of a small group of Egyptian Jews, working for Israeli intelligence, who tried to set fire to public
buildings and U.S. embassy libraries in Cairo and Alexandria in July
1954. Their object was to sabotage any improvement in U.S.-Egyp-
tian relations. Two of them were later executed by the Egyptian
government.

Israel, in turn, complained about raids from the Egyptian-ruled

Gaza Strip. Israeli civilian deaths from such attacks rose from 50 in 1954, to 192 in 1955. Egypt made some good faith efforts to stop the Muslim Brothers and the Mufti's men from such pursuits. Cairo cracked down on the Brothers after the assassination attempt against Nasser; the Mufti was also carefully watched and was threatened with deportation. The UN peace-keeping force also tried to gain Israeli-Egyptian cooperation in controlling the frontier.

On the night of February 28, 1955, however, two Israeli platoons crossed into Gaza, blew up military buildings and ambushed Egyptian troops sent as reinforcements. The assault left thirty-eight Egyptians killed (twenty-two of them from the ambush on an army truck) and thirty-one wounded, including two civilians. Israeli losses were five killed. Palestinian refugees in Gaza demonstrated against the Egyptian administration there.

Byroade arrived in Egypt just after the Gaza raid and was bombarded with aid demands. The Egyptians, already worried by French arms supplied to Israel, were convinced by the attack that Jerusalem possessed more advanced arms than did Cairo. Nasser said he would be unable to resist pressure from the public and from his own officers for retaliation unless he obtained arms. The CIA tried its "back channel," and Kermit Roosevelt escorted Nasser's personal representative, Major Hassan Touhamy, around Washington in search of supplies. But despite Allen Dulles' sympathy, no help was provided.

Nasser was equally angry about the founding of the "Baghdad Pact" as a regional security system, at the end of 1954, with Iraq as a leading member. The West, Nasser concluded, was trying to divide the Arab world and was supporting a rival against Egypt's claims of primacy.[45]

The State Department and Byroade were unhappy with John Foster Dulles' decision and with the prominent role played by the CIA in U.S.-Egypt relations. Byroade himself was the direct target of Nasser's ire. Nothing would be better than for the United States to give a squadron of B-26s to the Egyptian air force, he told Secretary Dulles in April. He forwarded Nasser's list to Washington, but by the time the Egyptian leader was preparing to go to the Bandung nonaligned conference, the ambassador had no satisfactory answer for him.[46]

At the meeting, Nasser avidly favored "positive neutralism," and he asked Chou En-lai to contact the Soviets about Egyptian arms purchases. When Nasser returned to Cairo, Secretary of State Dulles ordered Byroade to punish him by joining the French and British ambassadors in boycotting the arrival; the Soviet ambassador was left occupying the airfield by default.[47]

Whether or not Egyptian-Soviet talks predated Bandung, serious negotiations began with the arrival of Dmitri Shepilov, *Pravda*'s editor-in-chief, in Cairo during July. While the State Department was generally skeptical about any arms deal, the CIA — with its better sources — disagreed. Byroade, who had been told by Egyptian Ambassador Husayn that Shepilov had offered Migs and other weapons, pressed for approval of $28 million in military equipment. But the State Department feared an arms race and pointed to Egypt's hard currency shortage. The Defense Department wanted to offer a small number of planes and tanks for credit or Egyptian currency, though this suggestion was overtaken by events.[48]

Nasser's policies also made Washington suspicious. When Nasser warned that unless he obtained American arms he would turn to Moscow, this was thought a deception to gain U.S. support. Egyptian newspaper reports claiming that Moscow's arms would be supplied for free, and the possibility that the USSR might itself be bluffing also raised questions.[49]

Secretary of State Dulles shared these doubts, and it was one of the few occasions when he disagreed with his brother. Finally, convinced by Byroade's cables and by the CIA's Roosevelt, he dispatched the latter to try to talk Nasser out of it. But it was too late. In September, the world learned that Czechoslovakia was trading Egypt $200 million in military equipment for Egyptian cotton. This deal included 150 to 200 jet fighters and 35 twin-engine bombers.[50]

This began the arms race which Dulles had feared. Israel thought that Egypt's all-weather bombers could bomb at night using radar, a tactic against which Israel had no defense. Thereafter, the United States secretly supported the sale of French Mysteres to Israel. By the following year, Washington was helping to make arrangements which later led to Canada's sale of F-86s to Israel.[51]

Yet news of the arms deal did not push Dulles into a hard-line shell. On the contrary, he accelerated efforts toward an Arab-Israeli settlement and sped up the Alpha group's work on the project. If the Russians began to move into the area and to gain support from Egypt, Dulles said privately, it would alter America's position from one of neutrality in the Arab-Israeli conflict; Washington might even have to back Egypt against Israel.

Dulles thought Moscow intended to jeopardize an Arab-Israeli settlement. Israel might start a war in response to Egypt's rearming, Dulles reasoned, and the United States might have to redress the balance. He had already foreseen the essential issue of the coming Suez war; his efforts were designed to prevent such an explosion.[52]

These considerations were reflected in Dulles' own speech of August 26, 1955, at the Council on Foreign Relations. The resolution of the Suez base conflict and the progress made on regional security, he said, now permitted an attempt to settle the Arab-Israeli issue. The Johnston Mission was well advanced, stated Dulles with excessive optimism. This was a plan to develop the Jordan River, reclaim desert lands, generate electricity, provide jobs, and resettle Palestinian refugees. The Arab states, however, opposed even mutually beneficial cooperation with Israel.

The United States, Dulles explained, favored a solution based on resettlement of the Palestinian Arab refugees with some repatriation, compensation based on an international loan to Israel, and a formal treaty guaranteeing borders. The USSR, Dulles seemed to argue, might supply the tools for war, but the United States could offer a more attractive, peaceful resolution of Arab grievances.[53]

British Prime Minister Anthony Eden, who had succeeded Churchill, made a parallel, though less favorable to Israel, speech in November at London's Guildhall. Arab reaction was cautiously positive, and the British ambassador met four times with Nasser within two days of the speech. London promised arms aid and pledged that it had no intention to further expand the Baghdad Pact, whose inclusion of Iraq had already antagonized Nasser. Other steps taken by the British and Americans to avoid any further rift included Washington's decision not to join the pact.[54]

Dulles had understood Nasser's position two years earlier and had opposed the inclusion of Arab states in the Northern Tier alliance. London's decision to support Iraqi membership and to urge Jordan to join—as a way of modernizing Britain's relations with those two countries —angered and embittered Dulles. The British, he later said of these events, wanted a "blank check" from Washington on the Middle East. When London got into a mess, Dulles complained, they demanded that America be a "true ally" and back everything they had done. The feeling that London was destroying American influence in the region through its heavy-handed policy had much to do with Dulles's behavior during the Suez crisis.[55]

Nevertheless, both Britain and America agreed on the importance of financing the Aswan Dam. Eden positively insited on it and was very agitated on the issue, fearing that failure to do so would irreversibly drive Egypt into Moscow's arms. Nasser was also enthusiastic about the project. During a conversation with Byroade, Nasser pointed out the window to the Nile and said, "Mr. Ambassador, we're worrying about all these details while all that water is flowing by into the Mediterranean. That's more important."[56]

Dulles was of course aware that Nasser's neutrality was designed to play off Washington and Moscow, but he overestimated American leverage. The secretary of state apparently believed the Soviets were too overextended to undertake the Aswan project. While President Eisenhower thought that the USSR would outbid Washington, Dulles disagreed.[57]

The Anglo-American strategy, then, was to press forward on Aswan Dam financing and on Egypt-Israel peace, believing that the former could be used as leverage to gain the latter. The main hope was placed on the mission of Robert Anderson, a former secretary of the navy and a personal friend of President Eisenhower. In January 1956, Anderson visited Nasser and Israeli Prime Minister Ben-Gurion. Despite the optimism of Anderson and Dulles, his trip was a failure. Nasser could not meet with the Israelis, he told Anderson, because it might result in his overthrow or assassination. Ben-Gurion, though more positive, wanted direct talks, which were harder to arrange, and was not interested in making further concessions.[58]

Whatever the proper distribution of responsibility for the mission's failure, Ben-Gurion's response to Eisenhower charted his path toward the Suez war. Israel was operating under a six-month time limit, Ben-Gurion wrote, before the Soviet bloc arms could be absorbed by the Egyptian military. Nasser was not interested in a cease-fire, claimed the Israeli leader, and was simply stalling.[59]

While most American military experts still thought Israel was better armed, even after the Czech sale, they saw the new IL-28 bombers as a real threat. Admiral Arthur Radford, chairman of the Joint Chiefs of Staff, thought that without outside interference Egypt would be able to defeat Israel.[60]

Yet Nasser still held forth some hope of a settlement, hints that were eagerly received in Washington. "The establishment of Israel in Palestine was the gravest imaginable challenge to the peaceful preoccupation of the Egyptian and Arab people," Nasser wrote Eisenhower in February 1956. "But, despite the sense of injustice evoked by this development, in the interest of peace Egypt recognizes the desirability of seeking to eliminate the tensions between the Arab States and Israel." Eisenhower eagerly replied, "I believe that the present time may offer the best opportunity to work out a settlement."[61]

Arabs worried about Israel, not Russia, Dulles told the Senate Foreign Relations Committee. By seeking an Arab-Israeli solution, he explained, the United States was dealing with the real problem. Covert actions were more effective in responding to possible communist takeovers, as in Syria, than any direct confrontation with Egypt. To calm

Israel—and thus prevent border clashes with Egypt from escalating into war—Dulles concurred in the sale of Mystere fighters and considered providing Israel defensive weapons against the new Egyptian bombers— antiaircraft guns and radar.[62]

The immediate task was to persuade Congress to support aid for the Aswan dam. Although the American, British, and World Bank commitment would be $1.3 billion over fifteen years, the first phase only required a $56 million grant from Washington. The administration used all the arguments most likely to appeal to the legislators. "The salient fact remains," said Treasury Secretary George Humphrey, "that ... if the West does not do it ... the Soviet bloc will." But Egypt, he added, preferred the West, and if the United States helped Cairo devote its resources to domestic needs, it could avoid a local war or arms race.[63]

Neither the Egyptians nor Congress made Dulles's task easier. The Egyptians wanted firmer assurances of aid for the whole project and better credit terms as well as abandonment of the separate first phase, which had been suggested by the State Department because Congress did not want any long-term commitment.[64]

Nasser was also difficult to deal with in other areas. Anderson's report after his second trip was even more pessimistic. Nasser "is apparently seeking to be acknowledged as the political leader of the Arab world," wrote Eisenhower in his diary. Fearing to antagonize his base of support, Nasser was becoming more vocal in his attacks on Israel. As for the Israelis, the president wrote, they were anxious to talk to Egypt but wanted arms and were unwilling to give ground. Peaceful settlement seemed remote, despite Anderson's pledge of aid to both Ben-Gurion and Nasser. Johnston's efforts had also failed.[65]

Congress posed bureaucratic barriers. Earlier, a member of the CIA Board of National Estimates had written, "The niggling in Congress and its committees about our aid programs and the public debate about 'give-aways' contrasts very unfavorably with an executive decision made quickly by the Kremlin." The speedy conclusion of the Czech arms deal differed sharply from the three years of unsuccessful negotiations between Cairo and Washington.[66]

Angry at Nasser for his recognition of the Peoples Republic of China, the Czech arms deal, and his anti-Israel stance, legislators were not eager to give aid to Egypt. Representative Clarence Cannon, chairman of the House Appropriations Committee, told Dulles in a closed hearing, "I want you to understand, Mr. Secretary, that we will not approve one cent for any dam in Egypt. So please bear that in mind." Senator William Knowland said it would be difficult to get votes because increased Egyptian cotton production would compete with American growers. The Senate foreign relations and appropriations committees were also unenthusiastic.

Dulles tried to convince congressional leaders, including Senator Lyndon Johnson and House Speaker Sam Rayburn, that the dam would tie Egypt to America for ten years. Despite the arms deal, he insisted, Egypt was far from being a Soviet tool. Finally, on July 16, the Senate amended the annual appropriations bill so that Mutual Security Act money could not be used for Aswan. On June 30, the time would run out for the earlier financial offering.[67]

Yet powerful as these blows were, congressional opposition was not the principal reason for abandoning the Aswan aid project. Already, Dulles and the White House had developed a major departure for American policy. Its centerpiece was the secretary of state's memorandum of March 28, 1956, for the president and the establishment of Operation Omega. Efforts to bring Nasser to conciliation with Israel had failed, Dulles reported. Now the United States must show him "that he cannot cooperate as he is doing with the Soviet Union and at the same time enjoy most-favored-nation treatment from the United States. We would want for the time being to avoid any open break which would throw Nasser irrevocably into a Soviet satellite status and we would want to leave Nasser a bridge back to good relations with the West if he so desires."

Egypt would be punished by denying it arms' export licenses, delaying the conclusion of the Aswan negotiations, and other measures. At the same time, Jordan would be strengthened against a pro-Nasser coup, more American support would be given to the Baghdad Pact and its members, pro-Western elements in Lebanon would be strengthened, and Saudi Arabia would be assured of military aid. If these measures did not suffice, Dulles continued, "more drastic action" might be taken.[68]

This last point apparently referred to Plan Omega, an Anglo-American project for covert operations in the region. The British, who had tried to win over Nasser a few months earlier, were now taking a hard line. Nasser was, they concluded, the fountainhead of anti-British activities in the Arab world, particularly after General Glubb was fired as commander of Jordan's Arab Legion. Syria, which the Western allies thought to be heading toward a communist takeover, was the main battlefield, but Dulles had to restrain British intelligence from trying to overthrow Nasser as well.[69]

While Washington still hoped that Nasser would learn his lesson, both America and Britain had decided to stall indefinitely on providing aid for Aswan. Rumors of Soviet willingness to lend the money reinforced policy-makers' belief that Nasser was trying to play off the East and West. By June 26, Dulles was no longer pushing for American involvement. In the long run, he told the Senate Foreign Relations Committee, the dam might be a "white elephant," causing Egypt a painful period of austerity. "Whether the country which seems to be responsible for imposing that degree of austerity upon the Egyptian people for as long a period of time as that ... will end up as a country which enjoys the gratitude of the Egyptian people is highly doubtful." Senator William Fulbright agreed, he would be tempted to let Moscow do it. In short, Dulles was willing to call Nasser's "bluff," hoping it was still possible to avoid a real break.[70]

The scene was thus set for Ambassador Ahmad Husayn's arrival in Washington to meet Dulles on July 16. Moscow's denial of any intention to finance the dam two days earlier increased Washington's belief that Cairo was trying to fool the Americans. Dulles at first told Husayn that the United States remained undecided and that more time was needed. But when Husayn, who strongly favored U.S.-Egypt cooperation, brought up the alleged Soviet offer, an angry Dulles told him off. Egypt was not capable of financing the dam, the secretary of state said, and it seemed unlikely that the United States would do so.

Having sprung the first stage of his plan, Dulles felt the situation secure enough to set out on a trip to Latin America. Under-Secretary of State Hoover suggested to him over the telephone on July 23, that the Soviets might well have been bluffing on the dam. No one expected Nasser's bombshell only three days later: the nationalization of the Suez Canal company.[71]

The American press had shared the State Department's over-optimistic assessment of Dulles' action. It had shown neutrals "that it was no longer profitable to play the East against the West for economic aid," said *Newsweek*. *Time* called Dulles's challenge to Egypt a "gambit that took the breath of professionals for its daring and won the assent of kibbitzers for its instinctive rightness."[72]

Faced with the startling outcome of his serious miscalculation, Dulles still sought to avoid war. He quickly realized the eagerness of Britain and France to use force and to drag America along with them—an idea he called "crazy" in private conversations. Washington's main interest, he stressed, was on continued operation of the Suez Canal. While the United States was concerned about Nasser's activities in the Arab world, Dulles explained, it was better to confront those problems in the relevant countries, as suggested in the Omega plan.

Further, Dulles still saw some possibility of winning over Nasser, who he saw as the only Arab leader who could end the Arab-Israeli conflict. He and his brother, Allen, also understood that a Western-Arab confrontation over Suez would benefit Moscow's interests and would give the Soviets an excuse to act in central Europe.[73]

When Israel, Britain, and France invaded Egypt in October–November 1956, Dulles pressured them to withdraw and played a major role in saving Nasser's regime. Ironically, after this crisis Dulles seemed to have been won over to the analysis of his erstwhile allies who had wanted to overthrow the Egyptian leader. The CIA was now strongly anti-Nasser, and early in 1957 Allen Dulles and George Humphrey bet that Nasser would fall within six months. There is some evidence of British involvement in a 1957 anti-Nasser coup plan and U.S. intelligence might have known about this effort. Certainly, most policymakers in the State Department, CIA, and White House had come to see Nasser as little more than a Soviet tool.[74]

The Eisenhower Doctrine of January 1957, was intended to mobilize the Middle East against the perceived Soviet and Egyptian threat. The United States promised to help any nation protecting its integrity and independence against overt armed aggression from a communist or "communist-dominated" country. This was necessary, the secretary of state explained, because Britain's unwise attack on Suez had destroyed its credibility and had crippled the Baghdad Pact.[75]

The identity of the "communist-dominated nation" in question was not too well concealed. Though Dulles said that no country met that condition, Admiral Radford identified Egypt and Syria as the probable aggressors. The new American policy was perceived in Cairo as a virtual declaration of war.[76]

Why had U.S.-Egypt relations come full circle in only four and a half years? A great power's policy, wrote Albert Hourani at the time, "must attempt to reconcile, so far as possible, its relations with all the innumerable groups with which it is brought into contact and with which it needs to remain in contact. Any action it takes must necessarily be a compromise, and sometimes the search for a compromise leads it into a contradiction."[77]

Washington had tried to accomplish a variety of goals, some of them mutually exclusive. It wanted to show its sympathy and offer its partnership to the new Arab nationalism, it wanted to provide a Middle East regional defense against any Soviet intrusion, it sought to maintain the important alliance with Britain and France, and it wanted to promote a settlement of the Arab-Israeli conflict.

John Foster Dulles saw these as interrelated factors, each of which would help resolve the others. Yet while his understanding of Arab nationalism was greater than he has been credited with having, it was still insufficient to understand the problem he faced. Further, he tried to convince Egypt to do too much with too little benefit for the already suspicious Free Officers. Between May 25, 1950, and December 31, 1955, the United States exported only $1.2 million in arms and only $6.1 million in spare parts and aircraft to Egypt.[78]

American policy in the Middle East was also trapped between its bilateral relations with the local countries and its close alliance with Great Britain. Dulles realized, as had American policy-makers since 1941, that association with European colonial powers damaged U.S. prestige and limited American maneuverability in the region. Arab involvement in the Baghdad Pact, which proved so costly in relations with Nasser and the new nationalists, was due to British insistence and not to Dulles's "pactomania."[79]

There are a number of fascinating parallels between U.S.-Egypt relations during this period and U.S.-Iran relations during the overlapping Mossadegh era. In both cases, Washington was initially in sympathy with the nationalist movements. Similarly, Washington became mediator between Britain and Iran on the nationalization of the oil company and between Britain and Egypt on the Suez base issue. In both cases, it was a thankless task. The failure of Anglo-Iranian negotiations led to the CIA-organized anti-Mossadegh coup of 1953; the Suez base talks succeeded, but they left behind them a residue of lost opportunities and nascient mistrust.[80]

Nasser and Mossadegh had a similar analysis of U.S. policy, and both sought to use the USSR to gain leverage in their dealings with the United States. In each case, this orientation so frightened and outraged Washington as to lead to a clear break. Yet Nasser, so far away from the Red Army and with no considerable Communist party to seize power from him, was not deemed an equivalent danger to his Iranian colleague. Also, for various reasons, the sharp break visible between Truman-Acheson and Eisenhower-Dulles policies over Iran was muted in the case of Egypt.

Even at this distance, it is difficult to evaluate Nasser's intentions toward the West and toward Israel in the early 1950s. The argument that his ambitions in the Arab arena would have led him toward increased hostility on both fronts seems persuasive. Yet, at the time, there was a margin for trial; the future may not have been so predetermined.

Some evidence implies that Nasser might have been led to maintain a much closer relationship with the West. If Egypt-Israel peace was impossible at that time, perhaps war might have been avoided. The subsequent history of the Middle East—and of the world—would have been quite different. As Professor J. C. Hurewitz noted in December 1956, "When the historians of the future come to write the history of our times, they may well select the crucial period from July to September 1955, as marking the turning point in the evolution of the Cold War."[81]

Nasser's alliance with Saudi Arabia against the Iraq-Jordan Hashemite bloc was not inherently in conflict with U.S. interests; the same might be said of his proposal for a U.S.-sponsored, Egypt-led Arab bloc. Despite his antagonism toward Israel and anti-Israel rhetoric, Nasser did not favor war. As for the effect of American support for Israel, other Arab states, including Lebanon, Jordan, and Saudi Arabia, did not find this an insuperable barrier to maintaining good relations with Washington.

Under different circumstances, Egyptian nonalignment might have followed a pro-U.S. rather than a pro-Soviet tilt. After all, Nasser's highest priority was not strict nonalignment as an end in itself but as a means of strengthening Egypt while, at the same time, pursuing Cairo's primacy in the Arab world. For instance, though Nasser refused a small American military mission in the mid-1950s, he accepted thousands of Soviet advisors and *de facto* bases a decade later.

In following this course, however, Nasser was also subject to the patterns of domestic politics and of interstate rivalry already present in shaping Arab policy toward Palestine. While Nasser's experience in the 1948–49 war made him skeptical on the outcome of a second round, his past as a student demonstrator on the anniversaries of the Balfour Declaration and as a military officer who volunteered to train Muslim Brotherhood units in 1947 also affected him.

Nasser knew that at least rhetorical militancy toward Israel was necessary to protect his domestic flank from the still-powerful opposition forces. The palace/Wafd competition had been ended by the revolution but the Wafd, the Communist party, and the Muslim Brotherhood were all looking for an opportunity to topple him. Having made the bases' treaty with Britain, Nasser was vulnerable to the extremists' appeals.

Given his broader ambitions in the Arab world, Nasser also inherited the Palestine question's legacy to that broader sphere. To compete with other Arab leaders, he would have to carry the banner on that intensely emotional issue. In practice, Nasser was often extremely cautious but the interstate aspect of his foreign policy played a major role in pulling him over the brink in June 1967.

Of course, after 1948 the actual existence of the state of Israel was a new factor in regional politics. For decades, Arab leaders in Egypt and elsewhere had worried about the presence of a Jewish state on their borders as a security threat. The Suez War seemed to confirm these past nightmares. After 1956, the Arab-Israeli conflict emerged more clearly on the international stage, superficially becoming a "normal" state-to-state dispute. Such a conclusion, however, would have been misleading. The issue's historical complexities, emotional appeal, involvement with the aims and principles of all those involved, and deep roots in domestic and international Arab politics gave it unique and remarkable characteristics.

It would be erroneous to see modern Arab politics only in terms of the Palestine question. Despite its importance, this issue has functioned as part of the framework of politics, within and among the Arab states. The struggles over power, leadership, ideology, identity, and economic policy which characterized these relationships have determined the framework for coping with the conflict. There is every reason to believe, however, that it will play as important a role in the future as it has in the past.

$\mathcal{N}$otes

INTRODUCTION

1. For Muhammad Abdu's views, see Rashid Rida, *Tarikh*, vol. 2, p. 250, cited in Charles Adams, *Islam and Modernism in Egypt* (London: 1933), p. 59.

2. For an early example of Amin al-Husayni's use of religion for political purposes, see Elie Kedourie, "Samuel and the Government of Palestine," in *The Chatham House Version and other Middle-Eastern Studies* (London: 1970), pp. 62–63. See also Nadav Safran, *Egypt in Search of Political Community* (Cambridge: 1961), pp. 41–42.

3. A particularly graphic discussion of this is given in Bernard Lewis, "Egypt and Syria," *Cambridge History of Islam*, vol. 1, ed. P. M. Holt (London: 1970), pp. 191–92.

4. While Arabs in the Maghreb and Yemen played marginal roles in the issue, this book will not fully consider their participation. Muslims in India were also very active, and their sentiments were an important consideration for British policy in the 1930s and 1940s.

5. Arnold Toynbee, *Survey of International Affairs*, vol. 1 (London: 1927), p. 210.

6. Vernon Walters, *Silent Missions* (New York: 1978), p. 262. This problem is discussed at length in Barry Rubin, *Paved with Good Intentions: The American Experience and Iran* (Oxford University Press, 1980).

7. Safran, pp. 103–104.

8. The obvious difference here lies between states with multiparty systems and those with centralized monarchies. See Chapter 4 below.

9. One must bear in mind Professor Kedourie's warning that the history of political ideology in the Middle East should not be overattributed to the nature of Islam or Arabism, since events often owed more to the intrigues and ambitions of those in political life. Kedourie, p. 385. See also his *Arabic Political Memoirs* (London: 1974), p. 46.

1—THE BITTER LEGACY OF DEFEAT: 1948–81

1. Walid Khalidi, "Thinking the Unthinkable: A Sovereign Palestinian State," *Foreign Affairs*, July 1978, pp. 695–98.

2. Michael Hudson, *Arab Politics: The Search for Legitimacy* (New Haven, Conn.: 1978), pp. 27–28, 54.

3. For instance, Clovis Maqsud: The "Arab Left was not a political force of importance until the Arab defeat in Palestine when the traditional leadership failed." Cited in Kamel Abu Jaber, *The Arab Ba'th Socialist Party* (Syracuse: 1966), p. 104. Morroe Berger: "Arab liberalism, never more than a tender shoot... finally withered just after World War II in the white heat of the West's insistence upon maintaining its special position in the Near East and the creation of Israel in 1948 and the ensuing War." *The Arab World Today* (New York: 1962), p. 328.

4. RG59 890E.00/7-2748, July 27, 1948.

5. RG319 472533 Memminger to Marshall, June 15, 1948.

6. Musa al-Alami, "The Lesson of Palestine," *Middle East Journal* 1, no. 3 (October 1949):380–81.

7. Kirkbride, *A Crackle of Thorns* (London: 1956), p. 31. See also pp. 29–36, and RG59 111.20A/7-2049 Stabler to Acheson, July 20, 1949.

8. For example, *Foreign Relations of the United States 1949*, vol. 6 (Washington, D.C.: 1977), p. 748, and *1950*, vol. 5, pp. 658–888, 1043–61, 1483–86; DOS 320/9-1752, Davis to Dulles, September 17, 1952; Russell to author, and Ben-Gurion.

9. CCP General Progress Report A/1367 and Add. 1, October 23, 1950, cited Earl Berger, *The Covenant and the Sword* (London: 1965), p. 59.

10. Constantine Zurayk, *The Meaning of the Disaster* (Beirut: 1956), p. 2.

11. Text in Sadat, *Revolt on the Nile* (New York: 1957), p. 152; Nasser, pp. 26–29; Neguib, p. 17. The arms scandal became public in 1950 and eventually thirteen people were indicted for stealing hundreds of thousands of dollars. The palace, however, obstructed press coverage and hindered the investigation. Neguib, pp. 83–85; Quraishi, p. 178.

12. Abu Iyad, *Palestinians without a Country*, reprinted in *New Outlook* 22, no. 1 (January–February 1979):53–54.

13. Weizmann, *Trial and Error* (New York: 1966), p. 395.

14. Cited in Eban, *An Autobiography* (New York: 1977), p. 94.

15. Arnold Toynbee, *Survey of International Affairs 1925*, vol. 1 (London: 1927), pp. 6–7, 19.

16. Kirkbride, *From the Wings* (London: 1976), pp. 102–103.

17. Glubb, *A Soldier with the Arabs* (New York: 1957), p. 96. For a similar view, see George Kirk, "More Lessons of Palestine," *The 19th Century and After*, vol. 144 (December 1948), p. 337.

18. Weizmann, p. 435; Ben-Gurion cited in Moshe Sharett, *Political Diary*, p. 58, quoted in Eli Sha'altiel, "Moshe Sharett, The Diaries, and the St. James Conference," Forum #32 (Fall 1978), p. 51.

19. Cleveland, *The Making of an Arab Nationalist* (Princeton: 1971), p. 129.

20. Hisham Sharabi, p. 131.

21. Walter Laqueur, *Terrorism* (Boston: 1977), p. 192.

22. John Glubb, "Transjordan and the War," *Journal of the Royal Central Asia Society* 31, pt. 1 (January 1945), p. 31.

23. Sharabi, p. 41.

2—ZIONISTS, HASHEMITES, AND PAN-SYRIANS: 1897–1930

1. Cmd. 5479, Palestine: Royal Commission (London: 1937), ch. 23, para. 5.

2. Theodor Herzl, *The Diaries of Theodor Herzl* (New York: 1962), p. 204.

3. On Arab-Zionist relations during this period, see Neville Mandel, *The Arabs and Zionism Before World War I* (Los Angeles: 1976); Isaiah Friedman, *Germany, Turkey, and Zionism 1897 – 1918* (London: 1977); Moshe Perlman, "Chapters of Arab-Jewish Diplomacy 1918–22," *Jewish Social Studies* (1944); Yaacov Ro'i, "The Zionist Attitude to the Arabs 1908–1914," *Middle East Studies* (April 1968).

4. Albert Hourani, *Arabic Thought in the Liberal Age* (London: 1962), p. 279; Kedourie, "The Politics of Political Literature: Kawakabi, Azoury and Jung," in *Arabic Political Memoirs*. In 1897 Rida suggested his compatriots learn from "the weakest of people" who still "have so much knowledge and understanding of civilization ... that they can take possession of your country." Mandel, p. 45.

5. Hisham Sharabi, *Arab Intellectuals and the West* (Baltimore: 1970); Kedourie, "Young Turks, Freemasons and Jews" and "The Impact of the Young Turk Revolution in the Arabic-Speaking Provinces of the Ottoman Empire," in *Arabic Political Memoirs;* Bernard Lewis, *The Emergence of Modern Turkey* (New York: 1969), pp. 207–208. See also Sylvia Haim, *Arab Nationalism: An Anthology* (Berkeley: 1962).

6. Mandel, pp. 107–112.

7. Ibid., pp. 145–49; ESCO Foundation for Palestine, *Palestine, A Study of Jewish, Arab and British Policies* (New Haven, Conn.: 1949), 1:524, 566–67, 585; George Antonius, *The Arab Awakening* (London: 1945), pp. 437–39.

8. Hochberg to Jacobson, cited in Walter Laqueur, *A History of Zionism* (New York: 1972), p. 212. A few contacts did continue. Faris al-Khouri met Zionist delegates in 1914 saying that while Jewish immigrants would be a good thing for Palestine, the Jews would eventually try to oust the Arabs. Zionist leader Nahum Sokolow went to Beirut and Damascus in 1914, but Turkish pressure discouraged further talks. See Aharon Cohen, *Israel and the Arab World* (New York: 1970), p. 105.

9. Leonard Stein, *The Balfour Declaration* (London: 1961), Isaiah Friedman, *The Question of Palestine, 1914–1918* (New York: 1973); Elie Kedourie, *Britain and the Middle East 1914–1921* (London: 1956); Howard Sachar, *The Emergence of the Middle East 1914–1924* (New York: 1969); Antonius; and Elie Kedourie, *In The Anglo-Arab Labyrinth* (London: 1976).

10. William Yale report, December 10, 1917, cited Kedourie, *Britain and the Middle East*, p. 40; Laqueur, p. 236–37; Perlman, p. 131.

11. Sachar, p. 199; Christopher Sykes, *Two Studies in Virtue* (London: 1953); Sykes letter of November 16, 1917, cited in Kedourie, p. 86; Chaim Weizmann, *Trial and Error* (New York: 1966), p. 189.

12. Cohen, pp. 135–36; D. G. Hogarth, "Wahabism and British Interests," *Journal of the British Institute of International Affairs* 4 (1925): 72–73; Elie Kedourie, "Cairo and Khartoum on the Arab Question," in *The Chatham House Version*, pp. 13–32.

13. Lawrence wrote on November 4, 1918, "In Palestine the Arabs hope the British will keep what they have conquered. They will not approve Jewish independence for Palestine but will support as far as they can Jewish infiltration, if it is behind a British, as opposed to an international facade." But if Sykes-Picot was carried out, Lawrence continued, Faysal would press for self-determination in Palestine. Kedourie, *Britain and the Middle East*, p. 152; *Chatham House*, p. 30; Weizmann, pp. 232–36, 293; Cohen, pp. 136–39; Laqueur, p. 240.

14. Text is in Antonius. See also David Garnett, *Letters of T. E. Lawrence* (London: 1938), pp. 268–69; Perlman, pp. 123–54; Cohen, p. 141; Weizmann, pp. 245–46; *The Egyptian Gazette*, January 21, 1919; and Richard Meinertzhagen, *Middle East Diary* (London: 1959).

15. David Miller, *My Diary at the Peace Conference*, vol. 4 (New York: 1921), pp. 262, 297–300; Howard M. Sachar, *A History of Israel* (New York: 1976), p. 166. Weizmann was optimistic about the talks, but the Jewish community in Palestine was skeptical over his "Pan-Arab" strategy. See Neil Caplan, *Palestine Jewry and the Arab Question, 1917–1925* (London: 1978), pp. 17–19.

16. Kedourie, *Britain and the Middle East*, pp. 113–17; Cohen, p. 143; Headquarters Egyptian Expeditionary Force to Foreign Office, March 3, 1919, Foreign Office (hereafter FO) 608/98; Nadi al-'Arabi and Muntada al-'Arabi letter to British authorities, December 8, 1919, Israel State Archives; Lt. Col. Kinahan Cornwallis, "Political Situation in Arabia," May 16, 1919, in Lawrence Evans, *United States Policy and the Partition of Turkey* (Baltimore: 1965), p. 265.

17. *Documents of British Foreign Policy*, 1st ser., 4 (London: 1952):364–65; Antonius, p. 267.

18. Ronald Storrs, *Orientations* (London: 1943), p. 355; Ann Dearden, *Jordan* (London: 1958), p. 59; Kedourie, *England and the Middle East*, p. 159; Sachar, *A History of Israel*, pp. 166–67; Chaim Kalvarisky, *Al Parashat Darkhenu* (Jerusalem: 1939), pp. 25–35; Rony Gabbay, *A Political Study of the Arab-Jewish Conflict* (Paris: 1959), p. 33; Antonius, pp. 293–94 and text of the resolutions on pp. 440–42; ESCO, p. 474; J. C. Hurewitz, *The Struggle for Palestine* (New York: 1968), p. 56; and Harry Howard, "An American Experiment in Peace-Making," *Moslem World* 32 (April 1942).

19. Meinertzhagen to War Office, March 12, 1920, WO 106/195; E. L. Woodward and R. Butler, *Documents on British Foreign Policy*, pp. 265, 364–65, 421–22. Lawrence even suggested that to have Jews in Palestine would be to Faysal's advantage since if he found the townsmen of Syria slipping from his control, he might find support from the Jews. Elizabeth Monroe, *Britain's Moment in the Middle East* (London: 1963), p. 65; Kedourie, "The *Capture of Damascus*," in *Chatham House;* and Z. N. Zeine, *The Struggle for Arab Independence* (Beirut: 1960), pp. 132–41.

20. See FO 371/5121 and Allenby's telegrams of March 8 and 18, 1920, in *Documents on British Foreign Policy,* 1st ser., 13, nos. 216 and 223; Meinertzhagen, p. 56; Storrs, pp. 329–32; Montagu to Wilson, March 19, 1920, cited in *England and the Middle East*, p. 178.

21. Cohen, p. 162; FO371 E9379/85/44 Samuel to Curzon, April 2, 1920.

22. Suleiman Mousa, "A Matter of Principle: King Hussein of the Hijaz and the Arabs of Palestine," *International Journal of Middle East Studies* 9, no. 2 (May 1978):185–87; Yehoshua Porath, "The Palestinians and the Negotiations for the British-Hijazi Treaty, 1920–1925," *Asian and African Studies* 8, no. 1 (1972):20–48.

23. Mousa, pp. 188–94. In their final offer, made in 1923, Britain pledged to do nothing to "prejudice the civil and religious rights of the Arab community" in Palestine.

24. Aaron Kleiman, *The Foundations of British Policy in the Arab World* (Baltimore: 1970), p. 227; Mousa, p. 188; for text, see FO406 E930/248/91.

25. Kleiman, pp. 68–76; Benjamin Shwadran, *Jordan, A State of Tension* (New York: 1959), pp. 123–27; Munib al-Madi and Suleiman Mousa, *Tarikh al-urdun fi al-qarn al'ishrin* (Amman: 1959), p. 54; FO406 E16167/13556/44 Deedes to FO, December 5, 1920. Lawrence, too, thought union with Palestine would provide the best future for Transjordan; FO406 E1062/401/88 Samuel to Curzon, January 8, 1921; King Abdullah, *Memoirs* (London: 1950), p. 204n.

26. See Abdullah, and Kleiman, pp. 129–31. In 1919 Abd al-Hadi had been a member of the Hijazi delegation to the Versailles conference.

27. *Palestine* 9, no. 7 (April 30, 1921):49–51, and no. 14 (June 18, 1921), p. 106; Abdullah, *My Memoirs Completed* (New York: 1954), p. 97.

28. Weizmann to Eder, December 8, 1921, Weizmann Archives, cited Kleiman, p. 198; Elizabeth Monroe, *Philby of Arabia* (London: 1973), p. 126; Clinton Bailey, *The Participation of the Palestinians in the Politics of Jordan,* (Ph.D. diss., Columbia University, 1966); British White Paper CMD 1499; *Palestine* 9, no. 24 (September 10, 1921):192.

29. In November 1921, a secret meeting of Zionist leaders discussed methods for Arab-Jewish entente, and resolutions urging negotiations were passed at the Twelfth Zionist Congress.

30. Cited in Kleiman, p. 260.

31. On Abdallah's 1922 meetings with Weizmann, see M. Medzini, *Ten Years of Palestine Politics* (Hebrew) (Tel Aviv: 1928).

32. Fred Kisch, *Palestine Diary* (London: 1938), pp. 46–47, 109–110, 167, 317–18.

33. The minutes of this meeting were presented to the Peel Commission in 1936. Cohen, pp. 184–90, *Palestine* (April 30, 1922), p. 52, and (September 10, 1921), p. 188; ESCO, p.

477; Stephen Longrigg, *Syria and Lebanon under French Mandate* (New York: 1958), pp. 140–86; Weizmann, p. 289; Kisch, pp. 122–24; Susan Lee Hattis, *The Bi-National Idea in Palestine During Mandatory Times* (Tel Aviv: 1970), p. 39.

34. Hurewitz, p. 56.

35. Y. Porath, *The Emergence of the Palestinian Arab Nationalist Movement* (London: 1974), pp. 205–206.

36. Fred Sherrow, *The Arabs of Palestine As Seen Through Jewish Eyes 1925 – 29* (M.A. thesis, Columbia University), pp. 25–34. Among those involved were Ahmed Zaki, a noted Egyptian scholar, Emir Amin Arslan, and Lebanese philosopher Amin al-Rihani; see also Kisch, pp. 168–74.

37. Longrigg, pp. 186, 295.

38. Bailey, pp. 25–26; Kisch, pp. 63–65; P. J. Vatikiotis, *Politics and Military in Jordan* (London: 1967), p. 50.

39. Kisch, pp. 97–106.

40. Emir Abdallah to Dr. Saul Mizan, August 18, 1926, cited Cohen, p. 192. For their part, the right-wing Revisionist Zionists about this time began to claim Transjordan as part of the Jewish state, *Basic Principles of Revisionism* (London: 1929), p. 3.

41. Sherrow, p. 51; Cohen, pp. 192–94, 299. When Azmi was invited to head the law faculty at Baghdad, he was dissuaded by right-wing student demonstrations against him.

42. Cohen, pp. 247, 265. On the Istiqlal, see Yehoshua Porath, "Social Aspects of the Emergence of the Palestinian Arab National Movement," in *Social and Political Structure in the Arab World*, ed. Menahem Milson (New York: 1974), pp. 127–28.

43. On Damascus, see FO file 10838 and FO371 E2293/1065/65, Satow to FO, April 6, 1925, and Smart's memos of April 14 and 15, E2446/1065/65 and E2514/1065/65, respectively. Iraqi demonstrations were ostensibly organized by faculty at the Teachers Training College but received support from Yasin al-Hashimi and Rashid Ali al-Gailani. King Faysal might also have been involved since at that time he was pressuring Britain for an end to the Iraq mandate. Peter Sluglett, *Britain in Iraq 1914 – 1932* (London: 1976), pp. 159–60.

44. Sherrow, pp. 48–49.

45. Ibid., pp. 41–45.

46. Christopher Sykes, *Crossroads to Israel* (Bloomington, Ind.: 1965), pp. 99–128.

47. FO371 E6450/318/65 Transjordan intelligence summary, October 10, 1929; Parr to FO August 29, 1929, E4865/4198/65 and September 17, 1929, E5290/4198/65; E4614/4198/65 Colonial Office report of September 10, 1929; E4785/4198/65 Ellison to FO, September 6, 1929; E4866/4198/65 Satow to FO, August 30, 1929.

48. FO371 E4575/4198/65 Hoare to Henderson, August 31, 1929; E4860/4198/65 al-Maraghi to Loraine, September 14, 1929. Repercussions were felt as far away as Morocco. See John Halstead, *Rebirth of a Nation: The Origins and Rise of Moroccan Nationalism* (Cambridge: 1969), p. 155.

49. Kisch, pp. 317–18, 445; FO371 E5686/4198/65 Bond to FO, October 15, 1929, and E5178/4198/65 Colonial Office memo, October 8, 1929.

50. Kisch, pp. 338, 361, and 374; Sykes, pp. 116–19; FO371 E4754/4198/65 Colonial Office report, September 16, 1929. The October 1930 Passfield White Paper, though publicly watered down by Ramsey MacDonald, marked the new trend in British policy.

3—ENTRANCE OF THE ARAB KINGS: 1931–36

1. Yehoshua Porath, *The Palestinian Arab National Movement, 1928 – 1939* (London: 1978), p. 8. (hereafter, Porath, vol. 2).

2. H. A. R. Gibb, "The Islamic Congress at Jerusalem in December 1931," in *Survey of International Affairs* (London: 1935).

3. Porath, vol. 2, p. 72. On early Palestine Arab-Hashemite relations see Porath, vol. 1, pp. 79–103.

4. *London Times*, November 27, 1931.

5. Porath, vol. 2, pp. 9–12; Porath, "Social Aspects," ibid., pp. 128–30.

6. FO371 E5831/1205/65 and E5920/1205/65, Colonial Office reports of November 24 and 30, 1931, and E5784/1205/65 Clerk to FO, November 12, 1931.

7. FO371 E5667/1205/65 Gill to FO, November 14, 1931; E5382/1205/65, E5665/1205/65, E5696/1205/65, E1713/17/31, E5701/1205/65, and E5712/1205/65; U.S. State Department Record Group (hereafter RG) 59 Jardine to Kellogg, 883.00 General Conditions/7, December 28, 1931, and 867N.00/132, November 24, 1931; RG59 867N.00/128 Knabenshue to Kellogg, November 17, 1931; Gibb, p. 105; *New York Times*, November 9, 1931; *Egyptian Gazette*, November 5, 1931.

8. Gibb, p. 102; FO371 E6216/1205/65 and E6276/1205/65. Azzam's speech earned the Mufti a reprimand from the high commissioner.

9. RG59 867N.00/133 Knabenshue to Kellogg, December 17, 1931.

10. Nahum Sokolow, Jewish Agency president, was invited to attend and express the Zionist viewpoint but declined. Gibb, p. 108; M. V. Seton-Williams, *Britain and the Arab States* (London: 1948), p. 218; *New York Times*, December 14, 1931; Haim Arlosoroff, *Yoman Yirushalayim* (Tel Aviv: 1949), pp. 131–32. For texts, see Muhammed Khalil, *The Arab States and the Arab League: A Documentary Record*, vol. 2 (Beirut: 1962), pp. 7–9.

11. Gibb, p. 108. Sources differ on the exact role played by the delegation. See ESCO, vol. 2, p. 776, and Ernest Main, *Palestine at the Crossroads* (London: 1937), p. 56.

12. *New York Times*, January 28, 1932, and January 8, 1933; Stephen Longrigg, *Iraq 1900 – 1950* (New York: 1953), p. 265; RG59 890.G001 Faisal/50 #123, Knabenshue to Stimson, June 21, 1933, 867N.00/163 Sloan to Stimson, Feb. 3, 1933; FO371 E444/44/65 Colonial Office, January 23, 1930; Khaldun Husry, "King Faysal I and Arab Unity 1930–1933," *Journal of Contemporary History* 10, no. 2 (April 1975):332–37. Yasin al-Hashimi called for annexing Transjordan and Palestine to Iraq "so as to remove the Zionist menace." RG59 867N.9111/89.

13. Hurewitz, pp. 62–63; ESCO, vol. 2, 778–79; Bailey, pp. 14, 23–24.

14. David Ben-Gurion, *My Talks with Arab Leaders* (New York: 1973), pp. 30–97; Eliahu Elath, *Shivat Zion ve-Arav* (Tel Aviv: 1974), pp. 422–42.

15. Eliahu Elath, *Zionism at the UN* (Philadelphia: 1976), pp. 254–55; Ibid., pp. 301–314.

16. *New York Times*, September 12 and November 26, 1931; Laqueur, p. 498. On Abbas Hilmi, see *New York Times*, February 5, 1932, and RG59 867N.9111/92.

17. Kisch, pp. 387, 396, 404, 422–23, 431, 438; RG59 867N.00/103 Knabenshue to Kellogg, June 20, 1931.

18. Porath, vol. 2, pp. 70–75; *Haaretz*, October 13, 1933; RG59 867N.9111/109; Shwadran, pp. 190–92. For details of the negotiations, see Emanuel Neumann, *In the Arena* (New York: 1976), pp. 121–30. Text of the lease is on pp. 325–30.

19. Porath, vol. 2, pp. 70–75.

20. *Mir'at al-Sharq* March 7 and March 14, 1934, and May 1, 1935. One tribal chief explained that his people were hungry and that the Husayni-controlled Supreme Muslim Council had refused them a loan. "I would have negotiated with monkeys to save my people from starvation," he said. See also RG59 867N.9111/145, Porath, vol. 2, p. 65, and I. Chizik, "The Political Parties of Trans-Jordania," *Journal of the Royal Central Asian Society* (April 1935), p. 98.

21. Cohen, p. 254.

22. Arnold Toynbee, *Survey of International Affairs* 1934 (London: 1935), pp. 281–82; RG59 867N.9111/109, October 15, 1933; al-Madi and Mousa, p. 453; Abdullah, *My Memoirs Completed*, pp. 88, 92–96.

23. Chizik, p. 98; RG59 890I.001 Abdullah/8 and /5, August 23 and June 27, 1934; RG59 890F.0011/19 Palmer to Stimson, September 3, 1935; *Palestine Post*, October 17, 1935; Husry, pp. 328–29.

24. Gerald de Gaury, *Faisal* (New York: 1967), p. 61.

25. Alec Kirkbride, *A Crackle of Thorns* (London: 1956), p. 42; Seton-Williams, pp. 291–93. For the treaty, see British Parliamentary Paper CMD 2951, 1927; Hisham Sharabi, *Government and Politics of the Middle East in the Twentieth Century* (Princeton: 1962), p. 238; D. C. Watt, "The Foreign Policy of Ibn Saud 1936–39," *Journal of the Royal Central Asian Society*, 1 (April 1963):152; H. St. John Philby, *Arabian Jubilee* (London: 1954), p. 122; Elizabeth Monroe, *Philby of Arabia*, p. 214.

26. Arnold Toynbee wrote at the time that the king seemed to be "achieving the common Arab ambition of bringing together at least the ex-Ottoman part of the Arab-speaking world." *Survey of International Affairs 1936* (London: 1937), pp. 783–93.

27. British Parliamentary Paper CMD 3069 (1928); London *Times*, November 14, 1935.

28. ESCO, vol. 2, p. 777; Bailey, pp. 14–15.

29. Cohen, p. 190, 252; Caplan, pp. 172–82; Kisch, pp. 36, 65, 93–104, 236, 338, 387–96. Abdallah wrote about these negotiations, citing the Koran, "If they incline toward peace then do you incline toward peace also, and put your trust in God." *My Memoirs Completed*, p. 11. See also Shwadran, pp. 224–40; *New York Times*, January 18, 22, 24, and 26, 1933; London *Times*, January 27 and August 23, 1933.

30. Tawfiq Canaan, *Conflict in the Land of Peace* (Jerusalem: 1936); London *Times*, February 27, March 1 and 5, and June 4, 1935.

31. Porath, vol. 1, p. 149; Dearden, p. 56; Amin Mahmoud, *King Abdullah and Palestine,* (Ph.D. diss., Georgetown University, 1972), pp. 47–50; Zionist Organization, *Report to the Eighteenth Zionist Congress* (London: 1933), pp. 218–19; Abdullah, *My Memoirs Completed*, pp. 9–13. For the spread of Palestine tensions to Transjordan, see Abdullah, pp. 94–95; Vatikiotis, p. 73; FO371 E814/89/31, Wauchope's report, February 13, 1936. Abdallah to Wauchope, July 1936, cited by Abdullah, p. 93.

32. Dearden, p. 49; J. C. Hurewitz, *Diplomacy in the Near and Middle East*, vol. 2 (New York: 1956), pp. 156–59; A. Konikoff, *Transjordan: An Economic Survey* (Jerusalem: 1943), pp. 78–83.

4 — DOMESTIC POLITICS AND PALESTINE: IRAQ AND EGYPT

1. Hourani, p. 307.

2. Zeine N. Zeine, *The Emergence of Arab Nationalism* (New York: 1973), p. 95n.

3. Sluglett, p. 4. Of the three main towns, Mosul looked toward Syria and southern Turkey, Basra was connected through trade to India and the Persian Gulf, while Baghdad itself was the center of the Persian transit trade. The inclusion of the Kurds and the Mosul district added to the complexity and potential centrifugal forces.

4. Elie Kedourie, "The Kingdom of Iraq," in *Chatham House*, pp. 253–54.

5. *Hadhihi Ahdafuna* (These Are Our Aims) (Baghdad: 1939), pp. 1–3.

6. *Al Akha al-Watani*, July 14, 1932; Taha al-Hashimi, *Mudhakkirat* (Beirut: 1967), p. 358.

7. Sati al-Husri, *Mudhakkirat*, vol. 1 (Beirut: 1967), pp. 215–16; William Cleveland, *The Making of an Arab Nationalist* (Princeton: 1971), pp. 60–66; Khalil Kanna, *Al-Iraq Amsuhu wa Ghaduhu* (Beirut: 1966), p. 52.

8. CO730 119/40199 Dobbs to Amery, March 31, 1927.

9. Majid Khadduri, *Independent Iraq* (London: 1951), pp. 47–48.

10. *Al-Bayan* April 7, 1936. See also Robert Woolbert, "Pan Arabism and the Palestine Problem," *Foreign Affairs* 16, no. 2: 309–22.

11. Khadduri, pp. 66–68; Kedourie, *Chatham House*, pp. 248–49.

12. Khadduri, p. 65.

13. *New York Times*, February 7, 1935. For early Iraqi protests see FO371 E306/24/31 for the Chamber of Deputies declaration.

14. Arnold Toynbee, *Survey of International Affairs 1934*, p. 264.

15. (British) Syria Naval Intelligence Division, *Syria* (London: 1943), p. 287. See also *Palestine and the Near East*, 4, no. 13 (September 30, 1929), and no. 14 (October 20, 1929): 449–50; "Syrian-Palestine Trade," *Palestine* (October 12, 1938), pp. 324–25; Said Himadeh, *Economic Organization of Palestine* (Beirut: 1938); Michael Shefer, "The Effect of the Arab-Israeli Rupture on the Economy of the Arab Countries," (Hebrew) *Mizrach Hadash* 14, no. 2–3 (54–55) (1964):158–84.

NOTES

. Ibid.; D. Freeman, "The Jewish National Home and the Arab States," *Palestine and the Near East* 9, no. 5, (1939):119–23.

17. Longrigg, *Iraq,* p. 265; Toynbee, 1934 *Survey*, p. 187. See also C. Empson, *Economic Conditions in Iraq* (London: 1933). While beneficial for Iraq and Transjordan, the opening of Haifa harbor was a disaster for Lebanese ports. Its closure to Arab traffic after 1948 aided the growth of Beirut.

18. ESCO, vol. 2, p. 753; London *Times*, February 4, 1931, November 22, 1933, October 15 and 26, 1934, December 21, 1934, and January 15, 1935; Sluglett, p. 164; Toynbee, 1934 *Survey*, pp. 265–66.

19. Weizmann, p. 408; Main, pp. 57–58.

20. Laqueur, p. 262; Longrigg, *Iraq,* p. 252; Sluglett, p. 212; London *Times*, May 20 and October 3, 1932; Sylvia Haim, "Aspects of Jewish Life in Baghdad Under the Monarchy," *Middle Eastern Studies* 12, no. 2 (May 1976).

21. See al-Said's memorandum of December 15, 1940 in Khadduri, p. 284, and *Iraq Times*, November 21, 1941. On al-Said's career, see Majid Khadduri, *Arab Contemporaries* (Baltimore: 1973), pp. 19–42, and Lord Birdwood, *Nuri al-Said, A Study in Arab Leadership* (London: 1958).

22. Khadduri, *Independent Iraq*, pp. 157–59.

23. Waldemar Gallman, *Iraq Under General Nuri* (Baltimore: 1964), p. 3.

24. In Holt, pp. 191–92. See also Watt, p. 166, and Toynbee, 1934 *Survey*, p. 264.

25. In *Rida Tarikh*, vol. 2, p. 250, cited Adams, p. 59. See also Safran, pp. 41–42, 103–104.

26. Cited in Cleveland, p. 134. See also pp. 134–40.

27. Ibrahim Ghali, *L'Egypt Nationaliste et Liberale* (The Hague: 1969), p. 157; Christina Harris, *Nationalism and Revolution in Egypt* (The Hague: 1964), p. 134; Anwar Chejne, "Egyptian Attitudes Toward Pan-Arabism," *Middle East Journal* 11, no. 3 (Summer 1957):253; Hourani, pp. 324–40.

28. See for instance, Emil Lengyel, *Egypt's Role in World Affairs* (Washington, D.C.: 1957), p. 22; Virginia MacLean, *Domestic and Foreign Factors in Egyptian Foreign Policy 1919–1939*, Ph.D. diss., Fletcher School, 1955.

29. As in Sir Miles Lampson's 1938–39 dispatches, for example FO371 J3501/5/16, J4131/5/16, and J4690/5/16.

30. Afaf Lutfi al-Sayyid-Marsot, *Egypt's Liberal Experiment 1922–1936* (Berkeley: 1977), pp. 81, 214; Abdullah, *Memoirs Concluded*, p. 8.

31. Kisch, pp. 376–92, 408–409.

32. For example, *Al-Risalah,* August 26, 1935; Zaheer Quraishi, *Liberal Nationalism in Egypt* (New Delhi: 1967), pp. 126–27; Mahmoud I. M. Ismail, *Nationalism in Egypt Before Nasser's Revolution*, Ph.D. diss., University of Pittsburgh, 1966.

33. Richard Mitchell, *The Society of the Muslim Brothers* (New York: 1959), pp. 15–18; Jacques Berque, *Egypt: Imperialism and Revolution* (New York: 1972), pp. 410, 463; Quraishi, pp. 132–33; al-Sayyid-Marsot, pp. 152–53, 190.

34. For Azzam's views, see his, *The Arab Nation: Paths & Obstacles to Fulfillment* (Washington, D.C.: 1960), pp. 5–14.

35. Abdullah, *Memoirs Completed*, p. 8; Chejne, pp. 237–38; Harris, p. 178; Berque, p. 506.

36. Berque, pp. 410, 460–65.

37. Al-Sayyid Marsot, pp. 111–13; Ibid., pp. 406, 563. On Alluba and Mahmud and their split with the Wafd see Quraishi, pp. 45–67.

38. Gamal Abdul Nasser, *The Philosophy of the Revolution* (Buffalo, N.Y.: 1959), pp. 62, 103. On the student demonstrations see, for instance, *New York Times*, October 9, 1937 and London *Times*, April 29, 1938.

39. Elie Kedourie, "Pan-Arabism and Egyptian Politics," *Political Quarterly* 28, no. 1 (January–March 1957):139. See also Majid Khadduri, *Political Trends in the Arab World* (Baltimore: 1970).

40. *Palestine & Transjordan*, July 9, 1938; London *Times*, September 10, 1937, and October 13, 1938.

41. H. Heyworth-Dunne, *Religious and Political Trends in Modern Egypt* (Washington, D.C.: 1950).

42. *Jaridah Misr al-Fatah*, May 23, 1938, cited James Jankowski, *Egypt's Young Rebels* (Stanford, Calif.: 1975), pp. 53–54.

43. Al-Sayyid-Marsot, pp. 191–92.

5—THE GENERAL STRIKE AND THE BRITISH INVITATION: 1936

1. Howard Sachar, *Europe Leaves the Middle East* (New York: 1973), pp. 41–42.

2. J. Rives Childs, *Foreign Service Farewell* (Charlottesville, VA.: 1969), pp. 84–85; On Italian propaganda in Egypt, see FO371 J4189/2/16 Lampson to FO, May 7, 1936.

3. Porath, vol. 2, pp. 160–61.

4. *Al-Liwa*, March 23, 1936; F0371 E1993/19/31, March 14, 1936; Central Zionist Archives S25 5632 Sassoon report, March 12, 1936, and Epstein-Cohen, February 10, 1935.

5. *Palestine & Transjordan*, June 4, 1938.

6. Cited in Norman Rose, "The Arab Rulers and Palestine 1936: The British Reaction," *Journal of Modern History* 44, no. 2 (June 1972):215; Ben-Gurion, p. 104; Porath, vol. 2, p. 200.

7. FO371 E2653/94/31 Kerr to FO, May 5, 1936; *Al-Bilad* May 3, 1936; *Al-Iraq*, May 2, 1936; and *Al-Alam al-Arabi*, May 2, 1936; RG59 867N.00/324 Knabenshue to Hull, May 20, 1936.

8. FO371 E2585/2585/31, May 19, 1936; E3314/2585/93, May 27, 1936; E3399/2585/93, June 3, 1936, all Kerr to FO.

9. FO371 E3679/2585/93, June 20, 1936; E3800/2585/93, June 23, 1936; E3986/2585/93, June 25, 1936; E4774/2585/93, Bateman to FO, July 14, 1936. For text, see RG59 867N.00/339 Knabenshue to Hull, July 7, 1936.

10. FO371 E3452/3217/31, June 11, 1936; E3453/3217/31, June 11, 1936; Porath, vol. 2, pp. 199–201; Gabriel Sheffer, "The Involvement of Arab States in the Palestine Conflict and British-Arab Relations before World War 2," *Asian and African Studies* 10, no. 1: 61–62.

11. FO371 E3483/3217/31 Kelly to FO, June 4, 1936, J5232/2/16, June 9, 1936, and J5575/2/16, June 11, 1936; RG59 867N.00/320 Fish to Hull, June 15, 1936; *New York Times*, May 30, 1936.

12. FO371 E1357/94/31, J4727/2/16, and E3507/3217/31. See also E3629/3217/31, June 17, 1936; E3680/3217/31, June 20, 1936; E3704/3217/31 on projected delegation. On fund-raising, see E4415/3217/31, July 3, 1936, and E5113/3217/31, August 13, 1936.

13. FO371 E3598/3217/31 Kelly to FO, June 16, 1936, and E3753/3217/31 Kelly to FO, June 22, 1936.

14. *Egyptian Mail,* June 12, 1936; FO371 E4667/3217/31 and E4940/3217/31.

15. FO371 E4293/94/31, July 9, 1936; E5160/3217/30, August 12, 1936; E6376/94/31, October 8, 1936. See also E5207/3217/30.

16. RG59 867N.00/309 Farrell to Hull, May 2, 1936; 867N.00/325 Farrell to Hull, May 18, 1936, pp. 6–7; and 867N.00/328 Kelsey to Hull, June 15, 1936. See also Porath, vol. 2, pp. 176, 199.

17. Shwadran, pp. 187–88, 208; Abdullah, *My Memoirs Completed*, pp. 94–95; al-Madi and Mousa, p. 455; *New York Times*, October 27, 1936.

18. Rose, pp. 63–82; Mahmoud, pp. 104–121. See also *Palestine Royal Commission Report* (London: 1937), Hurewitz, *The Struggle for Palestine*, and Ben-Gurion, pp. 104–21.

19. Ibid.; London *Times,* June 8 and 10, 1936.

20. Michael Cohen, "Secret Diplomacy and Rebellion in Palestine 1936–9," *International Journal of Middle East Studies* 8, no. 3 (July 1977):382–88; Avraham Sela, "Conversations and Contacts between Zionist and Palestinian Arab Leaders 1933–1939," (Hebrew) *Mizrach Hadash* 22, no. 4 (88) (1972):401–23, and 23, no. 1 (89) (1973): 1–21.

21. FO371 E3466/2585/93, June 11, 1936; E4291/2585/93, June 28, 1936; Porath, vol. 2, pp. 202–203.

22. Michael Cohen, "Diplomacy and Rebellion," p. 380.

23. FO371 E3783/94/31, June 23, 1936, and E4109/94/31, July 3, 1936, on Ibn Saud's offer; E4257/94/31, July 8, 1936, and E4293/94/31 July 9, 1936, on Transjordan and Egypt; E6376/94/31 October 8, 1936, on reasons for omitting Egyptian participation.

24. London *Times*, July 24, August 7 and 18, 1936; Rose, pp. 219–20.

25. FO371 E5201/2585/93 August 17, 1936, E5264/2585/93 August 19, 1936; Ormsby-Gore to Wauchope, April 27, 1936, cited Rose, p. 221.

26. Porath, vol. 2, pp. 206–216; London *Times*, September 1 and 8, 1936.

27. FO371 E5551/19/31 September 2, 1936; Rose, p. 226; Porath, pp. 225–26.

28. FO371 E6404/94/31 and E6633/317/33 October 9, 1936. For text of the appeal, see Marlowe, p. 166, and Sachar, *Europe Leaves*, p. 74. See also *New York Times*, October 11, 1936, and London *Times*, September 25, 28, and 30, 1936. For Shertok's note to Nuri al-Said, see Central Zionist Archives 899/J3 S25 5632, November 9, 1936.

29. *Al Difah* October 13, 1936; *Palestine Royal Commission Report*, p. 105; *New York Times*, October 12 and 13, 1936.

30. London *Times*, October 13, 1936.

31. Rose, p. 231; Kedourie, *Chatham House*, p. 80; FO371 E5379/94/31 and E5422/94/31.

32. Khadduri, *Arab Contemporaries*, pp. 110–11; *Cumhuriyet*, September 13, 1936; FO371 E5098/94/31 August 11, 1936, E5206/94/31 August 15, 1936, for Ibn Saud's contribution; E5860/94/31 September 16, and E5954/94/31 September 21, 1936, for Mufti's dependence on Ibn Saud; E5455/9431 August 27, E5539/94/31 September 1, and E5695/94/31 September 8, 1936, for Ibn Saud's complaints about Nuri. See also E5474/94/31 Calvert to FO, August 11, 1936, on public opinion in Saudi Arabia, and E6453/94/31 Bullard to FO, October 13, 1936, for London's thanks.

33. For British criticism see E5427/94/31 Williams to FO, August 27, 1936; For Nuri's proposals, E5435/94/31 Williams to FO, August 28, 1936, and E5446/94/31 Bateman to FO, August 28, 1936.

34. FO371 E6036/94/31; E6374/94/31 Kerr to FO, October 8, 1936; E6507/94/31 Bateman to Rendel, September 30, 1936; E5551/19/31, August 18, 1936; Hattis, pp. 158–59.

35. Central Zionist Archives 899/J3 S25 5632 Kallay memorandum January 24, 1935, and memorandum of conversation, February 4, 1935. FO371 E6060/2585/93 Bateman to FO September 25, E6494/2585/93 Wedgewood inquiry, September 30; E6620/2585/93 Kerr to FO October 17, and E6702/2585/93 October 23, 1936, conversation with Weizmann. See also RG59 890G.4016 Jews/12 Moose to Hull October 14, 1936, for texts of Thabet's petitions; *Al-Istiqlal,* October 8, 1936.

36. Ibid.; *Palestine & Transjordan*, October 3, 1936.

37. Ibid., Sachar, *Europe Leaves* p. 72.

38. FO371 E6085/1419/93 Bateman to FO, September 17, 1936.

39. *Al Balagh,* October 12, 1936; *Egyptian Gazette,* October 13, 1936.

40. FO371 E6523/94/31 October 15, 1936; E7090/94/31 November 11, 1936; E7185/94/31 November 16, 1936; Porath, vol. 2, pp. 224–25.

41. Ibid.; FO371 E7108/94/31 November 12, 1936.

42. FO371 E6971/94/31 Kerr to FO November 6, 1936, and E172/172/93 January 1, 1936. Khadduri, *Arab Contemporaries,* pp. 128–42; London *Times*, August 13 and 14, 1937.

43. Majid Khadduri, "The Coup d'Etat of 1936," *Middle East Journal* 2, no. 3 (July 1948): 270–92; *Palestine & Transjordan*, November 7, 1936; FO371 E7203/317/31 November 6, 1936.

44. FO371 E7356/94/31 November 23, 1936; Porath, vol. 2, p. 226; Longrigg, *Iraq*, pp. 250–51; Khadduri, *Independent Iraq*, pp. 97–109; RG59 867N.00/422 and /424 Knabenshue to Hull, November 18 and December 3, 1936.

45. Kedourie, *Chatham House*, pp. 79–80.

6—OPPOSITION TO PARTITION, SUPPORT FOR REVOLT: 1937—38

1. CO733 326/75023/2 Cox to Moody, February 11, 1937; *Palestine*, March 10, 1937, pp. 74–75; FO371 5551/19/31, August 18, 1936.

2. *Falastin*, April 16, 1937; Shwadran, p. 227; Elie Eliacher, "An Attempt at Settlement in Transjordan," *New Outlook* 18, no. 5 (1975):71–75.

3. RG59 867N.00/509 Wadsworth to Hull, June 8, 1937, and 867N.00/522, June 26, 1937: *Falastin*, June 15, 1937.

4. RG59 867N.00/488 Wadsworth to Hull, June 12, 1937.

5. *Documents on German Foreign Policy 1918–1945*, ser. D, 5 (Washington, D.C.: 1953); Foreign Ministry to Neurath, June 1, 1937, p. 746; von Bulow-Schwante circular, June 22, 1937, pp. 750–53; Dohle to Foreign Ministry, June 15, 1937, p. 756; Grobba to Foreign Ministry, July 1, 1937, p. 756.

6. Elath, pp. 137, 238–41, offers a first-hand account.

7. Laqueur, pp. 516–21; Weizmann.

8. RG59 867N.01/780, July 9, 1937, Division of Near Eastern Affairs, "The Partition of Palestine and an Arab Entente."

9. *Documents on German Foreign Policy*, July 29, 1937, memo. After the Nazi defeat von Hentig became an adviser to Ibn Saud. Germany did oppose partition in the league. See pp. 758–62.

10. John Glubb, *A Soldier with the Arabs* (New York: 1957), p. 153. See also Hurewitz, *Struggle for Palestine*, p. 62.

11. Arnold Toynbee, *Survey of International Affairs 1937*, vol. 1 (London: 1938), p. 555; *Palestine*, July 21, 1937, pp. 230–31, and July 28, 1937, p. 239; *New York Times*, July 9, 1937.

12. *Palestine & Transjordan*, July 17, 1937; *New York Times*, July 14, 1937; Porath, vol. 2, pp. 225–30.

13. FO371 E3906/22/31 Ormsby-Gore to Secretary of State, July 2, 1937.

14. RG59 867N.01/775, 890D.9111/154 and /155 all Marriner to Hull, July 12, July 24, and August 7, 1937; London *Times*, July 22, 26, and 30, 1937.

15. Trefor Evans, *The Killearn Diaries* (London: 1972), pp. 83–84.

16. The first Egyptian response was not unfavorable, Lampson wrote Wauchope, FO371 E4146/22/31 July 12, 1937; E4194/22/31, E4320/22/31, E4668/22/31; *Egyptian Gazette*, July 21, 1937; RG59 867N.01/869 Fish to Hull, July 22, 1937.

17. Ibid.

18. FO371 E3854/22/31, July 7, 1937; E3885/22/31 Bullard to FO July 10, 1937; E4063/ 22/31 Wahba-Rendel meeting, July 14, 1937; E4078/22/31, July 17, 1937; E4166/22/31, July 20, 1937; *Palestine & Transjordan*, July 17, 1937. On the Saudi-Transjordan territorial dispute see Shwadran, pp. 154–59, and RG59 890I.014/11, October 15, 1937. See also Gabriel Shefer, "Saudi Arabia and the Palestine Problem 1936–39," *Mizrach Hadash* 22, no. 2 (86) (1972) (in Hebrew).

19. FO371 E4390/22/31, July 29, 1937.

20. FO371 E4167/22/31 Wahba-Rendel meeting.

21. Watt, p. 155.

22. Evans, pp. 368–69; RG226 OSS 104552, November 15, 1942. On the other hand, even Saudi diplomats would meet with Zionist leaders, see Ben-Gurion, pp. 121–27, 196.

23. FO371 E3919/22/31 Kerr to FO, July 10, 1937; E4495/14/93 Kerr to Oliphant, July 24, 1937; RG59 867N.00/488 Wadsworth to Hull, June 12, 1937 and /522, June 26, 1937; 867N.01/870 Satterthwaite to Hull, July 22, 1937; Porath, vol. 2, pp. 230–31.

24. London *Times*, July 12, 14, and 16, 1937. For more reactions, see *Survey of International Affairs 1937*, pp. 551–57.

25. Lukasz Hirszowicz, *The Third Reich and the Arab East* (Toronto: 1966), p. 34, cited Grobba's report of July 17, 1937; Longrigg, *Iraq*, p. 272.

26. *Al-Istiqlal* July 9 and 14, 1937; *Al-Bilad* July 12 and 15, 1937. See also Y. Taggar, "Iraq Reaction to the Partition Plan for Palestine 1937," in Gabriel Ben-Dor, *The Palestinians and the Middle East Conflict* (Haifa: 1976), pp. 195–213.

27. *Al-Difa*, July 19, 1937; FO371 E4193/22/31, July 19, 1937; *Jewish Telegraphic Agency*, July 19, 1937; *New York Times*, July 18, 1937.

28. RG59 867N.01/868 Wadsworth to Hull, July 23, 1937; 867N.01/861 Satterthwaite to Hull, August 6, 1937; 867N.01/1003 Steger to Hull November 27, 1937; 867N.01/858 August 4, 1937.

29. Khadduri, *Independent Iraq*, pp. 111–12, 134; RG59 867N.01/903, August 19, 1937; London *Times*, October 20, 1937.

30. League of Nations, *Official Journal of Plenary* 13th Session, p. 49; *Official Journal of Sixth Committee* 15th Session, p. 50; London *Times*, July 30, August 5, 7, and 9, September 21, and November 11, 1937. For full text of speech, see *Palestine & Transjordan*, September 30, 1937. Details of Iraqi statements are found in Abid al-Marayati, *A Diplomatic History of Modern Iraq* (New York: 1961).

31. On Nuri al-Said, see FO371 E4985/22/31 Kelly to FO, August 25, 1937; on al-Suweidi see E5392/22/31, September 13, 1937.

32. RG59 867N.01/960 Allen to Hull, October 11, 1937; *Palestine* 12, no. 38 (September 22, 1937): 302, and no. 39 (September 29, 1937):305; *New York Times*, September 19 and 22, 1937.

33. Ibid.

34. Robert Woolbert, "Pan-Arabism and the Palestine Problem," *Foreign Affairs* 16, no. 2 (January 1938):316–17; Hurewitz, *Struggle for Palestine*, pp. 89–93; Porath, vol. 2, pp. 89–93. Between 350 and 500 delegates attended. A partial tally showed 119 from Palestine, 75 from Syria, 60 from Lebanon, 35 from Transjordan, 13 from Iraq, 4 from Egypt, and 1 from Saudi Arabia. A list of delegates is given in FO371 E5516/22/31 Mackereth to FO, September 15, 1937.

35. FO371 E5633/22/31 Harvard to FO, September 10, 1937; E5515/22/31 and E5602/22/31 MacKereth to FO, September 15 and 17, 1937; E5784/22/31 Trott to FO, September 13, 1937; and E5942/22/31 Colonial Office memo, October 12, 1937; RG59 890D.00/675 Marriner to Hull, September 3, 1937; *New York Times*, September 2, 1937; London *Times*, October 20, 1937.

36. Ibid.

37. RG59 890D.00/676 and /677 Marriner to Hull, September 15 and 20, 1937. al-Suweidi had been an Ottoman officer who joined Sharif Husayn's revolt. He later participated in Rashid Ali al-Gailani's coup, Eliezer Be'eri, *Army Officers in Arab Politics and Society* (New York: 1970), p. 330.

38. This account is taken from FO371 E5515/22/31, E5550/22/31 Scott to FO, September 17, 1937; *New York Times*, September 9, 10, and 12, 1937; *Survey of International Affairs 1937* 1, p. 552; ESCO, vol. 2, pp. 859–60; and *Palestine & Transjordan*. A British agent inside the closed meeting gave detailed reports. The secret meeting is discussed in Scott's E5514/22/31 report. On Naji al-Suweidi, see FO371 E5781/22/31, Scott to FO, September 23, 1937, and E5916/22/31 Scott to FO, October 6, 1937.

39. Porath, vol. 2, pp. 233–34; *New York Times*, November 28, 1937.

40. FO371 E5567/22/31 Colonial Office report, September 22, 1937; Porath, vol. 2, p. 275; RG59 867N.01/971 and /1019 Knabenshue to Hull, October 28, 1937, and January 8, 1938. For a Zionist view, see "The Assembly," *Palestine* 12, no. 39 (September 29, 1937): 305–306. *Al Istiqlal*, October 3 and 4, 1937; *Al Bilad*, October 3, 1937.

41. Taha al-Hashimi, *Memoirs* (in Arabic) (Beirut: 1967), p. 225; London *Times*, February 20, 1938; Longrigg, *Iraq*, p. 273; ESCO, vol. 2, pp. 882–84; Hattis, pp. 176–93; Cohen, "Secret Diplomacy," p. 398; RG59 890G.00/434 Knabenshue to Murray, November 27, 1937; 867N.01/1011 Murray to Hull January 15, 1938; 867N.01/1021, /1055, and /1079, Knabenshue to Hull, January 22, March 3, and March 31, 1938; *Al Istiqlal*, June 9, 1938.

42. Porath, vol. 2, pp. 243–44, 251–55, 274–75.

43. Text in RG59 867N.9111/181.

44. Alec Kirkbride to League of Nations, *Permanent Mandates Committee Minutes* 36th session, p. 94; Dearden, p. 55; *New York Times*, November 7, 1937; Glubb, p. 155. For an earlier incident, see *Palestine & Transjordan*, September 26, 1936.

45. Porath, vol. 2, p. 275; *Rose al-Yusuf*, February 4, 1938; RG59 867N.01/960 Allen to Hull, October 11, 1937.

46. FO371 E7201/22/31 Walton to Rendel, October 25, 1937.

47. *Documents on German Foreign Policy*, Grobba to Foreign Ministry, November 9, 1937, pp. 767–72; Watt, pp. 155–57. Ibn Saud's envoys told Grobba that all Arabs were sympathetic to Britain except on the Palestine issue.

48. Reader Bullard, *The Camels Must Go* (London: 1961), pp. 198–214.

49. Michael Cohen, "British Strategy and the Palestine Question 1936–39," *Journal of Contemporary History* 7, nos. 3–4 (July–October 1972): 162–67.

50. Ibid., pp. 170–78.

51. FO371 E6750/22/31 Rendel to FO, November 11, 1937.

52. Ibid., pp. 12–14.

7—PARTITION ABANDONED, COMPROMISE DENIED: 1938—39

1. FO371 E2982/10/31 Downie to Baxter, May 20, 1938, and Iraq memorandum E2312/10/31, April 21, 1938; RG59 867N.01/1021 and /1055 Knabenshue to Hull, January 22 and March 3, 1938; Hattis, p. 188.

2. FO371 E2362/10/31 Peterson to FO, April 11, 1938.

3. *Palestine & Transjordan*, June 4, 1938; RG59 867N.01/1108 Wadsworth to Hull, June 27, 1938; *New York Times*, May 8, 1938.

4. Abdullah, *My Memoirs Completed*, pp. 96–99; ESCO, vol. 2, p. 857.

5. *Palestine & Transjordan*, June 4, 1938; "Egypt's Attitude towards Zionism," *Palestine*, April 20, 1938, pp. 122–23; On British reaction, FO371 E5651/10/31 Downie to Baxter, September 28, 1938, and E5787/10/31 FO to Lampson, October 3, 1938.

6. FO371 E2575/10/31 Lampson to FO, May 3, 1938; E6906/1/31 and E5898/10/31 Bateman to FO, November 10 and September 26, 1938; on Palestine day in Aleppo, see E5899/10/31 Davis to FO, October 3, 1938. For a summary of fund-raising events, see E5914/10/31, October 10, 1938.

7. FO371 E5247/10/31 and E5474/10/31 Houstoun to Boswall, August 18 and September 7, 1938; E5651/10/31 Downie to Baxter, September 28, 1938; E5655/10/31 and E5791/10/31 Trott to FO, September 26 and October 4, 1938; E5849/10/31, E5816/10/31, and E5787/10/31 Lampson to FO, October 6, 4 and 3, 1938. See also E4786/10/31, E5473/10/31, E5479/10/31, and E5330/10/31.

8. Abdullah, *My Memoirs Completed*, pp. 96–100. For Nuri's view, see FO371 E5924/10/31 Colonial Office report, October 11, 1938.

9. FO371 E6508/10/31 Lampson to FO, October 24, 1938, p. 3; RG59 867N.01/1250 Merriam to Hull, October 21, 1938; London *Times*, October 13, 1938; Hurewitz, *Struggle*, p. 89; Chejne, p. 258.

10. RG59 883.00 General Conditions/82, December 23, 1938; FO371 E5931/10/31 Lampson to FO, October 8, 1938; Ibid.; and E5849/10/31. For Mahmud's speech see E6179/10/31 Lampson to FO, October 14, 1938.

11. FO371 E5942/10/31 Lampson to FO, October 11, 1938. For accounts of the meeting, see E5931/10/31, E5942/10/31, E5951/10/31, E6179/10/31; CZA 899/51 S25 10385 Sassoon to Shertok, October 4 and 9, 1938; Toynbe, 1938 *Survey*, pp. 441–42; London *Times*, October 8, 10, 12, and 21, 1938.

12. Ibid.; FO371 E5951/10/31 and E5925/10/31 Lampson to FO, October 10 and 12, 1938 has texts of the resolutions. See also E7541/1/31 Lampson to Oliphant, December 6, 1938; RG59 867N.01/1472 Bullitt to Hull, March 10, 1939 and /1485 Kennedy to Hull, March 20, 1939 on British perceptions.

13. Interview with C. W. Baxter, head of the FO Eastern Department in RG59 867N.01/1459 Johnson to Hull, February 21, 1939; London *Times*, November 20, 1938.

14. *Palestine*, October 19, 1938, p. 330, and April 13, 1938, pp. 114–16; Ben-Gurion, p. 197.

15. FO371 E3791/10/31 Bullard to FO, June 6, 1938.

16. Text of treaty in Hurewitz, *Diplomacy* vol. 2, pp. 216–18; Hurewitz, *Struggle* pp. 87–99; *Documents on British Foreign Policy 1919–1939*, ser. 3, 3 (London: 1950): 312–13; London *Times*, October 19, 20, and 21, 1937; *New York Times*, October 17, 1937; Hirszowicz.

17. Ibid., ser. 3, 6, Henderson to Halifax, June 1939, p. 197, and ser. 3, 4:12; *Documents on German Foreign Policy*, von Hentig memorandum, August 27, 1938, pp. 789–91; Grobba to Foreign Ministry, November 2, 1938, pp. 793–97. For further Saudi approaches see pp. 798–807. On German propaganda, see CZA 899/51 S25 10385 Vilensky to Weizmann, June 17, 1938.

18. Porath, vol. 2, pp. 278–79; Michael Cohen, "The Palestine White Paper, May 1939: Appeasement in the Middle East," *The Historical Journal* 16, no. 3:576.

19. FO371 E7541/1/31 Lampson to Oliphant, December 6, 1938; CZA 899/51 S25 10385, memorandum of January 29, 1939.

20. Porath, vol. 2, pp. 279–81.

21. *New York Times*, October 6 and 7, November 10 and 24, and December 7, 1938; London *Times*, October 6, 7 and 8, December 7, 1938; Sykes, *Crossroads*, pp. 192–93.

22. Ibid., Hurewitz, *Struggle*, p. 96; *New Judea*, November 1938; Weizmann, p. 391. According to Musa al-Alami's biographer, he worked out with the British a protocol roughly along the lines of the later White Paper. When he told the other Arab delegations before the conference they commented that "half the battle for Palestine had been won in advance." Geoffrey Furlonge, *Palestine is My Country* (New York: 1969), p. 122.

23. *Documents on German Foreign Policy*, pp. 746, 754, 779. See also David Yisraeli, "The Third Reich and Palestine," *Middle East Affairs* (October 1971).

24. FO371 E244/6/31, E304/6/31, E482/6/31, E1371/6/31, and E1372/6/31; *New York Times*, December 13, 1938 and January 20, 22, and 23, 1939; London *Times*, July 13, 1939.

25. RG59 867N.01/1280 and /1346 Knabenshue to Hull, November 14 and 25, 1938.

26. Ibid.; RG59 867N.01/1384 and /1429 Knabenshue to Hull, December 30, 1938, and January 20, 1939; Be'eri, p. 23. The Palestine Defense Committee warned of corruption in fund-raising. British pressure later forced al-Hashimi to resign from the committee leadership. Maurice Peterson, *Both Sides of the Curtain* (London: 1950), p. 143.

27. RG59 867N.01/1364 King Ibn Saud to President Roosevelt, December 15, 1938. See also 867N.01/1365 and *New York Times*, January 15, 1939.

28. *New York Times*, November 12, 1938.

29. RG59 890G.911/15 Knabenshue to Hull, February 16, 1939; *New York Times*, February 7, 1939; *Al Difa Al Qawmi*, February 1, 1939.

30. *Great Britain and the East*, February 2, 1939.

31. RG59 890G.911/15 Knabenshue to Hull, February 16, 1939.

32. *Al-Istiqlal*, various issues; Porath, vol. 2, p. 283.

33. FO371 E754/6/31 Lampson to FO, January 20, 1939; *Journal d'Egypte*, January 19, 1939; RG59 867N.01/1446 Fish to Hull, February 9, 1939.

34. RG59 867N.01/1441 and /1417, Johnson to Hull, February 11 and 7, 1939; FO371 E1660/6/31 and E1661/6/31; Hurewitz, *Struggle*, p. 116; Ben-Gurion, pp. 219, 230–31; *New York Times*, February 8, 10, and 16, 1939.

35. FO371 E1668/6/31 and E1448/6/31, February 23 and 24, 1939; Cohen, "The Palestine White Paper," p. 584.

36. FO371 E1717/6/31 Peterson to FO, March 2, 1939; RG59 867N.01/1472 Bullitt to Hull, March 10, 1939, interview with Weizmann; /1485 Kennedy to Hull, March 20, 1939 interview with MacDonald. According to Philby's biographer, Ibn Saud sent him to London to meet with Weizmann and Ben-Gurion in order to suggest the king's son, Faysal, as king of Palestine. Monroe, p. 219.

37. FO371 E1253/6/31 and E1254/6/31 Bullard to FO, February 18, 1939; E1334/6/31 February 20, 1939; RG59 867N.01/1476 Knabenshue to Hull, February 16, 1939, and /1459 Johnson to Hull, February 21, 1939. Nuri was not altogether innocent: see RG59 867N.01/1472 Murray to Hull, March 2, 1939, and CZA 899/51 S25 10385 January 17, 1939, and interview, *Al Bilad*, January 22, 1939; *Al Zaman*, January 18, 1939.

38. FO371 E1875/6/31, March 7, 1939; Cohen, "White Paper," p. 586–88; *New York Times*, February 27, 1939.

39. Ibid.; *New York Times*, March 22, April 13, 27, and 30, 1939; London *Times*, April 1, 3, 14, 15, 24, and May 1, 1939.

40. FO371 File 23231 Lampson to FO, March 23, 1939; E2541/6/31 and E2724/6/31; E2691/6/31 Lampson to FO April 12, 1939; Cohen, "White Paper," pp. 590–91. On Ibn Saud, see E1878/6/31 February 20, 1939; RG59 867N.01/1545 Fish to Hull, April 17, 1939; CZA S25 899/51 10385 report of April 26, 1939.

41. FO371 E2956/6/31, E3029/6/31, and E3158/6/31 Lampson to FO April 23, 24, and 28, 1939; E3156/6/31 Houstoun-Boswell to FO, April 29, 1939.

42. FO371 E3160/6/31 and E3161/6/31 Lampson to FO, April 30, 1939.

43. Ibid., Baxter's minutes.

44. FO371 E3342/6/31 May 6, 1939. See also E3431/6/31.

45. Meeting notes are in FO371 E3945/6/31 Lampson to FO.

46. *Parliamentary Papers* 1939, CMD 6019, pp. 1–12.

47. *Documents on British Foreign Policy*, ser. 3, 4: pp. 208–209; Weizmann, p. 406.

48. FO371 E3619/6/31 Lampson to FO, May 17, 1939; Porath, vol. 2, pp. 291–92; *New York Times*, May 1 and 2, 1939.

49. *Survey 1939*, p. 466; London *Times*, June 14, 1939; Hurewitz, *Struggle*, pp. 102–103.

50. FO371 E3673/6/31 and E4904/6/31 Lampson to FO, May 18 and June 28, 1939; E4794/6/31 Newton-Butler to FO, June 28, 1939; RG59 867N.01/1557 Fish to Hull, May 20, 1939; *New York Times*, May 19, 1939; London *Times*, May 18, 1939.

51. Weizmann, p. 408; Berque, pp. 504–505; *Palestine & Transjordan*, July 9, 1938; *Jarida Misr al-Fatah*, July 8, 1939, cited Jankowski, p. 39.

52. *Survey 1939*, p. 466; RG59 867N.01/1603½, /1613, /1622, /1632 Knabenshue to Hull, May 25 and 26, June 8 and 29, 1939; FO371 E3700/6/31 Houstoun-Boswell to FO, May 19, 1939; E4788/72/93 and E4929/6/31 Newton to FO, June 28 and July 4, 1939; E5422/6/31 Bennett to FO, July 29, 1939.

8—FORTUNES AND MISFORTUNES OF WAR: 1939–42

1. Watt, pp. 157–60; *Documents on German Foreign Policy*, pp. 807–814.

2. Ibid; RG59 890F.0011/25 Murray memorandum, March 1, 1939; Barry Rubin, "Anglo-American Relations in Saudi Arabia, 1941–1945," *Journal of Contemporary History* 14, no. 2 (April 1979).

3. *Iraq Times*, July 7, 1939; RG59 890G.00/463 and /465 Knabenshue to Hull, January 4 and July 11, 1939.

4. Glubb, p. 159; Hurewitz, *Struggle*, pp. 146–55; American Christian Palestine Committee, "The Arab War Effort: A Documentary Account," (New York: 1947), pp. 35–40. Hurewitz suggests the British might not have objected to the Mufti's "escape." Documents on this and other matters concerning the Mufti during this period have been almost without exception withdrawn from the Public Record Office. For the Mufti's account see *Akher Sa'a* (Cairo), no. 1977 (September 13, 1972), pp. 11–13.

5. Ibid.; Khadduri, *Arab Contemporaries*, p. 239n.

6. FO371 E7760/6/31 Newton to Butler, November 20, 1939; RG59 867N.01/1646 July 18, 1939.

7. *Al Istiqlal*, January 18, February 18, March 11 and March 13, 1940. On demonstrations, see FO371 E1004/50/31, February 26, 1940; for Egyptian amnesty efforts, E1010/50/31, March 2, 1940.

8. FO371 E1551/50/31 and E1639/50/30 Newton to FO, March 25 and 28, 1940 contain transcripts. The debate took place at a time British authorities were executing several men sentenced for terrorism.

9. FO371 E1684/50/31, E1742/50/31, E1829/50/31 Lampson to FO April 14, 18, and 24, 1940; E1730/50/31 and E2076/50/31 Newton to FO May 2, and June 3, 1940; E1952/50/31 Butler to FO, May 2, 1940. See also File 24566 and E50/50/31, January 3, 1940. For Saudi requests on reconfirmation of the White Paper, see E1944/50/31 May 2, 1940, and Ibn Saud's views, E624/50/31. On Nuri's appeal over death sentences, E839/50/31, February 24, 1940. *Al-Istiqlal* editorialized on January 18, "Where are the results of the efforts exerted by Arab governments on behalf of Palestine?" It answered, "They have failed."

10. FO371 E1970/367/31 March 5, 1940; File 2080, p. 53, and Downis to Baggalay, May 30, 1940, pp. 87–89; File 2080B p. 91, June 18, 1940; File 2801 Newton to FO, October 16, 1940, E2900/367/31, pp. 120–27.

11. FO371 E2220/20/31, June 15, 1940. For Lampson's views see E578/31/31. See also minutes of June 3, 1940, E2077/50/31 and WP (G) (40) 149, debate in the June 15 War Cabinet meeting, pp. 215–41.

12. George Kirk, *The Middle East in the War* (London: 1952), pp. 6–11.

13. To my knowledge, this important study has never before been cited. See RG59 F. W. 811.43 Institute of World Affairs/15 Wadsworth to Berle, October 30, 1940. For an overview of the military situation in these years, see Geoffrey Warner, *Iraq and Syria 1941* (London: 1974).

14. Khadduri, *Arab Personalities*, pp. 240–43; Furlonge, pp. 127–28; Khadduri, *Independent Iraq*, pp. 170–71; Hirszowicz, p. 82; Hurewitz, *Struggle*, p. 147.

15. Evans, pp. 125–27, diary entry August 19, 1940; Kirk, p. 64; Khadduri, *Arab Personalities*, p. 238.

16. *Documents in German Foreign Policy*, ser. D, 11:241; Khadduri, *Independent Iraq*, pp. 166–69. Text is on pp. 281–85.

17. Anwar el-Sadat, *Revolt on the Nile* (New York: 1957) pp. 18–44; Mahir received direct Axis subsidies, funnelled through the Dresdener Bank, at least up to the start of the war. See Dunne, pp. 25–26; Warner, pp. 24–27.

18. London *Times*, May 30, 1941; Michael Cohen, "A Note on the Mansion House Speech," *Asian and African Studies* 11, no. 3 (1977):375–86.

19. Sadat, p. 39; Sachar, *Europe Leaves*, p. 175.

20. On the Arab Legion see Vatikiotis, p. 78. This account is taken from Gen. Hellmuth Felmy and Gen. Walter Warlimont, *German Exploitation of Arab National Movements in World War 2*, U.S. Army European Historical Division, Manuscript P-207, RG338, Modern Military Records, National Archives.

21. On these events' impact in Egypt, see Sadat, pp. 48–58; for the Iraq pogrom see Ruth Bondy, *The Emissary: A Life of Enzo Sereni* (Boston: 1977) p. 193; Hayyim Cohen, "The Anti-Jewish Farhud in Baghdad," *Middle Eastern Studies* 3, no. 1 (October 1966).

22. London *Times*, September 20, 1941; *New York Times*, August 13, 1941.

23. OSS 14286; Schwadran, pp. 233–34; *New York Times*, March 12, 1942.

24. Nuri al-Said, *Arab Independence and Unity* (Baghdad: 1943), p. 11. See also Paul Hanna, *British Policy in Palestine* (Washington, D.C.: 1942).

25. Bailey, p. 46.

26. See as examples, OSS 25681, Kirk to Hull November 20–26, 1942, report of December 6, 1942, and Kirk to Hull December 3, 1942 in OSS 26373, December 11, 1942, on propaganda activities. *New York Times* correspondent C. L. Sulzberger wrote a detailed account of Axis Middle East involvement in April 1942, Office of Naval Intelligence C-9-E 25524 Box 116, National Archives; see also Felmy and Warlimont. Detailed accounts of Arab activities in Germany are contained in OSS XL14167, interrogation of Carl Rekowski of the German Foreign Office, August 14, 1945. The Foreign Office paid 65,000 Reich Marks a month to Rashid Ali, 50,000 RM to the Mufti a month, and spent 80,000 a month on their expenses. See also Anthony R. De Luca, 'Der Grossmufti' in Berlin: The Politics of Collaboration,'' *International Journal of Middle East Studies* 10, no. 1 (February 1979).

27. See, for example, Ehud Avriel, *Open the Gates* (New York: 1975) pp. 66–189; Yehuda Bauer, *From Diplomacy to Resistance* (New York: 1970).

28. Bondy, pp. 192–206.

29. A. Cohen, pp. 322–28; CZA 899/51 S25 5632 Ruth Kleiner report October–November 1943 on conversations with Nuri and 3552 on Egyptian contacts of Eliahu Sassoon.

30. Cordell Hull, *Memoirs*, vol. 2 (New York: 1948), pp. 1512–32.

31. RG165 MID 000.3 Palestine, Gen. George Strong report of August 5, 1943.

32. Weizmann, pp. 427–32; *Foreign Relations of the United States 1943*, vol. 4 (Washington, D.C.: 1964), pp. 795–827; Monroe, pp. 221–25; Philby, *Arabian Jubilee* (London: 1952), pp. 216, 412–13. Monroe implies that Ibn Saud had to denounce the scheme because it leaked to courtiers, but also argues he never favored it in the first place. The latter interpretation became the official British view, FO371 E3327/506/65, June 8, 1943.

9—THE DIVISION OVER UNITY: 1943–45

1. Sykes, p. 265.

2. FO371 E1513/506/65 MacMichael to Colonial Office, March 13, 1943; E1524/506/65, March 2, 1943; File 34956; Shwadran, p. 234.

3. For text, see Khalil, pp. 12–16; Abdullah, *Memoirs* pp. 255, 263.

4. Khalil, pp. 9–12. See also S. F. Newcombe, "A Forecast of Arab Unity," *Journal of the Royal Central Asia Society* 31, pt. 2 (May 1944): 158–64; Harold Beeley, "The Middle East in 1939 and in 1944," *Journal of the Royal Central Asia Society* 32, pt. 1 (January 1945).

5. OSS Report 39032, "Egyptian Political Situation," June 18, 1943; Cohen, p. 315.

6. FO371 E209/84/25, December 30, 1943, gives Prince Faysal's views; *Life* magazine, May 31, June 21, and July 19, 1943.

7. Barry Rubin, *The Great Powers in the Middle East, 1941–1947: The Road to Cold War* (London: 1980); Michael Cohen, "American Influence on British Policy in the Middle East During World War Two," *American Jewish Historical Quarterly* 67, no. 1 (September 1977):61–67. On Arab lobbying in Washington, see RG59 867N.00/628, May 11, 1943, and 867N.01/1365½ and /2315.

8. See the summary and report on the resolution in Edward Stettinius Papers Box 229, University of Virginia Library; OSS Report 60920, February 1, 1944; *New York Times*, October 4, 1943.

9. Henry Stimson diary, Stimson papers, Yale University Library, pp. 52–56, February 14 and 17, 1944 entries; Murray to Stettinius, November 7, 1944, Stettinius papers Box 217 and report of November 30, 1944, Stettinius papers Box 229; RG59 867N.01/1-1045 Henderson to FO, January 10, 1945, #574 and #575.

10. State Department reports of January 10 and 17, 1945, Stettinius papers Box 229; FO371 E162/119/31 Jordan to FO, December 21, 1944; RG59 867N.01/3-1045 Henderson to Stettinius, May 10, 1945. For texts of letters, see 867N.01/3-1245.

11. RG59 867N.01/2-145 Eddy to Stettinius, February 1, 1945; OSS 114278, February 4, 1945. See also OSS 115569; James Byrnes, *All in One Lifetime* (New York: 1958), p. 242.

12. *New York Times*, March 2, 1945; Cohen, "American Influence," pp. 67–68. For a British perspective on the meeting, see FO371 E3669/119/31 Grafftey-Smith to FO, May 21, 1945. An overview of American objectives in the Arab world is found in Philip Baram, *The State Department in the Middle East 1918–45* (Philadelphia: 1978).

13. OSS L42785, May 4, 1944; L44219, August 15, 1944, and L44470 August 17, 1944. See also OSS 89863, August 9, 1944. On Nuri's Palestine visit, see OSS L38565. Detailed minutes of the meeting are in OSS 101239, October 12, 1944; OSS 95754 Henderson to Stettinius, September 1, 1944; and OSS 114101, January 18, 1945.

14. For Palestinian appeals to Syria, OSS 107196, December 15, 1944; Palestinian-Lebanese talks are in OSS 92822, August 14, 1944. Text of Abdallah's August 14, 1944 letter to Nahhas is in Khalil, pp. 19–20. An excellent analysis of wartime Palestinian Arab politics is in OSS 54614, January 6, 1944. See also OSS L54614, January 6, 1944.

15. Ibid. See also OSS L37012, May 15, 1944. There are some discrepancies between this account and Khadduri, *Independent Iraq*, pp. 255–56. On Iraqi activities, see OSS 37366, June 5, 1944 and 93065, August 20, 1944.

16. Abdullah, *Memoirs*, p. 253; For text of the Palestine resolution, see Hurewitz, *Struggle*, p. 192; OSS L52079, December 29, 1944.

17. OSS reports 109185, December 21, 1944; 93065, August 20, 1944; 109267, January 8, 1945; 95729, September 14, 1944; 109679, November 24, 1944; 112413, February 2, 1945; and XL25569, October 21, 1945. RG59 867N.01/2-645 and /2-945 Henderson to Stettinius, February 6 and 9, 1945.

18. OSS 115993 "Sympathy Toward Arab League and Palestine," January 23, 1945; FO371 E9859/84/25 Grafftey-Smith to FO, December 1, 1945.

19. Evans, pp. 282–83.

20. RG59 867N.01/6-2745 Memorandum of Conversation, June 27, 1945; OSS L46311, September 11, 1944, and 92906, August 31, 1944.

21. Ibid., OSS L53717, February 18, 1945; 54415, February 19, 1945; and XL22601, October 2, 1945. See also XL22600, L53717, L58590, L58435, and XL23962.

22. OSS L22518, March 20, 1945; 11304 Hadary to Langer, August 6, 1945; XL27404, November 15, 1945.

23. CZA 899/51 S25 9024 and 9031 provide a number of reports on meetings with Maronite clergy, Lebanese political parties, and unions; *Palestine Post*, March 11, 1946; OSS XL 18078, September 10, 1945. See also Bauer, pp. 121–22.

24. Andre Chouraqui, *Between East & West: A History of the Jews of North Africa* (Philadelphia: 1968), S. D. Goitein, *Jews and Arabs: Their contacts through the Ages* (New York: 1964); Bat Ye'or, "Peuples Dhimmis: Nations Mortes-Vivantes" (Geneva: 1977); M. J. Eugene Daumas, *The Ways of the Desert* (Austin, Tex.: 1971), pp. 15, 33–39, 69; OSS 89114, report of Major Duncan MacBryde, August 11, 1944.

25. Statistics in OSS Research & Analysis Branch 2689, "Present Position of the Jews in the Arab World," April 4, 1944.

26. OSS 133299 Naval Intelligence report, May 23, 1945.

27. Maurice Forgeon, *Les Juifs en Egypt* (Cairo: 1938), p. 179; *Al Balagh*, September 13, 1944; *Egyptian Gazette*, September 14, 1944.

28. OSS 23466, November 2, 1945; XL41496, January 30, 1946; 46458, February 21, 1946; FO371 J4006/3/16 Kellar to Scrivner, November 20, 1945, and J4078/3/16 Killearn to FO, November 18, 1945.

29. OSS 45124, August 31, 1944; XL34839, December 22, 1945; 29673 Moreland to Stettinius; XL509884 Moose to Byrnes, April 12, 1946; XL25569, October 21, 1945. The Anti-Zionist League had only about fifty members, but Jews played an important part in the early Iraq Communist party.

30. On contemporary events in Palestine see Elath, pp. 194–96, 258; Hurewitz, *Struggle*, pp. 193, 219.

31. RG59 867N.00/6-245 Pink to Merriam, June 2, 1945. The fund was used by Istiqlal for political purposes. See also 867N.00/1-1446 Pinkerton to Byrnes and /1-1246; OSS L52978, "Musa Alami and the Husseinis," January 30, 1945.

32. OSS L58624, August 1, 1945; XL16849, August 17, 1945; XL18074, August 18, 1945; and XL20860, August 31, 1945; RG59 867N.00/11-345 Hooper to Byrnes, November 3, 1945.

33. OSS XL29724, November 26, 1945; XL30447, November 20, 1945; Hurewitz, *Struggle*, pp. 239–40. The Mufti's escape is still shrouded in mystery. After American intelligence found documents buried in Bavaria which documented the Mufti's collaboration, the Foreign Office attempted to play down the information. There has been speculation that the French allowed him to escape as vengeance against Britain's Levant policy. Some data is in FO371 files 52587-88, 1946. File 52588 was withdrawn from the Public Records Office in 1978.

34. Elath, p. 85.

35. FO371 E5080/3/65 Farquhar to FO, July 4, 1945.

36. FO371 E7111/3/65 Young to FO, September 22, 1945; E7611/3/65, October 8, 1945; E8255/119/31 Melville to Dixon, October 23, 1945; OSS XL22754 Kitchen to Langer, October 24, 1945.

37. OSS XL22600, September 27, 1945 and XL31531, November 26, 1945; On the National Bloc's partisan Palestine committee, RG319 283997, June 4, 1946; FO371 E809/3/65

Jordan to FO, February 3, 1945; E63/3/65 Jordan to FO, January 3, 1945; E7207/119/31 Grafftey-Smith to FO, September 26, 1945; E7903/3/65 and E8096/3/65 Bird to FO, October 18 and 19, 1945; E9499/119/31 Killearn to FO, December 5, 1945. On Arab lobbying in Washington, see RG59 867N.01/10-345, /10-245, and /10-1245.

38. Jacob Robinson, *Palestine and the United Nations*, (Washington, D.C.: 1947), pp. 11–14; texts are in Robert MacDonald, *The League of Arab States* (Princeton: 1965), pp. 315–18.

39. Between 1939 and 1967, writes Elie Kedourie for example, the Palestinians "had no say or control over their affairs," while the Arab League and the Arab states undertook to defend their interests, *Arabic Political Memoirs,* p. 224. In general, this analysis is accurate, but it does not apply at a minimum to the years 1939–40 and 1946–48. In both cases, the leadership of Amin al-Husayni and his lieutenants was most evident, as the Arab governments were well aware. On the league's efforts, see MacDonald, pp. 325–26 and Khalil, pp. 161–62. On the emotional importance of Palestine to the Arabs, see for example the remarks of Iraq's prime minister to Lord Gort, RG59 867N.01/2-245 Henderson to Stettinius, February 2, 1945.

10—THE FAILURE OF ARAB DIPLOMACY: 1946–47

1. George Kirk, *The Middle East 1945–1950* (New York: 1954), p. 6.

2. See particularly such recent archival work as Joseph Heller, "Anglo-Zionist Relations 1939–1947," and Michael Cohen, "Why Britain Left: The end of the Mandate," both in *The Wiener Library Bulletin*, n.s. 45–46, 31, (1978). The earlier debate is in Jon Kimche, *Seven Fallen Pillars* (London: 1953), and Elizabeth Monroe, *Britain's Moment in the Middle East 1914–1956* (Baltimore: 1963), and "Mr. Bevin's Arab Policy," *St. Anthony's Papers* #11 (London: 1961).

3. Edward Grigg, *British Foreign Policy* (London: 1944), pp. 149–50. The misgivings of some Foreign Officials are shown in M. Cohen, "A Note on the Mansion House Speech." For Zionist complaints, see Jewish Agency to Foreign Office, March 21, 1945, and Weizmann to Eden, March 27, 1945, cited in Kedourie, *Chatham House*, p. 220.

4. Khalil, p. 508.

5. Monroe, "Mr. Bevin's Arab Policy," p. 12.

6. FO371 E797/797/65 Roberts to FO, January 25, 1946; Harry Truman, *Memoirs*, vol. 2 (London: 1956), pp. 149–51, 159.

7. Government inefficiency in dealing with violent and subversive opponents is well illustrated in Sadat, *Revolt on the Nile*, pp. 65–110. See also Raoul Makarius, *La Jeunesse Intellectuelle D'Egypt au Lendemain de la Deuxieme Guerre Mondiale* (The Hague: 1960).

8. Muhammad Hussayn Heikal, *Memoirs,* vol. 2 (in Arabic) (Cairo: 1951), p. 319. See also RG319 379696, May 20, 1947, and Berque, p. 573.

9. Safran, pp. 201–204. George Dangerfield, *The Strange Death of Liberal England 1910–1914*, offers a classic case of how domestic tensions can lead to the welcoming of a cathartic war.

10. CIA documents 420364, 420368, and 435228, intelligence reports on Transjordan, December 8 and 9, 1947, and February 6, 1948. See also Kimche, *Seven Fallen Pillars*, p. 46.

11. RG59 867N.00/1-1246 Pinkerton to Byrnes, January 12, 1946. For Zionist views on Transjordan see: Moshe Sneh, "What are the Facts," *Zionist Review*, March 15, 1946; Moshe Shertok in the *Palestine Post*, January 25, 1946; RG59 890I.01/1-3146 Silver to Byrnes; Paul Riebenfeld, "Israel, Jordan, Palestine," *Midstream* 22, no. 3 (March 1976): 30–44.

12. *Rose al-Yusuf*, April 20, 1947; CZA 899/71 S25 9033 Zaslani to Meir, January 29, 1947; RG59 867N.01/9-2645 Moreland to Byrnes, September 26, 1945.

13. Khalil, pp. 161–62; OSS XL 31040, December 6, 1945; Kirk, *The Middle East 1945–1950*, p. 209n; FO371 E6041/4/31, June 22, 1946. Syria's Law 273, confirmed May 1946, for example, provided a sentence of imprisonment at hard labor for anyone buying, selling, transporting, or smuggling Zionist goods.

14. RG59 867N.01/1-746 Tuck to Byrnes, January 7, 1946.

15. For text of Azzam's letter, see Kimche, pp. 48–49; *Al-Misri*, January 16 and 21, 1946.

16. Hurewitz, *Struggle for Palestine*, pp. 237–48.

17. Text of testimony is in RG59 867N.01/3-1346 and of the Arab League memorandum is in 867N.01/6-1946. See also Ibid., pp. 250–51 and FO371 E3754/4/31. Arab reactions are documented in FO371 E4049/4/31 May 4, 1946 (Azzam); E4050/4/31 May 6, 1946 (Iraq); E4269/4/31, May 8, 1946 (Saudi Arabia); E4270/4/31 Shone to FO (Syria and Lebanon), May 8, 1946; E4279/4/31 and E4313/4/31 Bird to FO, May 8 and 3, 1946 (Iraq). Abdallah's comments are in E5702/4/31, June 19, 1946, while Egypt's refusal is in E5782/4/31, June 21, 1946. For a general survey, see E5239/4/31 Shone to FO, June 7, 1946.

18. Text in Khalil, pp. 224–26; see also pp. 515–17.

19. Khalil, pp. 517–18. See also Leila Kadi, *Arab Summit Conferences and the Palestine Problem* (Beirut: 1966), pp. 29–31; MacDonald, p. 349; CZA 899/71 S25 9031, p. 253, May 6, 1946; Jon and David Kimche, *A Clash of Destinies* (New York: 1960), p. 47–52.

20. Hurewitz, *Struggle for Palestine*, pp. 249–53.

21. Bailey, pp. 57–58; Joseph Nevo, "Abdullah and the Arabs of Palestine," *Wiener Library Bulletin*, n.s. 45–46, 31 (1978):52.

22. FO371 E8106/4/31 Kirkbride to FO, August 11, 1946; E8424/4/31 Campbell to FO, August 26, 1946; E8409/4/31; David Horowitz, *State in the Making* (New York: 1953), pp. 117–18.

23. FO371 E8615/4/31 Cunningham to Secretary of State for Colonies, August 27, 1946; E9844/4/31 Bevin to Kirkbride, September 30, 1946. See also Transjordan's Foreign Ministry defense of November 19, 1946, Khalil, p. 27.

24. Khalil, pp. 518–22.

25. *Al Alam al-Arabi*, January 17, 1947. Iraq gave two-thirds of the information bureau budget. FO371 E9140/9140/80 Kirkbride to FO, August 22, 1946; E12103/8140/80 Stonehewer-Bird to FO, December 2, 1946; E12168/9140/80, December 14, 1946; RG59 867N.00/4-2147 Macatee to Marshall, April 21, 1947; 867N.01/1-2247 Moose to Marshall, January 22, 1947.

26. FO371 E1682/982/89 Houstoun-Boswell to FO, February 24, 1947; El725/892/89, February 25, 1947; E2052/892/89, March 5, 1947; and E10460/892/89, November 3, 1947.

27. *Al-Kutla*, February 4, 1947; *Akhbar al-Yom*, February 1, 1947; *Al-Moqattam*, February 3, 1947; FO371 E225/49/31, December 27, 1946, E622/49/31, January 14, 1947, and File 61834.

28. For Jamali's account, see RG319 354494, February 27, 1947; Hurewitz, *Struggle for Palestine*, pp. 272–73; Sykes, *Crossroads to Israel*, p. 310.

29. FO371 E3096/951/31, April 12, 1947; Robinson, p. 39; Hurewitz, p. 285.

30. Khouri, pp. 123–26; RG59 867N.01/2-2747 Wadsworth to Marshall, February 27, 1947 and /3-2647 Tuck to Marshall, March 26, 1947; MacDonald, pp. 349–50, Resolution #167; Albert Hourani in Richard Frye, *The Near East & The Great Powers* (Cambridge: 1951), pp. 123–26, 175n.

31. For treaty text see RG319 371109, May 8, 1947. Jamali's views are in 365147, April 16, 1947. Abdallah had managed also to recruit some support in Syria, see RG319 250424, March 2, 1946; 228456, February 6, 1947, and 339842, January 26, 1947.

32. RG319 Wadsworth to Marshall, June 23, 1947, #386103. On Transjordan's confidence in obtaining British support, see RG319 337850, November 1, 1946, and 333731, December 4, 1946.

33. RG319 343019 Moose to Marshall, January 22, 1947; 383648, July 11, 1947, and 397690, September 9, 1947. Saudi Arabia was terrified that Abdallah might also try to grab Syria, see 890D.00/8-1947 Childs to Marshall, August 19, 1947.

34. Khouri, pp. 132–35; Hurewitz, *Struggle for Palestine*, p. 286; Robinson, pp. 50–175.

35. For Saudi objections to UNSCOP, see their statement in RG59 501.BB Palestine/7-2347, July 23, 1947. See also /7-2347 and 867N.01/6-1847 Marshall to Iraq Embassy. The sole exception was Monsigneur Mubarak who called for an alliance between a Jewish state and a Christian Lebanon. Of Palestine, he wrote, "In less than 20 years, the country has been transformed. It is prosperous in culture, in the installation of large industries.... The presence on the border of Lebanon of a people so developed and hard-working can only contribute to the well-being of all." FO371 E9424/951/31, September 30, 1947, for text. See also E9030/951/31 Evans to FO, September 29, 1947.

36. Hurewitz, *Struggle for Palestine*, pp. 295.

37. Jon Kimche, a journalist who set up the meeting, was also present. Although he says it took place in October, internal evidence suggests the first half of September. Abba Eban, *Autobiography* (New York: 1977), pp. 86–87; David Horowitz, pp. 232–35; Jon Kimche, *The Second Arab Awakening* (New York: 1970), pp. 242–43. Eban and Horowitz appeal was echoed by Ben-Gurion. See Avraham Avi-hai, *Ben-Gurion: State-Builder* (Jerusalem: 1974), p. 176.

38. A biography is in RG319 350096, February 13, 1947.

39. RG319 358722, February 27, 1947, p. 14; 291346 Mattison to Byrnes, July 17, 1946; Gorden Torrey, *Syrian Politics and the Military* (Columbus, Ohio: 1963), pp. 103–106; CZA 899/51 S25 9031 p. 63, June 16, 1946. On factionalism in the Syrian National Bloc see RG319 345706, February 26, 1947; 346397, January 30, 1947; and 460590, April 20, 1948.

40. FO371 E9219/951/31 Evans to FO, October 4, 1947; File 61493. Nuri al-Said thought the same of Saudi Arabia, RG59 790F.90G/6-1145.

41. For Creech-Jones speech and al-Sulh's response see FO371 E9146/951/31; E9445/951/31, October 10, 1947 on Arab confidence in British support; E9193/951/31 and E9444/951/31 Evans to FO October 2 and 8, 1947.

42. FO371 E9372/951/31 Evans to FO, October 8, 1947. Syria's President Quwatly tried to reach such an agreement in advance with London. E9382/951/31 Dundas to FO, October 7, 1947.

43. FO371 E8773/951/31 cabinet report, September 18, 1947; File 61881, FO to Dominions, October 7, 1947.

11—THE PERILS OF PARTITION: 1947–48

1. Text of UPI interview in FO371 E8124/951/31, August 16, 1947; E10460/892/89, November 3, 1947.

2. FO371 E9482/951/31, Kirkbride to FO, October 11, 1947.

3. Nevo, p. 53; Kimches, p. 59.

4. Glubb, p. 48.

5. RG59 890I.00/11-1947 Macatee to Marshall, November 19, 1947. Elections were held under the new constitution on October 20.

6. FO371 E9696/49/31 Wright to FO, October 8, 1947. In case of partition, Azzam told a journalist, "I do not think anyone could protect the Jews of the various Arab states." Sachar, *Europe Leaves*, p. 489.

7. FO371 E9051/951/31, September 18, 1947.

8. Khouri, pp. 141–52.

9. Ibid.; FO371 E8750/951/31 Evans to FO, September 20, 1947.

10. Editorial cited Sykes, *Crossroads*, p. 325. On Lebanon, see FO371 E9065/951/31 Evans to FO, September 29, 1947; on Syria, E9206/951/31 Beaumont to FO, September 24, 1947. For a survey, see E11471/46/31; RG59 867N.01/9-647 Dorsz to Marshall, September 6, 1947.

11. George Brownell, "American Aviation in the Middle East," *Middle East Journal* (October 1947), p. 407.

12. RG59 501.BB Palestine/9-2247 Loy Henderson memorandum, September 22, 1947; 501.BB Palestine/9-2647, September 26, 1947, and /10-347, October 3, 1947; Donovan, p. 325.

13. Robinson, pp. 179–227.

14. Khalil, pp. 164–65; Robert John and Sami Hadawi, *The Palestine Diary*, vol. 2 (New York: 1970), pp. 280–83.

15. RG59 890D.00/10-1047, /10-1547, /10-2247, /11-647, and /1-448, October 10, 15, and 22, November 6, 1947, and January 4, 1948, all Memminger to Marshall, and 890D.00B/ 10-2247, Memminger to Marshall, October 22, 1947.

16. FO371 E9442/951/31 Bowker to FO, October 9, 1947; E10959/49/31, November 14, 1947.

17. FO371 E10851/10851/80 Kirkbride to FO, November 18, 1947; E10962/10851/80, minute of November 25, 1947; E11611/49/31, November 27, 1947; File 11678.

18. FO371 E11426/49/31, November 21, 1947. In December, Abd al-Hadi reportedly predicted that Abdallah would be assassinated if he identified himself with partition by annexing the Arab portion of Palestine. Central Intelligence Group Report 10247, December 11, 1947.

19. For texts of letters between Ibn Saud and Truman, see RG59 867N.01/10-3047; Khouri, pp. 160–62; Khalil, pp. 532–33.

20. RG59 890D.00/12-147, /12-447; 890B.00/12-1047.

21. Torrey, p. 104; RG59 890D.00/12-947; 867N.01/12-1147.

22. RG59 867N.01/11-2847 Memminger to Marshall, November 28, 1947. See also John Devlin, *The Ba'th Party* (Stanford, Calif.: 1976), pp. 49–51. The party's January 1948 attempt to send its own unit to Palestine was stopped by the Syrian army, since it was seen as a partisan effort aimed against the National Bloc. See also FO371 E11545/11280/65 Dundas to FO, December 4, 1947; E11675/951/31 Armanazi to Bevin, December 8, 1947.

23. FO371 E11280/11280/65 Kirkbride to FO, November 29, 1947; E11477/11280/65, December 2, 1947; E11544/11280/65 Kirkbride to FO, December 6, 1947; E12045/ 11280/65, December 4, 1947.

24. RG59 867N.01/11-2147 Memminger to Marshall, November 21, 1947. Abdallah's interlocutor was Greek diplomat Nicholas Vasselou.

25. Alec Kirkbride, *From the Wings* (London: 1976), pp. 4–5; Zeev Sharef, *Three Days* (New York: 1962).

26. FO371 E12050/951/31, Aide-Memoire to Iraq, December 6, 1947; E11675/951/31 Busk to FO, December 8, 1947.

27. FO371 E9442/951/31 Bowker to FO, October 9, 1947; E11909/11280/65, December 12, 1947; Berque, p. 601.

28. *Al Ikhwan*, December 10, 1947; Texts of many articles are analyzed in RG59 867N.01/12-447 and /12-2047, respectively Tuck to Marshall, December 4, 1947, and Patterson to Marshall, December 20, 1947. On Egypt's Zionist movement see 867N.01/ 12-2247.

29. FO371 E1244/1244/93 Stonehewer-Bird to FO, January 28, 1947; RG59 867N.01/12- 1647 Childs to Marshall, December 16, 1947.

30. RG59 867N.01/12-947 Pinkerton to Marshall, December 9, 1947. The shaykh, who had been a leader of the 1925–26 Druze revolt against the French, recalled that the neighboring Arabs had not given much aid to his efforts and suggested that Lebanese and Syrian Druze remain neutral. Central Intelligence Group Report 106729, September 3, 1947.

31. RG59 867N.01/11-2547 McNown to War Department, November 25, 1947; Strategic Air Command, "Implications of the Arab-Jewish Conflict in Palestine," December 8, 1947, #421555, RG318.

32. Letter from Quwatly to Faris al-Khuri, text in RG59 890B.00/12-547.

33. FO371 E10611/49/31 Kirkbride to FO, November 3, 1947.

34. RG59 867N.01/12-347 conversations with Azzam, December 3, 1947.

35. Israel State Archives S44/708, Sassoon to Azzam, December 5, 1947.

36. For text of public resolution, see Khalil, pp. 550–51. This account is taken from detailed interviews with delegates in RG59 890B.00/12-2047 Tuck to Marshall, December 20, 1947; Israel State Archives 93.03/2267/26 Sassoon to Shertok, December 11 and 20, 1947; and General Clayton's reports in FO371 E12064/951/31, December 18, 1947 and E11726/, 11741/, and 11775/11280/65, December 10, 1947.

37. FO371 E11260/951/31 Campbell to FO, December 24, 1947; E12081/11280/63, December 18, 1947.

38. FO371 E11260/951/31 Campbell to FO, December 24, 1947; E12081/11280/63, December 18, 1947; E12064/951/31, December 18, 1947; E11775/11280/65, December 10, 1947.

39. A. Cohen, pp. 408–409.

40. For example, FO371 E12131/11604/65 December 20, 1947, E12144/11604/65 December 22, 1947; E12092/11604/65 Kirkbride to FO, December 19, 1947. On Abdallah's efforts to win U.S. support, see RG59 867N.01/12-2347.

41. FO371 E11264/3765/80 FO to Amman, January 10, 1948, and E12416/3765/80.

42. For Ibn Saud's complaint to William Eddy, see RG59 890B.00/11-1547 Memminger to Marshall, November 15, 1947; Philby's views are in 867N.01/12-3047 Child to Marshall, December 30, 1947.

43. The following dispatches provide extensive clippings from the Syrian press RG59 890D.00/12-1547, /12-1947 through /12-2347, /12-2647, /12-3147, /1-248, /1-1148, and /2-1248. FO371 E12263/3765/80 discussed Syrian objectives in Palestine.

12—THE SLIPPERY ROAD TO WAR: January–May 1948

1. RG59 890D.00/1-248 and /1-3148 Memminger to Marshall, January 2 and 31, 1948. Jewish merchants were forced to contribute to a liberation fund, and one holdout's store was bombed. None of this money would, however, go to the Mufti, see RG319 428074.

2. Kimches, Clash of Destinies, pp. 85–88. Taha al-Hashimi in his book Diary of the War, estimated al-Qawukji's forces at seven thousand. Al-Madi and Mousa, pp. 467–71, estimate 350 Transjordan volunteers in the force. Relations between the army and Amman are described by al-Qawukji in "Memoirs 1948," Journal of Palestine Studies 2, no. 1 (1972):3–33. See also Kirkbride, From the Wings, pp. 6–7.

3. Kirkbride, Crackle of Thorns, p. 154; Hurewitz, p. 312.

4. See Israel State Archives (ISA) Memorandum of Conversation March 26, 1948, and Locker to Martin, January 23, 1948; Harry Sacher, Israel: *The Establishment of a State* (London: 1952), p. 119.

5. Gabbay, pp. 65, 73; Monroe, "Mr. Bevin's Arab Policy," p. 15; Khalil Kanna, *Iraq Yesterday and Tomorrow* (in Arabic) (Beirut: 1966), pp. 82–83.

6. ISA, Cornay to Gering, December 3, 1947; Ben-Gurion to Shertok, December 9, 1947; Shimoni to Meyerson (in Hebrew), December 10, 1947; Ben Gurion to Shertok (in Hebrew), December 14, 1947.

7. ISA Danin to Sassoon (in Hebrew), January 4, 1948; Sassoon to Shertok, January 19, 1948; Locker memorandum of conversation, January 18, 1948; Epstein to Jewish Agency, February 1, 1948.

8. RG59 890D.00/1-1048 Memminger to Marshall, January 10, 1948.

9. RG59 890I.01/1-1648 Tuck to Marshall, January 16, 1948. See also 890I.00/1-2448 Macatee to Marshall, January 24, 1948.

10. *Al Misri*, December 30, 1947; *Al Ikhwan*, December 29, 1947, and January 7, 1948; *Rose al-Yusuf*, December 30, 1947; RG59 883.00/1-1348, /1-2248, and /1-3148 Tuck to Marshall.

11. RG59 890E.00/1-1348 Pinkerton to Marshall, January 13, 1948.

12. RG59 890E.00/2-1648 Pinkerton to Marshall, February 16, 1948; Torrey, p. 105.

13. This series of events is the most controversial issue in U.S. Palestine policy. The key question is over how much Truman knew and approved of Austin's actions. Donovan, pp. 369–87, suggests that the president approved the measures taken but did not entirely understand their ramifications.

14. RG59 501.BB Palestine/3-448 Tuck to Marshall, March 4, 1948; John and Hadawi, vol. 2, pp. 312–16.

15. ISA Hurewitz to Ben-Gurion December 31, 1947 (in Hebrew), evaluates Arab rulers' attitudes toward a settlement; RG59 501.BB Palestine/3-948 Marshall to Damascus, March 9, 1948; /3-1348 Childs to Marshall, March 13, 1948; /3-1448 Kopper to Austin, March 14, 1948; /3-2648; and /4-1848 Tuck to Marshall, April 18, 1948. See also *Foreign Relations of the United States 1948* 5, pt. 2 (Washington, D.C.: 1976):827–28.

16. Ibid., *Foreign Relations*, pp. 836–37. On Bevin's position, see RG59 501.BB Palestine/4-2248 Douglas to Marshall, April 22, 1948. See also 501.BB Palestine/4-2948.

17. RG59 501.BB Palestine/4-2248 Austin to Marshall, April 22, 1948; 867N.01/4-2648 Memorandum, April 26, 1948.

18. RG59 883.00/3-2948, /4-2348, and /4-2648 Tuck to Marshall, April 26, 1948.

19. RG59 883.00/4-1248 and /4-2548 Tuck to Marshall, April 12 and 25, 1948; 867N.01/4-2648 Tuck to Marshall, April 26, 1948; Mohammed Naguib, *Egypt's Destiny* (New York: 1955), p. 20. See also Raymond Baker, *Egypt's Uncertain Revolution* (Cambridge: 1978), pp. 19–23.

20. On Weizmann, see Eban, p. 105. On the Egyptian military's situation, see Nasser; Sadat; and Naguib, pp. 14–28.

21. Nevo, p. 55; Kimches, pp. 107–108.

22. Kubba, p. 260; Longrigg, *Iraq 1900–1950*, p. 260.

23. RG59 890E.9111/4-2148 Pinkerton to Marshall, April 21, 1948; 890E.918/5-448 Pinkerton to Marshall, May 4, 1948.

24. RG59 867N.01/4-2748.

25. Glubb, p. 113n; Kimches, p. 108.

26. RG59 501.BB Palestine/4-2848 Marshall to Tuck, April 28, 1948.

27. ISA Shertok to Ben-Gurion, April 21, 1948; Sassoon and Berman, "Outline of Policy Toward the Arab States," (in Hebrew), March 13, 1948.

28. RG59 867N.01/4-2848 Tuck to Marshall, April 28, 1948. For last-minute Saudi and Egyptian attempts, see 501.BB Palestine/5-348 and /5-548. For U.S. truce efforts, see *Foreign Relations* 1948, pp. 877–1000.

29. Ezra Danin, "Meetings with Abdallah," (in Hebrew), March 9, 1975; Sharif; ISA, Goldman to Ben-Gurion, May 13, 1948; Golda Meir's report, *Minutes and Protocols April 18 – May 14, 1948,* Israel State Archives, May 1979 (in Hebrew).

30. ISA Meeting of the Arab section of the Political Department of the Jewish Agency, May 13, 1948; Nevo, pp. 56–58; 800.00 Summaries/5-1348 Marshall to Arab capitals, May 13, 1948; 867N.01/5-1448 Tuck to Marshall, May 14, 1948.

31. ISA Goldman to McNeil, May 11, 1948; Heikal, *Memoirs*, vol. 2, pp. 330–31; Folke Bernadotte, *To Jerusalem* (New York: 1951), p. 24; RG59 867N.01/5-1348 Tuck to Marshall, messages of May 13 and 15, 1948. Heikal quotes Nuqrashi as saying that he "would not commit the Egyptian army to a position such that the British troops stationed on the Canal would attack them from the rear."

32. RG59 867N.01/5-1548 Tuck to Marshall (two dispatches); 883.00/5-1548 Tuck to Marshall (two dispatches).

33. Glubb, p. 82.

34. Ibid., pp. 84–93; Kubba, p. 259. Earlier, Egypt opposed offering command to Abdallah.

35. Kirkbride, *From the Wings*, p. 22–24.

36. Glubb, pp. 99; Nathaniel Lorch, *The Edge of the Sword: Israel's War of Independence 1947–49* (New York: 1951), p. 177.

37. Kirkbride, *From the Wings*, pp. 28–30; see also Heikal, pp. 336–37. On Iraq's optimism, see Kubba, pp. 260–61. RG59 867N.01/5-1548 (three dispatches) and /5-1748.

38. Sykes, p. 350.

39. Glubb, pp. 93–94; al-Madi and Mousa, p. 467.

40. Cohen, p. 422.

41. Khalil, pp. 557–61.

13—ABDALLAH'S PERILOUS PEACE-MAKING: 1948–51

1. U.S. State Department records (hereafter DOS) 785.00/7-2451 Memorandum of Conversation, July 24, 1951. This document and the other DOS reports cited in this chapter were obtained under provisions of the Freedom of Information Act.

2. This story was confirmed by Francis Russell, Dulles' aide for the project, in a letter to the author, June 9, 1979.

3. See above, particularly ch. 3.

4. See above, particularly ch. 6.

5. FO371 E12264/3765/80 FO to Amman and E12416/3765/80; RG59 890D.00/1-1048 Memminger to Marshall, January 10, 1948; 890I.01/1-1648 Tuck to Marshall, January 16, 1948, and 890I.00/1-2448 Macatee to Marshall, January 24, 1948. See also Glubb, p. 66 and Kirkbride, *From the Wings*, pp. 12–13.

6. See above, chs. 11, 12.

7. Interview with Wells Stabler, American diplomat in Transjordan July 1948–August 1949, March 7, 1979; A. David Fritzlan to author, April 2 and May 13, 1979. Fritzlan was first secretary of the U.S. Legation in Amman 1949–52, and served as charge d'affaires, January–July 1951.

The British Foreign Office had concluded by the end of 1948 that the Arab parts of Palestine should be incorporated into Transjordan. Otherwise, it reasoned, they would either be absorbed by Israel or would form an unviable state under the anti-British (and anti-Transjordan) Mufti. London suggested to Amman, however, that any absorption of the West Bank be postponed until after a settlement with Israel. Washington, more distantly and to some extent relying on British judgment, took a similar position but also urged that an overall settlement be negotiated between Transjordan and Israel. Consequently, another reason for Amman's willingness to negotiate might have been that this was an Anglo-American precondition for accepting annexation. See FO 371 E6695, E6789, E6324, and E2377/1081/80.

At the same time, British analysts wanted to avoid any rift between Transjordan and Egypt, recognizing that the latter country was more important in their strategic plans. Mutual cooperation among pro-British Arab states might be facilitated, they believed, by a common Egypt-Transjordan border in the Negev and by Egypt's taking over of the Gaza Strip. Thus London urged Egypt-Transjordan negotiations and was restrained from strongly supporting Abdallah out of fear of antagonizing Cairo. These secret talks made no progress, however, and Egypt actually sent some arms to the Mufti's forces and played some role in stirring up Palestinians in the West Bank against Amman's rule. FO 371 E4150, E4284, E11015, E1281, and E2287/1015/31, E407/1013/80, and E6866/1015/31.

Amman was particularly worried about support for the Mufti from other Arab regimes. King Farouk had, however, stopped the Mufti from forming a Palestinian provisional government before the mandate ended and neither Saudi Arabia nor Syria recognized his later Gaza government. The Saudi decision was influenced by British intervention at Transjordan's request. E12022/1015/31 and E7336/3/31. There was some fatalism in other Arab governments after the 1948 war about any pursuit of the conflict. In December 1948, for example, Ibn Saud said that the communist danger should lead the British and Americans to force Jews and Arabs into an agreement. Syria's president thought the Jewish state would last and expected that an economic boycott might harm Syria more than it would damage Israel. But none of these concerns would prompt them anywhere nearly so far as Transjordan considered going. See, for instance, E1475/1015/31.

8. For first-hand descriptions of the early negotiations, see Moshe Dayan, *Story of My Life* (New York: 1976), pp. 132–43; Kirkbride, *From the Wings,* pp. 42–44; Walter Eytan, *The First Ten Years,* (New York: 1958), pp. 39–43; and Abdallah al-Tall, *Qadiyat Filastin* (Cairo: 1959). See also RG59 867N.01/1-1149, /1-2449, and /2-749 Stabler to Acheson, and 501.BB Palestine/1-449 Holmes to Acheson. The United States was an early supporter of annexation. Under-Secretary of State Robert Lovett wrote in December 1948, "Department believes that most satisfactory solution disposition greater part Arab Palestine would be incorporation in Transjordan." He added, "U.S. would like to see Transjordan negotiate armistice and final peace with Israelis," but the United States could not become overly involved in inter-Arab politics. RG59 867N.01/1-249 McDonald to Acheson and /12-2848 Memorandum by Lovett.

9. RG59 867N.01/1-1949; 890I.001/1-649, /1-1249, /4-2049, and /4-2249.

10. RG59 890I.001/9-149; 501.BB Palestine/10-2249 Jessup to Acheson.

11. RG59 867N.01/11-1149 and /11-1649 Fritzlan to Acheson.

12. RG59 867N.00/11-2149 Burdett to Acheson, and /11-2449 Ford to Acheson.

13. RG59 867N.00/12-149 Ford to Acheson; /12-549 Stabler Memorandum of Conversation; 767N.901/12-1349 Holmes to Acheson; 767N.90I/12-1549 and /12-2749 Fritzlan to Acheson; 867N.01/12-2249 Holmes to Acheson; and 867N.01/12-2949 McDonald to Acheson.

14. RG59 684A.85/2-1650 Gibson to Acheson; 784.00/1-1650 Fritzlan to Acheson; 684A.85/2-1050 Fritzlan to Acheson; 784A.00/1-2450 Memorandum of Conversation; 785.00/2-150 Fritzlan to Acheson; 684A.85/2-750 Fritzlan to Acheson; and 684A.85/2-750 McDonald to Acheson; Bunche to McDonald, February 24, 1950, McDonald Papers, Lehman Library, Columbia University.

15. RG59 684A.85/2-1950 McDonald to Acheson; /2-2050 and /2-2150 Fritzlan to Acheson; 684A.85/2-2650 McDonald to Acheson; 785.00/3-2450 Drew to Acheson.

16. P. J. Vatikiotis, *Politics and the Military in Jordan* (New York: 1967), pp. 99–108; Glubb, p. 256; Kirkbride, pp. 129–31; Eliezer Be'eri, *Army Officers in Arab Politics and Society* (New York: 1970), pp. 230–31.

17. DOS 785.00/2-750, /2-1350; 785.11/3-2450; 786.00/4-450.

18. DOS 785.00/2-850 Pinkerton to Acheson; 684A.85/3-1450 Keeley to Acheson, /3-1150 Webb to Acheson, 3-2550 Childs to Acheson.

19. For the resolutions' texts, see Schwadran, pp. 293–97, 784A.02/4-450, DOS.

20. DOS 684A.85/3-350 Drew to Acheson, and /3-650 McDonald to Acheson.

21. DOS611.85/4-1750; 684A.85/4-750 Keeley to Acheson; 786.00/5-450 (two dispatches); Childs to Acheson and Webb to Childs; "Conversation with the President," March 9, 1950, Acheson Papers, Harry S. Truman Library.

22. DOS 684.85/4-2550 Drew to Acheson; 785.022/4-2450 Memorandum of Conversation; 684A.85/4-2750 McDonald to Acheson; 785.02/5-550 Drew to Acheson.

23. Text in DOS 784.02/5-1950 Caffery to Acheson; 786.00/5-1550 and /5-1750.

24. DOS 684.85/5-350 Drew to Acheson, /7-2650 Gibson to Acheson; 684A.85/8-150 Drew to Acheson.

25. DOS 785.00/6-2750; 884A.85/6-3050 McDonald to Acheson; 684A.85/10-250 Ford to Acheson; 320.2AA/11-3050 Drew to Acheson.

26. DOS 684A.85/12-450, /12-550, /1-1251, /2-851, /2-951, and 2-1351; 785.13/12-1350.

27. DOS 684A.85/2-1551 Ford to Acheson, /3-2551 Davis to Acheson.

28. On the murder conspiracy, assassination, and trial, see "King Abdullah's Assassins," *The World Today*, October 1951; RG228 #838381, August 8, 1951; King Hussein, *Uneasy Lies the Head* (New York: 1962), pp. 5–19; Kirkbride, pp. 34–39; Be'eri, p. 234; DOS 785.11/8-2351 Drew to Acheson, and other reports cited below.

29. Fritzlan to author, April 2, 1979; DOS 785.11/7-2451 Drew to Acheson.

30. DOS 785.11/7-2151 and /7-2251 Tyler to Acheson.

31. DOS 785.11/7-2051 McGhee to Acheson, /7-2151 Caffery to Acheson; 785.00/8-551 Hare to Acheson, /8-751 Caffery to Acheson, /8-951 Drew to Acheson; 786.00/3-2152 Warren to Acheson and /9-1252 Minor to Acheson. During the preceding seven years, twelve prominent Arab politicians had been assassinated, including two sovereigns, one president, and five prime ministers. King Ibn Saud's gallant reaction to his old enemy's death was to recommend that Abdallah's sons inherit the kingdom: "Maintaining the status quo will help to avert endless crises."

32. DOS 785.11/7-2151 Tyler to Acheson; Bar-Zohar, p. 191.

14—EGYPT'S REVOLUTION, ISRAEL, AND AMERICA: 1950–56

1. Raymond Hare oral history, Columbia University Oral History Collection, p. 56. See, for example, U.S Department of State, *Foreign Relations of the United States 1950*, vol. 5 (Washington, D.C.: 1978), pp. 239, 744. Useful background works on U.S./Egypt relations in this period include: John Campbell, *Defense of the Middle East* (New York: 1961); Charles Cremeans, *The Arabs and the World* (New York: 1963); M.A. Fitzsimmons, *Empire by Treaty* (South Bend, Ind.: 1964); Faiz Saleh al-Jaber, "Egypt and the Cold War 1952–1956: Implications for American Policy" (Ph.D. diss., Syracuse University, 1966); Walter Laqueur, *Communism and Nationalism in the Middle East* (New York: 1956); Tom Little, *Modern Egypt* (New York: 1968); Kennett Love, *Suez: The Twice-Fought War* (New York: 1969); Peter Mansfield, *Nasser's Egypt* (London: 1965); Gail Meyer, *Egypt and the United States: The Formative Years* (E. Brunswick, N.J.: 1980); Mohammed Naguib, *Egypt's Destiny* (Garden City, N.Y.: 1965); Gamel Abdel Nasser, *The Philosophy of the Revolution* (Buffalo, N.Y.: 1959); Anthony Nutting, *Nasser* (New York: 1972); Shah A. Qayyum, *Egypt Reborn* (New Delhi: 1973), Anwar el-Sadat, *Revolt on the Nile* (New York: 1957); Haim Shaked and Itamar Rabinovich, *The Middle East and the United States* (New Brunswick, N.J.: 1980); Robert Stephens, *Nasser* (New York: 1971); and Keith Wheelock, *Nasser's New Egypt* (New York: 1960).

2. On the background of U.S.-Soviet conflict in the region, see Barry Rubin, *The Great Powers in the Middle East 1941–1947: The Road to Cold War* (London: 1980).

3. There were periodic hints of Egyptian willingness to negotiate with Israel and persistent Egyptian statements of disinterest in any second round with the Jewish state. For example, Nelson to Berry, February 24, 1950, in *Foreign Relations of the United States 1950* (hereafter FRUS) pp. 285–86.

4. The most comprehensive report is, "Stability versus Instability in Egypt," 774.00/8-1351, August 13, 1951. This, like most of the other State Department documents cited below, was obtained through the Freedom of Information Act. See also 774.00/11-650, /1-1251, /7-1651, /8-751, and /9-751. One American diplomat in the embassy, Keith Adamson, recounts how a young Egyptian officer came into his office in the summer of 1951, closed the door, and whispered that a group at the Officers' Club had discussed overthrowing King Farouk the previous evening. During the talk, Nasser had come in and criticized them, saying they did not know how to plan a revolution and that, in future, they should have less public gatherings. This, and other such information, was passed on to Caffery. Adamson to Rubin, 2/1/79, and C. Robert Payne to Rubin, 2/18/79.

5. *FRUS 1950*, pp. 291, 298, 327–28; Dean Acheson, *Present at the Creation* (New York: 1969), pp. 562–68; Acheson Papers, Memoranda of Conversation for 10/16/51 and 1/27/52, Truman Library; and *Executive Sessions of the Senate Foreign Relations Committee* (hereafter, *Executive Sessions*) 4 (1952) (Washington, D.C.: 1976):26.

6. Acheson Papers, Memorandum of Conversation, 1/27/52, Truman Library; Acheson, pp. 562–68; J. Wesley Adams, "Black Saturday: The Burning of Cairo," *Foreign Service Journal* (March 1980).

7. On Sudan see, for example, Meeker to Jessup, 774.00/1-752, and L. A. Fabunmi, *The Sudan in Anglo-Egyptian Relations* (London: 1961). On aid, see Berry to Acheson, 774.00/2-2752.

8. On the base issue, see "Princeton Seminar," 5/16/54, Dean Acheson Papers, reel 6, track 1, pp. 13–15, and track 2, pp. 1–4, 11, Truman Library; Foster to Acheson, 611.74/6-2952; Bruce to U.S. Embassy/London, 611.74/6-2552; and Byroade to Acheson, 774.00/7-2152. Byroade later testified that he never heard of Nasser before July 1952. *Executive Sessions* 9 (1957) (Washington, D.C.: 1980);217.

9. The most influential account has been Miles Copeland, *The Game of Nations* (New York: 1969), pp. 48–59. Copeland, the CIA Cairo station chief, argues that his superior, Kermit Roosevelt, tried first to work with King Farouk and, giving him up for lost, met with and assisted the Free Officers after March 1952. Copeland does not claim that the United States organized or supported the coup, but his account is often erroneously interpreted that way, particularly in Egypt. Author's interviews with Egyptian scholars and journalists, August 1979, in Cairo.

10. Interview with Kermit Roosevelt, March 20, 1980, and off-the-record discussions with other participants.

11. Interview with William Weathersby, 2/12/79, and with Evans, 1/12/79. See also note 4 above. Sabry, who had just returned from a training course in the United States, said he was inspired by American democracy and modernity.

12. Ibid.

13. Ibid.; Holmes to Acheson, 774.00/7-2352; Acheson to Caffery, /7-2452; interview with Wells Stabler, then Egypt desk officer, March 7, 1979; Memorandum of 7/24/52, Acheson Papers, Truman Library.

14. Caffery to Acheson, 774.00/7-2452. See also Wright to Acheson, /7-2452, and Caffery to Acheson, /7-2552. Caffery later compared Naguib's appeal to that of Walter Cronkite, but added the general's problem was that he tended to believe the last man to whom he spoke. John Badeau oral history, Columbia University, p. 236. Even the conspirators were confused. Ali Mahir, their choice for prime minister, told Americans that Anwar al-Sadat was the coup leader, /7-2552, Caffery to Acheson. As far as can be judged by his early dispatches and by interviews with his closest aides, Caffery was surprised by the coup and lacked prior knowledge of its leaders. For a British analysis, see Caffery to Acheson, /7-2852, and also Caffery to Acheson and Wright to Acheson, /7-2652 and /7-3152, describing the "controversial figure" Sadat (two dispatches including Evans' report).

15. 774.00/8-152, /8-552, and /8-952, all Caffery to Acheson.

16. Meeting with Amin and Zacharia Mohieddin, /8-1152; *New York Times*, 8/7/52; *Washington Post*, 8/21/52.

17. "Egypt's New Era — The First Three Weeks," 774.00/8-1852, see also /8-2052, /8-2252, and /9-252; *Washington Post*, 8/21/52; *Time*, 9/8/52, *U.S. News and World Report*, 3/27/53, p. 28; For the State Department's suggested public statement encouraging cooperation, see Bruce to Caffery, 611.74/8-1852. One sign of the emerging special relationship was Egypt's informing the United States in advance of important moves, including the removal of Mahir. See Acheson to Caffery, 774.00/9-752, and Byroade to Acheson, /9-852.

18. David Ben-Gurion, *My Talks with Arab Leaders* (Jerusalem: 1972), pp. 269–70; Memorandum of Conversation, 9/22/52, Acheson Papers, Davis to Acheson, 320.00/9-1752; and Caffery to Acheson, 774.00/12-1152.

19. Memorandum of Conversation, Acheson Papers, 9/8/52, Truman Library; Gifford to Acheson, 611.74/8-2052, /8-2152, Caffery to Acheson, and 611.74/9-1752.

20. Caffery to Acheson, 774.00/9-952 #622; Acheson to Caffery, /9-752, and Caffery to Acheson, /9-1152. In Caffery's words, "Once cooperation firmly established it may be possible (to) persuade Egypt's need for joint defense and inevitability British partnership therein."

21. Caffery to Acheson and Acheson to Caffery, 611.74/9-2652; see also /10-252. Public gestures might include a nonaggression statement toward Israel, support for UN action in Korea, compensation for victims of the "Burning of Cairo." Furnishing arms before an Egypt-Israel settlement was delicate, wrote Acheson, but not impossible.

22. See 611.74/9-2652, /9-2752, /10-852, /11-1052, /11-1352, and /11-1052, Byroade to Mathews, as well as /11-2152, Mathews to secretary of defense. See also 774.00/10-2152, /11-2152, Caffery to Acheson, 774.00(w)/11-2952, Caffery to Naguib 11/24/52 in 774.56/11-2852, and Ortiz to Stabler, 774.00/12-252.

23. Mohamed Heikal, *The Cairo Documents* (Garden City, N.Y.: 1973), pp. 36–42; Anwar el-Sadat, *In Search of Identity* (New York: 1978), pp. 126–27; Interviews with Stabler and Parker Hart, then director of the Office of Near East Affairs.

24. Caffery, Byroade, and Acheson favored giving Egypt $10–11 million in interim aid even before the base talks were completed. This might have prevented the rift which later occurred. But London opposed any such aid lest it be used against them or encourage Egypt to take a hard line on the base negotiations. In January 1953, London persuaded Truman to wait a while longer. On May 7, Prime Minister Churchill asked President Eisenhower to continue to delay arms aid; again Washington agreed. In late November, just before the Anglo-American Bermuda meeting, Eden wrote: "In my view an allotment to Egypt at this juncture could not fail to give publicity to a major divergence of British and American policies, and thus to have a serious effect on Anglo-American relations. It would have the appearance of encouraging the Egyptians to stand out in their demands against us and it would remove an important inducement to them to reach an agreement with us." Apparently, the British again won their point.

Caffery pointed out the dangers of delay. Nasser said that he wanted to cooperate with the United States but that America's failure to provide arms seemed to fulfill the prophecy of the regime's critics that "the only thing Egypt will get back from America will be Ali Sabry." Nasser had personally visited army units and told officers to expect American arms aid. Unless Washington was prepared to face the facts, Caffery wrote, Egypt would become neutralist.

See 774.5 MSP/1-452, /11-1852, /12-1652, /1-353, /1-1053, /2-1453, /2-1753, /3-3053; 110.11-DU/5-853 and briefing papers for Bermuda meeting (12/4-8/53), "U.S. Military Assistance to the Middle East."

Even more ominous — and prophetic — was Caffery's warning of January 7, 1953. Whenever Nasser visited military units, officers asked him, "Have you requested arms from Russia?" Caffery wrote, "I hope Department will ponder well implications of [the] fact that Nasser felt obliged to reply (untruthfully) that he had tried to get arms from Soviets but had been refused." 774.5/1-753. Caffery to Acheson, 774.00/1-353; Ortis to Dorsey, /1-653; E. K. Fryer memorandum in 361.2 Naguib X500 TCA, U.S. Embassy files, Washington National Records Center (WNRC); Naguib to Eisenhower in Caffery to Dulles, 4/11/53, Eisenhower Library; and Dulles Memorandum for the President, 4/3/53, Ann Whitman File, Box 8, Folder 3, Eisenhower Library. See also Ambassador Ahmad Husayn's views in 611.74/4-2453 and Memorandum of Conversation, 5/4/53, Eisenhower Library. For Churchill's views, see J. F. Dulles Memoranda for the President, 6/15/and 6/17/53, John Foster Dulles Papers, Eisenhower Library.

25. Caffery to Dulles, 611.74/3-253. See also /3-453, Caffery to Dulles. Nasser's domination became increasingly obvious, particularly after his appointment as deputy president of the Revolutionary Command Council in May 1953. One report to Dulles estimated that Naguib might only last six months more. Dulles also received reports stressing the danger of a communist takeover in Syria and the need to solve the Arab-Israeli conflict to prevent Moscow's exploitation of the dispute. See 774.00/5-1853, Caffery to Dulles, and Caffery's memorandum of 3/26/53, as well as Lowell Wadmond's report of 4/9/53, Eisenhower Library.

26. He feared, Heikal added, historians would later say, "During the most dangerous circumstances humanity ever confronted, the biggest country of the world behaved in a simple and idiotic way and with incomparable stupidity!" *Akhir Lahza*, 4/8/53, cited in 611.74/4-1153. Despite British complaints — and regardless of building tension in Egypt — the White House promised Chruchill that no arms would be given Egypt until after a Suez base agreement. Caffery to Dulles, 611.74/4-3053; 774.00/4-2953, /6-1653, /7-2053, and /8-553 on the internal situation. For Eden's charge, see Peter Mansfield, p. 133, and

NOTES   275

compare to Eisenhower to Churchill, 6/17/53, Eisenhower Papers, International Series, Box 8, Egypt Folder (3), Eisenhower Library.

27. Black's memo of 4/22/53, Ann Whitman File, Box 8, Folder 1, Eisenhower Library; Byroade to Smith, 611.74/4-2853.

28. "Conclusions on Trip," February 1953, and "Important Points of Trip," probably late May or early June 1953, John Foster Dulles Papers, Princeton University.

29. Heikal, pp. 31–32; Fitzsimmons, p. 120. Text in *Department of State Bulletin*, June 15, 1953, pp. 831–35, and in J. C. Hurewitz, *Diplomacy in the Near and Middle East*, vol. 2 (New York: 1956), pp. 337–42. Of this kind of thinking Eden complained, "the United States has sometimes failed to put its weight behind its friends, in the hope of being popular with their foes." *Full Circle* (Boston: 1960), pp. 374–75. Churchill, in contrast, thought Egypt was weakening and hence British concessions were not necessary. Dulles to U.S. Embassy/London, 6/17/53, Dwight Eisenhower Papers, International Series, Box 8, File Egypt (1) Eisenhower Library. The memoranda on Dulles' talks are in 110.11-DU/5-1253 #2417. For Egyptian press reaction to the visit, see /5-1253, /5-1353, and /5-1653.

30. *Executive Sessions*, vol. 5 (Washington, D.C.: 1977), pp. 439–43; Caffery to Dulles, 7/10/53, and Eisenhower to Naguib, 7/15/53, and Dulles to Eisenhower, 7/15/53, all in Eisenhower Papers, International Series, Box 8, File Egypt (1), Eisenhower Library.

31. U.S. Embassy files, Box 2667, file 320 Egypt-Israel, "Egyptian Policy on Palestine," 8/28/53; Ralph Bunche's report of 9/10/53 is in the same file.

32. 611.74/9-453, 774.13/11-2153, 774.00/12-353, and briefing paper on Egypt, 774.00/12/1853.

33. Copeland, pp. 64–108; Heikal, pp. 44–45; Kim Roosevelt and other interviews.

34. The specific issue in question was whether a Soviet attack on Turkey—as opposed to an Arab country—would allow British reoccupation of the base. On political developments, see 774.00/2-2654 #963 and #2054, /2-2754, /3-254, /3-354, /3-454, and /3-2354; also /3-2554 Payne to Dulles and /3-3054 #1224 and #1225.

35. RG84 Box 2672, 500 Economic Aid to Egypt, 1/3/54, 1/21/54, and 1/23/54 Smith to Caffery.

36. 774.00/3-3154 Caffery to Dulles. Parker Hart was far less impressed with Nasser, calling him "determined, very smart but basically immature," and more like a union boss than a statesman. Egypt's disorganization, Hart argued, increased Iraq's relative strength. See /3-3154 Hart to Byroade. See also /7-1254 Caffery to Dulles, and ibid., including Dulles to Caffery, 7/28/54 in 500 Economic Aid to Egypt.

37. *U.S. News and World Report*, 8/13/54. Similar views are expressed in his article, "The Egyptian Revolution," *Foreign Affairs*, January 1955.

38. 774.00/1023-54 Caffery to Dulles. See also /10-1954, /10-3054, /11-154, and 11-454; 774.13/10-2854, /11-254, and /11-1954.

39. Dulles to Eisenhower, 8/6/54, Eisenhower Library; John Foster Dulles to Stassen, 7/24/54 Box 2, file 3; Dulles and Byroade, Box 2 file 1, 8/24/54, and J. F. and Allen Dulles, Box 3 file 1, all John Foster Dulles, telephone memoranda, Eisenhower Library.

40. RG 84, Box 2672, 500 Economic and Military Aid to Egypt, 7/30/54, and Box 2671, 320 Israel-Egypt, memoranda of conversation, 8/5/54.

41. Ibid., Box 2671, 320 Israel-Egypt, 8/3/54. Caffery, 8/4/54, thought one day Egypt would have to face up to a peace treaty but that the time was not yet ripe. State suggested that the United States might seek some curbing of the Gaza-based guerrilla raids against Israel and some form of free passage through the canal for Israeli shipping, 611.74/11-1154.

42. Russell to Rubin, 6/9/79, and Eveland, p. 125.

43. U.S. Senate, *Hearings before the Committees on Foreign Relations and Armed Services*, 85th Congress, January–February 1957 (Washington, D.C.: 1957), pt. 2, p. 785; RG84 Box 2671, 320 Israel-Egypt, 8/29/54 and 8/30/54 Caffery to Dulles, 8/31 Conversation with Ambassador Hussein. Years later, Egyptian President Anwar al-Sadat said Egypt refused the military mission "because we had just carried out our revolution . . . against all kinds of foreign influence." Speech of 9/3/80, Foreign Broadcast Information Service, *Middle East & North Africa* 5, no. 173 (9/4/80):D4.

44. Interviews; Byroade to Allen, 7/10/54, George V. Allen papers, Duke University; Hare oral history; Copeland, pp. 123–31; Eveland, pp. 90–92.

45. On the border issue, see 674.84A/1-1955, /1-2055, /1-2855, and /2-555. On Nasser's reaction to the defense pact, see 123 Byroade, Henry A, March 1, 1955, #1261; Heikal, pp. 46–47; Eveland, pp. 136–38.

46. Ibid., and Dulles-Byroade conversation, 4/27/55, Telephone memoranda, John Foster Dulles papers, Eisenhower library.

47. John Badeau oral history, Columbia Oral History Collection, p. 298; Wyatt, pp. 117–18; and Chester Cooper, *The Lion's Last Roar* (New York: 1978), p. 68.

48. 774.56/8-2555, Trezise to Dulles, 774.56/8-2555, Cabell to Dulles; Eveland, p. 132.

49. Ibid. Khrushchev assured Dulles at the Geneva summit that there would be no Soviet arms sales to Egypt. Eveland, p. 147n.

50. Kermit Roosevelt interview; see also Eveland, pp. 132–33. Arms estimates are from Admiral Arthur Radford, chairman of the Joint Chiefs of Staff, U.S. Senate, *Executive Sessions of the Senate Foreign Relations Committee*, vol. 9 (1957) (Washington, D.C.: 1980), p. 147.

In announcing the deal, Nasser, speaking at the opening of an armed forces exhibit on September 27, recalled his attempts to obtain arms from the West compared with Israel's successful efforts. He noted Western press accounts that the Israeli army was superior to all the Arabs and could defeat them. Why, Nasser asked, did the United States, Britain, and France deny Egypt arms to equalize the situation? Text of his speech is in 774.56/9-2955.

Dulles sent a letter to Nasser that very day, indicating American disappointment in Egypt's decision. He warned that the USSR's record was clear: "Initial, supposedly friendly gestures, lead quickly to subversion, inextrioable involvement in the Communist orbit, and (the) loss of that independence of action which Egypt rightly values so highly."

A "talking paper," which accompanied Dulles' envoy, George V. Allen, to Cairo, warned that not only would Egypt become dependent on Soviet good will and cooperation for spare parts, but also that the inflow of arms would produce an arms race with Israel, possibly, "forcing issues at this time leading to all-out warfare in the area before Egypt is able to benefit from an increase in its arms." This is exactly what did happen in the Suez war.

"We have been and would continue to be willing *in the context* of an Egypt-Israel settlement, [emphasis in the original] to grant assistance, in addition to any loan the World Bank might make, in the construction of the Aswan Dam," Dulles continued. If Egypt cooperated in moving toward a settlement with Israel, American arms sales were still possible, added the talking paper: "The only thing, therefore, that separates you from acquiring the arms which Egypt needs from the West . . . is your cooperation in removing the obstacles mentioned in the Secretary of State's August 26 speech." Text of the letter and talking paper are in 774.56/10-655.

While Arab reaction to the arms deal with ecstatic—mainly based on the argument that Egypt should be able to buy any weapons it needed anywhere it chose to do so, Sharett called the deal a "revolutionary ominous change in Israel's security situation." He cited statements from Nasser, the Egyptian press, and Cairo radio calling for the mobilization of Arab resources to achieve Israel's final liquidation. Text in 774.56/10-1955.

Allen met with Nasser for an hour and forty-five minutes on October 1. Nasser assured him that he was determined to prevent communist influence within Egypt, but he reviewed Egypt's three years of efforts to obtain American arms. Since the Gaza raid, Nasser said, he had "been through a nightmare." He feared that Menachem Begin's Herut party which sought "Israeli domination from the Nile to the Euphrates" might take power. Nasser's attempts to obtain French arms after February produced no results. Allen's notes of meeting in 774.56/10-155.

51. Ibid., Radford testimony, pp. 154–55; Yaacov Herzog, oral history, John Foster Dulles papers, Princeton University, pp. 17–18. Hearing of Byroade's bad relationship with Nasser, Dulles dispatched George V. Allen to ask Nasser to reconsider the arms deal, but Allen's last-minute appeal was perceived as an ultimatum by Nasser, and his CIA friends had to mollify him. Roosevelt interview; Eveland, pp. 145–46.

52. Conversation with Eric Johnston, 8/18/55, Telephone Memoranda, and his discussions with Hoover, 9/20/55, 9/27/55, and 9/28/55, all John Foster Dulles papers, Eisenhower library. Sherman Adams, *Firsthand Report* (New York: 1961), p. 245.

53. Text of the Dulles speech in U.S. State Department, *A Select Chronology and Background Documents Relating to the Middle East* (Washington, D.C.: 1969), pp. 135–39.

54. Wynn, pp. 128–46; Harold MacMillan, *Tides of Fortune 1945–55* (London: 1969), p. 631; *New York Times*, 11/27/55.

The key discussion was at a meeting between Dulles and British Foreign Minister Harold MacMillan on October 3. Hare presented the State Department's analysis. It was too late to block the deal, and the logical steps were to try for an Egypt-Israel agreement and to prevent other countries from following Egypt's "unfortunate example." If this failed, other pressures might be brought to bear, but if Nasser was forced out, and there was no better candidate in sight, this might lead to complications. More immediately, there was a danger of forcing Egypt into a hostile position and the ominous prospect of a split in the Arab world with the West backing one group, the communists the other.

Dulles said that public action should be avoided and that any unpleasant events should appear to be happening naturally, otherwise all the Arabs would align against the West. Egypt wanted to be like Yugoslavia, enjoying the best of both worlds and playing off the two blocs against each other. Egypt as a neutralist nation would be more tolerable than as a communist satellite. It would be best to wait and see what developed.

He also suggested that the Soviets might antagonize Egypt through their implementation of the arms deal and that Egypt might become a liability for Moscow. Nasser could even be pushed along on the Johnston proposals and toward a settlement with Israel. MacMillan seemed to be in general agreement with Dulles' analysis. Notes of meeting in 774.56/10-355.

55. See the transcript of his interview with *U.S. News and World Report*, 4/21/56, John Foster Dulles papers, Princeton University. On the Baghdad Pact, see the following oral histories from the same collection: Loy Henderson, p. 20, and Yaacov Herzog, p. 14; see also Wilton Wynn, *Nasser of Egypt* (Cambridge: 1959), pp. 110–15.

56. Under-Secretary of State Herbert Hoover Jr., and Secretary of the Treasury George Humphrey were critical of the idea. See their oral history, John Foster Dulles papers, Princeton University, pp. 23–24. See also the oral histories in the same collection by Winthrop Aldrich, p. 6, Abba Eban, p. 30, and Lord Sherfield, p. 5; MacMillan, p. 642. On the background of the dam, see Wheelock, pp. 173–205; Eveland, p. 160. The Nasser-Byroade story is from Charles Cremeans who was present, interview, 2/23/79.

57. Eisenhower to Dulles, White House Telecommunications file, Box 11, file 3, Eisenhower Library. An intersting perspective on these issues is in Board of National Estimates to Allen Dulles, 11/29/55, "Reasons for the Impact of Soviet Orbit's Military, Economic, Cultural Drive in the Middle East" Allen Dulles papers, Princeton University. See also U.S. Senate Foreign Relations Committee, *Executive Sessions, vol. 9, p. 93*.

58. For President Eisenhower's letter to Nasser, carried by Anderson, see Eisenhower to Nasser, 1/9/56, and letter of 2/27/56, Eisenhower library; Russell, letter to author, Roosevelt interview, Ben-Gurion, pp. 294–325; Eveland, p. 161n.

59. Ibid. On Egyptian military infiltration, see Byroade to Dulles, 4/10/56, Eisenhower papers—International Series, Box 8, Egypt (1), Eisenhower Library.

60. Testimony of 2/27/56 to Senate Foreign Relations Committee, RG 46, Box 3, National Archives.

61. Nasser to Eisenhower, 2/6/56, Presidential papers — International Series, Box 8, Egypt (1); Eisenhower to Nasser, 2/27/56, Ann Whitman File, Box 8, Folder 4, Eisenhower Library.

62. Dulles testimony of 1/6/56, *Executive Sessions of the Senate Foreign Relations Committee*, vol. 8 (1956) (Washington, D.C.: 1978), pp. 10–11, see also p. 218. On CIA activities, see Eveland, p. 180. On arms sales, see Goodpaster to Whitman, 4/11/56, Presidential Papers—International Series, Box 8, Egypt (1); Dulles-Gray, 4/12/56, White House Telecommunications file; and Byroade to Dulles, 4/11/56, Eisenhower Library.

63. Ibid., *Executive Sessions*, p. 46, 49–56.

64. Hoover to Eisenhower, undated (probably April 1956), Ann Whitman file, Box 8, Folder 4, Eisenhower Library.

65. Eisenhower Diary, 3/12/56, Eisenhower Library.

66. Board of National Estimates report.

67. See the following oral histories in the John Foster Dulles papers, Princeton University: Henderson, pp. 23–24, 31–32, 41; Stassen, p. 28; Allen, pp. 33–35; Eugene Black, pp. 7–19; Sherfield, pp. 6–7; James Hollister, pp. 46–48. See also Paul Zinner, *Documents on*

American Foreign Relations 1956 (New York: 1957), pp. 272–75; and Milton Eisenhower, *The President is Calling*, (New York: 1974), p. 349.

68. Dulles to Eisenhower, 3/28/56, Eisenhower Library.

69. A symbol of this turnaround was the replacement of Byroade by Raymond Hare as ambassador to Egypt. George V. Allen was also replaced by his deputy, William Rountree. On intelligence activities see Eveland, p. 168ff.

70. *Executive Sessions*, vol. 9, pp. 514–15. See also pp. 618–19.

Byroade continually argued in favor of financing the dam and against Dulles' decision. He was deeply concerned that this action would push Egypt—and other Arab nations as well—into Moscow's arms. On the issue of a settlement with Israel, Byroade added, Nasser was simply "honest enough to tell us frankly and bluntly what he felt he could and could not do." See 874.2614/11-2855, /5-2656, and /6-1656.

Dulles had the State Department prepare a lengthy answer to the ambassador's complaints, putting the burden for the failure of cooperation on Cairo. Nasser purchased the Soviet arms in June 1955, the same month an agreement in principle was reached to approve $27 million in sales to Egypt. Cairo wanted to get American help while pursuing anti-American policies: the attack on the Baghdad Pact, the support of leftist elements in Syria, purchases and technicians from the Soviet bloc, active intervention in north Africa, and attempts to undermine American influence in Saudi Arabia.

As for Egypt-Israel relations, Fawzi expressed a desire to get along with Israel in August 1954 and stated his support for Washington's general approach and timing on the problem in April 1955. After Dulles' August 26 speech, Fawsi suggested further discussions and in November said that "Egypt (is) prepared to work towards settlement (of) Arab-Israeli issues at earliest date." Nasser confirmed this ten days later, and in January 1956, indicated a willingness to start definitive negotiations. But the Egyptian leaders had gone back on all these pledges. See 874.2614/6-1656.

71. Wheelock, p. 196; White House telecommunications file, Dulles-Hoover, 7/23/56; Eisenhower, *Waging Peace*, p. 33. Dulles assured Eisenhower that he was taking no gamble, since Congress would have defeated the proposal anyway. Indeed, a few days later, Shepilov, now Soviet foreign minister, was quoted at a Moscow reception as negative about Soviet aid for the dam: "We believe there are other things of more value to Egypt in industrial development than the Aswan Dam." Ibid., pp. 517–18.

In a meeting with British Ambassador Sir Roger Makins on July 13, Dulles still seems to have been debating what course to take. For a few days the United States would receive favorable headlines for agreeing to build the dam, he said, but during the twelve to fifteen years needed to construct it, Egyptians would have to put up with considerable austerity and fiscal controls. This might lead to resentment and was likely to be beyond Egypt's capacity. His inclination was to tell Nasser what the situation was and to hold out the chance of future assistance. He would not like to see Nasser go to Moscow with an American bid in his pocket. If Washington withdrew its offer beforehand, he reasoned, the Russians might overplay their position and ask so much of Egypt that it would lead to an anti-Soviet reaction in the Arab world. 874.2614/7-1356.

Byroade continued his debate with the secretary of state, complaining that Dulles judged Egypt "solely by whether—measured by our own criteria—she is for us or for the Soviets." Cairo could not be expected to forego its own interests to fall into line with Washington: "If we fail to develop means of fruitful cooperation" with the nonaligned, Byroade wrote, "and continue to consider them as being either in (the) enemy camp or as 'fellow travellers' I fear that before too long we will begin to appear" in their eyes "as being the unreasonable member of (the) East-West struggle." 874.2614/7-1356.

In his meeting with Ambassador Hussayn, Dulles stressed the project's burden for Egypt's economy, the lack of agreement with upriver states, and the likelihood that years of austerity would lead to Egyptian resentment. American public and congressional opposition were also mentioned. Essentially, Dulles concluded, the two countries were "out of step" in too many respects. Ambassador Hussein tried, unsuccessfully, to refute these various points, mentioning, among other things, Russia's "very generous" offer. 874.2614/7-1356.

One source close to Nasser said the Egyptian president was likely to curtail the American economic and technical aid program and attack U.S. influence in the region generally in his July 26 speech in Alexandria. This kind of response, rather than any move against the Suez Canal, is what the State Department expected. See 874.2614/7-2056 and /7-2456.

72. *Newsweek*, 7/30/56; *Time*, 7/30/56.

73. White House telecommunications file, J. F. Dulles-A. Dulles, 7/30/56, Box 5, file 5; Dulles-Nixon, Box five, file 5, 7/30/56; Dulles-Mansfield, and Dulles-Knowland, 7/31/56; Dulles-George, 8/3/56 in the same file; J. F. Dulles-Humphrey, 8/9/56 and -Allen Dulles, 10/29/56, Box 5, file 3. According to Eveland, though this cannot be confirmed, Dulles even warned Nasser that an Anglo-French attack on Egypt might be imminent. While Washington was certainly aware of French-Israel cooperation and of British military activity on Cyprus, there is no evidence that the United States knew of the planned attack in advance. See Eveland, p. 226.

74. Allen Dulles to George Humphrey, 9/29/57 and George Humphrey to Allen Dulles, 9/12/57, Allen Dulles papers, Princeton University; Kermit Roosevelt interview; *The Guardian* (London), 8/29/80, p. 2; Eveland, pp. 270, 292n. Eveland claims that a CIA assassination team was organized against Nasser after a misinterpreted remark from President Eisenhower. He also states that Dulles attributed the Egypt-Syria merger in early 1958 to Russian interests.

75. The text of the president's speech is in *A Select Chronology* pp. 144–50. See also *Executive Sessions*, vol. 9, pp. 3–10.

76. Ibid., pp. 10, 151, for Dulles and Radford testimony. One of the shrewdest critiques of the Eisenhower Doctrine came from Senator John F. Kennedy who saw the danger in failing to distinguish between ideological communism and tactical alliances with Moscow. He worried that the new American policy would push Egypt and Syria into the Soviets' arms and increase their antagonism to the West, pp. 174–75. On the other side, Eisenhower later wrote, "If (Nasser) was not a communist, he certainly succeeded in making us very suspicious of him." *Waging Peace*, p. 265.

77. Albert Hourani, "The Middle East and the Crisis of 1956," *St. Anthony's Papers* 4, *Middle East Affairs* 1 (London: 1958), p. 19.

78. *Executive Sessions*, vol. 8, p. 84.

79. The development of U.S.-British-Soviet relations is analyzed in Barry Rubin, *The Great Powers in the Middle East 1941–1947: The Road to the Cold War* (London: 1980).

80. On U.S. policy toward Mossadegh, see Barry Rubin, *Paved with Good Intentions: The American Experience and Iran* (New York: 1980), particularly Chapter Three. Just as

American aid refusal played a key role in Nasser's decisions on Czech arms and the Suez Canal, it also played an important role in pressing Iran toward nationalization of the British oil company. In both cases, the failure to obtain help abroad forced the nationalist government to make the best use of its potential assets at home.

81. J. C. Hurewitz, "Our Mistakes in the Middle East," *Atlantic Monthly* (December, 1956), p. 46.

Bibliography

ARCHIVAL AND DOCUMENTARY

American Christian Palestine Committee. *The Arab War Effort*. New York: 1947.

Arab League. *The Problem of Palestine*. Washington, D.C.: 1946.

British Foreign Office, archives, Public Records Office F0371.

British State Papers, 1904–48.

Central Zionist Archives.

Documents on German Foreign Policy, 1918–45.

Foreign Relations of the United States, 1931–48.

Golda Meir's report. Minutes & Protocols 4/18–5/13/48. Israel State Archives, May 1978 (in Hebrew).

Hurewitz, J. C. *Diplomacy in the Near and Middle East*. vol. 2. Princeton: 1956.

Iraq. *Taqrir Lajnat al-Tahqiq al-Niyabiyyah fi Qadiyyat Filastin* Report of the Parliamentary Committee of Inquiry on the Palestine Problem. Baghdad: 1949.

Israel State Archives.

Khalil, Mohammed. *The Arab States and the Arab League: A Documentary Record*. 2 vols. Beirut: 1962.

League of Nations. *Official Journal of Plenary*.

McDonald Papers. Lehman Library.

Office of Strategic Services, National Archives RG226.

Palestine Royal Commission Report Cmd 5479. London: 1937.

Stettinius Papers. University of Virginia Library.

Stimson Papers. Yale University Library.

U.S. Military Intelligence G-2. Washington National Records Center RG318.

U.S. State Department. National Archives RG59. General Records.
Woodward, E. L. and R. Butler. *Documents of British Foreign Policy.*
Zionist Organization. *Report to 18th Zionist Congress.* London, 1933.

PRIMARY SOURCES

Abdullah, King of Jordan. *Memoirs.* New York: 1950.
————. *My Memoirs Completed.* New York: 1954.
Amin, Ahmed. *Hiyati.* Cairo: 1950.
Antonius, George. *The Arab Awakening.* London: 1945.
Arlosoroff, Haim. *Yoman Yirushalayim.* Tel Aviv: 1949.
Avriel, Ehudm *Open the Gates.* New York: 1975.
Basic Principles of Revisionism. London: 1929.
Ben-Gurion, David. *My Talks with Arab Leaders.* New York: 1973.
Bentwich, Norman and Helen. *Mandate Memories.* New York: 1965.
Bernadotte, Folke. *To Jerusalem.* New York: 1951.
Bullard, Reader. *The Camels Must Go.* London: 1961.
Byrnes, James. *All in One Lifetime.* New York: 1968.
Childs, J. Rives. *Foreign Service Farewell.* Charlottesville, Va.: 1969.
Crum, Bartley C. *Behind the Silken Curtain.* New York: 1947.
Daumas, Eugene. *The Ways of the Desert.* Austin, Tex.: 1971.
Dayan, Moshe. *Story of My Life.* New York: 1976.
Eban, Abba. *An Autobiography.* New York: 1977.
Elath, Eliahu. *Zionism at the UN.* Philadelphia: 1976.
Evans, Trefor. *The Killearn Diaries.* London: 1972.
————. *Mission to Egypt, 1934–1946.* Cardiff: 1971.
Eytan, Walter. *The First Ten Years.* New York: 1958.
Felmy, Hellmuth, and Walter Warlimont. *German Exploitation of Arab
    Nationalist Movements in World War Two.* Washington, D.C.: 1946.
Gallman, Waldemar. *Iraq Under General Nuri.* Baltimore: 1964.
Garnett, David. *Letters of T. E. Lawrence.* London: 1938.
George, David Lloyd. *Memoirs of the Peace Conference.* vol. 2. London: 1921.
Gibson, Hugh. *The Ciano Diaries, 1939–1943.* New York: 1946.
Glubb, John. *A Soldier with the Arabs.* New York: 1957.
Haim, Sylvia. *Arab Nationalism: An Anthology.* Berkeley, Calif.: 1962.
al-Hashimi, Taha. *Mudhakkirat 1919–1943.* Beirut: 1967.
Heikal, Mohammed Hussein. *Mudhakkirat fi Siyassa al-Misr.* 2 vol. Cairo:
    1951.
Horowitz, David. *State in the Making.* New York: 1953.
Hull, Cordell. *Memoirs.* vol. 2. New York: 1948.
Hussein, King of Jordan. *Uneasy Lies the Head.* New York: 1962.
al-Jamali, Fadil. *Mudhakkirat wa-'Ibar* (Memoirs and Lessons). Beirut: 1964.
Kalvarisky, Chaim. *Al Parashat Darkhenu.* Jerusalem: 1939.

Kirkbride, Alec. *A Crackle of Thorns*. London: 1956.
——. *From the Wings*. London: 1976.
Kisch, F. H. *Palestine Diary*. London: 1938.
Kubba, Mohammed Mahdi. *Mudhakkirat fi Samim al-ahdath 1918–1958*. Beirut: 1965.
Lowenthal, Marvin. *The Diaries of Theodore Herzl*. New York: 1962.
al-Majali, Hazza. *Mudhakkirat*. Amman: 1960.
Meinertzhagen, Richard. *Middle East Diary 1917–1956*. London: 1959.
Miller, Aaron David. *Search for Security: Saudi Arabian Oil and American Foreign Policy, 1939–1949*. Chapel Hill, N.C.: 1980.
Miller, David. *My Diary at the Peace Conference*. vol. 4. New York: 1921.
Naguib, Mohammed. *Egypt's Destiny*. New York: 1955.
Nasser, Gamal Abdul. *The Philosophy of the Revolution*. Buffalo, N.Y.: 1959.
——. *The Truth about the Palestine War*. Cairo: 1956.
Neumann, Emanuel. *In the Arena*. New York: 1976.
Patai, Raphael. *The Complete Diaries of Theodor Herzl*. vol. 4. New York 1960.
Peterson, Maurice. *Both Sides of the Curtain*. London: 1950.
Philby, H. St. John. *Arabian Jubilee*. London: 1954.
al-Sabbagh, Salah al-Din. *Fursan al-Urubah fi al-Iraq*. Damascus: 1956.
Sachar, Harry. *Israel the Establishment of a State*. New York: 1953.
al-Sadat, Anwar. *In Search of Identity*. New York: 1978.
——. *Revolt on the Nile*. New York: 1957.
al-Said, Nuri. *Arab Independence and Unity*. Baghdad: 1942.
Sharett, Moshe. *Yoman Medini*. 4 vols. Tel Aviv: 1968–74.
Sidqi, Ismail. *Mudhakkirati*. Cairo: 1950.
Storrs, Ronald. *Orientations*. London: 1943.
Syria Naval Intelligence Division. *Syria*. London: 1943.
al-Tel, Muhammed. *The Palestine Question* (in Arabic). Cairo: 1959.
Walters, Vernon. *Silent Missions*. New York: 1978.
Weizmann, Chaim. *Trial and Error*. New York: 1966.
Zurayk, Constantine. *The Meaning of the Disaster*. Beirut: 1956.

SECONDARY SOURCES

Adams, Charles. *Islam and Modernism in Egypt*. London: 1933.
The Arab Nation: Paths and Obstacles. Washington, D.C.: 1960.
al-Arif, Arif. *Al-Nahda*. Beirut: 1956.
Assaf, Michael. *The Arab Movement in Palestine*. New York: 1937.
Avi-hai, Avraham. *Ben-Gurion, State-Builder*. Jerusalem: 1974.
Bailey, Clinton. *The Participation of the Palestinians in the Politics of Jordan*. Ph.D. diss., Columbia University, 1966.
Baram, Philip. *The State Department in the Middle East 1918–45*. Philadelphia: 1978.

el-Barawy, Rashid. *Military Coup in Egypt–An Analytic Study.* Cairo: 1952.

Bauer, Yehuda. *From Diplomacy to Resistance.* New York: 1970.

Be'eri, Yehuda. *Army Officers in Arab Politics and Society.* New York: 1970.

Ben-Dor, Gabriel, ed. *The Palestinians and the Middle East Conflict.* Haifa: 1976.

Berger, Earl. *The Covenant and the Sword.* London: 1965.

Berger, Morroe. *The Arab World Today.* New York: 1962.

Berque, Jacques. *Egypt: Imperialism and Revolution.* New York: 1972.

———. *North Africa: The Maghreb Between Two World Wars.* New York: 1963.

Birdwood, Lord. *Nuri As-Said: A Study in Arab Leadership.* London: 1959.

Bondy, Ruth. *The Emissary: A Life of Enzo Sereni.* Boston: 1977.

Caplin, Neil. *Palestine Jewry and the Arab Question 1917–1925.* London: 1978.

Chouraqi, Andre. *Between East and West: A History of the Jews in North Africa.* Philadelphia: 1968.

Cleveland, William. *The Making of an Arab Nationalist.* Princeton: 1971.

Cohen, Aharon. *Israel & The Arab World.* New York: 1970.

Cohen, Gabriel. *The British Cabinet and Palestine 1943* (in Hebrew).

———. *Churchill and Palestine 1939–42* (in Hebrew).

Cohen, Hayyim. *The Jews of the Middle East 1860–1972.* New York: 1973.

Cohen, Michael. *Palestine: Retreat from the Mandate 1936–45.* New York: 1978.

Darwaza, Mohammad Izzat. *Hawla al-haraka al-Arabiyah al-haditha.* Sayda: 1971.

Dearden, Ann. *Jordan.* London: 1958.

Devlin, John. *The Ba'th Party.* Stanford, Calif.: 1976.

Donovan, Robert. *Conflict and Crisis: The Presidency of Harry S. Truman 1945–1948.* New York: 1978.

Elath, Eliahu. *Shivat Zion ve-'Arav.* Tel Aviv: 1974.

Empson, C. *Economic Conditions in Iraq.* London: 1933.

ESCO Foundation for Palestine. *Palestine: A Study of Jewish, Arab & British Policies*, 2 vols. New Haven, Conn.: 1949.

Ettinger, Samuel, ed. *Zionists and the Arab Question* (in Hebrew). Jerusalem: n.d.

Evans, Lawrence. *United States Policy & the Partition of Turkey, 1914–1925.* Baltimore: 1965.

Friedman, Isaiah. *Germany, Turkey and Zionism 1897–1918.* London: 1977.

———. *The Question of Palestine 1914–1918.* New York: 1973.

Frye, Richard. *The Near East and the Great Powers.* Cambridge: 1951.

Furlonge, Geoffrey. *Palestine is My Country: The Story of Musa Alami.* New York: 1969.

Gabbay, Rony. *A Political Study of the Arab-Jewish Conflict.* Paris: 1959.

de Gaury, Gerald. *Faisal.* New York: 1967.

Ghali, Ibrahim. *L'Egypt Nationale et Liberale.* The Hague: 1969.

Gilbert, Martin. *Exile and Return.* New York: 1979.

Goitein, S. D. *Jews and Arabs: Their Contacts through the Ages*. New York: 1964.

Halstead, John. *Rebirth of a Nation: The Origins and Rise of Moroccan Nationalism*. Cambridge: 1969.

Harris, Christina Phelps. *Nationalism & Revolution in Egypt*. The Hague: 1964.

Hattis, Susan Lee. *The Bi-National Idea in Palestine during Mandate Times*. Tel Aviv: 1970.

Heyworth-Dunne, J. *Religious and Political Trends in Modern Egypt*. Washington, D.C.: 1950.

Himadeh, Said B. *Economic Organization of Palestine*. Beirut: 1938.

Hirszowicz, Lukasz. *The Third Reich & the Arab East*. Toronto: 1966.

Holt, P. M. *Cambridge History of Islam Vol. 1*. London: 1970.

Hourani, Albert. *Arabic Thought in the Liberal Age 1798–1939*. London: 1962.

———. *Syria and Lebanon*. New York: 1958.

Hudson, Michael. *Arab Politics: The Search for Legitimacy*. New Haven, Conn.: 1978.

Hurewitz, J. C. *The Struggle for Palestine*. New York: 1968.

Ismail, Mahmoud Ismail Mohamad. *Nationalism in Egypt before Nasser's Revolution*. Ph.D. diss., University of Pittsburgh, 1966.

Jamal, Mahmud et al. *Egypt and the Second World War* (in Arabic). Cairo: n.d.

Jankowski, James. *Egypt's Young Rebels*. Stanford, Calif.: 1975.

John, Robert, and Sami Hadawi. *The Palestine Diary*. 2 vols. New York: 1972.

Kadi, Leila. *Arab Summit Conferences and the Palestine Problem*. Beirut: 1966.

Kanna, Khalil. *Al-Iraq Amsuhu wa Ghaduhu* (Iraq Yesterday & Tomorrow). Beirut: 1966.

Kedourie, Elie. *Arabic Political Memoirs*. London: 1974.

———. *Britain and the Middle East 1914–1921*. London: 1956.

———. *The Chatham House Version & Other Middle East Studies*. London: 1970.

———. *In the Anglo-Arab Labyrinth*. London: 1977.

Khadduri, Majid. *Arab Contemporaries*. Baltimore: 1973.

———. *Independent Iraq*. New York: 1951.

Khouri, Fred. *The Arab States in the UN*. Ph.D. diss. Columbia, University 1953.

Kimche, David. *The Second Arab Awakening*. New York: 1970.

———. *Seven Fallen Pillars*. London: 1951.

———, with Jon Kimche. *A Clash of Destinies*. New York: 1960.

Kirk, George. *The Middle East in the War*. London: 1952.

———. *The Middle East 1945–1950*. London: 1954.

Kleiman, Aaron. *Foundations of British Policy in the Arab World: The Cairo Conference of 1921*. Baltimore: 1970.

Konikoff, A. *Transjordan: An Economic Survey*. Jerusalem: 1943.

Laqueur, Walter Z. *A History of Zionism*. New York: 1972.

———. *Communism and Nationalism in the Middle East*. New York: 1955.

———. *Terrorism*. Boston: 1977.

Lengyel, Emil. *Egypt's Role in World Affairs*. Washington, D.C.: 1957.

Lesch, Ann Mosely. *Arab Politics in Palestine 1917–39*. Ithaca, N.Y. 1979.

Lewis, Bernard. *The Emergence f Modern Turkey*. New York: 1969.

Longrigg, Stephen. *Iraq 1900–1950*. New York: 1953.

——. *Syria & Lebanon Under French Mandate*. New York: 1958.

Lorch, Nathaniel. *The Edge of the Sword: Israel's War of Independence*. New York: 1951.

MacDonald, Robert. *The League of Arab States*. Princeton: 1965.

MacLean, Virginia. *Foreign Factors in Egyptian Foreign Policy*. Ph.D. diss., Fletcher School, 1955.

al-Madi, Munib and Suleiman Mousa. *Tarikh al-Urdun fi al-qarn al-ishrin*. Amman: 1959.

Mahmoud, Amin. *King Abdullah and Palestine*. Ph.D. diss., Georgetown University, 1972.

Main, Ernest. *Palestine at the Crossroads*. London: 1937.

al-Majali, Hazza. *Mudhakkirat*. Amman: 1960.

Makarius, Raoul. *La Jeunesse Intellectuelle D'Egypt au Lendemain de la Deuxieme Guerre Mondiale*. The Hague: 1960.

Mandel, Neville. *The Arabs and Zionists Before World War I* Los Angeles: 1976.

al-Marayati, Abid. *A Diplomatic History of Modern Iraq*. New York: 1961.

Marlowe, John. *Rebellion in Palestine*. London: 1946.

——. *The Seat of Pilate*. London: 1959.

Medzini, Moshe. *Esser Shanim shel Mediniut Eretz-yisraelit* Tel Aviv: 1928.

Memmi, Albert. *Portrait of a Jew*. New York: 1962.

Mishal, Shaul. *West Bank/East Bank*. New Haven, Conn.: 1978.

Mitchell, Richard P. *The Society of the Muslim Brothers*. New York: 1959.

Monroe, Elizabeth. *Britain's Moment in the Middle East*. London: 1963.

——. *Mr. Bevin's Arab Policy*. London: 1973.

——. *Philby of Arabia*. London: 1973.

Nevo, Joseph. *Abdallah and the Arabs of Eretz Israel* (in Hebrew). Tel Aviv: 1975.

Patai, Raphael. *Jordan*. New Haven, Conn.: 1957.

Porath, Y. *The Emergence of the Palestinian Arab Nationalist Movement 1918–1929*. London: 1974.

——. *The Palestinian Arab Nationalist Movement 1929–1939*. London: 1978.

Pratt, Lawrence. *East of Malta, West of Suez*. London: 1977.

Quraishi, Zaheer. *Liberal Nationalism in Egypt: The Rise and Fall of the Wafd Party*. New Delhi: 1967.

al-Rafi'i, Abd al-Rahman. *Fi a'qub al-thawrah*. 3 vols. Cairo: 1951–66.

——. *Tarikh misr al-siyasi*. Cairo: 1967.

Robinson, Jacob. *Palestine and the United Nations*. Washington, D.C.: 1947

Rubin, Barry. *The Great Powers in the Middle East 1941–1947: The Road to the Cold War*. London: 1979.

——. *Paved with Good Intentions: The American Experience and Iran*. Oxford University Press, 1980.

Sachar, Howard M. *The Emergence of the Middle East 1914–1924*. New York: 1969.

———. *Europe Leaves the Middle East 1936–1954*. New York: 1973.

———. *A History of Israel*. New York: 1976.

Safran, Nadav. *Egypt in Search of Political Community*. Cambridge: 1961.

al-Sayyid Marsot, Afaf Lutfi. *Egypt's Liberal Experiment 1922–1936*. Berkeley, Calif.: 1977.

Seale, Patrick. *The Struggle for Syria*. New York: 1965.

Seton-Williams, M. V. *Britain and the Arab States*. London: 1948.

Sharabi, Hisham. *Arab Intellectuals and the West*. Baltimore: 1970.

———. *Government and Politics of the Middle East in the Twentieth Century*. Princeton: 1962.

Sharef, Zeev. *Three Days*. New York: 1962.

Sherrow, Fred. *The Arabs of Palestine as Seen Through Jewish Eyes 1925–1929*. M.A. thesis, Columbia University: n.d.

Shwadran, Benjamin. *Jordan, A State of Tension*. New York: 1959.

Sluglett, Peter. *Britain in Iraq 1914–1932*. London: 1976.

Stein, Leonard. *The Balfour Declaration*. London: 1961.

Sykes, Christopher. *Crossroads to Israel*. Bloomington, Ind.: 1973.

———. *Two Studies in Virtue*. London: 1953.

Torrey, Gordon. *Syrian Politics and the Military*. Columbus, Ohio: 1963.

Toynbee, Arnold, ed. *Survey of International Affairs 1925*. vol. 1. London: 1927.

———. *Survey of International Affairs 1934*. London: 1935.

———. *Survey of International Affairs 1937*. vol. 1. London: 1938.

———. *Survey of International Affairs 1938*. London: 1939.

———. *Survey of International Affairs 1939*. London: 1940.

Vatikiotis, P. J. *Politics and the Military in Jordan*. London: 1967.

Warner, Geoffrey. *Iraq and Syria 1941*. London: 1974.

Watt, W. Montgomery. *The Majesty that was Islam*. New York: 1974.

Ye'or, Bat. *Peuples Dhimmis: Nations Morte-vivante*. Geneva: 1977.

Zeine, Z. N. *The Struggle for Arab Independence*. Beirut: 1960.

ARTICLES

al-Alami, Musa. "The Lesson of Palestine." *Middle East Journal* 3, no. 3 (October 1949).

Arsenian, Seth. "Wartime Propaganda in the Middle East." *Middle East Journal* 2, no. 4 (October 1948).

Asadi, F. "Some Causes for the Rejection of the Partition Plan by the Palestine Arabs." *Middle East Forum* 48, no. 1 (1973):59–73.

Beeley, Harold. "The Middle East in 1939 and in 1944." *Journal of the Royal Central Asian Society* 32, no. 1 (January 1945).

Brownell, George. "American Aviation in the Middle East." *Middle East Journal* 1, no. 3 (October 1947).

Caplan, Neil. "Arab-Jewish Contacts in Palestine After World War I." *New Middle East* 27, nos. 1–2 (105–106) (1978):18–44 (in Hebrew).

Chejne, Anwar G. "The Egyptian Attitude toward Pan-Arabism." *Middle East Journal* 11, no. 3 (Summer 1957).

Chizik, I. "The Political Parties of Trans-Jordania." *Journal of the Royal Central Asian Society* 22, no. 2 (April 1935).

Cohen, Hayyim. "The Anti-Jewish *Farhud* in Baghdad, 1941." *Middle East Studies* 3, no. 1 (1966).

——. "Exodus from Iraq." *Jerusalem Quarterly* 9 (Fall 1978).

Cohen, Michael. "American Influence on British Policy in the Middle East During World War 2: First Attempts at Coordinating Allied Policy on Palestine." *American Jewish Historical Quarterly* 67, no. 1 (September 1977).

——. "The British White Paper on Palestine: The Testing of a Policy 1942–1945." *The Historical Journal* 19, no. 3 (1976).

——. "British Strategy and the Palestine Question." 1936–1939." *Journal of Contemporary History* 7, nos. 3–4 (July–October 1972).

——. "A Note on the Mansion House Speech." *Asian and African Studies* 11, no. 3 (1977).

——. "The Palestine White Paper, May 1939: Appeasement in the Middle East." *The Historical Journal* 16, no. 3 (1973).

——. "Secret Diplomacy and Rebellion in Palestine 1936–1939." *International Journal of Middle East Studies* 8, no. 3 (July 1977).

——. "Why Britain Left: The End of the Mandate." *Wiener Library Bulletin* 31, nos. 45–46 (1978).

Danin, Ezra. "Meetings with Abdallah." *Maariv* (March 9, 1975), p. 5 (in Hebrew).

Dann, Uriel. "The United States and the Recognition of Transjordan, 1946–1949." *Asian and African Studies* 2, no. 2 (1976).

Dawn, Ernest. "Pan-Arab Diplomacy: Romanticism or Calculation." monograph. Princeton: 1970.

De Luca, Anthony. "The 'Grossmufti' in Berlin: The Politics of Collaboration." *International Journal of Middle East Studies* 10, no. 1 (February 1979):225–38.

Eliacher, Elie. "An Attempt at Settlement in Transjordan." *New Outlook* 18, no. 5 (1975):71–75.

Gibb, H. A. R. "The Islamic Congress at Jerusalem in December 1931." in Arnold Toynbee. *Survey of International Affairs 1934*. London: 1935.

Glubb, John. "Transjordan and the War." *Journal of the Royal Central Asian Society* 31, no. 1 (January 1945).

Gottheil, Fred, "Arab Immigration into Pre-State Israel." *Middle East Information Series* 24 (Fall 1973):13–22.

Haim, Sylvia. "Aspects of Jewish Life in Baghdad Under the Monarchy." *Middle East Studies* 12, no. 2 (May 1976).

Heller, Joseph. "Anglo-Zionist Relations, 1939–1947." *Wiener Library Bulletin* 31, nos. 45–46 (1978).

Hogarth, D. G. "Wahabism and British Interests." *Journal of the British Institute of International Affairs* 4 (1925).

Husry, Khaldun. "King Faysal I and Arab Unity 1930–1933." *Journal of Contemporary History* 10, no. 2 (April 1975).

Jankowski, James. "The Egyptian Blue Shirts and the Egyptian Wafd 1935–1938." *Middle East Studies* 6 (1970).

———. "Egyptian Responses to the Palestine Problem in the Interwar Period." *International Journal of Middle East Studies* 12, no. 1 (August 1980).

Kedourie, Elie. "Pan-Arabism and Egyptian Politics." *Political Quarterly* 28, no. 1 (January–March 1957).

Khadduri, Majid. "The Coup d'Etat of 1936." *Middle East Journal* 2, no. 3 (July 1948).

———. "The Scheme of Fertile Crescent Unity." in Richard Frye. *The Near East and the Great Powers.* Cambridge: 1951.

Khalidi, Walid. "Thinking the Unthinkable: A Sovereign Palestinian State." *Foreign Affairs* (July 1978).

"King Abdallah's Assassins." *The World Today* (October 1951).

Kirk, George. "More Lessons of Palestine." *The 19th Century and After* 144 (December 1948).

Luntz, Joseph. "Diplomatic Contacts Between the Zionist Movement and the Arab Nationalist Movement at the Close of the First World War. *New Middle East* 12, no. 3(47)1962.

Luks, Harold. "Iraqi Jews during World War 2." *Wiener Library Bulletin* 30, nos. 43–44 (1977).

Mandel, Neville. "Attempts at an Arab-Zionist Entente 1913–1914." *Middle East Studies* 1, no. 3 (April 1965).

Morrison, S. "Arab Nationalism and Islam." *Middle East Journal* 2, no. 2 (April 1948).

Mousa, Suleiman. "A Matter of Principle: King Hussein of the Hijaz and the Arabs of Palestine." *International Journal of Middle East Studies* 9, no. 2 (May 1978).

Nevo, Joseph. "Abdullah and the Arabs of Palestine." *Wiener Library Bulletin* 31, nos. 45–46 (1978).

Newcombe, S. F. "A Forecast of Arab Unity." *Journal of the Royal Central Asian Society* 31, no. 2 (May 1944).

Perlman, Moshe. "Chapters of Arab-Jewish Diplomacy 1918–22." *Jewish Social Studies* (1944).

Porath, Yehoshua. "The Palestinians and the Negotiations for the British-Hijazi Treaty 1920–1925." *Asian and African Studies* 8, no. 1 (1972).

Porath, Y. "Social Aspects of the Emergence of the Palestinian Arab Nationalist Movement." in Menahem Milson. *Social and Political Structure in the Arab World.* New York: 1974.

al-Qawuqji, Fawzi. "Memoirs 1948." *Journal of Palestine Studies* 2, no. 1 (1972):1–26, no. 4:27–59.

Ro'i, Yaacov. "The Zionist Attitude to the Arabs 1908–1914." *Middle East Studies* 4, no. 3 (1968).

Rose, Norman A. "The Arab Rulers & Palestine 1936: The British Reaction." *Journal of Modern History* 44, no. 2 (June 1972).

Rubin, Barry. "Egypt and the Palestine Question, 1922–1939." *Wiener Library Bulletin* 31, nos. 45–46 (1978).

——. "Anglo-American Relations in Saudi Arabia, 1941–1945." *Journal of Contemporary History* 14, no. 2 (April 1979).

Safer, Naim. "The Integration of Arab Palestine in the Jordanian Kingdom." *New Middle East* 6, no. 3 (23):189–96 (in Hebrew).

Sela, Abraham. "Contacts and Conversations Between Zionist and Palestinian Arab Leaders, 1933–1939." *New Middle East* 22, no. 4 (88) (1972), and 23 (89) (1973) (in Hebrew).

Shefer, Michael. "The Effect of the Arab-Israeli Rupture on the Economy of the Arab Countries." *New Middle East* 14, nos. 2–3 (54–55) (1964):158–84 (in Hebrew).

Sheffer, Gabriel. "British Colonial Policy-Making Toward Palestine, 1929–1939." *Middle East Studies* 14, no. 3 (October 1978):307–322.

——. "The Involvement of the Arab States in the Palestine Conflict and British-Arab Relations Before World War Two." *Asian and African Studies* 10, nos. 1–3 (1974–75).

——. "Saudi Arabia and the Palestine Problem 1936–39." *New Middle East* 22, no. 2 (86) (1972) (in Hebrew).

Shimony, Yaacov. "The Arabs and the Approaching War with Israel, 1945–48." *New Middle East* 12, no. 3 (47) (1962):189–211.

Smith, Charles D. "The 'Crisis of Orientation': The Shift of Egyptian Intellectuals to Islamic Subjects in the 1930's." *International Journal of Middle East Studies* 4 (1973).

Watt, D. C., "The Foreign Policy of Ibn Saud 1936–39." *Journal of the Royal Central Asian Society* 1 (April 1963).

Woolbert, Robert G. "Pan Arabism and the Palestine Problem." *Foreign Affairs* 16, no. 2 (January 1938).

Ye'or, Bat. "Zionism in Islamic Lands: The Case of Egypt." *Wiener Library Bulletin* 30, nos. 43–44 (1977).

Yisraeli, David. "The Third Reich and Palestine." *Middle East Affairs* (October 1971).

PERIODICALS

Akhbar-al-Yawm (Egypt).
Al Alam al-Arabi (Iraq).
Al Balagh (Egypt).
Al Bilad (Iraq).
Al Difah (Palestine).
The Egyptian Gazette (Egypt).
The Egyptian Mail (Egypt).
Filastin (Palestine).
Great Britain and the East.
Al Ikhwan (Egypt).
Al Iraq.
Iraq Times.
Al Istiqlal (Iraq).
Journal d'Egypte.
Al Kutla (Egypt).
Life Magazine (1943).
Al Misri (Egypt).
Al Moqattam (Egypt).
New York Times.
Palestine.
Palestine and the Near East.
Palestine Post.
Palestine & Transjordan.
Rose al-Yusuf (Egypt).
Times (London).

INTERVIEWS

A. David Fritzlan. Letters to author April 2 and May 13, 1979.
Francis Russell. Letter to author June 9 , 1979.
Wells Stabler. Interview, March 7, 1979.

Index

THE ARAB STATES AND THE PALESTINE CONFLICT

was composed in 10-point VIP Times Roman and leaded two points
by Partners Composition, Inc.,
with display type in hand-set Foundry Legend by J. M. Bundscho, Inc.;
Printed sheet-fed offset on 50-pound, acid-free Glatfelter Antique Cream paper,
Smythe-sewn and bound over boards in Joanna Arrestox
and also adhesive-bound with laminated 10-pt. Carolina covers,
by Maple-Vail Book Manufacturing Group, Inc.;
and published by

SYRACUSE UNIVERSITY PRESS
SYRACUSE, NEW YORK 13210